THE PROBABILITY
OF THE IMPOSSIBLE

THE PROBABILITY
OF THE IMPOSSIBLE

Scientific Discoveries and
Explorations in the Psychic World

by Dr. Thelma Moss

A PLUME BOOK
NEW AMERICAN LIBRARY
TIMES MIRROR
NEW YORK AND SCARBOROUGH, ONTARIO

To Vip and all those like him; to Leland, Pauli, Tina, and all the young people; and with great thanks to Frances, John, Ken, Barry, Jack, Lois, and all the lab volunteers without whom the work could not have been done.

Library of Congress Catalog Card Number: 73-92094

This is an authorized reprint of a hardcover edition published by J. P. Tarcher, Inc. The hardcover edition was published simultaneously in Canada by Prentice-Hall of Canada, Ltd.

SIGNET, SIGNET CLASSICS, MENTOR, PLUME, MERIDIAN and NAL BOOKS are published *in the United States* by The New American Library, Inc., 1633 Broadway, New York, New York 10019, *in Canada* by The New American Library of Canada Limited, 81 Mack Avenue, Scarborough, Ontario M1L 1M8

Furst Plume Printing, October, 1975

4 5 6 7 8 9 10 11 12

Printed in the United States of America

Contents

Introduction

To venture beyond the fantastic accomplishments of
this physically fantastic age, sensory perception must
combine with the extra-sensory, and I suspect that
the two will prove to be different faces of each other.
                                        —Charles Lindbergh

SCIENTISTS' DISBELIEF

At UCLA's Neuropsychiatric Institute, where I am employed as
a medical psychologist, I also pursue research in parapsychology.
With the best of intentions, my superiors have occasionally taken
me aside to advise that I am committing professional suicide by
this sortie into the "occult." Such an interest brands me, they say,
as a member of the scientific lunatic fringe; and no matter how
many articles on my special subject I may publish (it is still
"publish or perish" in academia), such articles will never secure for
me professional advancement. A few kind colleagues have spent
considerable time with me in order to point out the absurdity of
my position.

They will ask, "Do you know *anyone* who can tell me what I
am thinking?" I must answer, "No." "Then why," they persist,
"do you choose to chase a wild goose like telepathy? Or prophecy? Do you know *anyone* who can tell me what tomorrow's
headline will read, or what will happen on August 29th, 1986?"
Again I must answer, "No." "Then why do you insist on investigating 'precognition,' as you call it? And don't tell me," someone
might add, "about the fashionable prophets of the moment. Oh,

yes, they may have predicted the assassination of President Kennedy, or the Los Angeles earthquake, but how many times have they made predictions which have not come true?" I admit that the accuracy of even the finest psychic is, at best, bad. I am sometimes further challenged to produce someone who can evoke spirits, or levitate tables, or read the numbers off concealed dollar bills. Before I can respond, I am assured that such are the tricks of the nightclub magician. I agree, and add that several magicians have told me (and I believe them) that there is nothing a psychic can do that they cannot do better and with 100 percent accuracy, whereas a genuine psychic is frequently, totally, wrong.

"What kind of fool are you?" they ask. One colleague tried to show me, by accompanying me on a field trip to a "haunted" house.

I am not sure, even now, whether her interest was prompted by a wish to help me or a wish to be amused. Throughout the evening, we were told of footsteps heard night after night in the hallway; of apparitions, particularly monks in hooded robes, seen by members of the household both individually and in groups; of moaning sounds outside the house, calling the name of the eldest son (a moaning verified by the neighbors); and of spots in rooms that were persistently cold and inexplicably clammy. At all these reports, my friend would smile and shake her head. Later she assured me that those phenomena were explainable in simple psychological or physical terms.

Obviously, she said, the immigrant Catholic family who had complained of the "ghosts" had brought to America their archaic beliefs and superstitions, which were accentuated by being confronted with our alien, highly technological society. In addition, she said that the marital situation was clearly one in which the husband and wife were strongly antagonistic to each other and that thus they were "projecting their repressed animosities as threatening apparitions of monks." Similarly, the whispers outside calling the name of the eldest son (of whom the mother seemed, in true Oedipal fashion, far too fond) were another sort of "projection of her repressed wish." The cold spots in the house offered no puzzle at all: they were undoubtedly due to the structure of the house which permitted air currents to settle in special areas, in accord with known physical laws. These explanations may have been valid for this particular "haunting." (We never did discover anything unearthly in our investigations.) At any rate, my colleague seemed satisfied with her one foray into psychical research and her analysis of the "true state of affairs." She dropped parapsychology into the wastebasket that contains such other scientific rubbish as phrenology, alchemy, and the search for a perpetual motion machine.

THE SCIENTIFIC REVOLUTION
AGAINST RELIGIOUS DOGMA

She was following a long and honorable tradition. Ever since the emergence of experimental science, some of the finest minds of man have developed astute arguments against the existence of what are called paranormal phenomena. The medieval Western world had its Knowledge of Divine Truth from the Bible, and its knowledge of secular truth in the encyclopedias inherited from the classical Greeks, especially Aristotle. And no further questions needed to be propounded.

It took enormous courage for anyone to question those unquestionable authorities. As an example, Aristotle had stated a fact which any thinking person immediately will realize is true: A heavy stone, dropped from a height, will hit the earth sooner than a light stone. How foolish it must have seemed to an intelligent man living in Pisa in the 1590s to watch someone actually climb to the top of the local tower and drop two stones, one heavy and one light, just to see for himself which one would land first. Galileo did exactly that, of course, and discovered that both stones landed at precisely the same moment. This was one of the first pragmatic experiments to yield measurable, quantitative data. But Galileo was guilty of still greater heresy, as were Copernicus and Kepler. These men did not accept the evidence their eyes clearly gave them: that the sun moves around the earth from east to west. They refused to accept the obvious, and the better to study heavenly bodies, they went so far as to employ telescopes. After many laborious measurements, they arrived at the preposterous conclusion that contrary to what was self-evident, the earth in fact revolved around the sun. With a swoop of the telescope (through which many eminent men refused to look), the earth was thrust from the center of the universe to become an insignificant planet moving, like all the other planets, in an orbit around the sun.

Could Aristotle be wrong?

Could the Bible contain untruths?

Anathema. Martyrdom.

No matter. These early men of science had turned the key in the lock, and others burst open the door to practical explorations of the world in which they lived. Alchemy, that bizarre search to transmute base metals into gold, gave way to chemistry, which eventually not only transmuted lead into gold (although uneconomically), but transformed chemicals into clothing, vitamins, and electrical power. And along every step of the way, men of unquestioned genius would scoff at each other's ideas. When Kepler, for instance, suggested that the tides of the ocean might be due to the influence of the moon, Galileo dismissed the idea as an "occult fancy."

And throughout, the established Divine Truth continued to wield its powerful influence on men's minds. Even that profligate genius Isaac Newton, who defined the law of gravity and invented a new mathematics, the calculus, to help his studies—even Newton believed that the world was created by God in 4004 B.C. and that He kept the Universe in order by correcting from time to time the slightly irregular movement of some planets.

THE EVOLUTION OF SCIENTIFIC DOGMA

Darwin and Pasteur and Einstein and Jeans and a host of scientists, year after year, with discovery upon discovery, made it less and less necessary to believe that Divine Truth ruled the world. In fact, it became untenable to accept Biblical "facts." Geologists made it perfectly clear that the earth could not have been created in seven days: rather the earth seems originally to have been a blob of incandescence which was tossed from the sun billions of years ago and took aeons to cool, develop vapors, condense into liquids, and eventually form the planet as we know it today. From its pinnacle as Divine Revelation, the Bible fell to the status of an allegory, ennobling in its sentiments perhaps (although how bloody and violent at times). It is permissible, surely, to interpret Adam and Eve as a parable of good and evil and possibly unbridled passion. But God did not create man from a handful of dust, nor woman from man's rib. We are reasonably sure that man evolved from his simian forbears, who evolved from their forbears, all the way back to the first creatures that emerged from water to make their homes on dry land.

No need to believe in Divine Miracles, either. Let the Bible tell of how Jesus walked on water, fed multitudes with a few fishes and loaves, healed the lepers and the blind and the crippled with a touch of his hand. We have created our own miracles, and they are far more impressive. We can levitate gigantic machines as far as the moon or Mars. We can feed multitudes with artificially manufactured foods, freezing the surplus for supply in years to come. Pasteur, Semmelwiess, Fleming, Salk, and many other men—not God—have delivered us from the scourges of plague and pox, cholera and scurvy and syphilis and a host of other diseases. For physical disease, physical remedy. No need to invoke a magic ritual like the "laying on of hands" or "spiritual healing."

Of course there still exist primitive societies with witch doctors, medicine men, shamans, and curanderos creating their special magic brews and rituals through which they claim miraculously to heal the sick, speak in tongues, prophesy, and destroy their enemies by sticking pins in dolls. Primitive men know no better.

But modern men do. Why regress to the cult of the occult? We live in a glorious age: Is it not a far better thing to study man as he is today, to understand better his behavior in this complex world in which we live? Why revive prescientific notions and superstitions about prophetic dreams, magical healing, and the like?

Such are the arguments with which parapsychology is persistently plagued.

A SCIENTIFIC REVOLUTION AGAINST SCIENTIFIC DOGMA?

By the end of the nineteenth century the kings of the scientific world, our physicists, believed that the basic laws of the universe (gravity, thermodynamics, electricity, etc.) had been deciphered. To be sure, there remained a few trivial irregularities to be untangled, but they believed that in the foreseeable future the science of physics could close forever its magnificent Bible of eternal, verifiable truths.

But an odd thing happened. In trying to tidy up those "trivial irregularities," vast new mysteries emerged, beautifully encapsulated in this paragraph from Nobel-prize-winner Albert Szent-Gyorgy:

> At the turn of this century, four important discoveries were made which marked the beginning of a new period in man's history. X-rays (1895), the electron (1895), radioactivity (1896), and the quantum (1900) were discovered, these discoveries being followed soon by relativity (1905). None of these were, or could be, revealed by our senses. They meant that surrounding man there was a world of which he had no inkling before, about which his senses could give him no information.

Suddenly the material universe of the physicist had begun to dissolve into smaller and smaller "bits" that could no longer justifiably be called matter. It was one thing for Galileo to drop stones that he could see, measure, and weigh. But physicists found themselves in a universe where not even their most sensitive instruments could detect the myriad, invisible essences unleashed by the smashing of the atom and christened positrons, neutrinos, mesons, etc. Like the genie let out of its bottle, these essences produced new mysteries for which there were no quick and tidy solutions.

Is it possible that there exist still other undiscovered energies? Are there biological energies in animals and man about which we still know nothing? Only after man invented radar and sonar did we discover that the bat and the dolphin had been equipped with those sophisticated communication devices all along. Man, after thousands of years, harnessed electricity, but the eel had been using it skillfully for thousands of years before man. Only sixty-odd years ago, when Hans Berger announced that electrical currents could be detected emerging from the heads of men, he was considered as funny as Pasteur had been when he announced that invisible bugs in milk carry disease.

Are there energies radiating from people, which might be channels of communication? Perhaps those radiations, as scientists are beginning to find, exist in the very cell itself. Have they always been there, or have they developed recently? Darwin's evolution, after all, brought us to the species of man, but Darwin did not state that evolution, like Harry Truman's buck, stops here. Are we evolving into another state of being?

In the recorded history of the world, several "trivial irregularities" have been regularly described in the realm of human behavior. Certain people were considered to have the ability to detect water, or oil, beneath the ground. Others reportedly were able to detect the thoughts or happenings of people miles away. Some persons, it was claimed, could predict the outcome of a future event. Others were supposed to be able to move objects just by thinking about them.

These all are rare occurrences, obviously. And perhaps they are trivial. But it was the "trivial irregularities" of planetary orbits that led to the discovery of unknown but existing planets. Thus, possibly those as yet inexplicable (unproven?) irregularities of human behavior may prove to have considerable significance in the study of man.

In a pioneering attempt to face such possibilities, a group of iconoclasts from several scientific disciplines, representing twenty countries of the world, met in 1973. What kinds of obscure, almost negligible forms of energy did they discuss, demonstrate, and puzzle over?

Let's begin there. And let us keep in mind that *nothing* presented at that conference or in this book is dogma. We will be examining inexplicable phenomena for which, happily, no dogma has as yet evolved. Your explanations about these happenings may be as valid as anyone's. The main point is that certain phenomena which according to classical science were impossible are now being regarded by some scientists as, perhaps, probable.

Part I: Bioenergy

1 Realms of Energy

The current fascination of scientists with possible
unknown energy fields. The eccentric history of man's
harnessing such energies as electricity and magnetism.
Is man himself capable of transmitting a form of
bioenergy which can influence matter?

THE FIRST INTERNATIONAL CONFERENCE
IN PSYCHOTRONICS

In June of 1973, eminent scientists from twenty countries and
many disciplines (physics, chemistry, electronics, biology, psychology, psychiatry, etc.) gathered together in Prague. Their purpose was to establish yet another field of scientific inquiry:
psychotronics, "the study of all interactions between man and
objects both animate and inanimate." This goal, in terms of
science as it has been studied, is highly unconventional. Physics,
for example, has for centuries attempted to understand the *objective* nature of the world in which we live. To this end, rigidly
controlled experiments have been designed with incredibly precise
instruments, so that human influences can be kept at a minimum
or, ideally, dispensed with entirely.

Human beings are subjective; machines are not. And the superi-
ority of machines in other ways has been well established. Everyone knows that a computer can be programmed to solve, in
seconds, problems on which a human being, no matter how
brilliant, would be forced to spend years of strenuous mental
effort to arrive at a solution. Election nights in the United States
are formidable examples of the near-infallibility of the computer.

Given a minimum of actual balloting, from a random sampling of polling places, long before the polls have closed and the actual votes been counted, the computer tells us on television the results of the election within a small percentage of error. The fact is that almost every facet of our daily living has become dominated by computer processes, whether payrolls, students' study programs, the ordering of theater, sports, or travel tickets. On rare occasions the computer has a "nervous breakdown," but generally it is infallible.

Why, then, organize a science in order to study the interaction of *man* with the machine, when the machine performs so brilliantly without him? The answer to this question became vividly clear as the conference got under way.

FROM OBJECTIVE TO SUBJECTIVE SCIENCE

In his welcoming speech, John Jungerman, a nuclear physicist from the University of California at Davis, offered his reasons for attending the conference. In the past decades, he declared, physicists have become aware that their ultimate goal of describing the objective universe can never be realized. It had been a basic tenet of classical physics that man must be the impartial observer of objective reality and that valid experiments should be repeatable by any competent observer. But, he said (quoting from Niels Bohr, the originator of quantum theory) if we were to produce a photograph of the entire world, showing where everything was, that photograph could only show us the world *at that moment in time.* A photograph taken a moment later would show us a slightly different world, and one taken weeks later would show us a radically different one.

We need not be physicists to appreciate this fact: Simply look at a photograph of yourself taken fifteen, ten, or even five years ago. Nineteenth-century science had likened the universe to a giant machine obeying with clocklike precision the laws of motion, gravity, etc., but that analogy no longer seems valid. Some scientists are beginning to appreciate the analogy offered by astronomer James Jeans: "The universe begins to look more like a great thought than a great machine."

FROM MACHINE TO MIND?

How can we follow this evolution in thinking of the universe as a machine to thinking of it as a mental phenomenon? Let us look at the world of matter as scientists saw it not too many years ago. It was a solid world, made up of tiny particles, the smallest of which was the atom. Then it was discovered that the atom was made up of still smaller particles, in a conformation often described as a miniature solar system with its nucleus like the sun, and with its electrons, like planets, revolving around it. Electrons had never actually been seen, but were imagined to be rather like tiny billiard balls of solid matter. However, in attempting to penetrate further into the mystery of matter, scientists found that electrons seemed to behave in a most unsolid fashion. In fact, Bertrand Russell felt compelled to write: "The idea that there is a hard little lump there, which is the electron or proton, is an illegitimate intrusion of common sense notions derived from touch. . . . For aught we know, an atom may consist entirely of the radiations which come out of it." At the Prague conference, for almost every speaker, radiations—energy fields—seemed to be the keynote.

Dr. Jungerman described his own beginning explorations. If the consciousness of man influences the nature of the world around him, then it may also influence the instruments with which he works. Perhaps, then, our instruments do not give a truly objective description of what we are measuring. To look for this possible influence of man on the machine, Jungerman decided to build a laser source "interferometer" which is sensitive to tiny forces of a few micrograms. He feels it is possible that certain persons may be able to influence the interferometer simply by their very presence.

Other speakers offered pragmatic demonstrations of such an influence. Dr. Harold Puthoff, physicist from the Stanford Research Institute, reported on a study with a gifted psychic, Ingo Swann. Puthoff and his colleagues encased a magnetometer (which shows magnetic field effects) in a special case that screens out all known radiations, and then buried the case deep in concrete. Swann, by doing something (concentrating? just being?), was repeatedly able to deflect the needle of the buried, encased magnetométer. Apparently Swann was influencing the machine at a distance.

THEORY AND PRACTICE: FIELDS INFLUENCING FIELDS

The Prague conference continually alternated between theory and practical demonstrations of man's interactions with the material world. Professor Alexander Dubrov, Soviet academician (academician is the highest rank a scientist can achieve in Russia), discussed his research into "biogravity," which he defined as "the ability of living organisms to generate and detect gravitational waves." Dubrov is a volatile young man, filled with excitement about the marvels he has explored in the mitosis of living cells. Characteristic of his resourcefulness was his handling of the crisis that occurred when he started to speak. As at the United Nations, there was simultaneous translation into the language of the participants. But at the start of his talk, there was a rustle of annoyance in the audience, as the English-speaking members began switching from channel to channel, looking for the English translator. It was clear that the translator was missing. Dubrov quickly saw what was happening and began his speech once more, this time in excellent English.

With wonder in his voice, he told us that in mitosis of a cell one can observe "an energetic radiation of photons," visible as a weak luminescence. At the same time, there is present a radiation of ultrasonic waves at a high frequency (between 10^6 and 10^7 cycles per second). And, during the process of mitosis, the liquid of the cell converts to a crystalline structure. "Imagine," he repeated with excitement, "the liquid of the cell turns into crystal!" For those of us whose juices might not be stirred by this fact, he pointed out that these characteristics tend to confirm his hypothesis that "biogravitational waves" emanate from cells, which in turn could account for such phenomena as telepathy, the movement of objects at a distance, and perhaps even levitation.

In further support of his hypothesis, Dubrov described some very recent research by Simon Shchurin, L. P. Mikhailova, and their colleagues at the University of Novosibirsk, the Soviet Union's most sophisticated technological institute. These experiments, repeated with variations more than 5,000 times, are fundamentally simple, but totally extraordinary. In these studies, normal cell cultures (typically chick embryos) were placed in two metal containers completely isolated from each other. Each container had a quartz "window" which screened out all known radiation but permitted "optical contact between cultures." Then, only one of the two cultures was infected with a lethal agent. As we might expect, the cells in the infected culture began to die off. But most unexpectedly, the cells in the noninfected culture also began to die in a "mirror image" of the contaminated cells. The authors write, "This mirror effect occurred whether the external agent was a virus, a chemical, or a lethal amount of ultra-violet radiation."

What was causing the spread of disease? The Soviet investigators surmised that these cells were communicating by an unknown radiation. To determine the nature of that radiation, they used a photomultiplier, which registers the flow of photons. They then observed that "when a tissue culture was infected with toxic viruses, the nature of the photon flow changed sharply. First the photon flow surged, then stopped, then surged again. . . . It is possible that the infected cells communicated to the non-infected cells by 'coded' information." Apparently different diseases radiate different *patterns* of energy, which patterns are "codes" conveying the disease to other cells at a distance. (Interestingly, the effect did not obtain when glass windows were used instead of quartz. Quartz, of course, is a crystalline structure, about which Dubrov had been so enthusiastic.)

It is perhaps not difficult to accept the possibility that cells transfer information at a distance from each other. But a skeptic might very well balk at making a comparison between that phenomenon and that of human beings presumed to interact with living and nonliving matter.

Yet the very next demonstration showed that man seems to have that capacity. Czech engineer Robert Pavlita performed informal experiments with his "psychotronic generators." These are metal objects which he has designed in various shapes (the shape determines the way in which the energy is to be used). Pavlita charges these generators with his own bioenergy; once charged, the generators are able to do various kinds of work. Putting a charged generator near a jar of muddy water speeds the precipitation of dirt, and setting a generator near a plant increases the plant's growth rate, etc. To show that the bioenergy which the generators are presumed to store is not exclusive in him, Pavlita asked his daughter, whom he has trained, to charge a generator. She did this by bringing the metal object to her temple, repeatedly, in a mild pulsing movement. Once charged, the generator was placed inside, but not touching, a copper shield near a device that looked like a horizontal windmill. The generator had been charged by pulsing it to the right temple, and the windmill began to revolve in a clockwise direction. After a time, Ms. Pavlita recharged the generator by pulsing it to her left temple, and the windmill began to revolve in a counterclockwise direction. After the demonstration, members of the audience were invited to try to charge the generator. Only a few of them were successful, a result that anyone familiar with other forms of bioenergy, like dowsing, would expect. For several years I have been working with such gifted persons as dowsers, magnetists, and healers, and although I have repeatedly tried to emulate their work, I have remained magnificently *un*able to perform any of the feats which they seem to do without effort.

After Pavlita came another Czech engineer, Julius Krmssky, who demonstrated a variation on Pavlita's form of bioenergy. Krmssky showed how emanations from his hands caused objects floating on water to move forward and backward; he also showed how an object suspended on a string inside a bell jar (to avoid the criticism that the movements were due to air currents or temperature changes) could be made to rotate clockwise or counterclockwise by rotating the hands at a distance of an inch or more outside the jar. Even more remarkable was a filmed demonstration of Krmssky's ability to turn on a light by focusing his eyes on a switch. His eyes apparently radiate some kind of force sufficient to trigger the switch.

Should all of this strike the reader as nothing more than magicians' tricks, let us depart briefly from the conference to describe an experiment reported by the celebrated English neurophysiologist E. Gray Walter in 1969. Walter attached to the frontal cortex of different persons electrodes which transmitted brainwave activities through an amplifier to a television set. Each person was told that if he pressed a certain button, an "interesting scene" would appear on the TV screen. About one second *before* he actually pressed the button, there appeared from the frontal cortex an "expectancy" brain wave of approximately 20 microvolts. This is a very tiny force, twenty millionths of a volt, but when amplified by Walter's circuitry, it was sufficient to trigger the switch which caused the "interesting scene" to appear on the TV screen without the person having to press the button at all. Walter concluded that there is an "effort of will" by which one "can influence external events without movement or overt action through the impalpable electrical surges of one's own brain." Walter, with this experiment, was demonstrating the interaction of man with a TV set; similarly Krmssky was demonstrating his interaction (involving the eyes, rather than—or in addition to—the frontal cortex) with an electric light bulb. Apparently man can influence an instrument by an act of "will."

An act of will, whatever that might prove to be, is an invisible force, undetectable with our present instrumentation. Undeniably it would seem to be a trivial force, compared with our awesome dynamos. But we sometimes forget that the world in which we live has been powered by invisible forces of nature which were at first undetectable, then noticed as trivial phenomena, and only very gradually isolated, harnessed, and put to use. Let's briefly examine man's incredible accomplishment in learning about the mysterious unseen forces which surround him.

OF ELECTRICITY AND MAGNETISM

The various known forms of energy—magnetic, electrical, gravitational, chemical—emerged separately into man's awareness and became his servants only after centuries of seemingly trivial (if not foolish) observations and experiments. As an example, two thousand years ago the Greeks had noticed that amber attracted to itself flimsy particles of matter. This phenomenon was considered an idle curiosity, ignored by Aristotle but mentioned casually by one of his disciples. The Greeks had a word for amber: *elektra*. (And for centuries the legend of Elektra, together with Oedipus, Orestes, and the whole damned family was of much more interest to the world than the capacity of the substance elektra to pick up bits and pieces of stuff.)

Not until the sixteenth century was it discovered, by the English Dr. William Gilbert, that other substances like crystal and resin also had the capacity to attract materials. This fact was reported by Gilbert and was apparently ignored by the scientific community of his time. A century later an Italian inventor, Guericke, built a machine that could produce a steady charge of electricity by friction. No one did anything with that machine, and it too was all but forgotten and had to be reinvented, with variations, by scientists of other countries. Interest in electricity increased during the eighteenth century, when some of its attributes, such as conduction, were observed and studied. It was learned that electricity could travel over wires and that the electric force (or "fluid," as it was often called) had the power not only to attract but also to repel. At first it was believed these were two separate "fluids," but the American scientist Benjamin Franklin suggested that the attraction and repulsion might be considered two polarities of one fluid, positive and negative. Franklin could not determine which pole was which, and to decide the matter, he arbitrarily tossed a coin, which delivered the wrong verdict. As a result, some textbooks to this day describe the flow of electricity as going from + to -. But with the acceptance of the electron theory in the twentieth century it was determined that the flow went in the opposite direction, from - to +. Franklin's flip of the coin has caused countless students (including me) anguish as a capricious, malicious sign kept changing directions in the textbooks.

Electrical experiments of the eighteenth century were very much like foolish games that children might play: stuffing jars with "electric fluid" which could give one a dreadful jolt, flying kites in thunderstorms to bring down lightning from the sky as Franklin did, or electrocuting little animals. In one extraordinary case, an admirer of Benjamin Franklin, an M. Riehman, emulated Franklin's experiments in obtaining a lightning discharge from a thundercloud over St. Petersburg and in the process, killed himself. But by the end of the century, some of the properties of electrical energy had been brought under experimental control. And as a result, the study of electricity began in earnest around the world. In Italy, Professor Galvani (to whom we are indebted for the word "galvanize") discovered, by accident, that a frog's legs hung from a copper wire would jerk about in odd contortions whenever they touched an iron railing. After fifteen years of research, he announced his discovery of "animal electricity," as evinced in the movements of the frog's legs. Galvani's announcement drew a salvo of derisive comments from his colleagues who promptly christened him "the dancing master of the frogs." One colleague argued more seriously that the frog's leg danced not because of any innate electricity, but because it was in contact with two different metals. This colleague, named Volta, went on to prove his point by using two different metals to form a cell battery, which produced electricity. This cell was named the voltaic cell for its inventor, and Volta has also been immortalized by having the electrical unit of power, the volt, named after him. Since it could produce a steady current of power, the voltaic cell gave electricity a potential practical value. So startling was this relatively constant flow of current that for a long time it was considered a very different form of energy from the sparks obtained from Leyden jars, or the energy that produced the dancing convulsions of Galvani's frog's legs. Slowly, through the nineteenth century, the various characteristics of electricity were tested in the laboratory. Eventually the study of electricity was combined with the study of magnetism and chemistry, each of which had been following its separate, similarly tortuous path of development.

At about the time the Greeks were playing at picking up bits of fluff with amber, they also noticed that magnetite, a special ore from Asia Minor, attracted to itself bits of metal. This finding was as trivial, in their estimation, as the attractive properties of amber. Despite the similarity of attractive force, no one seemed to ask whether the phenomena might be related. Some unknown hero discovered, however, that a piece of this rock, suspended on a string, always pointed north. Taking advantage of this oddity, travelers began to use this rock-on-a-string, or lodestone, to find their ways across the trackless deserts and seas. Otherwise, there seems to have been no further interest in the lodestone for more than a thousand years. That same Dr. Gilbert who had noticed the attractive qualities of crystals and resin, performed an ingenious experiment and discovered that the entire earth on which we live is a gigantic lodestone, or magnet, with north and south poles.

Gilbert's book *De magnete* was considered the classic work in the field of magnetism for the next two hundred years.

During the eighteenth century, paralleling Galvani's announce-ment of his discovery of "animal electricity," the Austrian physician Anton Mesmer announced his discovery of "animal magnetism." With iron rods and simple "magnetic passes" of his hands Mesmer demonstrated that he could "cure" his patients of a wide variety of illnesses. But his work, like Galvani's, was discredited, and animal magnetism was declared the trick of a charlatan by the august French Academy of Science. At the Prague conference, both Mesmer and Galvani were discussed as men of importance, whose work has subsequently been demonstrated as valid, and who can be considered as forerunners in the field of psychotronics.

But magnetism remained primarily in a small box labeled "For Navigational Purposes Only" until Ampere, and Faraday, and Oersted, and other pioneers of electricity came to realize that electrical current creates magnetic fields, and conversely, that magnets can be used to create electricity. These discoveries gradu-ally paved the way for the invention of the dynamo and electric motor, which led to the Industrial Revolution and to the Age of Technology, which has given the twentieth century its automatic heating and refrigeration, radio and TV, satellites and space ships, and of course those nearly infallible computing machines.

MODERN EXPLORATION OF ENERGY FIELDS

As a corollary to these marvels that came pouring, one atop the other, it was learned that the various energies could be trans-formed one into the other. Heat could turn into light, which could turn into electricity, which could turn into magnetism, which could turn into electricity, and so on. Knowledge of the vast realms of the electromagnetic spectrum grew rapidly. Charts were made, based on the new knowledge that all these forms of energy were electromagnetic waves. Each radiated at a different fre-quency, ranging from immensely long, slow waves at one end of the continuum to incredibly short, swift waves at the other. The ranges at which radiated light, heat, radio, TV, radar, sonar, x-ray, cosmic rays, gamma rays, etc., all found their places on these charts.

It comes as a great shock to find, on such a chart, the tiny range over which man's vision and hearing extend. We actually can see and hear only a microscopic section of the huge sea of invisible energies that surround us. And we have harnessed only a few of these energies. There still remain great gaps on these charts, indicating that there are unexplored, potentially usable energies at many frequencies. But whatever the wavelength, whatever the energy, it became clearer and clearer that all these energies were basically one. One what?

During this same outpouring of scientific discovery, man's concept of the smallest known particle of matter, the atom, underwent drastic revision. As we have already pointed out the ultimate "particle" of matter was found to be not a solid ball but a tiny solar system of protons, neutrons, electrons—which in turn were made up of tinier and tinier . . . what? . . . particles? . . . waves? It became a possibility that all matter could eventually be seen dissolving into nothing but energy. It was Einstein, of course, who for the moment at least, electrified the scientific world with his magnificently simple equation, $E = MC^2$, meaning that matter, multiplied by the speed of light, squared, becomes energy. If proved true, this meant that all matter can be made into energy or all energy can be converted into matter. The explosion of the atom bomb proved the truth of Einstein's equation. And with that explosion, we were forced to face the possibility that there is, in scientific reality, *no material world*—no matter how much our gross physical senses inform us otherwise.

Many experiments had demonstrated that when an electron collides with another particle, it bounces away like a hard little ball. But then came the classic experiment of Sir George Thomson and his colleagues. They caused a single electron to be fired at a screen containing two holes, expecting that the solid little electron would pass through one hole or the other. But it didn't. Instead the single "solid" electron passed through *both* holes at the same time, creating in the process an interference pattern of waves. This did not make sense. How could one particle pass through two holes at the same time? Further experiments only increased the confusion. Sometimes the electrons behaved like solid particles, but at other times they behaved like waves of energy. Sir William Bragg delightfully describes this dilemma: "Electrons seem to be waves on Mondays, Wednesdays, and Fridays, and particles on Tuesdays, Thursdays, and Saturdays." Some scientists even tried to effect a compromise by rechristening the electron a "wavicle." But more and more, scientists are beginning to accept the possibility that there is no "ultimate particle of matter." Now there have been discovered about one hundred particles smaller than the atom, particles which appear and disappear within fractions of a second. Our material world is evaporating into radiations, vibrations, wavelengths, energies, force fields. As Arthur Koestler has wryly observed, our physicists have acquired a new respect for the second commandment: " 'Thou shalt not make unto thee any graven images'—either of gods, or of protons."

Emanations. Radiations. Energy fields.

We have seen how scientists from various disciplines have recently been puzzling over types of energy which have escaped detection. At the Prague conference they spoke of "biogravity," of "bioplasma," of "orgone," of "energy fields" around objects animate and inanimate, of "mitogenetic radiation," of "bioluminescence," of "ultrasonic radiation." All these eminent biologists, physicists, and biochemists were looking for a definition of some kind of energy as yet undefined. Psychologists and psychiatrists were similarly puzzled, talking about "bioenergetics," about interactions between doctor and patient on a nonverbal "empathic" level, about experiments where the very presence and belief of the investigator seemed to influence the outcome of the experiments.

But an intangible, invisible energy can only be hypothesized until it can be observed at work. Is there any technique available to make visible this hypothesized bioenergy? One such possibility was discussed by several participants. It is a form of electrical photography, rediscovered and renamed Kirlian photography after its most recent, indefatigable inventors/researchers, Semyon and Valentina Kirlian. Let us next take a long look at this strangely beautiful, as yet inexplicable photography.

2 Bioenergy: Can It Be Seen through Kirlian Photography?

Electrical photography: its historical background; its rediscovery by the Kirlians; its current investigation in the Soviet Union, Czechoslovakia, England, and the Americas; and the controversies over what is being photographed.

WHAT IS KIRLIAN PHOTOGRAPHY?

News of Kirlian photography arrived in the United States in 1970, with the publication of *Psychic Discoveries behind the Iron Curtain,* by Sheila Ostrander and Lynn Schroeder. I was sent a prepublication copy of the book for review, and read it with mounting excitement. For, although written in extravagantly journalistic style, the book reported incisive developments by Soviet scientists in the field of parapsychology—a term which the Russians eschew in favor of more scientific terms like "bioenergetics" and "biocommunication." Paradoxically, that most materialistic of governments, according to Ostrander and Schroeder, had been exploring such nonmaterial domains as dowsing, psychokinesis, healing by the laying on of hands, and acupuncture. And of particular interest, a few Soviet scientists were claiming to obtain visible evidence of bioenergy through the use of an electrical photographic process invented by the Kirlians.

Quoting from the authors,

[The results of photographing a leaf] placed in the field of a high frequency current revealed a world of myriad dots of energy. Around the edges of the leaf there were turquoise and reddish-yellow patterns of flares coming out of specific channels of the leaf. . . . The pattern of luminescence was different for every item, but living things had totally different structural details than non-living things. A metal coin, for instance, showed only a completely even glow all around the edges. But a living leaf was made up of millions of sparkling lights.

In other words, this photography revealed a vast difference between inorganic and organic materials; the inorganic remained constant, whereas living things revealed a constantly changing luminescence. Could this difference be due to a form of bioenergy?

I gave the book an excellent review. Not surprisingly, there were colleagues who disapproved of my enthusiasm, for they considered *PDBIC* (as the book came to be known among parapsychologists) sensationalized reporting, if not pure fiction. Some skeptical parapsychologists with whom I talked considered that the Kirlian photographs of leaves, flower buds, and fingertips that had been published in the book were faked. Some went so far as to suggest that Kirlian photography did not exist at all but was a complex hoax perpetrated on the authors during their visit to the Soviet Union. (The history of psychic research has been plagued with phony claims and the tricks of charlatans; as a result, parapsychologists are perhaps the most cautious of scientists.) I could not share such skepticism, for there was an extensive bibliography in *PDBIC* which included the work of scientists for whom I had respect, and I had had extended correspondence with some of them. However, none of the researchers into Kirlian photography were familiar to me, and to learn about it first hand, I wrote to the scientist whose work was most liberally quoted in *PDBIC*, Professor Victor Inyushin, of Kirov University in Alma-Ata, Kazakhstan (in southern Siberia). I promptly received from him not only the proceedings of a symposium devoted to research into Kirlian photography, but also an invitation to visit his laboratory in Alma-Ata. I immediately made plans to incorporate a visit to the Soviet Union, and the remote outpost of Alma-Ata, into a previously arranged European tour. Before the journey, I had his papers translated so that I might study them in detail. I learned that on the basis of his research, which is primarily in biology,

Inyushin theorized that all living things have not only a physical body, but also an "energy body" consisting of "bioplasma," a word coined by Inyushin and his colleagues.

This concept of Inyushin was of great interest to me, because of the parallels that could be drawn between modern physics and certain occult literature. For example, plasma is considered by physicists to the fourth state of matter, the others being the more familiar solid, liquid, and gas. The ancients considered there were four states of matter too: fire, earth, water, and air. The analogy is striking. Further, modern physics presumes that plasma exists throughout the universe and is the substance of which the sun is composed. Ancient Yogic texts describe an invisible energy, "prana," which infuses the universe and is the substance of which the sun is composed. Another provocative parallel. To go further, an article by the Kirlians describes the energy which they believe they are photographing as "electrons and ions of the discharge flux in motion. . . . This electronic structure is not constant, since it depends on the condition of the organism . . . [and] by studying the geometric shapes, their spectra and the dynamics of their development, it is apparently possible to judge the biological (e.g. pathological) state of an organism." Occult literature too describes an "etheric body" which surrounds the physical body, and "it is by means of the etheric body that prana (energy) runs through the nerves. . . . The particles of the etheric body are being constantly changed."

Striking analogies. But analogies, as scientists have painfully learned, can often be deceptive. What evidence did Inyushin offer that the bioplasma body does, in fact, exist? He reported that a leaf, photographed with the Kirlian technique, reveals a brilliant pattern of bubbles and emanations which does not correlate with any known physical or anatomical structure. Further, he reported that if a leaf is plucked from a plant and photographed over a period of time, those emanations which are at first so brilliant and colorful gradually diminish in luminescence and eventually disappear, so that no photograph of the leaf can be obtained. Perhaps this signifies the "death" of the leaf, or rather, the death of its bioplasma body, since the leaf retains its physical, visible characteristics long after it ceases to produce a picture when photo-

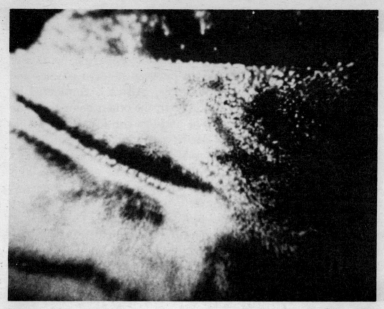

Figure 1. Soviet-made Kirlian photograph showing a "phantom." Part of the leaf (near the top of the photo) was cut off but is still visible as a phantom.

graphed by Kirlian techniques. Perhaps the most startling claim made by Inyushin and his colleague, biophysicist Victor Adamenko, was that when a small section of the leaf (from 2 to 10 percent) is cut away, the "phantom" body of the cut-away portion of the leaf can still be photographed!

This phenomenon, if true, might help to explain a medical anomaly that has existed for a very long time. In the practice of medicine it is not uncommon for a patient who has had a limb removed to feel intense pain where the limb *had been*. This phenomenon is called "phantom limb pain" for which there is no fully satisfactory anatomical explanation (nor any reliable relief for the pain, which can be almost intolerable). Was it at all possible, I wondered, that there might be an energy body not only in plants but in people? Could this energy body somehow remain after the physical limb has been amputated and be responsible for phantom limb pain?

My head buzzed with these and other questions: Did such photography really exist? Was it actually possible to take pictures without camera or lens? Were there in existence genuine pictures of "phantom" leaves, taken by Soviet scientists in their laboratories? Was there a bioplasma which could be seen changing its state due to disease and/or death? Hoping to learn some answers, off I went to the Soviet Union. (Figure 1 is a photograph of a "phantom leaf" obtained from a Russian scientist.)

VISITS WITH SOVIET RESEARCHERS

Unfortunately, the Kirlians live in a remote part of southern Russia, and it was not possible for me to meet them personally. But I did spend several days in Moscow with Victor Adamenko. As a child he had lived next door to the Kirlians, and he had grown up participating in their photographic research. Over the years their work had expanded to include techniques of making moving pictures, video tapes, and pictures through electron microscopes, as well as observing objects in real time. Adamenko provided me with his own research papers and those he had done with Inyushin and the Kirlians. They described dramatic photographic changes in human beings, which result from emotional or physical arousal or from different states of consciousness such as hypnosis. Surprising to me at that time was Adamenko's preoccupation with acupuncture in relation to Kirlian photography. (The explosion of acupuncture theory and therapy had not yet occurred in the United States.) Adamenko spoke of a possible correlation between the "invisible energy system" described by Chinese medicine and the "invisible energy body" made visible through Kirlian photography. Could they be the same thing? Were they, as he believed, photographing genuine acupuncture points?

Adamenko's enthusiasm for this esoteric thing called acupuncture gave me briefly that almost distasteful skepticism scientists feel when they think a colleague has carried his theories beyond any reasonable leap. But when he demonstrated on my hand a device of his creation which detects acupuncture points on the body, I was intrigued. However, this area of Russian research into acupuncture, which has been going on for several years, belongs properly to another chapter.

Most of Adamenko's research with Kirlian photography had been done with Inyushin at Alma-Ata. I arrived there at four o'clock one November morning, with the temperature at eight degrees below zero, and was brought safely by the Intourist guide to a delightful hotel—save for the fact that the hotel's heating system had broken down.

The next three days proved to be the most fascinating and frustrating of my entire journey. Inyushin and his wife were as hospitable as they could be with the restrictions that had been imposed. Since, for some unknown reason, permission had not arrived from Moscow for my official visit, I was not allowed to visit the laboratory or the university, and it was therefore impossible to see first hand the Kirlian apparatus or to observe experiments. (Inyushin told me the last official visit to the university by an American had been nine years earlier, when a lecture was given by the distinguished artist Rockwell Kent.) As solace, Inyushin and his colleagues devoted many hours to discussing their work with me. Inyushin is a huge, burly man with sideburns, a hearty laugh, and an encyclopedic knowledge not only of American science, but of American art, literature, and theater. And he was not yet thirty years old. I was constantly amazed at the youth of the Soviet scientists, their expertise, and their knowledge of recent scientific literature from the West. In fact, Inyushin put me to shame when he told me that some of his research had been inspired by "your great American scientist Szent-Gyorgy," whose two recent monographs, *Bioelectricity* and *Bioenergetics*, helped corroborate his ideas of a bioplasma body. I had to confess ignorance of those works, but on my return to California, read them promptly. Albert Szent-Gyorgy, a Nobel-prize-winner for his discovery of Vitamin C, has written in simple and witty prose this passage:

> If you would ask a chemist to find out for you what a dynamo is, the first thing he would do is to dissolve it in hydrochloric acid. A molecular biochemist would, probably, take the dynamo to pieces, describing carefully the helices of wire. Should you timidly suggest to him that what is driving the machine may be, perhaps, an invisible fluid, electricity, flowing through it, he would scold you as a vitalist.

Szent-Gyorgy goes on to describe a possible electron flow in the organism which may account for as yet inexplicable dynamic processes in people.

Like Adamenko, Inyushin was generous with his published work and other pertinent literature, which included a schematic diagram of the Kirlian apparatus so that we could build one in our laboratory for our own experimentation. When I left Russia, my luggage bulged with scientific literature obtained from Russian scientists. There was only one item that I could immediately read. It was a report on experimental electrical photography written in English and published in 1939 in the *American Journal of Biological Photography*. Adamenko had found it in a Moscow library while doing research for one of his degrees. Adamenko had told me that electrical photography had a lengthy history, which included this published work of Prat and Schlemmer, two Czech scientists who had reported their research on "electrography" with their own device. In this article were reproductions of photographs they had taken which looked remarkably like the Kirlian photographs I had seen. Far from being a hoax, Kirlian photography was apparently a recent evolution of a photographic technique that went back more than one hundred years.

A SHORT HISTORY OF ELECTRICAL PHOTOGRAPHY

As we have already seen, scientific instruments are invented, ignored, and reinvented in other countries by other, independent investigators. Apparently, such has been the fate of electrical photography. At the Prague conference an excellent historical survey of the field was given by the Czechoslovakian engineer Karel Drbal, who traced its origin to 1842, when an Englishman named Carsten used a condenser system to get "electric patterns" of coins on a mica plate. Some forty years later, in 1884, the German Jiri Lichtenburg described specific kinds of patterns (called today "Lichtenburg figures") which are commonly seen in electric photographs. Then in 1889 a Moravian, Bartholomew Navratil, described "a new kind of electric pattern" made visible by electrography, a word that Navratil coined. Other independent investigators from different countries included Iodko, Markovitch, and Baraduc, as well as Adamenko's discovery, Prat and Schlemmer of Czechoslovakia, who are still alive and working in Prague. Their most recent photographs were published in a Czech encyclopedia, in 1965.

The Kirlians, then, had independently reinvented (but with a different apparatus) the technique of taking photographs by means of electricity. According to Adamenko, Semyon Kirlian is an extremely curious, creative engineer who asks, "What if?" about all kinds of phenomena that most people take for granted. One day, some thirty-five years ago, he saw a machine emitting sparks and wondered, "What if I put my hand in that spark—would it make a photograph on a piece of film?" He tried the experiment, burned his hand badly, but obtained a picture. And that is how Kirlian photography originated, with no knowledge by its inventor of its previous history.

ITS BEGINNINGS IN THE UNITED STATES

Returning to California early in 1971, I was brimming with enthusiasm to begin research in these strange new areas only to find that colleagues received news of Kirlian photography, bio-energy, and acupuncture with apathy, or even amusement. As for the Kirlian photographs I had brought back with me, the general opinion was that the radiations that showed up on the film could be explained as an artifact, due to an electrical current surging through the object being photographed. Discouraging too was the response of electronics engineers to whom I showed the schematic diagrams. They were unanimous in saying that the diagrams for constructing a Kirlian machine were unfeasible because they were (1) highly dangerous, (2) unworkable, (3) lacking in enough information, or (4) crazy. A few experts condescendingly explained to me that the high frequencies and voltages required would burn to a frazzle any object like a leaf placed in the charged field. Moreover, a human being exposed to that kind of electrical voltage would in all likelihood be killed instantly.

Gradually I stopped talking about acupuncture and Kirlian photography to colleagues. They simply were not interested. But during a spring extension course, Psyche and Psychic Phenomena, at UCLA, I devoted a full evening's lecture to what I had learned of the Soviet research. At the end of the lecture, a student came to the podium, saying he would like to take some Kirlian photographs, to which I replied, "So would I!" All that I could offer him was some of the Russian literature which had been translated and a copy of the Prat-Schlemmer article, which was on a simpler technical level. He smiled broadly, thanked me, and left. I remember thinking, "Poor man, he just doesn't know. . . ."

The fact is, he just *didn't* know enough to know that it couldn't be done. At the next-to-last lecture that student, Kendall Johnson, handed me a photograph before class (Figure 2). It looked astonishingly like a Kirlian photograph of a leaf. Startled, I asked where he had gotten it, and he answered rather sheepishly, "In my father-in-law's garage." What Ken had done, I later learned, was to study the rather simple schematics given by Prat and Schlemmer and then go to an electronics "junk shop," where he bought things he thought "looked like" what was required. (How he knew even that much is curious, since he is by education a lawyer and at that time was an insurance claims adjuster.) That weekend I visited Ken

Figure 2. Kendall Johnson's first attempt at Kirlian photography.

in his father-in-law's garage and looked at what can only be described as an early Rube Goldberg arrangement of wires, batteries, copper plates, and even a doorbell. All that afternoon Ken tried, and failed, to take more pictures. The next weeks were ones of countless trials, many many failures, and a few shimmeringly beautiful pictures of leaves. More importantly, Ken learned how to improve his apparatus and devised various kinds of instruments to take the same kinds of pictures. For instance, the Russian literature described their basic power source as a Tesla coil. Not having one at the time, Ken tried a secondhand automobile spark coil, reasoning correctly that what was necessary was a spark. Later, we found that Tesla coils are readily obtainable, or buildable for very little cost, and Ken learned how to take equally good pictures with them. When he learned that piezocrystals produce good sparks, he used them. Then he thought of Van de Graaf generators, which also create large sparks, and made pictures with that power source. Eventually he even tried rubbing his feet along a nylon carpet to produce a spark and obtained pictures that way. (So can I. So can anybody.)

HOW TO MAKE ELECTRICAL PHOTOGRAPHS

The basic parameters of electrical photography are simple. Neither camera nor lens is used. In our standard procedure, a power source (in this instance, an automobile spark coil) is placed outside the isolation booth which is the most prominent feature of the laboratory. (This isolation booth, which has been used for sensory deprivation experiments, electrophysiological measurements, telepathy experiments, "primal" therapy, and other assorted studies also now doubles as our darkroom and photographic studio.) The power source is connected by cable to a film holder which lies on a wooden table inside the booth (Figure 3). Into the film holder we place an ordinary 4-by-5-inch piece of black-and-white or color film. The object to be photographed—leaf, coin, fingerpad—is placed directly in contact with the film emulsion. Then an electrical charge of one second's duration is pulsed through the photographic plate, and film, into the object. And lo, a picture has been made. We develop the black-and-white

Figure 3. Apparatus used in our lab for obtaining Kirlian photographs.

film as soon as we have taken the picture, so that in less than five minutes we can see the results of an experiment. The entire operation is so simple that a child can (and has) done it.

Because even a tiny electrical current can be lethal, the amperage must be kept at a minimum. We use less than one microampere. In designing any electrical equipment which is to be used with people, this is the one real danger that must be carefully avoided. Even taking an electrocardiogram (a standard procedure in many doctors' offices) can cause fatalities if the current is not properly controlled. Apart from that, the technical aspects of this photography are without risk to the experimenter.

Naturally there can be complex elaborations on this basic process. In our three years of research we have learned that changing just one parameter (voltage, pulse, frequency) will dramatically alter the picture. Figure 4A shows an ivy leaf taken with our standard apparatus; Figure 4B shows the same leaf taken at a much higher frequency, with all other variables held constant. As can be seen, the interior topography and the external coronas are

Figure 4A. Ivy leaf photographed by our standard procedures.

Figure 4B. Same leaf photographed at a much higher frequency.

radically different. This corroborates what the Kirlians reported many years ago, although no one yet knows why this change occurs. We have come to believe that certain frequencies *resonate* with specific characteristics of the object, but we are a long way from proving this to be true. We also discovered that at certain frequencies no picture at all is obtained. There may exist a still-to-be-formulated law of harmonics at work here because the pictures, as we go up the frequency scale from one cycle per second to millions of cycles per second, can be seen to emerge as clear and sharp, become blurred, change characteristics, disappear, and then emerge again with brilliant clarity. Different kinds of power sources give different pictures. Currently, we are comparing five different instruments. And while each gives its own characteristic picture, it is fascinating to see that they seem to show essentially the same kinds of changes when we manipulate one or another variable.

We were quickly able to confirm the Russian claim that inorganic objects, like coins, give a constant and unchanging corona,

whereas living materials (plants, animals, people) reveal a fasci-
natingly varied corona and surface structure depending on the
state of the organism (healthy or diseased, aroused or relaxed,
etc.). We also quickly confirm, the Soviet claim that when the same
leaf is photographed over a period of days, the image fades until
no picture at all can be obtained. We have performed this study
more than five hundred times with many species of leaves and
invariably found this to be true. Figures 5A, 5B, and 5C show a
campanula leaf photographed when freshly plucked and rephoto-
graphed over several days. One can observe how the inner bubbles
and lights are the first to extinguish, as if the energy were flowing
from inside *out*, to the periphery and corona of the leaf. In the
last picture, the image has just about vanished, except for the
corona. After that picture was taken, we obtained no image at
all, although the leaf was still green and looked fairly much the
same as when originally plucked. Are we watching, as the Russians
suggest, the energetic death of the leaf? What is it that has faded
away? No one can yet say with certainty, but several hypotheses
have been offered.

HYPOTHESES ABOUT THE NATURE OF KIRLIAN PHOTOGRAPHY

Look at the leaf in Figure 2. It looks like a Christmas tree lit up
with brilliant bubbles or balls. What are those bubbles? Biologists
tell us that there is nothing in the anatomy or cell structure of the
leaf to which they correspond. They simply do not exist in the
physiology of the leaf.

Do they represent, as Inyushin maintains, the bioplasma body
of the leaf? Inyushin rejects the theory that those emanations are
simply an electrical phenomenon due to the current pulsed
through the object. He has written, "The bioluminescence visible
in the Kirlian pictures is caused by the bioplasma, *not the electrical state of the organism. . . .* This bioplasma is not a chaotric
system: it has specific spatial organization." According to Inyushin, this consists of ionized electrons, photons, and possibly other
particles which react to the environment in which we live. He
states that even such exotic environmental influences as solar

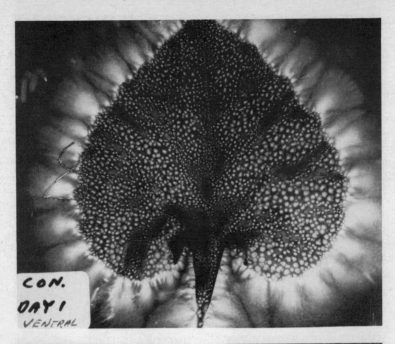

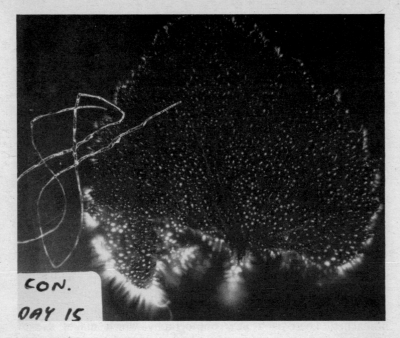

Figures 5A to 5C. The fading image. 5A (top left): Freshly plucked campanula leaf. 5B (bottom left): Same leaf 3 days later. 5C (above): Same leaf more than 2 weeks later.

flares and cosmic rays can cause changes in the bioplasma body. And he offers experimental evidence of changes in organisms due to more prosaic influences such as thunder storms, atmosphere charged with negative ions, and different colors of light.

As is typical in this field, biophysicist Adamenko disagrees with his colleague, biologist Inyushin. Adamenko believes that what we see in the pictures is the "cold emission of electrons" resulting from the electrical current passing through the object. Electrons are always being emitted from all objects, but that emission is strongly facilitated by electricity (as demonstrated in the process of gold plating). By studying the emission *patterns* of the electrons which appear on the film or which can be seen *in vivo* with special techniques, Adamenko is convinced it is possible to learn a great deal about the dynamic processes of living organisms.

Another hypothesis is offered by a few American scientists, the most prominent of whom is Professor William Tiller of Stanford University, an international authority on metals and crystals. After visiting the Soviet Union in 1971, Dr. Tiller also became interested in Kirlian photography and began his own research. On the basis of his findings, he believes that the photographs can be explained by the conventional concept of corona discharge. Examples of corona discharge are the flashes of lightning in thunderstorms; "St. Elmo's fire," an eerie light that glows on pointed objects of ships at sea; and ball lighting, which has sometimes been mistaken for unidentified flying objects by passengers and pilots on aircraft. Being neither physicist, biologist, nor electronics expert (what is a psychologist doing here?!), I can take no sides in this controversy. I simply do not know what happens when we take the pictures. Whatever it might prove to be, the photographs are beautiful, mysterious, and most importantly, capable of offering information not visible to the eye.

This is of course not an unusual aspect of photography. X-rays, for example, provide valuable information to the medical profession about bones and tissues *inside* the body. Infrared photography is used to photograph temperature changes, which are helpful in detecting invisible tumors, and, as Dr. Paul Ruegsegger informed us in Prague, in revealing the patterns of various kinds of headaches. There is a new photography which makes use of ultrasonic radiations, showing in moving pictures the interior processes of the body as they take place. Perhaps useful information about invisible processes may be obtained using Kirlian photography, when we learn what it is that is being photographed.

WHAT WE HAVE LEARNED ABOUT ELECTRICAL PHOTOGRAPHY

Naturally one of the first Russian experiments we tried to duplicate was the "phantom leaf"; and we kept trying, without success. Figures 6A and 6B show a typical early result. Figure 6A is a photograph of a freshly plucked coleus leaf, and Figure 6B is a photograph of the same leaf after the top of it has been cut away. Clearly there is no "phantom." But very clearly there can be seen remarkable changes in the patterning of the leaf before and after it has been mutilated. Look at the central spine of the whole leaf: it is clear and black. Now look at the cut leaf: the spine has filled up with those as yet inexplicable bubbles. (This effect, incidentally, does not always obtain. Sometimes the central spine is filled with

Figure 6A. Freshly plucked whole coleus leaf. Note the patterning and the appearance of the spine.

Figure 6B. Same leaf with the top cut away. Note how the patterning and spine have changed.

bubbles in the whole leaf, and becomes clear black after it has been cut!) A careful inspection of 6A and 6B will reveal other distinct differences in patterning, particularly the dramatic increase of black areas in the mutilated leaf as if the electrical, or energetic, characteristics of the leaf change *even though the physical leaf looks the same.*

This energy change (if that's what it is) becomes even more obvious when we photograph the fingertips of people. We began extensive research on our own fingertips, after Ken Johnson accidentally discovered his own peculiar variations. In his multiple attempts to get workable apparatus, he would typically use his fingertips as photographic objects. Sometimes he would obtain a vivid corona with clear fingerprints (Figure 7A), whereas at other times, he would obtain no corona at all, but a vague cloudlike "blotch" instead (Figure 7B). At first Ken thought the blotch was due to faulty apparatus. But as his work became more refined, he gradually realized that the apparatus was all right and that instead something in *him* kept changing the pictures. In an attempt to understand the nature of these changes, it became standard procedure for all of us in the lab to take pictures of our fingertips every day, and several times a day, if special events occurred. For example, our most devoted volunteer research associate, Frances Saba, would go into the isolation booth to take her picture if she had a headache or were coming down with a cold or if she felt drowsy or angry or in any state she thought might alter her picture. The photos we obtained were indeed very different, and this led us to believe that there exists a range, a continuum of pictures from deeply relaxed (large corona) to strongly aroused (blotch), with odd gaps in the corona indicating some kind of imbalance. With this basic hypothesis, after studying literally hundreds of volunteers' fingerprints, we have learned to predict with fair accuracy the kind of picture a stranger will take: blotch, thin corona, gaps, or wide aura. In color, these changes are dramatic: the fingerprint is typically blue (from azure to royal), and the corona a combination of blue and yellow/white. But the blotch always appears as a brilliant crimson. Other researchers have also found this continuum from blue-white corona to red blotch. A brilliant example is the photograph on the jacket of this book, made by Daniel Kientz and colleagues at the Psychotronic

Figure 7A. Fingerprint of a deeply relaxed subject.

Figure 7B. Fingerprint of a strongly aroused subject.

 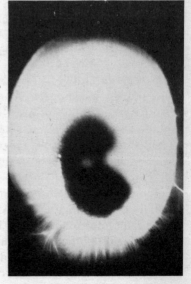

Research Institute. It is a picture of a finger pad revealing both vivid crimson blotch and blue-white corona.

WHAT THE PHOTOGRAPHS DO NOT REVEAL

At first, we explored standard physiological measures, according to the suggestions of various physiologists, each of whom had his particular theory as to what the photographs reveal.

One colleague believed that we were getting pictures of the state of blood supply to the finger. When we are relaxed, blood flows near the surface of the skin; and when we are anxious, it retreats from the surface. Technically, this movement of blood toward and away from the skin surface is called peripheral vascular dilation (near the surface) or constriction (away from the surface). To test this hypothesis, we used a plethysmograph, an instrument which accurately records blood dilation and constriction. We found absolutely zero correlation. In other words, when the finger was dilated with blood, we sometimes obtained a nice, wide corona but at other times, the blotch. We feel certain that it is not the supply of blood to the finger that is being photographed.

A skeptical colleague thought that the corona, with its characteristic bubbles (which occasionally can be seen detached from the corona), could be a picture of sweat and that the bubbles were, in fact, beads of sweat. We tested that suggestion two ways. One evening we all encased our hands in plastic bags until our fingers became very sweaty. Then we took our pictures. Our sweaty fingers invariably produced a big blotch! Exciting idea: Maybe the *blotch*, not the bubbles, was the result of sweat? We tried another tactic. We did strenuous physical exercise until we worked up a sweat and then took our pictures. This time, almost all of us showed the vivid blue/white corona. Could there be two kinds of sweat, one kind produced externally, from the lack of oxygen in the plastic bag, and the other internally produced through physical exertion? We asked a biochemist about sweat and were told that it comes in thousands of varieties. Different body reactions and diseases produce different kinds of sweat. If what we are photographing is, indeed, sweat, we will require biochemical analysis for each of our subjects. But it is obvious now that whatever those bubbles might prove to be, they are *not* tiny beads of sweat.

Another suggestion was that we were observing in the pictures changes in skin temperature; i.e., a hot finger could give a blotch, and a cold finger a corona. We attached little thermometers (called thermisters) to the subjects' fingers, and kept their entire arms in either ice water or very hot water until the finger temperature was either very low or very high. Again, we could find no relationship between temperature and whether the finger pad photographed as blotch or corona.

Still another suggestion was that the pictures were showing variations in electrical skin resistance, called galvanic skin response, or GSR for short. GSR has been a favorite electrophysiological measure among psychologists for nearly fifty years, because it shows dramatic changes between a relaxed (high resistance) and tense (low resistance) state. In fact, even the telling of a lie by an outwardly calm person is reflected in a precipitous drop in GSR. This change is so reliable that it has been used as a significant element in lie detection devices. We attached GSR equipment to our subjects as they were lying down, relaxed. When the GSR showed that resistance was high, we took pictures. Then, with the subject still relaxing, one of us would suddenly scream loudly, another favorite ploy of scientists looking for a "startle" or "fear" reaction, which sends the GSR plummeting down. At this point, we took pictures again. We could find no correlation here, either, between GSR and the photographs. (This GSR study has been duplicated by researchers at Sonoma State College, with the same results.)

The failure of these physiological studies to explain the changes in our photographs led us to believe that the changes were more the effects of mood, or the state of consciousness, than they were physical. And we began to shift focus from physiological states to altered states of consciousness, drug-induced and otherwise.

For example, Figures 8A to 8D show what happened to the fingertip of a medical student who volunteered to get drunk for us one night. He was delighted, particularly when we offered him his favorite bourbon. The conditions for the experiment were simple. We took pictures of our volunteer's finger pad when he came into the lab, before he had anything at all to drink. Then he had one ounce of whiskey every fifteen minutes, after which we again took his picture. During the time between drinks he was allowed to do as he wished, and he proved to be a jolly, lively drunk. Figure 8A

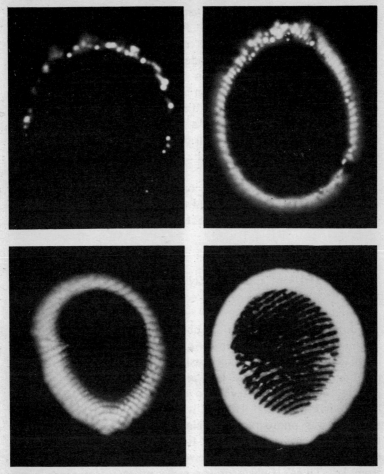

Figures 8A to 8D. Alchohol experiment. 8A (top left): Subject's fingerprint before he had any alcohol. 8B (top right): Subject's fingerprint after he had 1 ounce of alcohol. 8C (bottom left): Subject's fingerprint after he had 7 ounces of alcohol. 8D (bottom right): Subject's fingerprint after he had 17 ounces of alcohol.

shows his almost nonexistent corona before his first drink. Figure 8B shows his finger pad after only one ounce: in color, the blue took on a lavender tinge, and the corona got wider. After seven ounces (Figure 8C) he had achieved a "rosy glow," and the picture was a definite rose color combined with blue/lavender. This became considerably rosier, and by the seventeenth drink (!) he was obviously "all lit up" (Figure 8D). This picture, in color, is pure yellow/white. The experiment ended when our subject became quite sick.

This study led us to examine other states of consciousness. We learned that under hypnosis, under the influence of certain drugs (primarily the tranquilizers), in meditation, and in trance, the corona is generally large, with no blotch. Some of the staff experimented on themselves and learned that they could deliberately create either a blotch or a corona by changing their emotional states. In fact, two of our associates can arouse themselves to such a pitch that when the photograph is taken, nothing whatsoever appears on the film!

If this photography reveals corona discharge, then something can occur in the body to prevent the corona from discharging. No one at the moment has a satisfactory explanation for that ability.

THE "GREEN THUMB" AND "BROWN THUMB" EXPERIMENTS

About nine months into our research, Dr. Tiller, who had not yet begun his work in Kirlian photography, visited our lab, and was particularly interested in the changes we had discovered in our mutilated-leaf photographs. He asked to perform a similar experiment and after gashing a leaf, and seeing the resultant dimmer picture, he suggested trying to revivify or "heal" the leaf by holding it in his hand. He held it for a few minutes, after which the leaf was photographed again. The image was considerably brighter! It was not clear at that time whether the leaf had brightened because it had received moisture or some chemical from Dr. Tiller's fingers or for some other reason, but it was certainly something to be more fully explored.

We decided to conduct a rigorously controlled experiment on the "green thumb" phenomenon, that is, the apparent ability of some persons to make plants flourish. We sent out a call to anyone who believed he had this talent and eventually obtained the services of thirty volunteers. In a typical experiment our steadfast volunteer research associate, John Hubacher, known from then to now as "the leaf gasher," would take into the darkroom two leaves plucked from the same plant at the same time. One leaf was the experimental leaf, the other the control. John would photograph each leaf in its normal state, then gash them both and rephotograph them. Then he would set the control leaf aside and invite the volunteer "green thumb" person to treat the experimental leaf by holding his hand about two inches above the leaf, so that no physical contact existed between hand and leaf, until the volunteer thought the leaf had responded. Then both the "healed" leaf and the control leaf, to which nothing had been done, were photographed for a third time. In twenty-three out of the thirty experiments, there was a brilliant increase in the luminescence of the leaf after this "healing at a distance." Figures 9A to 9C show results of a "green thumb" experiment performed for us by Alan Vaughan, writer and editor of *Psychic* magazine. Figure 9A shows the freshly plucked leaf; Figure 9B the leaf after it has been gashed; and Figure 9C, the leaf after Vaughan's treatment. By contrast, Figures 10A to 10C show the control leaf freshly plucked, gashed, and left untreated for the same period of time. The luminescence has faded. It began to look very much as if we were photographing *an exchange of energy* between person and leaf, an interaction between living organisms that is the subject of the newly formed science psychotronics. In the other seven of the thirty cases, no visible change was observed, and no difference was found between control and experimental leaves.

Then—always a delight in laboratory work—an unexpected event occurred. A young psychic with whom we have been working for the past four years, Barry Taff, came into the lab one day during a leaf study. Barry mentioned that plants could not survive in his home, that he had a "brown thumb." He was promptly challenged to prove it, and he accepted the challenge. The results can be seen in Figures 11A to 11C; after the leaf was treated by Barry, the image all but disappeared. Later, Barry built his own photographic device and performed the experiment several more times, generally (though not always) with the same results. Since Barry, we have found other persons, including a woman physician from Great Britain, who have "killed" the leaf. It looks very much as though "green thumbs" and "brown thumbs" may not be old wives' tales, after all.

After this success with presumed bioenergy emanating from the hand, we tried another variation: the use of "magnetic passes," a

Figures 9A to 9C. "Green thumb" experiment. 9A (top left): Freshly plucked leaf. 9B (above): Same leaf after being gashed. 9C (left): Same leaf after being "healed at a distance."

controversial area ever since Anton Mesmer devised the technique in the eighteenth century. Jack Gray is another of our research associates who has volunteered his services for the past four years. Jack is a skilled hypnotherapist who sometimes uses magnetic passes in his work. The passes are simply movements of the hands around and above parts of the body, which sometimes relieve pain or effect a healing. Occasionally the passes are used to induce a deep hypnotic trance. In our lab, Jack had been using magnetic

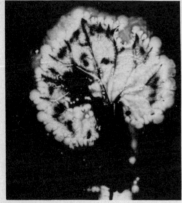

Figures 10A to 10C. "Green thumb" experiment—control. 10A (top left): Freshly plucked leaf. 10B (above): Same leaf after being gashed. 10C (left): Same leaf after being left untreated.

passes not only on people, but on plants. (In Prague, I learned that magnetic passes are now being explored by Czech and Russian scientists as a possible example of bioenergy.) Jack's "magnetized" leaves and flowers generally photographed more vividly than the controls.

In one study with chrysanthemums, for example, his magnetized chrysanthemum still gave vivid photographs eight weeks after having been magnetized (and kept for the entire period in a plastic container, without water). The control, nonmagnetized chrysanthemum could no longer be photographed after seven days (Figures 12A and 12B). About this time in the research, when we were

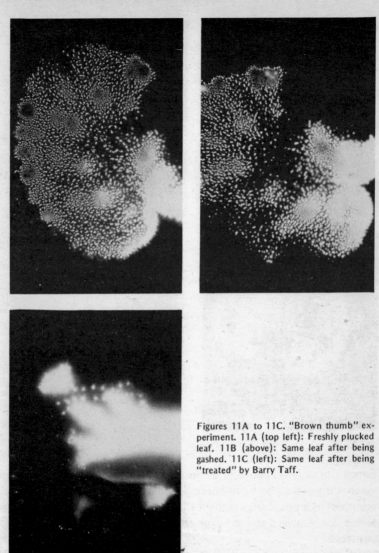

Figures 11A to 11C. "Brown thumb" experiment. 11A (top left): Freshly plucked leaf. 11B (above): Same leaf after being gashed. 11C (left): Same leaf after being "treated" by Barry Taff.

Figures 12A and 12B. Magnetism experiment. 12A (left) Magnetized chrysanthemum 8 weeks after being plucked. 12B (right): Nonmagnetized chrysanthemum after a few days.

wondering about these "transfers of energy" from person to plant, we received an unexpected impetus.

A CONTROLLED STUDY IN HEALING

A stranger entered my office one day, introduced himself as Dr. Marshall Barshay, and went directly to the purpose of his visit: "I hear you've taken photographs of a healer, and the photographs prove he can really heal." Then he added as a challenge, "Is that true?"

Only a small part of the statement was true. A "healer" had come to the lab, eager to demonstrate his ability with "the laying on of hands" under controlled laboratory conditions, because he did not know himself what he did that prompted relief from pain in the people he "treated." Since none of my experimental staff are medical doctors, and since doctors are usually reluctant to offer their patients for such unconventional treatment, we were unable to provide him with a patient. However, one of the staff volunteered to act the role of patient, and photographs were taken of the healer's finger pads and the "patient's" finger pads before and after treatment. These photographs showed, after treatment, a decrease in emanations from the healer's finger, and an increase from the patient's. This had been our only foray into "healing," and it was certainly no proof that the healer could really heal. This healer had told Dr. Barshay and us the same odd story about himself. He had been a mechanic most of his life and had known nothing of healing. Many years ago he had gone to a fortuneteller, who told him repeatedly that he had "healing hands." This had meant nothing to him until one day, driving through the desert, he was overcome by a headache so severe that he was forced to stop his car on the side of the blazingly hot road. At that moment he remembered the clairvoyant's words, and—feeling foolish, but with nothing to lose—he placed his hands on his head. Within thirty seconds, he reported, the headache had vanished. So startling was this experience that he wanted to see if he could repeat it with other people. He used the peculiar procedure of riding on a train for an entire day and going from car to car asking if anyone had a headache. Most passengers regarded him as a madman, but occasionally someone with a headache would permit the laying on of hands, and generally the headache would disappear. Encouraged, he expanded his activities successfully to treating persons with arthritis, toothache, back pain, and heart and stomach trouble. Both Dr. Barshay and I had seen letters he had received from reputable doctors, commending his ability.

Dr. Barshay, a kidney specialist, proposed a healing study. At that time he was treating several patients by means of dialysis. All dialysis patients are terminally ill, Dr. Barshay explained, in the sense that they cannot survive without dialysis two or three times each week. No one in the history of dialysis treatment (not a long history to be sure) has been able to stop treatment and survive. He volunteered to bring kidney patients into the laboratory for treatment by the healer. We could obtain pictures of them before and after treatment, and more importantly, we would learn if any of the patients could be released from dialysis. Medical science would be hard put to explain such a phenomenon except as "spontaneous remission" of an unprecedented type.

The study was begun, and for a period of three months, twelve patients received on the average eight treatments each. Treatment consisted of the healer placing his hands on the patient's lower back, in the area of the kidneys, for twenty minutes. Photographs were routinely taken of the fingertips of both patient and healer before and after each treatment.

The patients were enthusiastic and described various subjective sensations such as intense heat coming from the healer's hands, a tingling, a "force" entering them, and a sense of well-being after treatment. All these sensations, as we will learn in the next chapter, are typical of a healing experience. There were scattered indications of "improvements," such as lowered hematocrit and decreased blood pressure, both of which can and do occur spontaneously with dialysis patients. On several occasions, the healer relieved headaches (his specialty). On one occasion, so swiftly did the headache leave that the patient turned to me with goggle-eyes, saying, "That's hard to believe!" It was. Another healing occurred with a seventy-five-year-old patient, badly disturbed by the side effects of a drug he was taking. He felt such constant, intense dizziness ("like being drunk all the time") that he had to walk slowly with a cane. After his first treatment, the patient discarded the cane and did not use it for the duration of the experiment.

However, no one was able to stop dialysis treatment. That part of the experiment had to be considered a failure.

But the photographs provided very interesting data. Typically (though not invariably) the healer's corona grew smaller after treatment (Figures 13A and 13B), while the patient's grew larger and brighter (Figures 13C and 13D). To find out if this phenomenon was special to the healer, we instituted a group of control healers who claimed no healing talent, but who agreed to do exactly what the healer had done—keep their hands on the patient's back for twenty minutes. There was no indication of an energy transfer from any control healer to patient—except one. That was Dr. Barshay, himself. Perhaps in the future this kind of photography will provide a means of locating genuine healers.

There was another unexpected finding in this study, unpleasant to report. We have already described the "green thumb/brown thumb" effect. The same effect seems to have occurred in this healing study. Our healer had donated generously of his services and time. But he had also enjoyed the publicity and a number of patients had come to him on a paying basis outside the lab. One day a television company came to film the healing study. As usual,

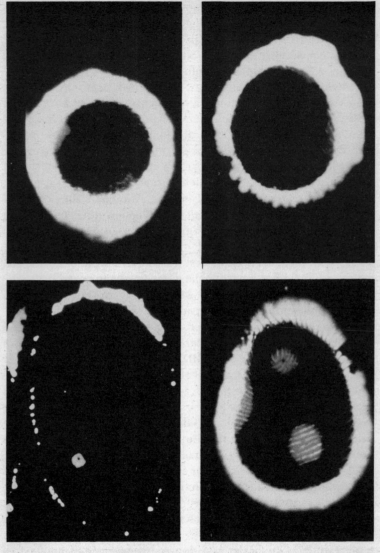

Figures 13A to 13D. Healing experiment. 13A (top left): Healer's fingerprint before healing. 13B (top right): Healer's fingerprint after healing. 13C (bottom left): Patient's fingerprint before healing. 13D (bottom right): Patient's fingerprint after healing.

both patient and healer were photographed before and after treatment. Before treatment the patient revealed a fairly bright corona, which after treatment just about vanished; while in contrast, the healer's emanations *increased* after treatment. It also happened that the patient had to be hospitalized two days later. I do not for one moment suggest there is a one-to-one correlation between these events: dialysis patients must frequently be hospitalized. But I do believe that the pictures show that the energy can travel not only from healer to patient but from patient to healer.

ELECTRICAL PHOTOGRAPHY IN ENGLAND

At the conclusion of the healing study, in September of 1972, I was to attend the Parapsychology Convention in Edinburgh. Before I left, Dr. Tiller suggested I visit two English scientists who for more than eight years had been doing their own version of Kirlian photography. Apparently Drs. Dennis Milner and Ted Smart, metallurgists at the University of Birmingham, had independently discovered electrical photography before news of the Kirlians' invention reached the Western world. (At Prague I discovered that a Brazilian scientist, Professor Henry Andrade, had also made his own electrical photographic device ten years before.)

In Birmingham, Dr. Milner showed me his device, very different from ours and also from the Kirlians'; the pictures taken with the apparatus were also different from any pictures I had seen. In his pictures, beyond the leaf and its aura there can be seen visible distortions in the atmosphere. This atmospheric phenomenon had become so intriguing to these investigators that they had abandoned their work with leaves, magnets, and fluids to concentrate solely on photographing air, just air! Depending on the parameters they use (frequency, pulse duration, etc.), they can reliably produce time and again the same *kinds* of extraordinary pictures which reveal highly intricate patterns (Figures 14A and 14B). Here indeed is a fascinating puzzle: What's in the air? The Yogis, as we have learned, postulate an all-pervasive energy; and contemporary physicists are discussing biological and electromagnetic fields which are everywhere around us. Are these pictures visible repre-

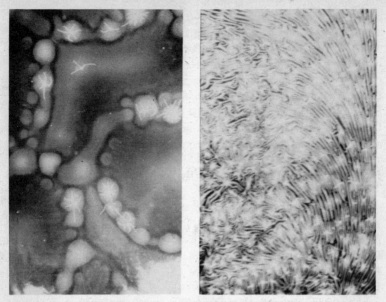

Figures 14A and 14B. Two examples of Dr. Milner's electrical photographs of air.

sentations of that invisible energy? Drs. Milner and Smart are attempting to find out.

Returning to my lab, I showed these "air pictures" to Ken Johnson and told him what little I could about the process by which they were taken. Ken, who had never stopped experimenting with different photographic techniques, was soon able to obtain similar effects with his apparatus. Figure 15 is one such photograph, revealing Zen-like patterns of a "forest," mysterious and beautiful. What are we looking at? It may be a long time before we know.

THE "PHANTOM" IS FOUND

Two and a half years after Ken brought me his first Kirlian photograph of a leaf, he brought to the lab the picture shown in Figure 16, a superb "phantom leaf," revealing both the internal structure and the edge of the section that had been cut off.

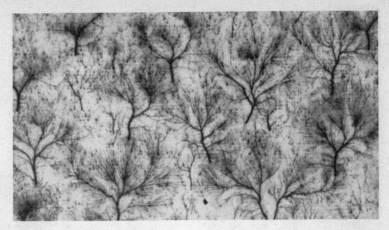

Figure 15. Ken Johnson's photograph of air.

Figure 16. Ken Johnson's phantom leaf. A portion of the side of the leaf (nearest the top in this photograph) was cut away before the picture was taken.

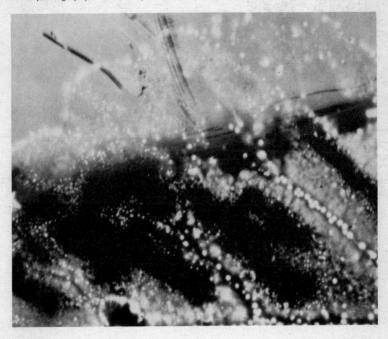

Figure 17. John Hubacher's phantom leaf. The top of the leaf was cut away before this picture was taken.

This success stimulated our research associate, John Hubacher, the "leaf gasher." He carried on his own explorations, and he, too, obtained several phantom leaf pictures. Figure 17 is one example.

The publication of these pictures, naturally, aroused a storm of controversy. Once more the cry of "Artifact!" was raised, with specific questions: Had the entire leaf been in contact with the film, and if so, then wasn't the phantom merely a residue from the entire leaf, a portion of which had later been cut away? Was the phantom just the exudation of liquids or gases from the cut leaf? In answer, John cut the leaf before placing it on the film, and obtained phantoms that way. He also tried deliberately to obtain the phantom by pressing the entire leaf firmly on the emulsion, cutting away a section, and then photographing the remaining leaf. A typical result of this method is the picture shown in Figure 18. Where the whole leaf had been squashed on the film, one can see the residue revealed in black detail, a very different effect from the white bubbles of the phantom. (It should be stressed that the

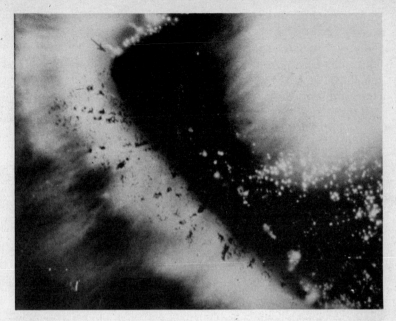

Figure 18. Effect produced by deliberately squashing a whole leaf on the film and then cutting away a part of the leaf. This is an artifact, not a genuine phantom.

phantom is rarely obtained, and almost as rarely the squashed-leaf effect.)

Further, John developed a technique so that observers can see the phantom *in vivo*. He attaches a transparent electrode (a large glass plate coated thinly on one side with Mylar) to the power source of the Kirlian device, places the cut leaf on the glass electrode, and turns on the electric power. One can then see the entire leaf scintillating for several seconds.

The first time John obtained this effect was when two film-makers were in the lab, hoping to make a movie of the Kirlian pictures. When they saw the phantom on the transparent electrode, the photographer said, "If that happens again, I'm getting out of here!" When it did happen again, he stayed right where he was, trying to record it on movie film. (We don't know if he succeeded; neither the photographer nor director ever returned.)

Very recently John Hubacher and Clark Dugger, a graduate

student of UCLA's cinema department, have succeeded in making moving pictures of the Kirlian effect using both black-and-white and color film. A new fascination is to watch, in these movies, the "phantom leaves" which sparkle brilliantly for several seconds, sometimes giving the impression that the entire leaf has been photographed. Unfortunately we still have no idea of what the "phantom" consists.

POSSIBLE APPLICATIONS OF KIRLIAN PHOTOGRAPHY

Doing research with this photography is like wandering down a corridor with many unopened doors. Thus far we have been peeping through keyholes, wondering which room to explore first. Three possibilities are medicine, metallurgy, and bioenergy.

Medicine

The Russians have claimed that the bioplasma changes dramatically in plants and in people before a disease is evidenced in the physical body. This is a challenging statement, which Dr. David Sheinkin and his colleagues at Rockland State Hospital, in New York, are beginning to explore. They have reported preliminary work with patients suffering from respiratory, gastrointestinal, and mental illnesses. To them the work looks promising, in that the corona can be seen to change radically with different illnesses. But these changes must be deciphered, a task which will require years of painstaking research.

There is promise of information to be derived from tissues and cultures, too. For our exploration in this area, we were asked by a radiologist at UCLA to photograph three different tissues taken from a patient's breast, tissues labelled simply "A," "B," and "C." We knew that "A," "B," and "C" were normal, fatty, and cancerous tissues, but we did not know which was which. Neither did the doctor to whom we gave the pictures, but he was able to identify them correctly. Pathologists may eventually find this photography as helpful as x-ray or thermography. Currently research is being conducted by John Hubacher and Ted Dunn, a pathologist at the University of Southern California, comparing the tails of tumorous and healthy rats by means of the Kirlian technique. More than 100 pairs of rats have thus far been photographed, and the tumorous rats seem to be easily distinguished from their healthy partners in double-blind studies. Naturally more research is needed before any conclusions can be drawn.

Metallurgy

Metallurgist Dr. William Tiller of Stanford University is conducting research that may furnish pertinent information in this area. We performed one interesting experiment for the National Aeronautics and Space Administration, which wished to learn if invisible fractures in metal could be detected through Kirlian photography. NASA gave us a piece of metal with a fracture less than one three-thousandth of an inch in its apparently smooth surface. After much trial and error, Ken Johnson was able to show the fracture clearly on film. Since that time he has helped the Los Angeles police by revealing the filed-off number of a pistol. These photographs required different techniques, which Ken will describe in detail in his soon-to-be-published, *An Adventure in Photographing the Non-Material World (Without a Camera).*

Bioenergy

This area is of special interest, obviously, to the new science of psychotronics. We have been examining the energy exchange which seems to take place between persons and leaves and between persons and coins. In one study, we learned that by placing our hands above a coin (as we did in the "green thumb" studies), we can make the coin become dimmer in the photograph. By breathing on the coin, we can make its picture entirely disappear.

We are also, of course, exploring the interactions between people, and again we have found a repeatable "disappearance" effect. If two people place their fingers simultaneously on a piece of film, generally both fingerprints will show clearly. However, if we ask them to look into each other's eyes until they feel a strong connection, and we photograph their finger pads during that·eye contact, typically we find that either one or the other of the pair has been "blanked out." His finger pad no longer takes a picture! (See Figure 19.) We have no explanation for this phenomenon, but we believe it may one day be correlated with the nonverbal transactions between people which today we describe as empathic or nonempathic feeling states.

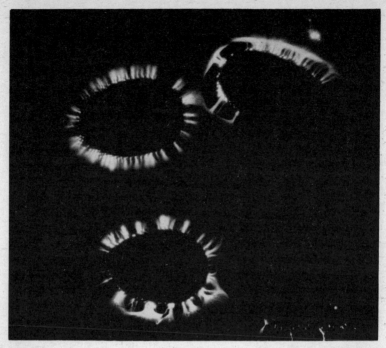

Figure 19. Eye-contact experiment. Fingerprints at top were photographed as two subjects looked away from each other. Fingerprints at bottom were photographed during strong eye contact between the same two subjects.

We have also learned that some people are able to direct the "energy flow" at will. Among our "green thumb" volunteers was Dr. Olga Worrall, a famous American healer whose work will be discussed in the next chapter. The day she performed her first leaf experiment, we had a shock. When we developed the film, we found that the image of the leaf Olga had "healed" had, in fact, all but disappeared: The "brown thumb" effect. Uppermost in my panicked mind was the question: "How can we tell her?" But tell her and show her we did. The next day she asked if she could repeat the experiment because she felt she might have given the leaf "too much." Of course we repeated the study. This time, with more gentle treatment, the leaf flared brilliantly. In other words, Olga Worrall was the first person we found who seemed able to direct the energy flow. Since then, a few other persons have demonstrated a similar ability.

AGAIN, WHAT IS KIRLIAN PHOTOGRAPHY?

As a result of these preliminary studies, we believe we are obtaining visible evidence of a flow of energy, an interaction, between human beings and their environment. Our studies are beginning to be repeated by other laboratories, independently, just as we have been able to duplicate several of the Kirlian effects reported from the Soviet Union: the phantom leaf, the photographic death of a leaf, the influence of a healer, etc.

Of what significance are such results? Oddly, the most succinct answer to that question was given in 1939 by Prat and Schlemmer when they wrote: "There can be no doubt about the complex nature of the radiation pictures. . . . Xylonite, an English fabric which is impermeable to infra-red, visible, and ultra-violet radiation, does not hinder reproduction of the corona." In other words, whatever this unknown radiation, it does not seem to belong to the range of frequencies with which we are familiar; we still cannot define it, twenty-five years after the Prat-Schlemmer article. Perhaps this unknown radiation is linked to the bioenergetic transfer which the Soviets and other researchers have observed in studies with healers. This is a category of unorthodox medicine which has existed for thousands of years, a category which has generally been ignored or derided by our rigorously scientific generation.

Suppose we explore those unorthodox methods of healing next.

3 Bioenergy and Healing

Types of unorthodox or unconventional healing. Healers throughout history. Fake healers. Scientific investigation into healing, and its possible relationship to bioenergy.

We have seen how, in the history of science, electrical photography and other inventions were discovered, lost, and rediscovered through the years. The same phenomenon seems also to occur in the history of ideas. In almost every civilization one can find the idea (discovered, lost, and rediscovered) of an invisible energy that can be channeled toward the sick, an energy that can heal directly, without any intermediary techniques. This healing energy repeatedly has been classified into three areas: healing through the laying on of hands, healing by the power of thought (and/or visualization), and healing at a distance. Let us look at some contemporary evidence for these types of healing: they are anecdotes, of course, and may seem to many readers incredible.

HEALING THROUGH THE LAYING ON OF HANDS

In 1972 the aeronautical engineer Ambrose Worrall died after having spent fifty years of his life, together with his wife, Olga, using their common gifts of healing for all who sought their help. Never once did they charge a fee for their services. Olga Worrall still continues her healing ministry at the New Life Clinic of the Mount Washington Methodist Church in Baltimore. She also travels around the world, lecturing and demonstrating her gifts to scientists, medical doctors, and religious organizations. In 1972, only months after her husband's death, Mrs. Worrall participated in the Dimensions of Healing symposium at UCLA, where she lectured, gave healing demonstrations, and took part in the leaf experiments with Kirlian photography described in the previous chapter. Olga is an energetic, knowledgeable, and witty person who describes herself as "an average housewife." She refers to her psychical ability and healing power as a "natural talent" which everyone has to a greater or lesser degree, just as everyone has some musical ability. However, although anyone can probably learn to play *Chopsticks* on the piano, only a real musician can play Gershwin's *American in Paris*.

Ambrose and Olga discovered their healing gifts independently of each other, before they met. Olga became aware of her talent as a child, when her mother would ask her to place her hands on a painful spot, which promptly removed the pain. As a result, her mother frequently sent Olga to "lay hands" on the sick people in the neighborhood. By contrast, Ambrose never realized anything unusual about himself until he was a young man. One day, as he put it, "an unknown power took control of my body and under its influence I placed my hands on my sister who suffered from a paralyzed neck resulting from an accident. She was instantly cured. I consider this to be the event that revealed to me my healing gift."

Among the best documented cases treated by Ambrose Worrall is that of a nine-year-old girl, brought to him in 1965, with presumably only months to live. She had been diagnosed as suffering from Von Hecklinghausen's disease, which is characterized by numerous subcutaneous nodules, that spread throughout the system, causing death rather swiftly. The existence of the disease had been verified by laboratory tests. For three weeks Ambrose treated the child daily with the laying on of hands, and as he described it, "during that time the soft nodules gradually disappeared, and the hard ones began to recede. The girl was not completely healed when she was taken home." But four years later, in 1969, her father wrote to the Worralls reporting that the child was in perfect health and "all symptoms of the terrible disease were gone."

In another case, a medical doctor brought his own daughter, who was suffering from a bone disease, for treatment. The disease had been verified by x-rays, and an operation had been declared imperative. In Mr. Worrall's words, "I placed my left hand under her knee and my right hand on her knee cap. I felt the healing current strongly, and in a few minutes, I knew the bone was healed. I reported my findings to Dr. G——, who thought it would be wise to have further x-rays taken because he did not want to delay the operation if it were needed." The x-rays showed no further evidence of the disease, and two years later the child was enjoying skiing and swimming, in excellent health.

One of Olga Warrall's most dramatic cases was witnessed by a friend of mine at the New Life Clinic in Baltimore. A woman with an ugly red tumor "as large as a goose egg" on her cheek came forward to Mrs. Worrall, who placed her hand on the lump. When she removed her hands, the tumor was still there, as red and ugly as before. The woman returned to her pew, where she had to pass two ladies who were seated on the aisle. When she asked permission to get by, the two women gasped (as did my friend, who was sitting nearby, watching), because they saw the tumor apparently melt away. By the time the afflicted woman had seated herself, the tumor was gone.

HEALING THROUGH THE POWER OF MIND, AND VISUALIZATION

Another personal friend, the gifted psychic Harold Sherman, has written about his own experience of being healed, in 1920. One day, after tennis, he developed a blister on his toe, which he did not treat carefully and which became infected. His family doctor, Dr. Garner, gave him medication, but gangrene developed and began spreading throughout Harold's system. Finally Dr. Garner called in a surgeon for consultation, and the decision was that if the condition had not dramatically improved by the next morning, the foot would have to be amputated. During the illness, Harold had been practicing a form of self-healing, described in Thomas Hudson's excellent book, *The Law of Psychic Phenomena*. In his mind's eye, Harold had been trying to visualize his toe restored to its normal, healthy condition, but the more he had tried to conjure up that image, the more pain he suffered. With the prospect of surgery imminent, Harold confided in Dr. Garner about what he had been doing, adding "I don't have the mental strength to rise above it. I feel I need the help of a healthy mind in a healthy body. . . . Doctor, when you get home tonight, will you sit quietly by yourself and picture in your mind what has to happen to my toe to make it well?" The doctor agreed—although, in Harold's words, "he looked as if he were wondering if my fever had made me delirious." Harold's landlady had been in the room during this talk, and asked if she could "think along" with the doctor that night, an offer Harold gratefully accepted. The "thought healing" was scheduled to last from 10 to 10:30 P.M. At ten o'clock, in Harold's words,

> I relaxed my body as best I could and made my mind passive. Then, as I had tried countless times before, I sought to see a picture of a healthy toe. Instead all that registered was this toe in its infected state. . . . I knew that Dr. Garner in his home, and Mrs. Walker, nearby, were both visualizing, so I let go of this wrong picture and tried again and again, but each time the picture was unchanged.

However, at twenty minutes past ten something happened:

> Suddenly, it seemed as though I had tuned in on the positive thoughts that were being projected towards me. For just an instant I glimpsed a fleeting picture of my toe as it had been before the infection. The mental relief was so great that I fell asleep and slept the night through for the first time since this gangrene had developed. . . . [The next morning] the swelling was almost gone and I had no pain. Not only that, I had no fever.

This was not an instantaneous cure. It was months before Harold's toe was back to normal, but he believes it was that night's healthy mind power from two friends that effected the cure. Dr. Garner, in corroborating Harold's story, adds: "In my more than forty years of medical practice, this was the nearest thing to a miracle that I have seen."

This technique, the power of visualization, has very recently been employed on cancer patients by a young medical doctor, Carl Simonton, at Langley Air Force Base in California. According to his report given at the Dimensions of Healing symposium at UCLA, Simonton had been practicing a form of meditation, and wondered if the visualization technique of his meditations could be used by patients as a healing force. He obtained permission to try his method on some cancer patients who were considered beyond medical help. At the 1972 symposium, Dr. Simonton presented slides of the patients' illnesses—rectal, mouth, and other forms of cancer in an advanced state—before and after treatment by his method. His special technique was to have his patients (and sometimes their relatives) visualize in their minds for a certain period each day exactly what had to happen in order for their health to return. The recovery rate was so high as to cause extreme reactions (both favorable and unfavorable) among his colleagues.

HEALING AT A DISTANCE

One of the best-known healers in America today is Katherine Kuhlman, who has been practicing since 1946, when the first of her healings took place. According to Miss Kuhlman, at that time she had given a sermon on the Holy Spirit, with no idea at all that she could perform healing. But the next day, a woman came to tell her that after the sermon, she had been cured of a tumor. Gradually others reported being healed. Eventually Miss Kuhlman learned to sense where in her vast audiences the healings were taking place. (It is not uncommon for the healer to be unaware of a healing; nor is it uncommon in this unorthodox healing for a person to be healed without his knowledge.) A medical man, Dr. E. B. Henry, attended one of Miss Kuhlman's services mainly to please his wife, because he had "no more faith than a rabbit." In a letter to Miss Kuhlman, he reported his recovery from a chronic sinus condition of more than thirty years' duration, the restoration of hearing in his right ear (deaf for fifteen years), and the healing of a fractured collarbone. Yet during the service, when Miss Kuhlman was calling out these events, he had not for one moment felt that she was talking about him. It was only when he

was driving home that his wife pointed out he had heard everything she had been saying, even though she had been speaking on
his deaf side. Later x-rays showed the fracture had disappeared;
and that night, with much pain, his sinuses drained, and they never
troubled him again.

One of the most extraordinary healings at a distance is documented in a recent film on the life of the Capucin monk Padre Pio.
The audience is introduced to a young woman who had been born
without pupils in her eyes, which would make it impossible for her
to see (at least, according to present-day medical science). And in
fact, for the first six years of her life, she had been totally blind.
In the film she is shown neatly dodging traffic, and preparing
dinner, both of which tasks demand fairly good vision. Optome-
trists, in the film, confirm that she does see quite well, without
being able to offer an explanation for the phenomenon. No one
can say how she sees, but details of when she began to see are
given by her family and herself. Like many people in Italy the
blind child's mother had read of Padre Pio's miraculous healings,
and in spite of the doctors' pessimism, she decided to send her
daughter to Padre Pio's church. Just before the pilgrimage, as a
treat, the girl was taken to the beach where the blue ocean waves,
the golden sand, and the tiny fishing boats on the horizon were
described to her. En route by train to Padre Pio, the child
suddenly pointed out of the window of the train, which was
chugging along the coast, and exclaimed, "Out there! It is the
beach and the water, isn't it?" By the time the pilgrims had
reached Padre Pio, the child was seeing quite well.

What had happened? Had the child's belief that Padre Pio would
heal her performed the cure? Did the padre know that the healing
had taken place? It is not made clear in the film. But the girl's
vision is abundantly demonstrated.

These are surely incredible, if not preposterous, anecdotes. Most
scientists are convinced that such miracles cannot and do not
occur. They know that for every effect there must be a cause. And
what could cause a tumor to disintegrate in a moment, or what
could cause pupil-less eyes to see? The fact is, such anecdotes have
been recorded in every culture throughout the world, wherever
records have been kept.

HEALERS THROUGHOUT HISTORY

More than twenty-five centuries ago yogis wrote of the healing energy (prana) which could be directed to a sick person by rubbing his body with the hands, by placing the hands on the surface of his skin, or by passing the hands above his skin. They also described a form of healing called "thought force" in which the cure is effected by the influence of mind on mind, in which distance was not a factor.

In Egypt, before the Christian era, ancient rock carvings show healers treating patients by placing one hand on the stomach, the other on the back (reminiscent, perhaps, of Ambrose Worrall's treatment of the child's knee, one hand below, the other above the bone). The Bible, of course, describes how Jesus made clean the lepers and made the crippled walk, by the laying on of hands.

The great Greek physician Hippocrates (whose code is still repeated by doctors today, as a statement of ethics, before they begin practice) wrote about healing hands in these words:

> It is believed by experienced doctors that the heat which oozes out of the hand, on being applied to the sick, is highly salutary. . . . It has often appeared, while I have been thus soothing my patients, as if there were a singular property in my hands to pull and draw away from the affected parts aches and diverse impurities, by laying my hand upon the place, and by extending my fingers toward it. Thus it is known to some of the learned that health may be implanted in the sick by certain gestures, and by contact, as some diseases may be communicated from one to another.

Apparently Hippocrates felt that not only can diseases be transferred from person to person, but also health can be transferred from the healthy to the sick.

Certain royal personages, like the Emperors Vespasian and Hadrian (and King Pyrrhus, who cured colic by the laying on of *toes*), claimed the power of healing. On special days the "king's touch" drew thousands of sufferers for healing both in England and in France as recently as the seventeenth century. During the seventeenth century, the Englishman Valentine Greatrakes (called "The Stroker") became so famous for his cures that in 1665 he worked twelve hours a day, three days a week, healing the sick who flocked to his home. Since he was a man of means, he took no money for his services. It was observed, with surprise, that skeptics were healed by Greatrakes as easily as believers. It was further noticed that when touched, the limbs of the sick often became so anesthetized that the patient could not feel "the deepest pinprick." Greatrakes himself was puzzled by his powers, which apparently faded away as swiftly as they had come to him.

In the late eighteenth century, Anton Mesmer discovered that making "magnetic passes" over his patients often resulted in remarkable cures. These included the restoration of sight to an eighteen-year-old girl, who responded by falling in love with him, thereby causing a scandal which perhaps prompted Mesmer to leave Vienna for Paris. There he not only published his thesis, *Animal Magnetism*, but captured a clientele so vast that he evolved a kind of group therapy, which took place in a large, brilliantly decorated room with mirrors, stained glass, incense and music. In the center of the room was placed a large tub filled with iron filings and bottles of water. The patients would sit in a circle around the tub, holding rods or each others' hands. At a suitable moment, rather like a star of the theater making his entrance, Mesmer would appear in violet silk robes, holding an iron rod with which he would make passes over one or another patient. This effect apparently produced a form of ecstasy. Reading accounts of these seances, one is given the impression of a revivalist meeting, in which uncontrollable emotional outbursts, fainting, "speaking in tongues," and occasional instant healings occurred. Probably because of his elaborate showmanship, Mesmer became an object of suspicion to his colleagues. He was twice investigated by the French Academy of Science, one of the two committees including the American scientist Benjamin Franklin. In 1784 the committee reported, unanimously, that Mesmer's successes (which did exist) were probably due to "suggestion," that his theory of magnetism was without foundation, and that occasionally his patients suffered adverse reactions. Mesmer was discredited, his clientele evaporated, and he retired for the last thirty years of his life to a small Swiss village.

In spite of this, other doctors took up Mesmer's work. A British surgeon in India, James Esdaile, wrote an almost unbelievable book, reporting his use of magnetic passes to produce a state of insensibility in his patients. (This phenomenon is reminiscent of the inability of Valentine Greatrake's patients to feel a deep pinprick. A pinprick test is still used today to determine the depth of hypnosis.) Esdaile trained assistants in making the magnetic passes, which anesthetized the patients so that he could perform major operations, including the amputation of whole limbs and the removal of tumors weighing as much as forty pounds. There are photographs in his book which lend credence to his reports. By a remarkable coincidence, at just the time Esdaile discovered the anesthetic properties of magnetic passes, ether was discovered in the Western world. Ether proved to be far easier and quicker to use for anesthesia than the tedious technique of magnetic passes, and mesmerism again faded from use.

But "animal magnetism" reappeared in the United States, swerving onto a curious course, due primarily to a remarkably inquisitive clockmaker of Portland, Maine, named Phineas P. Quimby. Quimby saw a stage performer give a demonstration of mesmerism, and he was so impressed that he tried to achieve the same effect. He had indifferent success until he found a remarkable young subject named Lucius. Lucius achieved a state of deep trance readily, and in trance was able not only to diagnose patients but to prescribe remedies to treat them. In fact, Quimby was healed of his own devastating illness by Lucius. Quimby described the diagnosis as follows:

> I had pains in the back which, they said, were caused by my kidneys. Under this belief, I was miserable enough to be of no account in the world. . . . On one occasion, when I had Lucius asleep, he described the pains I felt in my back (I had never dared to ask him to examine me there, for I felt sure my kidneys were nearly gone), and he placed his hand on the spot where I felt the pain. He then told me that my kidneys were in a very bad state—that one was half consumed, and a piece three inches long had separated from it, and was only connected by a slender thread.

Quimby then asked him if there was any remedy. He replied, "Yes, I can put the piece on so it will grow, and you will get well." According to Quimby, Lucius then proceeded to heal him:

He immediately placed his hands upon me, and said he united the pieces so they would grow. The next day he said they had grown together, and from that day I never have experienced the least pain from them. . . . Now what is the secret of the cure? . . . If he had said, as I expected he would, that nothing could be done, I should have died in a year or so. But, when he said he could cure me in the way he proposed, I began to think: and I discovered that I had been deceived into *a belief that made me sick*.

Possessed of a fine (uneducated) mind and a consuming curiosity, Quimby determined to learn how to become clairvoyant himself, without mesmerism, in order to understand better the mystery of illness and health he had experienced in his own body. He succeeded in training himself so that he could sit beside a patient and with full concentration learn the nature of and treatment for the disease. According to Quimby,

At first I found that my thoughts affected the subject, and not only my thought but my belief. *If I really believed anything, the effect would follow whether I was thinking it or not. . . .* I found that *belief in everything affects us, yet we are not aware of it. . . .* The creating of a disease is under the superstition of man's belief.

Quimby became a healer, using this method of getting rid of the false belief, which lies at a deep level of mind, *unknown to the patient.* Along with the disappearance of the belief, goes the disease. Thus Quimby postulated the subliminal or unconscious mind some fifty years before Freud, or Myers.

Quimby's work as a healer made him famous, and patients flocked to him from all over the United States. In 1861, he received a letter from a dentist, Dr. Patterson, asking for help: "My wife has been an invalid for a number of years; is able to sit up but a little, and we wish to have the benefit of your wonderful power in her case." When she arrived in Portland for treatment, she had to be carried to her hotel bedroom. In her own words:

The belief of my recovery had died out of the hearts of those who were most anxious for it. With this mental and physical depression I first visited P. P. Quimby; and in less than one week from that time I ascended a stairway of one hundred and eighty two steps to the dome of City Hall. . . . The truth which [Quimby] establishes in the patient cures him [although he may be wholly unconscious thereof]; and the body, which is full of light, is no longer in disease. At present I am too much in error to elucidate the truth, and can only touch the keynote of the master hand.

The lady who was cured was Mary Baker Eddy (then Mrs. Patterson). She remained in Portland to study with Quimby, worshipful of his teachings and grateful for his "miraculous cure," which lasted until a few years later, when, as she wrote in a letter,

I fell on a sidewalk, and struck my back on the ice, and was taken up for dead, came to consciousness . . . to find myself the helpless cripple I was before I saw Dr. Quimby. The physician attending said I had taken the last step I ever should, but in two days I got out of bed *alone.*

This letter was written to Julius Dresser, an associate of Quimby, asking for help, for Quimby now was dead. Dresser could not help her, and Mrs. Eddy was thus forced to help herself, which she certainly did! For Mrs. Eddy, as there had been for Quimby, there were years of searching, discovery, and disappointment. But eventually, as we know, she evolved her own method of mind cure and established the Christian Science Church. Controversy still rages over what was contributed by Quimby and what by Mrs. Eddy, to the "Science of Mind." It is unnecessary to take sides: both contributed, and both suffered unexpected, frequent failures. One of Quimby's patients wrote:

He asked me to concentrate my mind on him, and to think of nothing and nobody but him. . . . As the relief came to me, he suffered greatly himself, saying that he took on my pain. . . . After following his directions for about four years, I experienced only temporary relief.

(This "boomerang" effect, the healer taking on the pain of the patient, is not uncommon; many inexperienced healers have suffered this reaction.)

Although failures in the Christian Science Church have been legion, it must be remembered that practitioners have effected cures time and time again. The basic difference in the methods of Quimby and Mrs. Eddy is probably best described by Mrs. Eddy's biographer, Robert Peel: Quimby stressed the "God within," whereas Mrs. Eddy insisted that "God is not *in* man." Quimby's healing relied not at all on religious beliefs (in fact, he thought that religious beliefs could unknowingly bring illness to the patient), whereas Mrs. Eddy's healing resulted in the founding of a still-powerful church. Essentially, however, both agreed that there is a science of mind that heals.

There began to mushroom, all over the United States, churches and nonchurches of what William James, one of America's great pioneer psychologists, called the "mind-cure movements" in the guise of transcendentalism, spiritism, Hinduism, or the dogma of "healthy-minded attitudes." In 1900 James wrote:

> The mind-cure principles are beginning so to pervade the air that one catches their spirit second-hand. One hears of the "Gospel of Relaxation," of the "Don't Worry Movement," of people who repeat to themselves, "Youth, health, vigour!" when dressing in the morning. . . . These general tonic effects on public opinion would be good even if the more striking results were non-existent. But the latter abound so that we can afford to overlook the innumerable failures and self-deceptions that are mixed in with them. . . . To the importance of mind-cure the medical and clerical professions in the United States are beginning, though with much recalcitrancy and protesting, to open their eyes.

He tried to make peace between science and this kind of religion:

> Science gives to all of us telegraphy, electric lighting, and diagnosis, and succeeds in preventing and curing a certain amount of disease. Religion in the shape of mind-cure gives to some of us serenity, moral poise, and

happiness, and prevents certain forms of disease as well as science does, or even better in a certain class of persons. Evidently, then, the science and the religion are both of them genuine keys for unlocking the world's treasure house to him who can use either of them practically. Just as evidently neither is exhaustive or inclusive of the other's simultaneous use. And why, after all, may not the world be so complex as to consist of many interpenetrating spheres of reality?

Mind-cure movements flourished in the beginning of the twentieth century. They are beginning to flourish again under different names: Mind Control, Mind Dynamics, Yoga, Zen, Biofeedback, Transcendental Meditation. Some of these movements today are attempting to do exactly what William James suggested: to make a union between science and religion, both of them "genuine keys for unlocking the world's treasure house."

AN EXTENDED SCIENTIFIC INVESTIGATION OF HEALING

The oldest and most rigorous medical investigation of healing is that which has taken place at Lourdes, where more than a hundred years ago an illiterate, asthmatic fourteen-year-old peasant girl named Bernadette had a vision of a "beautiful lady" in a grotto. This subsequently became a shrine attracting people seeking to be cured of every conceivable kind of illness. In 1882 a medical bureau, staffed by physicians, began to examine the thousands of claims of "miraculous cures" made every year. It has been estimated that between 70 and 80 million people have sought healing at Lourdes; of that number, according to the English psychiatrist Louis Rose, who has written a careful and critical book, *Faith Healing*, the number of verified cures of organic illnesses "runs to only a thousand or so in all." Further, Dr. Rose reports that "the successes which are fully accepted by the church . . . are estimated at perhaps one in two million, and that even marked physical improvement as a whole runs at only about two percent." He concludes that the significance of the shrine appears to be more "religious than medical."

But how can we account for those one thousand persons who were judged medically to have recovered from incurable illnesses?

SPONTANEOUS REMISSION

Generally, one of two theories is offered to explain inexplicable cures: Either the patient has had a "spontaneous remission" or he has responded to the "power of suggestion."

Hospital records show, rarely (as rarely perhaps as the authenticated cases at Lourdes), that a patient who has been diagnosed as terminally ill can make a dramatic, complete recovery for reasons which are unknown. As a graduate student, I heard one of my professors discuss in class a case of spontaneous remission which he personally had observed. The patient had severe pain symptoms which sounded suspiciously like cancer, but the presence of cancer could not be verified without exploratory surgery. On the operating table, it was found that he had a malignant growth which had spread so widely that it was impossible to do anything more than sew him up again. The prognosis was that he could live a few weeks at most. Strangely, the medical decision was not to tell the patient's wife the true condition of her husband. Instead she was informed that "everything was fine" and that she could take her husband home. She was given powerful pain-killing medication for him. The expectation was that the patient would die, peacefully, in his sleep. The wife was told to telephone the hospital immediately should any problems arise; otherwise all that was required was a "checkup" in six months' time. To the amazement of the medical staff, at the end of six months husband and wife returned for the "checkup," the former patient apparently in excellent health. Examinations revealed no sign of a terminal cancer, and tests taken for several years after showed that he was cancer-free.

What had happened to the cancer? The medical term is "spontaneous remission," a nice term that explains nothing. Again, to use the statistics offered by Louis Rose, "there is evidence that between one in 10,000 and one in 100,000 cases are classified as spontaneous remission. The problem presented by this phenomenon is described by Louis Rose as "frightening and uncanny . . . and calls for more accurate statistics."

THE POWER OF SUGGESTION

The sudden alleviation under hypnosis of paralysis, stuttering, migraine headache, intractable pain, and many other illnesses is considered by the medical profession to be due to the power of suggestion.

Carl Jung describes a fascinating incident in which he was demonstrating hypnosis to a group of medical students. The patient was a middle-aged woman who had been suffering for seventeen years with a painful paralysis of the left leg. It was Jung's custom to elicit a brief history from the patient before inducing hypnosis. This patient obliged all too heartily, explaining her condition in laborious detail. In Jung's words:

> Finally I interrupted her and said, "Well, now, we have no more time for so much talk. I am now going to hypnotize you."
> I had scarcely said the words when she closed her eyes and fell into a profound trance—without any hypnosis at all! She went on talking without pause, and related the most remarkable dreams—dreams that represented a fairly deep experience of the unconscious. This, however, I did not understand until years later. At the time I assumed she was in a kind of delirium. The situation was gradually growing rather uncomfortable for me. Here were twenty students present, to whom I was going to demonstrate hypnosis!

Jung then attempted to awaken the women, and when he could not, he became alarmed:

> It took some ten minutes before I succeeded in waking her. All the while I dared not let the students observe my nervousness. When the woman came to, she was giddy and confused. I said to her, "I am the doctor and everything is all right." Whereupon she cried out, "But I am cured!" threw away her crutches, and was able to walk. Flushed with embarrassment, I said to the students, "Now you've seen what can be done with hypnosis!" In fact I had not the slightest idea what had happened.

That was one of the experiences that prompted me to abandon hypnosis. I could not understand what had really happened, but the woman was in fact cured. . . . I asked her to let me hear from her, since I counted on a relapse in twenty-four hours at the latest. But her pains did not recur; in spite of my skepticism, I had to accept the fact of her cure.

A repeated, demonstrable effect of the power of suggestion, which is in fact as inexplicable as Jung's cure with hypnosis, is the use of the placebo. As an example, it is not uncommon for a patient to return again and again to his doctor with a chronic complaint, such as migraine headache. The physician has prescribed every known pharmacological agent for the relief of migraine, and nothing has worked. In this situation, the canny doctor looks up with mystery and excitement as his patient comes in the next time, and announces that a new miracle drug, infallible in its relief of migraine, has just been made available. The doctor then gives the patient a bottle of placebos (generally pills containing nothing but a little sugar). The patient takes the placebo—and the migraine vanishes!

This phenomenon has been reported so frequently that it is a routine procedure, in testing new drugs, to try the new drug on one group of patients, and to give placebos to another group who are told they are receiving the new drug. The placebo group often shows just as high a cure rate as the experimental group. A most confounding phenomenon, this power of suggestion.

GENUINE VERSUS FAKE HEALERS

The medical profession, while believing in the efficacy of suggestion and spontaneous remission, is loath to accept the idea that an untrained, nonmedical person can heal a serious illness. That is a reasonable attitude. The healing procedures, so simple as to appear absurd, smack of magic. Which they often are.

Charlatan healers (and they are common) intensify this aura of mystery and magic as much as Mesmer did. Usually their offices are spectacularly decorated, with pictures of patients before and after treatment prominent on the walls, especially any patients who are well-known figures. Testimonials are also on display, from clientele and even medical doctors. (These are seldom valid; I have been quoted as recommending quacks whose names I have never heard.) The waiting rooms provide special kinds of music and lighting, as in a well-staged theatrical production. And sometimes the "healing instrument" is an impressive piece of equipment that looks like the latest thing in computer technology but in fact does nothing. The fees that are charged are exorbitant, and the patient is given complex explanations for why the treatment has to be prolonged for weeks or months. Such are the outward trappings of the fake healer.

Unfortunately, the genuine healer also resorts at times to subterfuge. For instance, both real and fake healers may ally themselves with a religious movement and acquire the title of "Reverend." This allows them to practice "spiritual counseling," in which such innocuous practices as the laying on of hands, or mind cures, are permissible. The reason such subterfuge is necessary is that it is a criminal offense in every state of the union to practice medicine without a license. The healer, genuine or fake, does exactly that because he has no education in the healing arts and no degree that can be hung on the wall. As a result, various kinds of healers have been persecuted by law. For example, until very recently the practice of acupuncture was outlawed everywhere in the United States (although it was practiced surreptitiously among the Oriental subcultures of every large city). The use of hypnosis was also proscribed by law, even in the medical profession, until 1957. The curanderos of Mexico, the kahunas of Hawaii, the "psychic surgeons" of the Phillipines, and other practitioners of folk medicine are also outside the law. Yet pharmacologists like Dr. Robert de Ropp admit freely that folk medicine, with its lore of medicinal herbs, has been productive of such invaluable drugs as quinine, ephedrine, digitalis, and rauwolfia, whose effectiveness was at first regarded as an "old wives' tale."

CHARACTERISTICS OF THE GENUINE HEALER

There appear to be a few characteristics common to genuine healers, past and present.

They Do Not Know What They Do

Typically, the healer uses no medication and no special rituals and he cannot explain in what his treatment consists. Kathryn Kuhlman is quoted by her biographer, Allen Spraggett, as saying: "Sometimes in the miracle service I stand there and see all those wonderful things happen and I don't understand *how* they happened or what happened to cause them to happen, and all I know is that we made contact some place but I don't know how.... I feel so stupid sometimes."

Healers' descriptions of their subjective experiences while healing are frequently very similar. They describe a "force" or "energy" or "spirit" traveling through them, going out toward the patient. Sometimes this force is felt as a tingling, sometimes as intense heat, and sometimes as a coolness. Ambrose Worrall has described his experience of the force in these words:

> During a healing treatment I do not turn my attention to some far-off place up in the heavens nor do I look for the source of power anywhere else or ask it to come to me.... When the power flows through my hands, I feel a heat and sometimes I feel pins and needles.

In the Soviet Union the healer Krivorotov has been studied intensively by scientists, among them Victor Adamenko, who describes Krivorotov's work in these words:

> Outwardly the process of treatment is as follows: Krivorotov prepares himself ... by concentrating in *thought* on the patient. Thereupon by forcibly rubbing one of the palms against the other he makes his hands dry and in a slow motion over the patient's hair electrifies his hands.... As Krivorotov passes his hands at some distance along the patient's body, there arises in the patient approximately at the site of the sick organ a strong subjective sense of heat, at times almost unbearable. Krivorotov also feels at this place an intensification of heat in his hand. Stopping his hand, he says, "You feel a pain here."

Compare that description with this passage in Yogi Rama-charaka's *Science of Psychic Healing* (published in 1906):

> Prana is the name given by Yogi philosophers to "Vital Force" or Energy. . . . Prana may be transferred or transmitted from one person to another in many ways. The usual method, and the most effective, is to use the hands and make passes over the sick person. . . . Rub the hands together briskly . . . until they have the un-definable feeling of "aliveness" and being full of energy. . . . Then bring the fingers down along the spine, slowly and firmly. . . . If you notice a point much colder or warmer than the neighboring points . . . [there is] pain and abnormal action.

In our laboratory work with more than twenty healers, sixteen of them have described the sensation of heat, tingling, and/or coldness. Jack Gray, who prefers not to call himself a healer, has been working with us for years, using hypnosis and magnetic passes in many experiments. While making his magnetic passes, he frequently hesitates at one or another part of the subject's body, describing a sensation of either intense cold or heat. On one occasion, while making passes over a research associate, he directed his hands above the head, moving them back and forth in an unusual manner. I asked what was going on, and Jack replied, "There's something wrong up here; it's very hot, I get strong tingling sensations." After the hypnotic session was finished, Jack casually asked the colleague if at any time recently he had suffered a blow on the top of his head. The colleague grinned sheepishly and confessed that the night before he had leaned out of his window to get a better look at the sunset, and the window had crashed down on top of his head. No bump, or other indication of the accident was visible.

They Have Often Never Been Taught How to Heal; They Discover Their Talents in Unexpected Ways

We have already learned how Olga Worrall's mother first became aware of Olga's talent as a child, how Ambrose Worrall felt "impelled" as a young man to help his paralyzed sister, and how Kathryn Kuhlman was informed she had unknowingly performed a healing during a sermon.

Many healers learn about their ability in some accidental way, often as a result of some crisis (like the healer in our laboratory who had found himself with an unendurable headache in the middle of a desert). A healer currently being studied in the laboratory of parapsychologist Douglas Dean is Mrs. Ethel de Loach. Mrs. de Loach has been doing healing work only for the past few years. The first time she tried it was when her daughter had been kicked in the leg by a horse, was suffering intense pain, and no physician was available. In desperation, she decided to try the laying on of hands. Within a few minutes, her daughter was free of pain. Since that time, Mrs. de Loach has performed healing successfully on patients with terminal illness, even being allowed, on one occasion, that still rare privilege in the United States of performing her services in a modern hospital.

They Claim No Ability of Their Own

Olga Worrall has said, "I must emphasize that I have no control over this ability." And Ambrose Worrall insisted that he was merely "a channel or conductor for the spiritual power that flows through me for healing. I have no control over the flow of healing current. I cannot turn it on." Phineas Quimby insisted that he possessed "no 'power' nor healing properties different from anyone else." Miss Kuhlman freely admits that she can't "demand or command God to do anything. In general, I believe it is God's will to heal. But I can't say absolutely what is or is not His will in a particular case." Padre Pio has answered to those who came to express gratitude for his healing, "I have done nothing. Good people, do not involve me. You, with the force of your faith, helped yourselves."

Again and again the healer speaks of making himself passive, a channel for the force or energy which does all the work. To quote once more from Ambrose Worrall, whose scientific training may make these concepts more acceptable, perhaps, to the modern audience:

I sit with a patient and do what I call a "tuning-in" operation. This is done by sitting in a relaxed state and fixing my attention on the patient, but not to any specific part of the body. . . . In many cases I have to talk to the patient and get his or her mind entirely away from the disease. I might talk about football, baseball, or some other subject of general interest. After a while I find it easier to tune in because I have caused the patient temporarily to forget about his affliction.

After the 'tune-in' has been accomplished, the conditions are such that the force can flow. It will flow provided the potential in the patient is lower than the potential in the healer. It will always flow from the high to the low potential. [Note: Is this the reason for the "boomerang effect" reported earlier?]

The power that flows is entirely impersonal. Although I am instrumental in creating the conditions which permit the force to flow, actually I have no control over it whatsoever.

They Do Not Claim to Heal Everyone

We have already learned that there is a 2 percent chance of physical improvement if one makes a pilgrimage to Lourdes. It is fairly safe to say that most healers have a higher percentage of cure; otherwise they would have given up, or their patients would have stopped coming for treatment. But healers freely admit that a large percentage of their patients do *not* respond to treatment. The Worralls have written:

Quite a number of deserving people fail to get the healings. We deeply regret this but there is nothing we can do about it. Miraculous, instantaneous healings seldom occur, but we have had tumors and malignant growths shrivel up and disappear beneath our hands.

Miss Kuhlman also is free to admit that she never knows who among her vast audiences will receive the curative power. It is not known what percentage of her audiences receive cures, but it seems not unreasonable to believe that the cured are a small minority.

The healer, then, makes no claim to infallibility. But of course, neither does the medical doctor.

They Believe in Working with the Medical Profession

Usually people who are seriously ill do not go to a healer unless medical treatment has failed. Healers are very much aware of this fact, and most of them believe that the medical treatment received prior to their work may have greatly contributed to the healing. Again to quote from the Worralls:

> We never interfere with medical treatment. We insist that physicians be consulted in all cases. We believe prayer and medicine do not stand unalterably opposed. . . . We recognize that in practically every case of illness, medical or other treatment has been administered before spiritual healing is tried; that in cases where recovery follows both spiritual healing and medical treatment, it may be the result of the two methods. . . . We believe spiritual healers should work in association with other healing professions.

And, in fact, the Worralls participated for many years in healing experiments with scientists and doctors at Wainwright House in New York, an organization doing research in unorthodox healing.

Padre Pio is reported by one of his biographers, Oscar de Liso, as recommending operations to several of his parishioners. He himself underwent surgery. And his great goal was to establish at San Giovanni Rotando, where he lived most of his life, a modern hospital with the best of facilities—a goal which was completed in 1956.

Some medical men do not share this cooperative feeling. It was only after some thirty years of struggle that the famous English healer Harry Edwards won permission for his National Federation of Spiritual Healers to minister (with proper medical sanction) to patients in over fifteen hundred British hospitals.

In the Soviet Union, the healer Krivorotov has been working with his son, a medical doctor, on particularly recalcitrant cases. Even more remarkable is the fact that Krivorotov's healing has been the subject of an official investigation by the Georgian Republic's Ministry of Health. According to an article by Adamenko in the *Journal of Paraphysics,* "The conclusive evidence, obtained by a commission presided over by the Academician Pyotr Kavtaradze, was positive."

BIOENERGY AND HEALING

Is there a common thread that can be discerned through these various phenomena of healing? I believe so. The Hindus call it "prana," the Hawaiians "mana," the Chinese "ch'i," and Hippocrates called it the "heat oozing out of the hand," Mesmer "animal magnetism," and Quimby "mind force." I believe they were all referring to the same invisible energy.

Recently scientists have invented other words to describe essentially the same force: the German von Reichenbach believed he had discovered an invisible energy which he christened "od"; an English couple, Marjorie and George de la Warr, describe a method of diagnosis and treatment based on "radionics"; psychoanalyst Wilhelm Reich believed that the invisible energy which he discovered and christened "orgone" could be accumulated in a box built of alternating conductive and nonconductive materials. Reich built "orgone boxes," much like empty telephone booths, in which he had patients sit. He believed the accumulated "orgone" had a beneficial effect on emotional and physical disorders, including cancer. Reich was accused of advertising false cancer cures and was jailed. His researches into orgone are now being intensively investigated by scientists.

A still-unanswered question was raised at the Prague conference: Can it be that all forms of energy (from that which moves a muscle to that which propels a rocket, to gravitational, electromagnetic, and cosmic energies) derive from one basic energy, an energy about which we still know almost nothing? The question is reminiscent of the one propounded by the Greek Democritus some two thousand years ago: Is it possible that all matter, whether air, earth, fire, or water, is composed of one basic substance, the atom?

SCIENTIFIC INVESTIGATIONS OF A "HEALING ENERGY"

Only very recently, as we have learned, has the concept of bioenergy been subjected to laboratory experiments. To my knowledge, the most extended, rigorous, and successful series of studies on a "healing energy" has been performed by Dr. Bernard Grad, a biochemist doing research in gerontology at McGill University in Canada. In 1957, Dr. Grad met a Hungarian emigré, Colonel Estabany, a former cavalry officer who first discovered his healing powers by noticing the unusual calming and curative effect his hands had on injured horses. Impressed by Estabany's sincerity and apparent ability, Grad began to wonder if this faculty, the laying on of hands, could be tested with standard biomedical procedures. Grad writes, "The problem may reside in the very simplicity of the procedure. . . . Another problem may be the belief that the person with the healing gift (if one accepts this possibility) and the mountebank cannot be distinguished." Mountebank and healer, as we have said, both simply place their hands upon the sick.

Grad proceeded to design several sophisticated experiments to find out, empirically, if Estabany could speed up healing, and if so, to try to understand the process by which such accelerated healing had occurred. Although Estabany had only treated large mammals (horses, dogs, people), he agreed to try his hand with the laboratory mice Grad had at his disposal. Grad describes one study:

> Skin wounds were made on the backs of mice, some of whom were treated by Colonel E. simply by having the mice in suitable containers placed between his hands for two fifteen-minute periods daily, five and a half days per week, until the wounds were healed twenty days after they were made. Control mice were placed in similar containers and either were left untreated or were treated in the identical manner of Col. E., but by persons making no claim to a healing gift. The results showed that the rate of wound healing was significantly faster (by a statistical analysis) in the group treated by Col. E. than in the other two groups.

Estabany, then, did show a healing gift, but no instantaneous healing of the mice wounds had taken place. Many other studies were made with mice, during some of which the mice were given goiters, which dissolved under Estabany's hands in a significantly shorter time than the goiters of the control mice.

Grad then turned Estabany's talents to several triple-blind studies with plants. The only variable manipulated was the water used for watering the plants. Three kinds of water were used: water held by Estabany, untreated water, and water held by a nonhealer. Again,

> Significant stimulation in plant growth was obtained when Mr. E. held in his hands, for thirty minutes, the vessels containing the solutions with which his plants were later watered, and such results were obtained not only when the solutions were treated in open beakers, but also in closed reagent bottles. The laying on of hands directly on the plants themselves was found to be unnecessary.

Whatever the energy might be, it could apparently be transferred, through the glass, into the water. Grad became convinced (and admits his astonishment at being convinced) that there was a special force or energy emanating from Estabany which promotes healing and growth.

Grad then began to wonder if one's mental or emotional state might have a similar effect on plants. Since Grad works in a medical center, he had access to patients with mental and emotional disturbances. Using that advantage, he devised an ingenious study in which jars of water were held in the hands for thirty minutes. Grad asked three people to perform that chore: a man suffering from psychotic depression, a woman diagnosed as being neurotically depressed, and a lab assistant who had demonstrated he could perform healing in a manner similar to Estabany. In addition, of course, there was a control bottle of water which nobody held. Some of the most interesting effects occurred at the beginning of the experiment, when Grad asked the patients' cooperation. As he approached the man with psychotic depression, the patient looked at him and said, "But, doctor, I told you I don't want electroshock treatment." Dr. Grad explained he had not come to give shock treatment; he simply wanted the man to hold a jug of water in his hands for thirty minutes. The patient passively took the bottle, and held it for thirty minutes with no change of expression, until Grad returned to get the bottle, when the patient again said, "But, doctor, I told you I don't want electroshock treatment." Grad assured him again that he was not going to administer shock, and retrieved the bottle. Things went differently with the neurotically depressed woman. When Grad asked her to hold the jug of water for thirty minutes, she wanted to know why he wanted her to do such a foolish thing. When he explained the experiment, she smiled and said, "What a marvelous idea!" And for thirty minutes, she cradled the bottle in her lap as if it were a baby. (When Grad saw her do that, as he tells the story, *he* got depressed, because her mood of "depression" which he was attempting to study had been transformed into enthusiasm). Results of the study showed that the water held by the lab assistant grew plants that were significantly larger and grew faster. The plants treated by the water held by the psychotically depressed man grew slowest by far. And as might be expected by the mood of the neurotic woman *at the time she was holding the water jug*, plants treated with this water performed better than those watered from the control jar and those watered from the jar held by the psychotic patient, but not as well as those watered from the lab assistant's jug. Grad believes, on the basis of his study, that one's mood can affect the health of plants. This effect is reminiscent of our own photographic studies of "green thumbs" and "brown thumbs."

Grad also believes that the results of these and other studies may help to explain the placebo effect. As we have learned, many patients when given a placebo have reported relief (even when given an active placebo—a drug with an action opposite that of the real drug). Grad suggests that the mood or belief of the experimenter might also have a direct, measurable effect on the influence of the placebo. He quotes the case of

> two investigators [who] measured gastric secretions in healthy humans in response to an oral placebo. In one group of subjects, a 12% increase in gastric acidity was observed and in another group an 18% decrease was observed following administration of the placebo. These differing results were consistent when each of the experimenters was used.

Grad points out that a general explanation of the placebo effect is the power of suggestion, the same explanation being offered for

the healing effects of the laying on of hands. He disagrees, point-
ing out that the growth rate of plants cannot be accounted for by
the power of suggestion since barley seeds (used in his plant
studies) "by all normal criteria are not suggestible." Then Grad
offers his alternative explanation:

> The fact that such (growth) effects were produced in
> the plant experiments, via a saline solution treated in
> closed or sealed bottles strongly implicates a physical
> agent—an *energy*. The strongest evidence comes . . .
> from the laying on of hands, because the majority of
> so-called healers have frequently claimed to experience a
> vibration or flow of energy during the laying on of
> hands.

Although Grad's studies were published steadily from 1958
through 1967, they were generally ignored until Sister Justa Smith
read them. Sister Justa is a practicing nun who, in her own words,
"kicked the habit." She obtained her Ph.D in biochemistry and
has served as chairman of Rosary Hill College's Department of
Natural Sciences. It occurred to her that what Estabany had done
with mice and barley seeds, he might also be able to do with
enzymes, her particular field of study. Estabany accepted Sister
Justa's invitation to work in her lab one summer. At that time her
work load would be at a minimum and she could supervise the
experiments herself.

Sister Justa's idea was simple but splendid. Enzymes are cata-
lysts which regulate the reactions of our cells; thus, Sister Justa
reasoned, any change from illness to health would be regulated by
enzyme activity. She planned to compare the effects of Estabany's
hands on enzyme activity, with the activity produced by a high
magnetic field, and also with the activity of control enzymes not
subjected to any treatment. After many sets of experiments, Sister
Justa reported, "It is interesting to note that the qualitative effect
of a high magnetic field and a paranormal 'healer' are the same."
In other words, Estabany affected enzyme activity in much the
same way as did a strong magnetic field, suggesting a form of
energy similar, in effect, to magnetism. (Remember Mesmer's
discredited theory of animal magnetism?) Since those first experi-

ments, Sister Justa has worked with three other psychic healers, and obtained similar results. She reports now, "These results, together with those obtained with Mr. Estabany, would indicate that a person blessed with healing power can affect the enzyme trypsin by increasing its activity. . . . It is possible that this effect can contribute to over-all good health."

These experiments by Grad and Sister Justa demonstrate that the healing energy can affect both water and chemicals. An interesting study reported by Dr. Francois Leuret of the Lourdes Medical Bureau and performed at the Naples Institute of Hygiene is relevant here. Animals injected with microbes, and given Lourdes water, do not develop disease, while similarly infected animals given local water die within a few days. But the Lourdes water was demonstrated to be *no different chemically* from the local water.

It is important to add that Sister Justa repeated her studies with Estabany during a fall semester, when she could devote very little time to the work. A lab assistant replaced her as Estabany's colleague, and this "different experimenter" (as in the placebo study) achieved results that did *not* show an increase in activity in Estabany's treated enzymes. The problem of the effect of the experimenter on the experiment is one that has plagued psychological (and biological) research for many years. Psychologist Robert Rosenthal of Harvard University, in a very long series of experiments, has shown that experimenters who are told their subjects are slow, or fast, learners actually obtain slow, or fast, learning rates, although both groups had been carefully selected to be of the same learning ability. Thus, the *belief* of the experimenter may prove to be one of the most crucial variables in any study. As you may remember, one of the keynotes at the Prague conference was the subjective influence of the experimenter on the experiment.

A LABORATORY STUDY OF "HEALING AT A DISTANCE"

There have been, to my knowledge, only two laboratory studies of "healing at a distance." They were conducted by research chemist Dr. Robert Miller, in Georgia. Dr. Miller met the Worralls when they visited Atlanta, and he showed them his laboratory, where he was conducting experiments on the growth rate of rye grass under different lighting conditions. The Worralls expressed interest in this research, and Miller expressed, in return, interest in conducting a "distant-prayer" experiment when the Worralls returned to their home in Baltimore, more than six hundred miles away. The Worralls agreed. Quoting now from Dr. Miller's article:

> On January 4, [1967] the growth rate of a new blade of rye grass had just been stabilized at 0.00625 inches per hour. During the night of January 3rd the growth rate on the strip chart recorded was a straight line. The straight line continued with little or no deviation during the night of January 4th. At 8:00 P.M. on the evening of January 4th a long distance call was made to Baltimore and the Worralls were asked to hold the plant in their thoughts at their usual 9:00 P.M. prayer time. They said they would do so. Their method of "praying" for the plant was to visualize it as growing vigorously.
>
> The trace on the strip chart recorded was carefully examined the next morning. Dr. Miller describes the results: All through the evening and up until 9:00 P.M. the trace was a straight line with a slope which represented a growth rate of 0.00625 inches per hour. At exactly 9:00 P.M. the trace began deviating upward and by 8:00 A.M. the next morning the growth rate was 0.0525 inches per hour, a growth rate increase of 830%.

In 1974, collaborating with Dr. Philip Reinhart and Anita Kern, Miller discovered that Olga Worrall could create a wave pattern in an Atomic Laboratories cloud chamber by holding her hands near the chamber. Mrs. Worrall was then asked to try to affect the cloud chamber from her home in Baltimore, hundreds of miles away, and she succeeded on two occasions. Photographs taken during the second experiment reveal pulsating wave patterns which continued to occur for the eight minutes Mrs. Worrall was concentrating. (Other persons acting as controls were unable to affect the cloud chamber in any way.) Miller writes, "Additional experiments under still more rigorously controlled conditions are now being conducted to establish statistical validity."

These remarkable effects are perhaps not examples of healing at a distance. More properly they might be considered cases of bioenergy affecting objects at a distance. This bioenergetic influence, if that is what it is, has been examined by some scientists as a means of either *transmitting* information or its opposite polarity, *receiving* information. We'll examine this latter concept in the next chapter.

4 Receiving Bioenergy: Dowsing, Skin Vision, Acupuncture

Information received bioenergetically.

We have seen in Kirlian photography that there seems to be a visible transfer of energy from healer to patient. Before treatment, the healer has a wide corona and the patient a narrow one; whereas after treatment, the healer's corona has decreased and the patient's has increased. This visible shift suggests that the patient is *receiving* energy, which is sometimes reported as a subjective sensation of heat, or cold, or tingling, and is occasionally translated into a feeling of well-being. It might be assumed, then, that the human organism is capable of receiving energy, which can be transduced or translated into special kinds of information.

In addition to healing, there are other areas, controversial to be sure, in which information seems to be received bioenergetically. These areas include dowsing (water witching or divining), skin vision (eyeless sight or dermo-optical perception), and that recent bombshell in Western medicine arrived from China, the theory and therapy of acupuncture. Let's investigate these fields.

DOWSING

It has been claimed since Greek and Roman times that certain people have the faculty of being able to locate underground water by walking with a forked twig (or metal coat hanger or divining rod) held in their hands in front of them. When passing over water, the twig makes sudden strong deflections. This skill has been used in finding not only underground water, but mineral deposits, oil, and other treasures hidden in the earth.

Soviet research has been rigorous in this area, beginning perhaps in 1916 when Professor Kashkarov, of the Tomsk Institute of Technology, published a report which contains this passage:

> Holding in his hands a simple forked branch of a nut tree, a man endowed with an aptitude for water-divination can, by the turnings of this branch (brought on by his reflex tremorous movements), point to the place where an underground stream may be found; can estimate its width, the approximate depth of the channel under the surface of the earth, and the direction of flow of the water, and can trace its course. Many water-diviners, if they are within the field of influence, sense the presence not only of streams of underground water, but also of gas pockets and electric currents, and, finally, they detect the presence of metal deposits and veins of ore. After prolonged training, some diviners develop the ability to distinguish the sensations elicited in them by various substances and to determine what is acting on them.

Since that time, according to the pioneer Russian parapsychologist L. L. Vasiliev, more complex electronic and radio instrumentation had been used for prospecting. However, he writes,

> It must be acknowledged that cases have been reported in which physical instruments do not generate reliable findings, while the water- or ore-diviner solved precisely the task set. . . . The diviner's organism (seems to) react to changes in ionization and to descending electric currents. . . . But the true reason for the diviner's motor reactions remains unknown.

Vasiliev goes on to make the wry, but true observation that

> We do not know why only a few, rarely-met representatives of the human race possess the aptitude of water and ore divination. Such exclusiveness of possession is characteristic of all parapsychological phenomena—a fact which greatly impedes their study.

The most comprehensive scientific study of dowsing undertaken in the United States, to my knowledge, was published in 1971 by Professors Chadwick and Jensen of Utah State University, titled *The Detection of Magnetic Fields Caused by Groundwater and the Correlation of Such Fields with Water Dowsing.* The authors begin by saying, "Few people could have approached the subject of dowsing with more skepticism." Then they go on to report that groundwater can cause a perturbation in the earth's magnetic field; that dowsing devices are held in a way that they can be considered "unstable mechanical amplifiers"; and that if the human body can be shown to be influenced by magnetic fields, then this could help to explain the dowsing phenomenon. They offer the hypothesis that the body as it moves causes "small electrical potentials to be generated, leading to the question: Is the magnetically induced potential large enough to cause the characteristic hand motion of the dowser?" In this study, dowsing tests involving 150 men and women were conducted in four different areas. Dowsing reactions were compared with known magnetic field perturbations, and a statistical analysis was made. The result showed that quantitatively there was a strong correlation linking magnetic fields with dowsing reactions. This research may remind us of Sister Justa's studies with enzymes, in which she found a remarkable similarity between the influence of a magnetic field and Estabany's healing hands on enzyme activity. Whether the magnetic field is a necessary and sufficient cause of the dowser's talent is as yet unknown. The fact remains, however, that oil and water companies pay dowsers to locate such resources, and recently the Soviet government has employed dowsers not only to find these assets, but to locate archeological ruins.

A PERSONAL EXPERIENCE WITH A DOWSER

One day a dowser visited the laboratory in order to demonstrate his discovery of the "polarities" in the human body. He showed us how his instrument, a pendulum-type rod, moved rapidly in a clockwise direction over his left foot, and counterclockwise over his right foot. It was not at all clear whether the pendulum was responding to polarities or to the fact that the dowser could clearly see when the pendulum was over the right or left foot and could either consciously or unconsciously manipulate the pendulum appropriately. I suggested that he return for a double blind study. We would blindfold him and see if the pendulum still followed the same movements, and we would also have him try his dowsing skill, blindfolded, in locating metal objects concealed in various places. Unfortunately, he did not return for that experiment. However, about a year later, a friend of mine called in desperation, trying to locate water on a summer camping site where the wells had run dry. Geologists had told him there was no more water in the area, and now, as a last resort, he was hunting for a dowser. I told him about the dowser who had visited the lab, with the warning that I had no real evidence that he could actually locate water. My friend nevertheless called the dowser, who went to the camping site, and within half an hour located a rich spring which has been providing water there for the past three years. Empirically, dowsing has worked for thousands of years, *sometimes*. As Vasiliev points out, unfortunately when, and where, it will work is unknown. At any rate, it seems beyond questioning that on occasion, the human organism receives (via magnetic fields?) information about what lies under the earth. At times, this information has proved to be more accurate than that obtained from specialized electronic instrumentation.

SKIN VISION

A more highly debated area involving bioenergetic information received by a few gifted individuals is that of skin vision, a field which belongs in the province of (1) physiology, (2) neurology, (3) parapsychology, (4) physics, (5) stage magic, (6) all of the above, or (7) none of the above. Scientists had paid little attention to the phenomenon, in spite of sporadic reports in the literature on hypnosis of persons able to read newspapers, or detect colors, while deep in hypnotic trance with their eyes closed. The Soviet investigator Vasiliev reports this case history of a middle-aged intellectual man suffering from alcoholism, as described by Drs. Shilo and Lopitsky of Polotsky Psychiatric Hospital in 1957:

> A newspaper is picked from a great pile of newspapers and magazines on a bookstand and given to the patient with the command to read the name of the newspaper with his eyes shut. The patient is silent and does not

open his eyes. Then the doctor draws the right index finger of the patient along the name of the newspaper, as if to direct his attention mentally to the given spatial area with the aid of the kinesthetic sense of the hand (without the finger touching the text). The patient correctly pronounces the name of the Byelorussian newspaper *Zvezda* (Star). Then in the same way the patient reads headlines, single sentences, words in smaller type. Finally, with eyes shut, he reads the headlines of *Pravda*—first through a single sheet and then through double sheets of unlined blank paper. Upon awakening, he remembers that he saw the large print of the headlines as if "through a fog" and that the small print of the text "blurred in his eyes." ... The possibility of a prior acquaintance with the newspaper on the part of the patient was completely excluded, since he did not have access to the room in which they were kept and he was not forewarned about the nature of the experiment.

Not until Rosa Kulasheva, in 1962, did skin vision become another prominent battlefield on the frontiers of behavior research. Headlines all over the world heralded the fact that Rosa had been tested rigorously by the Moscow Academy of Science and had demonstrated that she could detect colors, and even read newspapers, with the tips of her fingers. As so frequently happens, within months headlines once again appeared, first in the Soviet Union and then around the world, denouncing Rosa as a fraud.

I was surprised, then, that the scientists whom I met in the Soviet Union accepted skin vision as a genuine phenomenon which was being seriously investigated. I asked Edward Naumov, a well-known Soviet parapsychologist, what had become of Rosa Kulasheva. He told me that Rosa had, in fact, been remarkably gifted (and self-taught) but that she had also been emotionally unstable. She had begun demonstrating her abilities before theatrical audiences, had conceived grandiose ideas of being supported for her entire life for the purpose of scientific investigation, had made more and more extravagant claims—which she could not support—and eventually suffered a mental breakdown, during which she lost her ability. Naumov informed me that his secretary, Larisa Vilenskaya, had learned skin vision and that she was also teaching the ability to students. Larisa offered to give me an informal demonstration, with the apology that she might not be successful for she was out of practice. The cards, which she used in teaching, were of heavy cardboard with the letters of the Russian alphabet printed in characters about two inches tall. To make sure that the letters were not embossed, or differentiated in any way from the paper on which they were printed, I felt them carefully and could detect only a glossy overall surface. Larisa blindfolded herself, turned her head away, and then proceeded, by passing her fingertips lightly over the cards, to "read" the letters I presented her randomly. This was, as Larisa emphasized, *not* a controlled experiment, merely an informal demonstration. And to substantiate the amount of scientific rigor with which skin vision is being explored in Russia, she presented me with the book *Problems in Dermo-Optical Sensitivity*, as reported by Goldberg, Novomeisky, and their colleagues. The book also contains an extensive bibliography of research papers from many Soviet universities and institutes. Further confirmation of the detailed Soviet study of skin vision was forthcoming when I was presented with another Soviet book, written in English, by the well-known Soviet psychologist K. Platonov. In this work, titled *Psychology: As You May Like It*, Platonov writes:

> In November, 1963, I chanced to meet Lena Bliznova, a nine-year-old very capable pupil of a Kharkhov music school, and to carry out several experiments with her. Completely guaranteeing the elimination of telepathy, these experiments not only confirmed that Lena had this still mysterious ability, which nobody had developed in her, but also showed that she had it to an even greater extent than the formerly investigated people.

Even more persuasive evidence was offered to me when Naumov took me to see a film called *Seven Steps beyond the Horizon*, being shown publicly in Moscow. One step was devoted to current Soviet research in skin vision. The most dramatic episode in this section of the film shows the experimenter placing in one of six identical aluminum cassettes a strip of red paper, then covering all of the cassettes, which were presented to a pleasant-faced young woman. She proceeded to place her hand about two inches above each of the cassettes in turn, eventually stopping at one with a nod of her head. The cassette was opened to reveal the red paper. This study seemed more than skin vision; information was being conveyed to the subject *at a distance* from the skin. Was this a form of bioenergetic communication, in much the same way perhaps as the dowser receives information about what lies buried, not in an aluminum cassette, but underneath the earth?

These questions occurred to me in Moscow, but I had no special interest in skin vision at that time. However, when I returned home, I faced an unexpected challenge in the form of a telephone call from a stranger, Mary Wimberley, who became a central figure in our laboratory research.

THE REMARKABLE BLIND MARY WIMBERLEY

Mary introduced herself over the telephone, saying she had "read" (by listening to tapes) *Psychic Discoveries behind the Iron Curtain*. She was fascinated by the accomplishments in skin vision that had been attributed to Rose Kulasheva, and wondered if she could possibly develop the same faculty. Mary offered herself as a guinea pig, suggesting that she might be a good candidate since she had been totally blind since the age of eighteen. The fact that she was totally blind, callous as that may seem, was a strong inducement to us, since so much criticism about skin vision resides in the likelihood of fraud, particularly if blindfolds are used. Blindfolds, as parapsychologists have learned through painful experience with charlatans, are a strategy employed with great success by magicians around the world. Try an experiment yourself: Put on a double or triple blindfold and then look directly down. You will see what is beneath your eyes with fine clarity.

In our initial interview, Mary told us that she had been born with cataracts but that for the first years of her life, she did see colors—which she enjoyed enormously. Unfortunately, she developed glaucoma, and was subjected to a series of eye operations over the years, during which one eye was removed, and the optic nerve of the other eye severed. In spite of her complete blindness, Mary earned an M.A. in Russian and learned four other languages besides. She served as a typist for the United Nations organization, and was teaching Braille, but still felt she needed to do more. Now she wanted to try to learn skin vision. I had already told Mary that none of us had experience in teaching skin vision, but that we would improvise. I brought to the lab ten pieces of construction paper of identical quality except for the color: five were black, and five were white. I suggested that Mary try to discriminate between the black and white, using any kind of subjective clues that might come to her. While she felt the paper, we chatted; after about ten minutes, Mary reported that she could tell no difference between the black and white. A run of ten trials proved she was right, she made four correct calls out of ten (pure chance would give five calls out of ten). After a coffee break and more touching of the papers by Mary, she made a second run of ten trials. This time she had eight correct calls. We were encouraged, but Mary felt she had merely made some "lucky guesses."

Probably she had. It was months before Mary learned to discriminate black and white 100 percent of the time. To avoid boredom, we introduced other colors: red, blue, green, yellow—the whole spectrum; as well as other materials of various textures, including plastic, wool, cardboard, and tissue paper. The work went slowly, and progress was sporadic. Some days Mary performed brilliantly; other days it was as if she had learned nothing. She never believed she was doing anything more than "guessing," well or badly. Fortunately we found one task at which Mary proved a master. I had found, in a hardware store, black letters printed on a gold background, similar to the letters Larissa had demonstrated with in Moscow. None of the experimenters could distinguish the letters by touch, when they were blindfolded, but Mary became so adept so quickly that we devised a game of anagrams which we all enjoyed. For example, an experimenter would give Mary two letters, S and A, and Mary would make the word AS; then she would be given a T and she would rearrange the letters to form SAT; add C to make CATS; add E to make CASTE; add H to make CHASTE; and add E to make TEACHES.

Eventually, Mary agreed to try controlled experiments to learn by means of a statistical analysis how well she could discriminate colors. We ran 1,500 trials, with Mary making many mistakes, but scoring so high that the odds of her doing that well (simply by "lucky guessing" or chance) were less than 5 million to one. But

Mary still did not know how she made her choices, and she remained pessimistic about her ability, which she honestly believed was nonexistent.

To make matters more difficult, colleagues had made various suggestions about cues that Mary might be using unconsciously. For example, the light in the lab could radiate differently with the different colors. To eliminate that possibility, we put Mary in the isolation booth, in total darkness, with a stack of papers of four different colors, which she was required to sort into four different piles according to color. She performed just as well in total darkness as she did in the light of the lab. (This was an unexpected finding: According to the Soviet investigators, Rosa could *not* distinguish colors in total darkness.) Another suggestion was that Mary was responding to the *textures* of the materials, which could receive the dyes differently. To eliminate this possibility, we followed the Russian practice of enclosing the materials in plastic. Mary found this a disagreeable condition, and made a counterproposal: She would prefer to *sense* the colors, keeping her hand at least an inch above the materials. In her attempts to sense the colors, her performance deteriorated sharply to chance. But after arduous, tedious practice, she was able to perform equally well with sensing as with feeling the materials. It was not, then, the texture of the materials that gave her information.

Two years went by, with Mary faithfully returning for weekly practice sessions. It became clear to us that she could discriminate colors, but that she could not define for herself or us how she made her discriminations. Mary has not been successful when given a totally new material, nor is she interested in the questions which her ability raises. We would like to know if the information she receives is a form of energy, emanating from the materials, which her skin translates into meaningful data. If so, what is the nature of that energy? What message is she receiving?

These are the same questions with which the Soviet researchers have been concerned since the discovery of Rosa's ability. Although they still cannot explain how the information is obtained, they have been able to teach blind children to detect colors with their fingertips. And that is Mary's goal. She has already begun experiments (despite objections by conservative schools for the blind) in trying to teach her skill to children who were born blind.

Should she succeed, as Mary points out, it will not matter in the least how the faculty is possible; what is important is to give blind children a new dimension of experience.

But my curiosity remains: Is there a special energy, a bioenergy about which we know almost nothing, that helps us to receive information about color through the skin?

BIOENERGY AND ACUPUNCTURE

It is astonishing that in spite of their materialistic philosophy, the Communist countries of China and Russia have shown a scientific surge of interest in that ancient "mythology" of medicine, acupuncture. As we know, in 1971 four of America's most distinguished physicians, Drs. Paul Dudley White, E. Grey Dimond, Samual Rosen, and Victor Sidel were invited to the Republic of China to observe modern Chinese medical practice. These doctors were amazed to witness, in Chinese hospitals, not only the use of acupuncture as a therapy but the recently discovered use of acupuncture as an anesthetic agent. They made films of operations in which lungs and tumors were removed from patients who remained wide awake, even sipping tea and eating fruit while the surgeries were being performed. The only anesthesia administered to them was strategically placed acupuncture needles, either twirled by hand or stimulated electrically by small machines. When these films were first shown in the United States, many eminent doctors refused to accept the phenomenon as genuine, even expressing suspicion that the good American doctors had been the victims of a hoax. (Cries of "Hoax! Fraud! Charlatan!" will be heard more and more often in the chapters to come, sometimes justifiably, sometimes not.) But as more American doctors visited China and brought back verification of the phenomenon, with slides, films, and personal reports in the news media, the subject of acupuncture became a household excitement in the United States.

For years before this, Soviet scientists had been engaged in basic research on, and clinical applications of, acupuncture, using modern technological equipment. In Moscow, Victor Adamenko had shown me an instrument of his invention which he claimed detected acupuncture points on the human body, as well as on animals and plants. His instrument, which he calls a "tobiscope," looks very much like a pocket penlight (its nickname in Russian is the "light pencil"). When this small, battery-powered, transistorized gadget is moved over the surface of the body, it lights up whenever it arrives at a place on the skin where an acupuncture point is presumed to exist. Adamenko demonstrated his tobiscope on my hand, and sure enough, the light flashed on and off at different spots. However, since acupuncture (like skin vision) was remote from my interests at that time, I simply filed the information without any thought of possible future use.

In Alma-Ata, I discovered that Professor Inyushin and his young colleague Nicholas Shuisky were also deeply involved in acupuncture research. At that time they were experimenting with a startling treatment for chronic arthritis. Traditionally, for the relief of arthritis, acupuncture uses needle stimulation on the point between thumb and forefinger called "hoku." (This hoku point is among the most important for the treatment of numerous conditions, from toothache to chronic pain of different varieties, and is used to obtain total anesthesia.) Instead of needle stimulation, Inyushin and Shuisky had been focusing a laser beam on the hoku points of eight patients suffering from crippling arthritis, none of whom had responded to any conventional medical treatment. All eight patients had made remarkable recoveries. However, Shuisky, who was in charge of the project, was not going to report his findings until a much larger number of patients had been treated. This was a wise precaution. Modern medicine sometimes announces a "miracle" drug or cure prematurely, only to discover after a few years that the "miracle" was probably the placebo effect, due to the discoverer's enthusiasm and belief in his discovery. Whether the laser treatment for arthritis will survive this test remains for time to tell. Very recently, I was surprised to receive from Alma-Ata the proceedings of a symposium in which no less than fourteen articles discussed the use of laser beams in the treatment of several illnesses.

Why so much research into acupuncture in Alma-Ata? Perhaps because it is situated very close to the Chinese border, and the natives of the region, Kazakhstan, have an Oriental heritage. (In fact, Alma-Ata, the capital, is directly on the caravan route which Marco Polo had used on his journeys from Italy to China and back again. It is not unlikely that he made at least one gift to Kazakhstan. One night, I was treated by Inyushin and his colleagues to a dinner of "national foods." I cannot pronounce or spell their names, but when two of the dishes were served, they proved to be very spicy, and delicious versions of spaghetti and ravioli!) This nearness to the Chinese border makes Alma-Ata a place where defectors from the Chinese Republic seek refuge. One defector was a medical doctor who had been trained in medicine and acupuncture at the University of Peking. This doctor had agreed to locate, in the traditional way with his fingers, the 700-odd acupuncture points on a human subject, as taught in China and as published on Chinese acupuncture charts. This was done with neither Shuisky nor Inyushin present. Then, at a different time, on the same subject, these investigators used Adamenko's tobiscope to detect the points. The points located by the tobiscope correlated remarkably with those located by the Chinese doctor. Nick Shuisky, when he told me about this investigation, said with amazement, "Can you imagine? The Chinese could find all those points, just with his fingers!" Shuisky was not quite twenty-four years old then, and like so many of his generation, seemed to think that the only accurate measurements that can be taken are with machines. One might wonder if this ability of the Chinese doctor could be similar to the method of receiving bioenergetic information in dowsing or skin vision.

ACUPUNCTURE RESEARCH IN OUR LAB

Shortly after returning to work in 1971, I was asked to give a lecture to UCLA medical students on parapsychology. En route to the lecture hall, I passed several bulletin boards which announced a discussion/demonstration on acupuncture which was to be held in the Department of Psychology. I was surprised, for at that time there had been no report about Chinese acupuncture work released in this country. The announcements on the bulletin boards probably triggered something in me, for during the lecture I found myself speaking of the acupuncture research I had learned about in the Soviet Union. My comments about laser beams, arthritis, and acupuncture points seemed to be greeted with icy incredulity, but that may not have been the case, because shortly after that lecture one of the medical students met an acupuncturist recently arrived from Taiwan. He invited the acupuncturist to UCLA to give a demonstration and asked me to attend. I was impressed with the skill of this young Taiwan practitioner, as revealed in this incident:

A volunteer from the audience of medical students was requested to demonstrate the insertion of the needles. After long hesitation, a first-year medical student volunteered to be the guinea pig. (It is usually the first-year students, like the army rookies, who volunteer; as they learn more, they volunteer less.) This young man became visibly nervous when the acupuncturist removed from his box of needles a very sharp-looking needle about four inches long. He expressed concern about the needle not being sterilized and the possibility of hepatitis. In Taiwan and China, too, according to the English physician and acupuncture expert, Felix Mann, sterilization of needles is considered unnecessary. In deference to American customs, the man from Taiwan carefully wiped the needle with cotton which had been thoroughly doused with alcohol. The student was still obviously frightened, and so the acupuncturist suggested he turn his head to the wall so that he would not have to watch the needle being inserted. The student replied, "I wasn't going to watch anyhow!" and turned his face to the wall. The acupuncturist asked him to announce when he felt the needle going in, and to tell him to stop if it became too painful. "You're damned right I will!" the student answered sharply, his head still averted. By this time the needle was already about an inch into the student's forearm. It was inserted about another inch when the acupuncturist again asked the student to announce when he felt the needle being inserted. Again the student answered, "Don't worry, I will!" At this point the audience of students broke into laughter. The "patient" turned around, saw the needle deep in his arm, and could only stare at it, open-mouthed and unbelieving.

It wasn't long before the acupuncturist was working in our lab, helping to begin our research. During this time, again due to the ingenuity of Ken Johnson, our lab had acquired an instrument similar, we believe, to Adamenko's tobiscope. When an acupuncture point is located, Ken's device lights up and makes a beeping sound. Basically, Ken uses a measurement of current flow between an electrode of one metal placed on the earlobe and one of a different metal used as a probe for locating the points. As we pursued our research, we learned that there are other methods for locating the points. There are temperature differences (slight, but seemingly genuine) at the points. And the Japanese, many years ago, invented an instrument which they call a "neurometer" which locates the points by measuring the characteristic drop in skin resistance at the points as compared with adjacent skin surfaces. In other words, the use of electronic instrumentation for acupuncture research and therapy has been in existence for quite some time.

Now, with our man from Taiwan, we tried to duplicate the Inyushin-Shuisky study by making a comparison of acupuncture points located in the Taiwan manner, with the fingers, as against locating them with Ken's instrument. We also found a high correlation between the points located manually and those found with the device. The machine was a great fascination to the acupuncturist, because he claimed that the most difficult part of acupuncture treatment, in his opinion, is correctly locating the points to be manipulated. The machine also found many points not included in the traditional acupuncture taught to the young man from Taiwan. (This also corroborated a statement by Inyushin that the tobiscope had now located over a thousand points, much more than the 700-odd points which are classically taught.)

The Taiwanese technique of acupuncture had been passed from father to son for eleven generations in Mongolia. Mongolian acupuncture differs from Manchurian acupuncture, which in turn differs from Japanese acupuncture, etc. Our young man's technique was limited to needle therapy; he did not know about moxa, an herb which is burned on the points; nor did he know anything about electrical stimulation. With his particular knowledge, however, he did claim to treat a variety of problems, such as toothache, arthritis, migraine headache, back pains, impotence, eye and ear problems, and to achieve Caesarian childbirth without anesthesia. Indeed, in the sheer range of ailments he claimed to be able to cure, he sounded to us like a patent medicine man of an earlier American era.

Actually, in his clinical work, he was successful with some symptoms, *sometimes*. For example, one of our group had been in an automobile accident and suffered a whiplash for which no amount of medication afforded relief from pain. One brief acupuncture treatment left him pain-free for days. Another of our group still has chronic bursitis of the shoulder despite a long series of acupuncture treatments. A swollen, broken toe, badly discolored, responded overnight. A tennis elbow required several treatments, and responded to acupuncture better than to other therapies (without, however, a complete remission).

It is vitally important to emphasize that acupuncture is *not* a cure-all. This is obvious, if one remembers that in the People's Republic of China, where acupuncture is a highly respected medical modality, the government has officially reported more than 400,000 operations performed using acupuncture anesthesia. These include heart surgery and the removal of appendices, tumors, and lungs. If acupuncture could cure everything, there would be no need for even one operation, let alone 400,000.

THE IMPORTANCE OF ACUPUNCTURE RESEARCH

For our laboratory, acupuncture theory, rather than therapy, is the important issue. We are not, after all, medical doctors. Our research work is in the area of bioenergetics, and it is in this regard that acupuncture theory is vastly intriguing. For according to this ancient system of medicine, there is a constant flow of an invisible energy, called "ch'i," which exists throughout the universe and interpenetrates with all matter, including our bodies.

We are, of course, already familiar with this concept of a universal energy, whether called "prana," "orgone," "od," "elan vital," "ch'i," "mana," or by any other name. And we have seen that some kind of force or energy has been used for healing, whether by the laying on of hands, by magnetic passes, or by the power of thought over distances. The concept of a universal energy, used in a healing capacity via needle manipulation, had evolved into a formal practice of medicine by the Chinese perhaps five thousand years ago. According to acupuncture theory, the universal energy is in constant flux, circulating in and out of the human body along invisible channels called in English "meridians." Ch'i is supposed to circulate in much the same way that blood and lymph circulate through the channels of their respective systems.

Naturally this concept of an invisible energy flowing through an invisible system is inadmissible to many Western doctors. They have been trained to believe that the anatomy of the body, its bones, organs, and systems, is the basis by means of which its physiological processes can occur. This is the materialistic model: There must be a machine through which the energy of gas or electricity or blood can flow, in order for the machine to operate. The body is our machine. Since there is a cerebral cortex composed of billions of neurons, it is possible for electromagnetic energies to circulate through them, by means of which we see, hear, feel, and think. Similarly, since there is a complex system of capillaries, veins, and arteries, it is possible for blood to flow through that system, vitalizing the machinery of the body. But there is no anatomical structure for the meridians through which an invisible energy is hypothesized to flow; therefore, there can be no ch'i. Thus, in Western medicine, disease and illness are considered to be the result of a malfunctioning of body parts, caused by bacteria, virus, trauma, or defective genes, all of which, however small, are material entities.

In contrast, acupuncture theory denies the concept of disease. Instead, it maintains that when the energy ch'i flows in and out of the body (through the acupuncture points) in a balanced way, the body is in a state of "health." But when, for whatever reason, that flow of ch'i is dammed up or pouring out too quickly, there arises an imbalance of energy, causing a state of "not-health." In acupuncture, there are no specific diseases. Bodily symptoms (whether we call them arthritis, sexual impotence, asthma, psoriasis, deafness, whatever) are regarded as an indication of *where* in the body the energy flow is out of balance. The acupuncturist is paid to maintain the balance, a state of "health"; and traditionally, the acupuncturist was required to pay his patients, if he had been so remiss as to permit them to become ill. His skill resides in his knowledge of the paths of the meridians and of the twelve pulses which can be taken along the wrists, and which inform him of where the imbalance of energy exists. The imbalance refers to the two energies, yin and yang, which together make up the ch'i. Yang and yin represent the masculine and feminine, the sun and the moon, the hot, dry and the cool, moist. In terms which are easier for the Western mind of today, yang and yin represent the positive and negative forces, in much the same way that electricity is described. In order to redress the imbalance of yin/yang, very thin needles, long or short, must be inserted properly in appropriate places. For example, acupuncturists relieve the pain of a severe toothache by inserting needles near the large toe and between thumb and forefinger (hoku point). Stimulation (either by twisting the needles or, more recently, by electrical stimulation through the needles) at these points far removed from the toothache is nevertheless supposed to reestablish the energy balance so that the toothache vanishes.

For Western medicine this is a bewildering phenomenon. There is, as yet, no physiological explanation for the treatment, which works empirically.

Another example of acupuncture therapy, at a site far removed from the actual injury, has been described by Dr. William McGarey, of the Association for Research and Enlightment Clinic in Phoenix, Arizona. Dr. McGarey has been doing extensive research in acupuncture for the past several years. He reports a treatment given by an associate, Dr. Urquhart, who studied acupuncture in Japan. A patient arrived at the Tokyo Clinic with a severe third-degree burn area of the left chest and axilla which they covered with a piece of ordinary kitchen aluminum foil.

> [They] then connected the foil by wire to an acupuncture needle which was inserted in the opposing contralateral extremity. . . . The patient had a full night's sleep after that without medication of any kind. She was pain free and did not wake up through the night. . . . They noted that the normal exudation of fluid from the burned area was lessened; and also, there was a much earlier appearance of the healing crustations. . . . The indications were that the treatment was not only a therapy for the relief of pain but was also an aid in the healing process itself.

Dr. McGarey adds that he has had a few opportunities to try this treatment in his practice; on one occasion, a nun suffering from severe sunburn from thigh to foot gave her permission for the experimental therapy. After treatment, Dr. McGarey reports, "she was walking more normally, gingerly feeling her sunburned areas to see if they were 'for real,' and shaking her head while she said, over and over, 'I don't believe it! I don't believe it!' "

This treatment for burns is a recent development of acupuncture, as is its use as an anesthetic. Acupuncture anesthesia, or analgesia as it is called in the United States, has been effectively accomplished in several centers already. One pioneer in this area is Dr. David Bresler, of UCLA. It was Dr. Bresler who was responsible for the placards I had seen in 1971, announcing a lecture and demonstration of acupuncture. At that time, Dr. Bresler had already been studying with a master Chinese acupuncturist for several years. His study had been considered a mild insanity by his colleagues, but he persevered, and is today probably one of the most knowledgeable acupuncturists in the country. His primary goal is to correlate, if possible, acupuncture effects with electrophysiological measures; meanwhile he has been able to make empiric use of acupuncture anesthesia (without yet understanding how or why it works).

Together with colleagues at the University of Southern California, Dr. Bresler has made a video tape showing the extraction of a badly infected tooth, where the only anesthetic was acupuncture needles inserted between the toes and in the hoku points. I watched this tape when it was presented at the first acupuncture symposium held by the National Institutes of Health, in Bethesda, Maryland, in 1973. During the operation, the tooth snapped in half while the dentist was making the extraction. The snap was almost grotesquely loud and evoked an empathetic "ouch!" from the audience, but the patient, who was fully awake, made no movement, and looked unconcerned.

Other findings are emerging about the effectivness of acupuncture stimulation, findings still inexplicable by Western standards, but reliable and repeatable phenomena. For example, Los Angeles obstetrician Dr. Charles Ledergerber attended a few acupuncture symposia (which are being offered in various places around the country), during which he learned some of the basic techniques, including acupuncture point stimulation with electrical current. In his research, Dr. Ledergerber accidentally discovered that electrical stimulation of specific points on the abdomen of pregnant women can induce labor. He has repeated this procedure more than twenty times, on twenty different women, and has induced labor each time. In the summer of 1973, Dr. Ledergerber presented his findings at a Swiss symposium. Before he left, he told me he was stopping in Paris on his way home, to confer with a French doctor who had discovered, at approximately the same time, that he could induce labor voluntarily by stimulating acupuncture points on the ear! Dr. Ledergerber remarked, rather ruefully, that the French technique of using the ear rather than the abdomen was a "more elegant" one.

WHY DOES ACUPUNCTURE WORK, WHEN IT WORKS?

As we have tried to emphasize, acupuncture is not a panacea, and frequently it does not cure a specific complaint. Dr. Marshall Barshay (who performed the healing study with his kidney patients in our lab) took a sabbatical to study acupuncture with doctors in England, and returned to use it as an adjunct to his practice of internal medicine. He reports that he gets good results only about 40 to 50 percent of the time. This for him is a disappointment; but since his cases had had no improvement with other therapies, it seems to me rather a good result.

However, the major question remains: How does acupuncture work? Our Western scientists have been grappling with this problem, and thus far have offered three major hypotheses:

A Form of Hypnosis

Since anesthesia can be evoked with acupuncture, the obvious analogy is hypnosis, which can also produce anesthesia for surgery. The reasoning goes like this: The doctor is an authority figure, especially in China, where he is supported by the enormous authority of Chairman Mao, who has declared acupuncture to be a uniquely Chinese technique of medicine. Thus, when the doctor says the needles will stop all pain, he is using very strong power of suggestion. The dramatic success of this technique, seen now on TV screens all over the United States, has in turn influenced the American public, whose belief is a form of hypnosis. Thus, essentially, acupuncture is considered in the same category as a placebo, which we have seen can alleviate many conditions.

The Gate Theories of Physiologists

Many American scientists consider it vital to find a mechanistic explanation for the cessation of pain when needles are manipulated in specific areas of the body. Some physiologists, of whom the best known are Patrick Wall and Donald Melzack, have proposed gate theories which involve the nervous system and its complex series of A, B, and C fibers. In its simplest form, the single-gate theory proposes that certain heavy fibers can block the flow of the smaller, narrow fibers which carry pain sensations. This single-gate theory has been extended to a double-, triple-, and quadruple-gate theory to account for the various sections of the body which can be anesthetized by remote needle stimulation.

Energy Flow through an Undiscovered System

A Vietnamese, Professor Kim Bong Han, is reported to have extensively investigated the "Kyungrak" system (of meridians), by linking it to vascular and lymphatic ducts, via special types of corpuscles. He is said to have injected a radioisotope, p^{32}, into an acupuncture point and traced its progress through the body. By following its path, Bong Han is supposed to have empirically shown that the meridian system is an independent one, carrying a liquor containing granules which were given the name "sanal." Extracting sanal (which is supposed to contain DNA, RNA, and protein), Bong Han reportedly injected it directly into different areas, traced it with radioisotopes, and found it penetrated deep into cell tissues. No one in the United States has been able to contact Professor Bong Han, and in some instances investigators have been told that his work is unsound and cannot be duplicated. Very recently however, Victor Adamenko of the Soviet Union is reported to have obtained similar effects using Bong Han's technique.

Apart from this controversial and unsubstantiated research, there have been in the past fifty years many studies by scientists around the world which have stressed the importance of electrical energy in the functioning of the human body. In 1922, a group of doctors showed that certain pathological conditions are accompanied by changes in the electrical conductivity of the cells. For many years, Dr. Robert Becker and his associates in Syracuse, New

York, have experimented with electrical and magnetic fields around the body. They have been able to cause partial regeneration of amputated legs in frogs and rats, which do not naturally grow new limbs, by implanting in the stump of the severed limb a bimetallic coupling. This produces a weak electrical field similar to that found in the salamander, which does naturally regenerate severed limbs. Dr. Harold S. Burr, together with psychiatrist Dr. Leonard Ravitz, spent more than thirty-five years of research in what he calls the "L" (life) fields which surround all living matter. These fields can be monitored with special equipment which measures the difference in voltage potential between two points either on or *close to* the surface of the body. According to Dr. Ravitz, who has studied more than four hundred normal subjects, these L fields vary rhythmically over time. When the person feels "on top of the world," his voltage is high, and vice versa. In Dr. Burr's words,

> The pattern or organization of any biological system is established by a complex electro-dynamic field ... which in part determines the behavior and orientation of those components.... It must maintain pattern.... Therefore, it must regulate and control living things.

Dr. Burr seems to be paraphrasing Professor Inyushin's concept of bioplasma. Perhaps this is another example of similar discoveries by scientists working independently, like Darwin's and Wallace's theory of evolution.

OUR LABORATORY FINDINGS ABOUT ENERGY FIELDS

As must be obvious, my own bias favors this third hypothesis of an invisible energy system, and we have conducted a few experiments which may eventually offer light on this complex subject. Again quite by accident, while working with Ken Johnson's acupuncture point detector, we began to notice that we could not locate the points on damp skin. The Taiwanese acupuncturist with whom we were working said that this dampness was not sweat, but the "juices" of yin energy, as opposed to the hot, dry energy of yang. Our colleagues, recognizing neither yin nor yang, disagreed and suggested instead that what we were locating with the instrument might not be acupuncture points at all, but aggregates of sweat glands.

This was a hypothesis that could be tested by finding someone who had had a sympathectomy, which is an operation on part of the nervous system that prevents sweating over specific areas of the body. There is also a way of producing a temporary, artificial sympathectomy by an injection of the drug xylocaine. We explored both methods. On one occasion we worked with a patient who had had a sympathectomy, and on other occasions we injected several volunteers in the lab with xylocaine underneath the shoulder, causing the right arm to be blocked and unable to sweat. We found out that the instrument located the points, even on those areas of the body which could not sweat.

In those experiments where we gave ourselves the injection, we took Kirlian photographs of each finger on both hands before, during, and after the xylocaine injection. The results were startling because of the implications for an energy *imbalance*, one of the tenets of acupuncture theory. Before the block, the fingers of both hands were in balance, showing about the same amount of emanations. During the sympathetic block of the right hand, there were revealed brilliant emanations in that hand, whereas the emanations from the unblocked, presumable normal left hand, all but disappeared! Is this the energy imbalance that acupuncture describes? After the effects of the xylocaine had worn off, pictures were taken again. Once more the distribution of emanations appeared to be equal in both hands.

We are continuing to work along these lines, studying the energetic processes of the body by manipulating acupuncture points and taking photographs before and after manipulation. Results are encouraging, and follow along the lines reported by the Soviet investigators Adamenko, Inyushin, and others.

In this chapter, the idea of an energetic process in the body has been examined from the point of view that the human organism can act as a *receiver* of bioenergetic information from the environment and objects in the environment, as evinced by dowsing, skin vision, and acupuncture needle stimulation. Now it is time to explore the possibilities of the opposite process: the human body acting as a *transmitter* of information to its environment and the objects which inhabit it.

5 Transmitting Bioenergy: Psychokinesis

Physical mediums of the past and present. Laboratory studies of "hot dice," necessitating a brief excursion into the laws of probability. Levitation.

A TV DEMONSTRATION OF PSYCHOKINESIS

Captain Edgar Mitchell, an astronaut of the Apollo-14 flight to the moon, startled the world when he conducted, in 1971, the first ESP experiment from space to earth. Some time later, he resigned from the Navy and organized the Institute of Noetic Sciences at Palo Alto, California, in order to give serious study to paranormal phenomena. These phenomena include psychokinesis, or PK for short, the movement of objects at a distance through "the power of mind." One of his research projects, conducted at the prestigious Stanford Research Institute, is laboratory study of the psychokinetic abilities of Uri Geller, probably the best known psychic in the Western world. Introducing Geller on a local television program, Dr. Mitchell explained that the informal demonstration Geller was about to give might fail, since Geller could never be sure when his capricious talent would be available to him (a fact which investigators at SRI had frequently observed). As I listened to Edgar Mitchell, I was impressed by his last statement for, as we have seen, genuine psychics are never sure that they can produce an effect.

When Geller, a handsome young Israeli, appeared on the TV screen, he looked nervous, which was to be expected. He had recently received national publicity in two news magazines, one commenting favorably on his work, the other giving a devastating critique. It accused investigators Russell Targ and Hal Puthoff of poor methodology and insinuated that Geller might be much more magician than psychic. The inevitable controversy over whether he was a psychic or a charlatan was already breaking over his head.

Geller began that evening by successfully selecting out of ten identical metal jars placed before him the one which contained a metal screw. He did this by holding his hand approximately two inches above each jar and gradually eliminating all but the one which contained the screw. We have become familiar with this process, and have already discussed the Soviet film in which a young lady, trained in skin vision, picked from among six aluminum cassettes the one that contained a red piece of paper. This is an example of *reception*, rather than *transmission*, of information through some form of bioenergy. After this demonstration, Geller tried to perform one of his special PK effects: bending a very strong, thick four-inch nail simply by stroking it gently with one finger. This would involve the *transmission* of energy to an object. Geller was unsuccessful on the first trials, but eventually when one of the guests (a beautiful woman) held the nail in her hand while Geller stroked it with his finger, the nail was seen to bend, and it continued to bend after it was placed on the table, although no one was touching it. Geller then held a ring in his hand. First it bent, and then it snapped in two. The audience and guests applauded loudly.

A few nights later, Geller appeared on a nationally televised talk show and was unable to perform any of these feats.

Question: Is Uri Geller charlatan, magician, or gifted physical medium? We shall need to digress a bit into history before attempting to answer that question.

PSYCHOKINESIS AMONG THE PRIMITIVES

In countless reports anthropologists for many years have described PK-like phenomena among the primitive peoples they have studied. Probably the most familiar of these is the voodoo or black magic practice among Haitians and Africans, in which sticking pins into dolls is presumed to bring about the sickness or even death of the person whom the doll represents. Among the American

Indians, and certain Pacific Islanders, in special ritual dances, warriors have been observed to hurl arrows or knives at the bodies of other warriors, who, in a state of ecstasy or trance, somehow deflect the weapons with their bodies, no wounds ever being made. A psychiatrist colleague of mine at the Neuropsychiatric Institute spent an evening in Bali, witnessing for himself how sharp knives, violently hurled at the bodies of entranced men, simply fell limply to the ground, glancing off the flesh of the chest, almost "like feathers." In India, fakirs lie on beds of nails which do not puncture the flesh; they pierce their bodies with long needles and do not flinch or bleed; they walk on coals of fire and their feet remain unburned. Sai Baba, a holy man of India today, "materializes" seemingly out of the air rings, gold, and statuary which he gives to his disciples.

Where, in all the legend and lore of black and white magic lies the truth? How many, if any, of these (and thousands more) phenomena are genuine? We do not know yet; but for almost one hundred years a few scientists have spent much time and effort to find out.

THE SOCIETIES FOR PSYCHICAL RESEARCH

In England, in 1882, an organization was formed called the Society for Psychical Research (SPR for convenience, from now on). Its purpose was to discover, through systematic investigation, whether "supernormal" or psychical phenomena are actually manifested. This was a bold step for scientists in the materialistic nineteenth century, when the brain was supposed to secrete thought the way the liver secretes bile. The founders and members of SPR (and its American counterpart, the ASPR, headed by the renowned psychologist William James a few years later) included some of the finest and most inquiring minds of the time, such as physicists Sir William Barrett, Sir Oliver Lodge, and Sir William Crookes and philosophers and scholars like Henry Sidgwick and F. W. H. Myers. Years later, Sigmund Freud was a member of both organizations. The SPR and ASPR continue to exist in spite of constant isolation and ridicule from the more "respectable" scientific community. It was, in fact, not until 1969 that the Parapsychology Association was admitted to membership in the august American Association for the Advancement of Science.

Early SPR work was devoted to collecting and classifying anecdotal data about paranormal events, in much the same way that the science of biology evolved out of the collecting and classifying of flora and fauna. In addition, whenever possible, the SPR investigators studied at first hand those few gifted psychics who would agree to work under controlled conditions.

Probably the most remarkable of these psychics was the physical medium D. D. Home. According to sworn testimonies of witnesses from many countries in Europe, he was able to make lamps and tables jump into the air merely by looking at them; to hold a bar of iron in his hand and cause one end to become cold and the other hot; and to "materialize" brandy into a glass held over his head while a hand was held over the mouth of the glass. Sir William Crookes published a report of his laboratory research with Home, in which he measured Home's ability to influence the balance of a scale at a distance of three feet, by "willing" the pointer to move. It did, making a tracing on a smoked glass plate. On reading Crookes' article, Charles Darwin is said to have commented: "I cannot disbelieve Mr. Crookes' statements, nor can I believe the results." (Indeed, it is on the horns of this dilemma that many scientists are still dangling today.) Unlike almost every other medium of that era, Home was never exposed as a fraud. It must be admitted that most (if not all) of the feats just described could probably be duplicated by a good magician today, without having to evoke the concept of PK. Unlike a good magician, however, Home could not always give an impressive demonstration.

For decades this was the handicap which the SPR researchers faced: They could not provide a "repeatable experiment," the criterion by which any discovery or invention must be tested. In order for any scientific discovery to be recognized, be it an invention (TV, radio, aircraft), a drug (aspirin, antibiotic, anesthesia), or a law of nature (gravity, thermodynamics, the flow of electric current), the effect must be capable of being repeated by any scientist in any laboratory at least a significant percentage of the time. In order to determine what a "significant percentage of the time" might be, the formidable science of statistics evolved in the early twentieth century.

THE THEORY OF PROBABILITY AND
THE LAW OF LARGE NUMBERS

As briefly as possible, let us investigate probability theory and its offspring, the law of large numbers. One of the basic, startling facts in statistics is that something which seems unpredictable, such as the whereabouts of one particular electron, can neverthe-less be neatly predicted by means of an *average*. We see this phenomenon beautifully illustrated with a baseball batter: We never know, when a batter comes to the plate, whether he will make a hit or strike out. But we know that a star batter, *on the average*, will score a hit once out of every three times he comes to bat; his batting *average* is .333. (This fact, incidentally, would be astonishing to someone who did not know baseball: How can someone be a *star* performer when he misses the ball twice as often as he hits it?) We'll have more to say about performance levels later.

The mysterious consistency of the law of averages is dazzlingly described by Warren Weaver:

> The circumstances which result in a dog biting a person seriously enough so that the matter gets reported to the health authorities would seem to be complex and un-predictable indeed. In New York City, in the year 1955, there were, on the average, 73.3 reports per day to the Department of Health of bitings of people. In 1956 the corresponding number was 73.6. In 1957 it was 73.2. In 1958 and 1959 the figures were 74.5 and 72.6.

Deriving from this law of averages (which holds true for astonish-ingly varied events), there has evolved the familiar "bell curve" which tells us that of all the crops harvested (or of all student scores on a nationwide aptitude test or of all electric light bulbs manufactured in a factory, etc.), 68 percent will be of average quality, 13.5 percent will be somewhat better and 13.5 percent somewhat worse than average, 2.5 percent will be definitely in-ferior, and 2.5 percent will be definitely superior. Out of every large group, 1 percent will be outstandingly good (and 1 percent outstandingly bad); or expressed another way, the odds against any member of a group falling into this category are 100 to 1.

Professional gamblers, as we know, have made a deep study of the odds for and against practically every event, from the winner of the heavyweight championship or the Kentucky Derby to the rolling of a 7, 11, or 8 "the hard way" at the crap table. (Statistics, interestingly, originated with the brilliant Pascal, when an aristocratic friend, addicted to gambling, asked for his help so that he could do better at the gaming tables.) With the throw of one die, which has six sides, statistics tell us that the odds of your calling the face of the die that will turn up when you toss it are 6 to 1; that is, if you predict that a 5 will turn up when you toss a true die, your chances of being correct, just by chance, are 1 in 6. You might like to try the experiment. In your first six throws, you might get three hits or none, but if you were to throw the die 600 times, you would probably get close to 100 hits, plus or minus 10, perhaps; and if you were to throw the dice 60,000 times (try it! you'll hate it), you will probably get very close to 10,000 hits. This is the law of large numbers at work: the more trials, the closer the results will be to chance expectation.

The laws of probability and large numbers are used in scientific research in biology, genetics, physics, psychology, etc., but in the field of parapsychology, SPR researchers had not been able to evolve an experiment which would yield reliable, repeatable statistical information that such a thing as PK does, actually, exist.

Enter Dr. Joseph Banks Rhine.

THE RHINES AND THEIR PIONEER LABORATORY STUDIES IN PK

When Drs. J. B. and Louisa Rhine, husband and wife, were invited in the 1930s to join the psychology department at Duke University by the chairman of the department, William McDougall, they were encouraged to pursue psychical research. This was an extraordinary invitation from a university (and would still be equally extraordinary today). The Rhines wanted to satisfy science's demand for a rigid experimental procedure, with controls, double blinds, and statistical analysis. Eventually they succeeded. A brilliant example of their careful, painstaking work is their research into PK using one of the gambler's favorite tools, dice.

We have seen that the odds against calling the face of a true die correctly are 1 in 6 and that as the number of trials increases, the closer the results will be to this prediction.

In real life, of course, things are not that simple. Even the best-made dice have some imperfections which create a built-in, though negligible bias, which could affect the results in a laboratory experiment utilizing hundreds of thousands of trials. To control against this criticism of their work, the faces of the dice in Rhine's experiments were changed, randomly, with a marker. To prevent against a tricky throwing procedure, all Rhine's subjects were required to throw the dice from containers, and then through various mechanical releasing devices, so that no one ever touched the dice with his hands. The subjects were mostly students at Duke University who volunteered to try their luck at "influencing" the dice mentally. They were asked to call out beforehand which numbers would appear on the dice when they came to rest. The object was to obtain as many hits as possible through PK. Sometimes 6, or 12, or 24 dice were thrown at one time, with all guesses recorded before the throw. There were variations in the procedure, but essentially the technique consisted in filling up score sheets with 240 trials per sheet.

An interesting study evolved when a divinity student named William Gatling (who preferred to think of PK as similar in its effects to prayer) asked for a competition between a group of divinity students and the "best crap shooters on campus." The Rhines obliged. In Louisa Rhine's words:

> History does not record the atmosphere or the intensity with which each side worked. Only the mathematical outcome is on record. But presumably the young divinity students were just as determined to beat the crap shooters as the latter were not to be outdone by fledgling preachers.
>
> Both sides, of course, worked under standard conditions. . . . The result was that both sides won—against chance, but not against each other. Their scores were so nearly the same, in fact, that . . . neither group could be called the winner.

The average number of hits scored in the study seems unimpressive; instead of the expected average of 4 hits out of 24, these crap shooters achieved an average of only 4.5 hits out of 24. Yet when the law of large numbers comes into play, this figure has enormous statistical significance. Indeed, both groups together achieved so many hits that the odds against their combined scores were much more than 1 million to 1.

Eventually, Dr. Rhine pooled all the dice-throwing studies conducted by his lab from 1934 to 1943. The number of correct calls out of 651,216 throws of the dice was so high that the probability against such a score by chance was truly astronomical (10^{-115} to 1).

How can we appreciate the meaning of that number? A Yale biologist, G. E. Hutchinson, gave an excellent analogy: Let us agree, he said, that the age of the earth is three thousand million years, and let us assume that for every minute of every one of those years there had been conducted one Rhine experiment and that all of those minute-by-minute experiments gave only chance results, except for this PK series. Just pooling this PK study together with all those chance results would still result in extremely high statistical significance. It boggles the mind.

And it boggled the minds of scientists when Dr. Rhine published the results. He had already published results on his ESP card studies to outraged cries of "Lies!" "Poor controls!" "Bad statistics!" "Fraud!" Patiently, criticism after criticism, Rhine had tightened his experimental designs and obtained approval of the statistical models he used. He had even obtained the services of the most competent statistician of the era, Dr. R. A. Fisher. Fisher had publicly announced that the statistics used were exactly right (they are, in fact, the statistics that are used in all the sciences up to this very day). When even Dr. Fisher's approval did not stop the critical barrage, Dr. Rhine presented his case to the American Institute of Mathematical Statistics. Their statement, after examining the data, was clear: "Mathematical work has established the fact that, assuming the experiments have been properly performed, the statistical analysis is essentially valid. If the Rhine investigation is to be fairly attacked, it must be on other than mathematical grounds." This statement was delivered in 1937; yet

I have recently attended psychology classes where Dr. Rhine's research is still being dismissed by professors with an amused chuckle as "poorly controlled, with a gross misuse of statistics."

Despite blatant, persistent hostility, Dr. Rhine has continued for more than forty years with crisp, clean laboratory experiments, and he is considered by parapsychologists as the patriarch who brought scientific methodology to the study of psychic phenomena, and bioenergy.

After accumulating this "hot dice" data, Dr. Rhine wrote: "This is the human mind doing *physical* work. . . . It is as simple as that so long as we do not ask, 'How is it done?' " Seeking the answer to that question, however, is the major thrust of psychic researchers throughout the world.

Along with "How is it done?" (a question for which we have no answer), people frequently ask, "Why is it done?" Of what use is it, this rolling of little cubes down inclined slopes millions of times? (The same question may very well have been asked of Galileo as he rolled balls down inclines, year after year, in order to learn the mathematical laws that govern their rate of speed.) To the question of what practical use are these parapsychology studies, it has become my custom to reply with an anecdote credited to Thomas Faraday, genius of electrical theory.

The Queen of England subsidized his researches for years, and Faraday happily used the money, year after year. He built ever more complicated coils and magnets and did more and more intricate experiments, which usually resulted in sparks flying and little else. Eventually, the Queen grew uneasy at pouring out large sums of money for what seemed no more than complicated "games," and she sent two gentlemen of the exchequer to inquire about Faraday's researches. Faraday genially showed off his contrivances. Finally, one of them asked, "But, Mr. Faraday, of what use is all this electrics?" To which Faraday replied, astonished: "Of what *use* is it?! Gentlemen, I haven't the remotest idea. But perhaps one day Her Majesty can put a tax on it."

Another version of the story had Faraday replying to the queries of the practical gentlemen from the exchequer: "Of what *use* is it?! Gentlemen, of what use is a newborn baby?" Both versions beautifully make the point.

RECENT LABORATORY RESEARCH IN PK

Uri Geller is now a subject of intensive research in the United States. It is doubtful that such research would have been sponsored in this country had it not been for the Soviet Union's Madame Nina Kulagina, a physical medium who apparently can move objects at a distance in much the same way as D. D. Home—simply by looking at them. Having read extensively about her laboratory experiments, conducted at Leningrad University under the eminent brain physiologist Dr. Sergeev, I had included a trip to Leningrad on my 1970 itinerary in the hopes of meeting her and the scientist. Happily, I was able to meet Mme. Kulagina. Having seen her work on film, and having read papers on her PK performances, I did not ask her to demonstrate for me. Neither success nor failure would have been as meaningful as exploring her subjective feelings.

When Mme. Kulagina arrived, accompanied by her engineer husband who has conducted several studies with her, she proved to be a diminutive, extremely attractive middle-aged woman, smartly dressed and made up, who spoke (only in Russian) in a lovely contralto voice. She told me she had had no talent for, nor interest in, psychic phenomena for the greater part of her life. She had always been a housewife except during the siege of Leningrad in World War II, when she had driven a tank to defend the city. I had read that she first discovered her remarkable ability to move objects at a distance when, one day working in her kitchen, she got very angry—and noticed a pitcher moving closer and closer to the edge of a shelf. As she watched, the pitcher, seemingly of its own volition, made a sudden movement and fell to the floor. Both Mme. Kulagina and her husband smiled. She explained that they had heard this story many times, but it was apochryphal. The true story of her development in PK came when she was practicing skin vision! (One form of bioenergy apparently led to another.) One day, as she held her fingertips a few centimeters above a piece of colored paper, trying to sense its color, she got the impression that the paper was making little, jerking movements. She then deliberately tried to get the paper to move, still keeping her fingers at a distance from the paper. After many abortive attempts, she found that a small percentage of the time she could get lightweight objects to follow—or move opposite to—the movements of her hands. Her husband encouraged her work, and eventually Mme. Kulagina was introduced to Russia's pioneer parapsychologist, L. L. Vasiliev of Leningrad University. He asked her to expand her efforts, by trying to move a compass needle which was encased in glass, keeping her fingers about two inches *above* the compass. She learned to do this successfully, in public demonstrations. I have a film in the lab, in which Kulagina is seen to move the compass needle in a complete 360-degree circle, in both directions. When she does this, she cannot predict in which direction it will move.

Madame Kulagina is not the first person to have this ability. This particular PK demonstration was reported, more than one hundred years ago, by the celebrated German psychologist and physiologist Gustav Fechner. He worked in his laboratory at the University of Leipzig, with a German woman named Mrs. Ruf. She was able to cause wide deflections of a compass needle by holding her hands at a distance. Fechner eventually published a report of this "abnormal power" which caused "the deflection of a magnetic needle by attractive and repulsive passes made merely in its vicinity by her fingers. . . . The fingertips of one hand held closely together deflected the needle from 40 to 50 degrees . . . and . . . Reichenbach had seen her cause the needle to make a complete revolution through all 360 degrees of the circle." This passage is of interest because of the mention of "passes," again evoking the concept of animal magnetism postulated by Mesmer.

After the death of Vasiliev, Mme. Kulagina's work was further researched by his successor, Professor Sergeev. It took years of intensive practice before Kulagina acquired a measure of control over her ability to move such diverse objects as matches, cigarette cases, fountain pens, and even cigarette smoke! In one of the films of her work, Mme. Kulagina is seen passing her hands above a glass ball filled with cigarette smoke. Gradually the smoke parts in two, very much as the Red Sea was supposed to have parted when Moses led the Jews out of Egypt. Mr. Kulagin's favorite experiment, which he told me about and later reported at the Czechoslovakian symposium on psychotronics in 1970, is the one in which Mme. Kulagina was able to tilt a pair of scales balanced with thirty grams of weight, simply by concentrating with her eyes. She was able to hold one scale down, even after ten additional grams had been added to the other scale to make it heavier. But as soon as she stopped concentrating and moved her eyes, the heavier scale sank.

What is it that Kulagina does?

There are the usual insistent claims that what she does is nothing more than a brilliant magician's trick, and her work from time to time has been criticized in the Soviet press. But distinguished Soviet scientists, like Professor Sergeev, have encased her in electrophysiological equipment (after examining her from inside the skin out, to eliminate the possibility of concealed magnets), and have pronounced her work genuine, though inexplicable according to the postulates of physics as they are understood today.

I asked Mme. Kulagina if she had any idea how she does what she does, and like almost every genuine psychic with whom I've talked, she answered that she does not. She added, with a sad shake of her head, that she can only do what she does *on some occasions*. There seems always to be that qualification with star psychics. There have been times, Mme. Kulagina told me, when she has been called on to give official demonstrations and has totally failed. If there are openly hostile skeptics in the audience, Kulagina feels constrained and is often ineffectual. Even under the most favorable of circumstances she may have to spend hours warming up, before objects will begin to move for her. On a recent visit, an American psychiatrist and parapsychologist from Maimonides Medical Center in Brooklyn, New York, Dr. Montague Ullman, spent an evening with the Kulaginas and Professor Sergeev. Dr. Ullman reported that it was hours before Kulagina moved anything at all; but by the end of the evening he was convinced that he had seen the most extraordinary PK of his experience.

Mme. Kulagina told me of a most interesting, subjective feeling she sometimes gets, which is a clue for her that she will have a good session. She described the feeling as "like a current of electricity" or heat rising up from her spine, localizing at the base of her neck and remaining there as if waiting for her to direct it. Her most successful sessions are physically exhausting; she has lost as much as five pounds in one sitting, and sometimes finishes with a devastating headache. (The most recent news of Mme. Kulagina is that she has suffered a heart attack as a result of trying to levitate certain objects.)

Her description of a "current of electricity" or heat rising along the spine sounds reminiscent of the "kundalini," about which the yogis have written for many centuries. Kundalini may prove to be a source of bioenergy, but more about that phenomenon in a later chapter.

OTHER CONTEMPORARY PHYSICAL MEDIUMS: GELLER AND SWANN

In 1970, when I met Mme. Kulagina, she was the only person in the world known to perform such feats. Since that time, a New York artist, Ingo Swann, has demonstrated his ability under controlled laboratory conditions supervised by Dr. Gertrude Schmeidler of the City University of New York. Dr. Schmeidler is one of America's most indefatigable parapsychologists. In one experiment, she asked Swann to raise the temperature of an object sealed inside a vacuum bottle, a feat he was able to perform on several occasions. Recently, at Stanford Research Institute, Swann has been able to deflect the needle of a magnetometer encased in a superconductive substance and buried in concrete. This truly extraordinary feat seems more dramatic than Kulagina's deflecting a compass needle with her hand. Swann's work at SRI was reported at Prague by Dr. Harold Puthoff, but somehow it faded into the background when Dr. Puthoff presented a film made at SRI on research with Uri Geller.

MORE ABOUT URI GELLER

At about the same time I was talking with Mme. Kulagina in Leningrad, in 1970, Dr. Andrija Puharich was acting as chairman of an international conference titled "Exploring the Energy Fields of Man" in New York City. At that conference, Dr. Puharich was elected to travel around the world to find persons genuinely gifted with PK. On his trip he met several mediums, but none who were willing, or perhaps even able, to perform under strict laboratory conditions until, in Israel, he met Uri Geller. At that time, Geller was performing on stage as a "mentalist." (Immediately, one is tempted to cry, "Fake! Fraud! Magician!") Dr. Puharich watched Geller's performance more than one hundred times and persuaded him to do some laboratory work. After seeing Geller, under controlled conditions, raise the temperature of thermometers 6 and 8 degrees, break a gold ring clenched in another person's fist, and move compass needles, Dr. Puharich believed he had found the ideal person for strenuous laboratory research.

Actually, none of the PK work performed by Geller was shown in the SRI film at Prague, because none of it passed the stringent criteria set up by Puthoff and his collaborator, Russell Targ. At Prague, Hal Puthoff told me that Geller cannot always perform in the lab (sic semper psychics!), but on several occasions, when Uri spontaneously feels "the power" in him, he has demonstrated remarkable things. One feat, which dazzled Puthoff, took place one day when he and Uri were walking past an electronics lab; the door to the lab happened to be partially open, revealing complex equipment which included several large functioning oscilloscopes. Suddenly, like a mischievous child, Geller pulled Puthoff inside the lab and cried, "Watch this!" He lifted his hand up and then dropped it down. Ten feet away, obediently, the oscilloscopes raised their tracings high, then dropped them low. Then Geller walked out of the lab, followed by a bemused scientist.

Elaborate trick? (Many accomplices would have been needed.) Sleight-of-hand? (Is there a magician who could perform that feat? None has volunteered to do it.) PK? If so, how does it work?

Scientists are pondering that last question. And in Russia, Victor Adamenko has offered a promising lead.

ELECTROSTATICS TO PK?

Adamenko has been able to train his wife, Alla, and a few other gifted subjects to move objects at a distance. Initially they are aided by an electrostatic field, but eventually they are able to move objects even when that field no longer exists. Electrostatics is a complex study in itself. The only thing we need know about electrostatics to understand Adamenko's research is the fact that certain surfaces, such as plastic, can be made to hold an electrical charge.

Adamenko uses a plastic cube about two feet in diameter for his experiments. On the surface of the plastic he places lightweight objects, which Alla can move easily, without ever touching them. I have seen films of Alla chasing table tennis balls, cigar tubes, and cigarettes all over the plastic surface. But she can do this only under special, limiting conditions. Typically, she rubs her hands together to create friction, or she may rub the object, instead. Then she passes her hand to and fro above the object until it begins to move. After that initial movement, she can cause the object to move very rapidly back and forth across the plastic surface. However, the object, guided by the force of repulsion, moves only in the direction that her hand is traveling. Kulagina, on the contrary, can move objects sideways or toward or away from her (though she cannot predict in which direction the object will move). And Kulagina can perform on various surfaces such as wood or glass that are not subject to holding an electrostatic charge. Probably the most important distinction between Alla and Kulagina is the fact that Kulagina can choose one particular match out of a group of fifty matches on the table in front of her, and make that *one* match move toward her, while the others remain motionless. She can also cause a group of matches, scattered helter-skelter on the table, to move in a unit (as if magnetized) toward her.

But Adamenko's work with his wife is an admirable beginning in the study of PK/electrostatic movements. He has already learned that only a few people are capable of doing what Alla can do. Interestingly, although he was able to teach his wife this skill, he himself is unable to evoke any movement with the balls or tubes or cigarettes which his wife can move so deftly.

At the parapsychology conference in Moscow in 1972, Alla gave a demonstration of her PK/electrostatic ability, and some scientists objected that this was simply electrostatic force, not PK. In order to refute this argument, Adamenko suggested that Dr. Stanley Krippner, cochairman of the conference, try to move the ball. At first he could not. But with Alla touching him gently on the shoulder, he soon found himself moving the ball deftly back and forth across the plastic surface. In fact, his performance was so good that one of the observers, fortunately, began filming it. Then, unexpectedly, Alla put her hand about three inches above Krippner's, and the ball immediately stopped dead. Nor could

Krippner get it to move again. Something more than electrostatic force seemed to be involved. But what?

When Ken Johnson, our ingenious inventor of photographic and acupuncture devices, learned about Alla's work, he got a plastic table top, packages of cigarettes, table tennis balls, and cigar tubes. (As you can see, we spare no expense in our unfunded research.) With practice, Ken obtained the same kind of movements as Alla Adamenko, but to get the action going, he has to rub the surface of the plastic with either silk or wool to generate electrostatic force. When I first tried to emulate Ken's performance, even with the silk-created friction, I got no action at all. Eventually, with practice, I could get very respectable movements indeed, but for a far shorter period of time than Ken, who can keep a ball rolling back and forth almost indefinitely. Adamenko believes that the first movements (of which even I am capable) are primarily due to electrostatic force. But after a short time, that force is discharged and the objects stop. With a few rare persons (like Alla, Ken, and Jeff Franklin, another research associate in the lab, who learned the skill), another kind of force seems to take over. Adamenko relates this other force to a bioenergy, possibly the same bioenergy with which acupuncture is concerned.

Using his tobiscope, and other instruments, Adamenko has been able to measure the amount of energy (as measured in nano-amperes of current flow) which is emitted at specific acupuncture points. He learned that this energy not only varies in intensity from person to person but can vary in the same person from day to day. (In our preliminary work in this area, we have found the same effect; interestingly, young people show a greater intensity than older people, as a general rule.) Both Adamenko and Inyushin discovered that by aiming a laser beam at an acupuncture point or by stimulating the body with electricity, the intensity of energy emitted at the points can generally be increased. As he was working in this area Adamenko asked himself a provocative question: Could subjects be trained to increase or decrease the energy of their acupuncture points at will?

The possibility of such control immediately brings to mind recent research in biofeedback, in which subjects are trained to vary at will their heart rate, muscle tension, and brain wave activity. (Research in biofeedback has been going on for many years in Russia, in the wake of Pavlov's work with conditioned reflexes.) Learning to control one's blood pressure or the alpha rhythm of one's brainwaves seems extraordinary enough for most of us, but learning to control the flow of an invisible energy which is presumed to be admitted at presumed acupuncture points?! Remarkably, it seems to work. At least, in one of Adamenko's most recent articles, he claims that those subjects who can control the energy intensity of their acupuncture points seem particularly suited to learn the bioenergetic/electrostatic PK which his wife has mastered. He hopes, eventually, that this area of research may help to explain the more mysterious capabilities of Mme. Kulagina.

LEVITATION

It is one thing for psychics, by an effort of will or bioenergy, to move light objects horizontally along a flat surface. It is quite another thing to *raise* an object from the surface on which it is resting. Such a phenomenon goes against Newton's law of gravity. But claims for "levitation," as the phenomenon is called, have existed for centuries. Most of these claims are anecdotal, and therefore dismissed by scientists.

As examples, the Bible tells us that Jesus walked on water; and the Catholic Church in its annals reports that Saint Joseph of Cupertino was seen by hundreds of people one great celebration day in Rome rising as high as the topmost spires of St. Peter's Cathedral; similarly, Saint Theresa and St. John of the Cross, while engaged in night-long meditations, were reported by nuns in the cloister as rising in the chairs on which they sat, until the heads of the two saints quite literally touched the ceiling. Such reports are not confined to the Catholic Church. Similar tales can be found in almost every kind of religious literature, making levitation seem hardly noteworthy. There is, in fact, a Zen story about a disciple who left his teacher to spend some years in solitary meditation. On his return, his guru asked what he had learned, and the disciple with some pride answered, "I have learned to walk across the river, on the water." Without surprise, in fact with a sigh of disappointment, the guru replied, "What a pity! For only one rupee, the ferry can carry you across."

A CONTROLLED EXPERIMENT IN LEVITATION

Documented cases of levitation, however, are among the rarest in the annals of parapsychologists. The nearest approach to documentation from the early SPR investigators was the case of the remarkable D. D. Home. On one notable occasion, witnessed by several reliable observers, Home was seen to float out of a window in a London home, seventy feet above the ground, and float in again through another window. But this feat was performed in a drawing room, in semidarkness, and it may well have been a case of legerdemain or magic, rather than levitation.

There is only one experiment, to my knowledge, that achieved levitation under controlled conditions. It is to be found in the September 1966 issue of the journal of the SPR, written by British psychologist K. J. Batcheldor, "Report on a Case of Table Levitation and Associated Phenomena." Batcheldor admits that "no skeptic worth his salt" would accept his experimentations as foolproof, but says he would be content if he succeeds "in inducing some few of my readers to suspend disbelief long enough to attempt sustained experimentations for themselves." Batcheldor knew very well that when a group of persons sit at a table with their hands resting on its surface, the table "can tilt and dance in a manner surprising to the uninitiated, but such movements can be caused by the combined unconscious muscular action of the sitters—a fact demonstrated by Faraday in 1853." (The phenomena produced at mediumistic seances, both genuine and phony, which were so popular during the spiritualist movement at the turn of the century will be discussed in detail in a later chapter.) Batcheldor and his colleagues therefore began their sittings "almost in a spirit of amusement." Batcheldor writes that this attitude

> changed sharply in the eleventh meeting, when the table, instead of merely tilting or rocking on two legs, as it had done so far, rose clear from the floor. The explanation of unconscious muscle action was suddenly no longer applicable, since one cannot push a table up into the air, either consciously or unconsciously, when the hands are on top of it.

Over the course of eighteen months, there had been two hundred sittings; but only eighty sittings were held with Mr. W. G. Chick, and these were the *only* occasions when phenomena occurred. According to Batcheldor, "positive results were almost guaranteed in the presence of W. G. C., even if there were only one other sitter." This observation coincides with the findings of parapsychologists: It is usually one person, the medium or sensitive, who has the "power" to manifest phenomena. But W. G. C. rejected the appellation "medium," because of its spiritualistic overtones.

Since the early sittings were in darkness, and trickery might have been used, after the first, unexpected levitation, the table was equipped as follows:

> Four switches, one on each foot, [were] joined in series to a battery lamp. . . . The [red] lamp would light if . . . and *only* if, all four legs came off the floor. . . . The apparatus stood up extremely well to the rough treatment it received during the more violent motions of the table . . . and a most vigorous deliberate rocking and tilting would not give a false signal.

This apparatus was used on various tables, ranging in weight from two to forty pounds. Here is Batcheldor's account of the twelfth sitting, when the apparatus had been attached to a fifteen-pound table:

> This twelfth meeting proved to be extremely colorful, containing the largest number of total levitations ever witnessed in one sitting. At first the table seemed to "try out" the device "tentatively" (it is difficult to resist such anthropomorphism). . . . Gradually the movements became bolder and the lamp was lit for longer periods. By its red glow we could clearly see our hands on top of the table. The table then seemed to act as an excited person would, and proceeded to execute all manner of very lively movements—rocking, swaying, jumping, dancing, tilting, oscillating, oscillating bodily both slowly and rapidly; it shook like a live thing even when totally levitated, almost shaking our hands off.

Batcheldor then describes the table's response to a command from him:

> Because the levitations were not very high, I said: "Come on—higher!" at which the table rose up chest high and remained there for eight seconds. . . . At one point the table levitated and floated right across the room: we had to leave our seats to follow it; it appeared to be about five inches off the floor, and the signal lamp remained alight until we crashed into some other furniture near the wall and the table dropped to the floor. When we had reseated ourselves in the center of the room, the table soon came to life again, and took to rising up and then banging itself down with tremendous force, so that we feared it would break.

LEVITATION IN OUR LABORATORY

Occasionally the lab will receive an excited phone call from someone who has attended a "sitting" and has seen "with his own eyes" a table lift all four legs from the ground. In the early days, we would pay house calls on such seances. When such a seance would begin, usually nothing at all would happen. Sometimes we could observe the table performing little jumping movements, and on rare occasions, we have seen a table tilt so that it was perched daintily on one leg, remaining there when no one was touching it. But none of these observations satisfied the criterion that all four legs must be off the ground at the same time. Whatever else it might be, such movement is not levitation. There is, though, a simple demonstration which suggests that levitation might not be so paranormal or "occult" as it might seem on reading Batcheldon's account. (Why not try it and see for yourself? The directions follow.)

AN EXERCISE IN LEVITATION

1. Any five people may serve as the subjects, and one more acts as the experimenter.

2. The largest and heaviest subject sits on a small chair, preferably one without arms.

The four other people stand around the seated person, two ind him and two a little forward on either side, adjacent to his knees.

4. The experimenter gives the following instructions: "The seated person simply remains seated where he is, and is not to do anything: not cooperate, not resist, not become active in any way. The four participants must perform a specific set of movements, in a rhythm which will be called out by me. The movements are simple and are divided into two parts. Person 1, at the seated person's right, places his right hand on top of the head of the person who is sitting down. Person 2, right rear, then places his right hand on top of Person 1's right hand. Person 3, left rear, places his right hand on top of Person 2's right hand, and Person 4, left front, places his right hand on top of the others." There are now four hands, one on top of the other. Continuing, the experimenter tells Person 4 to place his left hand on top of his own right hand; Person 3 to place his left hand on top of the pile of hands, and Person 2 and Person 1 to do likewise. These movements should be practiced until each person moves in an easy, rhythmic, flowing manner.

5. After a rhythm has been achieved, in this movement, the participants must make another set of rhythmic movements in unison. When the experimenter calls out, "Lift!" all will move their hands from the seated person's head, extend the forefingers of each hand, palm down, and place these fingers as follows: Person 1 will place his forefingers under the right knee of the seated person; Person 2 will place his under the right armpit; Person 3 will place his under the left armpit; and Person 4 will place his under the left knee. These movements should be practiced until they are effortless and smooth. Then the experimenter should explain, "When I say, 'Lift!' you will move to this last position (under armpits and knees) and you will easily lift the seated person up into the air."

Usually, when this statement is made, all five participants will laugh, because the idea is absurd. It is. To show how absurd it is, suggest that the four persons all place two fingers in the designated places under knees and armpits and try to lift the person seated in the chair. It will be obvious that it takes an enormous amount of effort to lift the seated person (if they can) by so much as an inch.

6. The success of the experiment is in the rhythm with which these simple movements are carried out. The experimenter chooses the tempo. It can be as slow or as fast as he wishes, *provided the rhythm is maintained.* Keep rehearsing until the flow is nice and easy. When it is, the experimenter should count out the rhythm until everyone is in the correct position and then cry: "LIFT!" At that point, *in unison,* each person moves to the next position and lifts.

It is to be expected that the first three or four attempts will be unsuccessful. People will laugh, movements will be out of synch, and the ridiculousness of the movements will cause embarrassment. But if you persevere, after three or four false starts, the group will become cohesive and rhythmical. When the experimenter cries, "LIFT!" the seated person will be lifted from two to four *feet* into the air, without any effort being experienced by the lifters. Usually, the participants are astonished, and the seated person experiences a sensation of lightness and exhilaration.

I have included this demonstration in several parapsychology classes I have taught and have met only once with failure. Therefore, it is with confidence that I offer the experiment. Furthermore, when some skill has been obtained (and this is easily achieved by having each of the four lifters become, in turn, the seated person), you may find it is no longer necessary to go through the procedure of placing the hands on top of the head. All that seems necessary is for the four persons to chant a phrase in unison five or six times. Any phrase will do, provided it is done *in rhythm.* We have used with repeated success the phrase "chocolate cake." Another good phrase is "hot fudge sundae." "Abracadabra" doesn't seem too successful.

What happens in this simple process that enables a hefty man to be raised several feet in the air, supported by the *backs* of eight fingers? Lifting him that way, without the rhythm, is almost impossible. Done with rhythm, there is little sensation of energy being expended.

This apparently age-old experiment, which can be done by just about anyone, may be a variant of the extraordinary feat performed by 123-pound Mrs. Maxwell Rogers, who, in 1960, lifted one end of a 3,600-pound automobile which, after the collapse of a jack, had fallen on her son. She was not aware, during that stress, that she had done anything remarkable. While performing this experiment, there is no sensation of doing anything remarkable.

(I am permitted a delicious side note here. The publisher of this book, a reasonable and conservative gentleman, was loath to print this recipe for Instant Levitation without proof that it worked. At first, he refused to attempt it; but eventually, without my being present, he did attempt it with wife and friends and found that it was [as he told me, brusquely, with averted eyes] "simple, very easy." Shortly after his experiment was successfully concluded, he was visited by a physicist friend, who was immediately asked to supply a reasonable, mechanical explanation for the phenomenon. The physicist answered that he himself had performed the experiment, but was at a loss to explain how it happened.)

LEVITATION IN THE SOVIET UNION

In 1973 an article titled "Autogravity" was published in the Soviet journal *Socialist Industries*. The author, V. Anisimov, describes an event in the Moscow laboratory of psychologist/professor V. N. Pushkin:

> Only a table stood in the middle—on it a tennis ball, a match box, and a few pencils. . . . A man extends his hand over the objects. . . . A minute passes. Another. Suddenly the ball on the table begins to move; the match box and pencils move from their places. The man has activated the objects without touching them with his hands.

The man was Boris Ermolaev, who was just warming up for the "significant part of the experiments." Ermolaev would take in his hands some object, squeeze it between his palms, and then slowly move his hands apart; the object would remain suspended in space. The distance between his hands could reach 20 centimeters.

The author points out that this is a phenomenon for which "Newton's law of gravitation is inapplicable." And he offers various hypotheses to explain "autogravity," hypotheses which include the concepts of bioenergy, bioelectric fields, and Dubrov's biogravity, all of which we have discussed. He then points out that one of the chief difficulties in studying this phenomenon is that "the person possessing this type of ability is not always able to control it." Anisimov concludes by stating, "One does not need to resist new facts and complex problems. In our world of jet planes and atomic reactors there remains much that is unknown. And science must uncover the secrets of the universe."

And so, once more we find that the Soviet Union is reporting experiments with a gifted psychic who apparently can, *only at times,* perform "impossible" feats in the laboratory, feats for which science has as yet no explanation.

REALMS OF BIOENERGY

We have been examining various "impossibilities": persons moving objects at a distance with their eyes or with motions of their hands; persons detecting minerals beneath the ground with divining rods or coat hangers; persons detecting colors with the tips of their fingers or sensing colors concealed in metal containers; persons conveying bioenergy to generators, which can then precipitate dirt from water or set paddle wheels in motion; persons healing the sick with the laying on of hands or with the power of mind; persons making plants grow faster by holding the jars of water which will water the plants; persons keeping suspended in space a tennis ball or a pencil. All these seemingly dissimilar events are presumed to involve some type of human energy which can be directed to influence objects in the environment.

And we have also seen how various hypotheses have been offered to account for these phenomena: biogravity, magnetic field effects, bioplasma, L fields, orgone, radionics. All are recent names for energies called in ancient times prana, mana, ch'i, etc. Some sages in those remote eras believed that these energies are all manifestations of *one* energy that derives from an even more evanescent stuff, the "mind stuff" of which Sir James Jeans conjectures that the universe was composed.

What do we know about mind? Science has scarcely begun to explore the reaches of mind, but already there has been charted a rough map of various states of consciousness in which equally "impossible" phenomena, like telepathy and precognition, seem to occur.

Realms of the mind will occupy our attention in the section to follow.

Part II: Biocommunication

6 Realms of the Mind

Levels of mind: Conscious, subconscious, preconscious, unconscious (personal and collective), and the superconscious.

Techniques to achieve the deeper levels of mind (both ancient and modern): Dreams; solitude or sensory deprivation; intoxication through mind-altering plants or chemicals; hypnosis; trance states.

THE CONSCIOUS MIND

Probably all of us can immediately give our names, addresses, and phone numbers; and some of us our area codes, zip codes, and possibly social security numbers. This information is contained in the rational, conscious mind, which of course is the repository of a great deal more: We know, consciously, to eat and exercise for health and pleasure; to study and work; to keep appointments, checkbooks, gardens, or pets; to raise a family and perhaps provide some comforts for our old age. This is the domain of the conscious mind, a domain so obvious and straightforward that little more need be said about it, except that our conscious minds are available to us only when we are awake and functioning normally.

THE SUBCONSCIOUS MIND

There are a great many functions which we perform every moment of our lives, night and day, without thinking about them: our lungs breathe in and out, our hearts pump blood, our stomachs and bowels digest and eliminate, and our senses remain available at all times. These functions are in the domain of the subconscious mind, which remains alert and discriminating, even though we are fast asleep. For instance, you may remain in a deep sleep, snoring comfortably, while traffic noises roar outside your window, but an unexpected, almost silent footstep in your bedroom may wake you instantly, with pounding heart. No conscious thinking was involved in your arousal.

The subconscious stays in control of these involuntary processes which go on in us from the moment we are slapped into birth until we die. Indeed, only if they cease functioning properly do we become aware of them. And in fact, until very recently it was believed by scientists that we are, most of us, slaves to these autonomic activities. Now, however, the control of such processes has become an object of serious study in the laboratory, under the name of biofeedback. People are being trained to control the temperature of their hands, the rhythm of their brain waves, the tension or relaxation of muscles they scarcely knew existed. (We will see where the development of these capacities may lead, at the end of this chapter.)

It has further been shown that animals can learn exquisite control over extremely subtle measures, such as the electrical activity in tiny areas of the brain. In one study at Rockefeller University, psychologist Neil Miller and his colleagues implanted sensors in both ears of a rat. The rat was rewarded with food only when there was a difference in the blood flow of one ear as compared to the other—and the rat learned to control its blood flow to each ear, differentially. Perhaps one day people will learn equally sensitive control over the subconscious mind.

THE PRECONSCIOUS MIND

Let's add a third level of mind, the preconscious. Perhaps the nature of the preconscious can best be exemplified by the experience of trying to remember an event or name that eludes us. Stop for a moment and try to remember the name of your second-grade schoolteacher. If your second grade was a delightful year, you may, without effort, remember her name. If so, then her name is in the domain of your conscious mind. The chances are, however, that her name escapes you. Were you to take the time to relax, settle comfortably wherever you are, close your eyes, and let the events of your early school years drift through your mind, you might catch a glimpse of the room in which you spent your second grade, or the face of the child who sat across from you, or the blackboard on which you might see the teacher's name. If you were to continue this reverie, you might hear the sound of her voice, and perhaps suddenly, with startling vividness, you might even see your teacher sitting at her desk, wearing a dress the colors of which would be just as clear to you now as they were when she was actually wearing that dress so many years ago.

This repository of memories which can be made accessible to consciousness is brimful with events and information which, with some effort, can be brought to consciousness. How often have you said in exasperation, "But I know that! It's on the tip of my tongue!" And only later, when you've ceased thinking about it, does the elusive fact come floating into your awareness? That is because the contents of the preconscious are not fixed. Sometimes our conscious mind loses information which slips into the preconscious, and we "forget." At other times the knowledge in the preconscious surges into awareness, and we "remember."

THE PERSONAL UNCONSCIOUS MIND

Despite the vast contents of the preconscious, its domain is trivial compared with the unconscious. A great deal of research in classical psychology has been directed to the domain of the personal unconscious, as outlined by Freud and his followers. (In exploring the deeper levels of mind, Freud became interested in psychic phenomena, and wrote several papers on telepathy, dreams, and the "occult." But before we explore those realms, let us return to conventional psychology.)

Specifically, let's return to your second-grade teacher, whose name, even after some effort, still remains lost to you. It may be that your second grade was filled with difficulties, and as a result almost the entire year has been blotted from your memory. In Freud's terminology, your memories have been driven back into the unconscious through repression. It is a basic premise of psychoanalysis that even though you cannot remember those experiences, they nevertheless remain alive in your unconscious, and affect your behavior now. It may be, for example, that the name "Elinor" has always been disagreeable to you and that "Elinor" was the name of the girl who sat in front of you in the second grade and tattled on you to the teacher for cheating on a test.

How many of our everyday reactions have been molded by early childhood experiences which have been totally forgotten? Most of us will never know. But psychiatrists are all too familiar with patients who present themselves for treatment because of some incapacitating fear which they realize is irrational and absurd, but which they cannot control, and for which they cannot account. This can be a fear of elevators, snakes, airplanes, cats, or even blueberry pie. At a recent seminar, in an attempt to demonstrate the origins of certain dislikes, I asked a psychiatrist to relax, close his eyes, and to visualize as vividly as he could a food he had a strong aversion for: its color, smell, texture, shape. (This technique is derived from the "method acting" exercise, "affective memory," devised by the great Russian regisseur Konstantin Stanislavsky.) When the visualization became strong, I asked him to describe the place in which he found himself. With rich detail, he replied that he was a child sitting at the kitchen table, and his mother was serving his favorite dessert, fresh blueberry pie. As he said that, his face suffused with pleasure, and I suggested he fantasy eating the pie. As soon as he began, he experienced intense revulsion, because as he bit into the luscious pie, his teeth clamped down into a unfortunate cockroach that had found its way into the blueberry mixture. This was an experience the psychiatrist had totally forgotten: All he knew was that he thoroughly disliked blueberry pie.

This of course is a trivial phobia, due to a repressed childhood experience. Psychoanalytic literature contains thousands of such revelations, many of far more terrifying childhood traumae. Sometimes they cannot be brought to the surface easily, and drugs like sodium amytal, or LSD, are used to break through to those deep levels of mind.

The domain of the personal unconscious, then, includes a wealth of experience which has been lost to our conscious memories. In fact, it has been proposed by serious scientists that the personal unconscious mind contains within it every one of our experiences, from the moment of birth. The eminent brain surgeon Wilder Penfield arrived at that conclusion as a result of his very special operating technique. He usually performed surgery under a local anesthetic so that his patients could remain conscious and cooperative while he used an electrode to probe for the diseased part of the brain. Quite by accident he discovered that electrical stimulation in the cortex sometimes caused the patient to relive episodes from early life. One patient heard, as if she were there, the singing of a Christmas carol in her church in Holland, experiencing the emotional beauty of the occasion exactly as she had originally so many years before. After observing many such incidents in the operating room, Penfield wrote:

> When by chance the neurosurgeon's electrode activates past experience, that experience unfolds progressively, moment by moment. This is a little like the performance of a wire recorder or a strip of film on which are registered all those things of which the individual was once aware. . . . As long as the electrode is held in place, the experience of a former day goes forward. There is no holding it still, no turning back, no crossing to other periods. When the electrode is withdrawn, it stops as suddenly as it began.

But there is more to be found in the unconscious mind, far more than even this treasure trove of barely noticed, forgotten, or repressed personal experience.

During his early explorations of repressed traumae in the unconscious, Freud believed, and published, that he had cured thirteen cases of "virtually incurable" hysteria, tracing the symptoms back to their childhood origin "which invariably proves to be an experience in the person's sexual life . . . a brutal [sexual] attempt committed by an adult." Later Freud learned to his chagrin that in several of these cases the sexual attacks, relived by patients during their therapy, had never actually occurred! Almost thirty years elapsed before Freud published his conclusion:

The majority of my patients reproduced from their childhood scenes in which they were sexually seduced by some grown up person. With female patients, the part of the seducer was almost always assigned to the father. I believed these stories, and consequently supposed that I had discovered the roots of the subsequent neurosis in these experiences of sexual seductions in childhood. . . . If the reader feels inclined to shake his head at my credulity, I cannot altogether blame him. . . . When, however, I was at last obliged to recognize that these scenes of seduction had never taken place, and that they were only fantasies which my patients had made up, . . . I was able to draw the right conclusions from my discovery: namely, *that the neurotic symptoms were not directly related to actual events but to fantasies,* and that as far as the neurosis was concerned, psychic reality was of more importance than material reality.

Psychic reality. Fantasies causing traumae. With this discovery Freud traveled beyond the realm of the personal unconscious with its repressed actual experiences, and found a domain of mind where fantasies and dreams exist on the same level of reality as actually lived events. As we know, Freud made a profound study of the dream, a part of human behavior that had been almost completely ignored in scientific research—which is not to say that the dream had been ignored in earlier societies.

DREAM INTERPRETATION IN ANCIENT TIMES

Even in primitive cultures men had considered (and do still consider) the dream to be an important source of information, when correctly interpreted by the witch doctor, medicine man, or shaman. In the more sophisticated societies of ancient Egypt and Greece, it was the oracles and priests who were consulted as authorities in this esoteric field of man's behavior. For the dream is not easily interpreted. The contents of so many dreams are apparently so outlandish and bizarre that the meaning, if any, is obscured and one is left to conclude that the dream is pure nonsense. It was only the oracle or prophet who could reveal its symbolic meaning. Gradually there grew an "occult" literature which tried to interpret the dream through the use of ready-made symbols. Dream books are purchasable today. In them one can read that "a dream of finding gold means an inheritance," or "a dream of a black lily means violent death to a woman," etc. Such recipe dream books served mainly to discredit the dream as a phenomenon worthy of study. And in fact, until Freud, scientists considered that dreams were no more than the excreta of the mind during sleep and that the horrifying imagery of a nightmare could in all probability be explained by too much pizza before bedtime.

DREAM INTERPRETATION: CONTEMPORARY

Scientific research into dreams began primarily with physiological studies which explored the possibility that the dream was caused by stimuli impinging on the brain from outside (an alarm clock going off might give rise to the dream of a fire engine's wailing sirens) or from within (the need to urinate might prompt a dream of flood waters rising).

But with the very gradual acceptance of Freud's monumental *Interpretation of Dreams* and his dictum that the dream is "the royal road to the unconscious," dream interpretation became an acceptable avenue for exploration by behavioral scientists. It was generally agreed, as Freud had pointed out, that dreams are prompted by the unconscious needs and desires of the dreamer, with particular emphasis on his sexual desires. Dreams of keys going into locks, or cigars placed into ashtrays, or spades digging into gardens became an almost international sex joke. Eventually Carl Jung made this pertinent comment:

A man may dream of inserting a key in a lock, of wielding a heavy stick, or of breaking down a door with a battering ram. Each of these can be regarded as a sexual allegory. But the fact that his unconscious for its own purposes has chosen one of these specific images—it might be the key, the stick, or the battering ram—is also of major significance. The real task is to understand *why* the key has been preferred to the stick, or the stick to the battering ram. And sometimes this might lead one to discover that it was not the sexual act at all that was represented, but some quite different psychological point.

FROM THE PERSONAL TO THE COLLECTIVE UNCONSCIOUS

At first, Freud believed that dreams could be completely understood on the level of the personal unconscious. But, as not infrequently happened in his long career, he changed his mind. Again, borrowing from Carl Jung to explain:

> We have to take into consideration the fact (first observed and commented on by Freud) that elements occur in the dream that are not individual and that cannot be derived from the dreamer's personal experience. These elements are what Freud called "archaic remnants"—mental forms which seem to be aboriginal, innate, and inherited shapes of the human mind.

Jung's word for Freud's "archaic remnants" was "archetypes," for which he gave many illustrative examples: The Wise Old Man, the Anima, the Eye, the Snake, the Earth Mother, the Big Fish who devours the dreamer/hero. Jung claimed that these, and other symbols, have appeared in the myths and legends of all mankind, independent of race, country, or culture. Let us explore one archetype, that of the Devouring Dragon or Fish, which philosopher Mircea Eliade has documented as it appears in various cultures. We are probably all familiar with the biblical story of Jonah being swallowed by a whale, living in its belly, and then reemerging from its mouth. In Lapland there is a legend in which the holy man (shaman) is found by his son, after a long sleep, in the guts of a whale, and then emerges from its mouth. In New Guinea, one of the rites of puberty has the child entering into an effigy of a monster (perhaps a crocodile or whale), then emerging out of its belly into manhood. In Finland a legend describes a blacksmith who, to win his love, must capture a large fish. The fish swallows him, but the blacksmith causes so much upheaval in its belly that the fish begs him to leave through its rear. The blacksmith refuses, "because of what people will call him," and eventually he bursts open the monster and emerges unscathed. Polynesian myth has the parents of the hero swallowed by a whale. The hero takes the mast of his boat, props open the whale's mouth, goes into its stomach to retrieve his parents from the whale's belly, and emerges with them through the mouth.

Jung believed that this archetypal motif of the hero being swallowed by the monster and emerging intact, symbolizes man's death and rebirth. As Jung was so well aware, his contemporaries disbelieved the archetype:

> My views about the "archaic remnants," which I call "archetypes" have been constantly criticized. My critics have incorrectly assumed that I am dealing with "inherited representations" and have dismissed the idea of the archetype as mere "superstition."

Shortly after this passage was written, the drug culture erupted around the world. And from every country came descriptions of psychedelic experiences in which emerged again and again the archetypes that Jung had so carefully tabulated. Here, for example, is the LSD experience of a forty-year-old American businessman, as reported by Masters and Houston in their valuable book *The Varieties of Psychedelic Experience:*

> A serpent with great jaws flicked out his tongue . . . draws me into his mouth. . . . I am swallowed. . . . Incredible demons line the shores of the snake's insides. Each tries to destroy me as I float by. . . . I reach the end of the tail and kick my way out. . . . An old fisherman has caught me. . . . The serpent rises out of the water, grown into a huge sea monster. . . . The sea monster pursues us. . . . Just as we reach the shore it snaps off the fisherman's leg. The fisherman crawls with me to a nearby hut. His wife is there. I am raised by this couple. . . . The years pass. . . . They tell me I must avenge myself on the sea monster. . . . I dive into the water . . . and finally find the monster. . . . It has grown gargantuan . . . opens its jaws to consume me but I get a stranglehold on his throat. For many days we battle together. . . . I am the conqueror . . . tear open its belly. . . . I find the leg of my foster-father. I take the leg back and fit it on its stump. It instantly joins and he is whole again.

Sometimes, without drugs, the poet or artist (or madman) has had similar archetypal visions. Under the pseudonym of John Custance, the author of *Wisdom, Madness, and Folly* gives a brilliant introspective account of a manic episode:

> One night a little patch of damp on the wall opposite my bed took on plainly the shape of a gorilla. It so happened that I knew a girl nicknamed "Gorilla," and I immediately associated the vision with her. . . . I spoke to her. "Who are you?" I asked. I did not actually hear her voice replying; I have never experienced true auditory hallucinations. Yet she spoke to me quite clearly in my inner consciousness. . . . "I am the Harlot Eye who fell. Satan, who is the Serpent in Man, tempted me to my fall, but I rose again. For I am Astarte, I am Ashtaroth, I am the Great Whore of Babylon, yes and Aphrodite of the Greeks, and Cleopatra and Helen of Troy, too. . . . I am all fallen women since the world began; I wantoned in the groves of Nineveh and Babylon; I danced before the Golden Calf of Bethel and upon the hillside of Greece in the wild worship of the young Dionysius; and as Mary Magdalene I loved the Lord Jesus and for once knew peace.

This was Custance's first meeting with what, in agreement with Jung, he calls the archetype of the Anima (the feminine part of every man). It appeared to him in many forms during the course of his illness.

If, as may seem more plausible now, such imagery exists deep within us, deeper than the personal unconscious mind, we ask: What is it? Why is it? What does it mean? Aldous Huxley, who experienced similar extraordinary visions under mescaline, evolved this hypothesis:

> A man consists of what I may call an Old World of personal consciousness and, beyond a dividing sea, a series of New Worlds—the not too distant Virginias and Carolinas of the personal subconscious; the Far West of the collective unconscious, with its flora of symbols, its tribes of aboriginal archetypes; and, across another, vaster ocean, at the antipodes of everyday consciousness, the world of Visionary Experience.

THE COLLECTIVE UNCONSCIOUS AND THE THRESHOLD TO THE SUPERCONSCIOUS

According to the mystics of every age, there exists a region deep within us which serves as a threshold to guard still another vast and almost unexplored realm, the world of Huxley's visionary experience. This threshold, perhaps like the Van Allen belt which guards the earth's borders from the cosmos beyond, seems to contain within it universal symbols of Heaven and Hell, good and evil, dragons and dakinis: all the opposites before they are fused into One. Those who follow the spiritual path through meditation may experience these opposites, as in these words of caution from Tao master Chao Pi Ch'en: "Demonic states will occur in the forms of visions of paradise in all its majesties, with beautiful gardens and pools or of hells with frightful demons with strange and awesome heads constantly changing their hideous faces."

Here, in this antipode of the mind, called the Devil Land by the Buddhists, Hades by the ancient Greeks, and a bum trip by the LSD taker, deep in the unconscious mind of all of us, there are found such mysterious, such fascinating phenomena that throughout history men have evolved various techniques to penetrate there. And today, in the laboratory, new techniques are being developed to better achieve those altered states of consciousness which, it seems, make penetration into the deeper levels of mind more available. Dreams are considered one such altered state of consciousness.

THE PROPHETIC DREAM AND THE CREATIVE DREAM

Freud was perhaps the first to point out the possible prophetic nature of the dream, in his analysis of the biblical story in which Joseph interpreted one of the Pharoah's dreams as indicating seven years of plenty, to be followed by seven years of famine although the Pharoah had not dreamed of feast or famine; he had dreamed merely that seven fat cows were being devoured by seven skinny cows. This use of symbols, distortion, and condensation was called by Freud "primary process" thinking, to which we will be referring frequently in this section, for primary process seems to be a strong characteristic of the unconscious mind.

Another prophetic dream expressed in primary process symbols is reported by Jung, who knew a man with "almost a morbid passion for dangerous mountain climbing," which Jung felt was his way of trying to "get above himself":

> In a dream one night, he saw himself stepping off the summit of a high mountain into empty space. . . . I told him that the dream foreshadowed his death in a mountain accident. It was in vain. . . . Six months later, a mountain guide watched him and a friend letting themselves down on a rope in a difficult place. . . . Suddenly he let go of the rope, according to the guide, "as if he were jumping into the air." He fell upon his friend, and both were killed.

This faculty of foretelling the future by means of·the dream was called, in ancient times, the gift of prophecy. Today parapsychologists call it precognition. Whether this is a valid concept remains for another chapter. Here it is merely suggested that a dream, the product of an altered state of consciousness, may have functions about which we still do not know very much.

Another little-recognized aspect of the dream is its ability to serve creatively both artist and scientist. On rare occasions, the dream has provided entire plots for novels. Robert Louis Stevenson tells us that he spent years looking for a story to illustrate his "strong sense of man's double being," when suddenly the plot of *Dr. Jekyll and Mr. Hyde* was revealed to him one night in a dream. Similarly, Mary Shelley dreamed one night the entire story of her famous novel, *Frankenstein*. Scientists, too, have recorded that some of their most important discoveries were revealed to them through dreams. The chemist Friedrich August von Kekule tells of a series of dreams and reveries:

> Atoms were gamboling before my eyes. . . . I saw how, frequently, two smaller atoms united to form a pair, how a larger one embraced two smaller ones; how still larger ones kept hold of three or even four of the smaller, whilst the whole kept whirling in a giddy dance. I saw how the larger ones formed a chain. . . . I spent part of the night putting on paper at least sketches of

these dream forms. [In the last of these dreams] again the atoms were gamboling before my eyes. ... My mental eye, rendered more acute by repeated visions of this kind, could now distinguish larger structures, of manifold conformation; long rows, sometimes more closely fitted together, all turning and twisting in snake-like motion. But look! What was that? One of the snakes had siezed hold of its own tail, and the form whirled mockingly before my eyes. As if by a flash of lightning I woke.

Through this dream symbol of a snake biting its own tail, von Kekule was able to derive his discovery that some organic compounds are composed of closed chains or rings, a discovery that has been called "the most brilliant piece of prediction to be found in the whole range of organic chemistry." A scientific prediction derived from a dream.

Obviously, there is still much we do not understand about the dream. Clearly, on rare occasions, the dream (which arrives when we are in a different state of consciousness, when we are, in fact, unconscious, or "dead to the world") has produced new knowledge for the dreamer, knowledge he may have been actively seeking in vain or knowledge which he was not seeking at all. Obviously we have no control over our dreams. Since they provide some of us with valuable information, it was probably inevitable that certain people, throughout history, sought to develop other techniques which might provide similar kinds of unknown information, techniques which could be consciously developed.

ANCIENT TECHNIQUES OF SOLITUDE AND SENSORY DEPRIVATION

In every civilization there have always been a few rare men so determined to learn about the universe within that they would leave the society in which they dwelled to seek silence and solitude in forests, mountains, or deep in desert caves. In India, Tibet, and China there exist sacred mountains and caves in which mystics like Naropa, Milarepa, and Juang Po dwelled for years in isolation, struggling to attain illumination. Among the Siberians and Eskimos there is a tradition that the shaman, in order to find his "power," must seek for it alone, in the wilderness. The great Danish explorer ismussen spent many years among the Tungus, and learned of one shaman's solitary vigil:

> I soon became melancholy. I would sometimes fall to weeping and feel unhappy without knowing why. Then for no reason all would suddenly be changed, and I felt a great, inexplicable joy, a joy so powerful that I could not restrain it, but had to break into song, a mighty song, with room for only one word: joy, joy! And then in the midst of such a fit of mysterious and overwhelming delight I became a shaman, not knowing myself how it came about. But I was a shaman. I could see and hear in a totally different way. I had gained my enlightenment, the shaman's light of brain and body, and this in such a manner that it was not only I who could see through the darkness of life, but the same bright light also shone out from me, imperceptible to human beings but visible to all spirits of earth and sky and sea, and these now came to me to become my helping spirits.

In the eleventh century, a respected doctor of religion in Bagdad, Al Ghazzali, renounced profession and family in order to understand better Sufi philosophy:

> I read [Sufi books] until I . . . recognized that what pertains to their methods is just what no study can grasp. How great is the difference, for example, to know in what drunkenness consists—as being occasioned by a vapor that rises in the stomach—and *being* drunk effectively. Thus I had learned what words could teach of Sufism, but what was left could be learned solely by giving one's self up.
>
> So I quitted Bagdad, with no other occupation than living in retreat and solitude. And in this situation I spent ten years. During this solitary state things were revealed to me which it is impossible to describe. . . . A blind man can understand nothing of colors save what he had learned by hearsay. Wherefore, just as an eye opens to discern various intellectual objects uncomprehended by sensation; just so in the prophetic the sight is illumined by a light which uncovers hidden things and objects which the intellect fails to reach.

There are those who follow this path of solitude today. Probably one of the most remarkable women of our time was the fantastic French lady Madame Alexandra David-Neel, who as a young woman (long before woman's liberation), traveled alone into the wilderness of Tibet, to do something no Westerner had succeeded in doing before: to study with a lama (gomchen), who had been living for seventeen years in a mountain cave thirteen thousand feet high. In Mme. David-Neel's words:

> At first the gomchen had lived in total seclusion. The villagers and herdsmen who brought his provisions left their offerings in front of his door and retired without seeing him. The hermitage was inaccessible during three or four months every year, for the snows would block the valleys leading to it. . . . A few Westerners had sojourned in lamaist monasteries, but none had lived with these gomchen about whom so many fantastic stories are told.

On meeting the lama, Mme. David-Neel requested that she be allowed to remain:

> I presented my request in a manner that agreed with Oriental customs. He objected that it was useless for me to stay in such an inhospitable region to listen to an ignorant man. I strongly insisted, however, and he decided to admit me on a trial as a novice. . . . The days passed. Winter came, blocking the village that led to the foot of the mountain. The gomchen shut himself up for a long retreat. I did the same thing. My single daily meal was placed behind a curtain at the entrance of the hut. . . . At last it was springtime in the cloudy Himalayas. Nine hundred feet below my cave rhododendrons blossomed. I climbed the barren mountain tops. . . . Solitude! Solitude! Mind and senses develop their sensibility in this contemplative life made up of continual observations and reflections. Does one become a visionary or, rather, is it not that one is blind until then?

Mme. David-Neel spent fourteen years traveling throughout Tibet, and became a foremost authority on its languages, customs, and spiritual practices. She died in 1969 at the age of one hundred and two.

Students from the West continue to make pilgrimages to India today, searching for similar instruction. Former Harvard professor Richard Alpert (Baba Ram Dass) has written of his experiences with his teacher, and probably is at least partially responsible for the exodus of neophyte psychiatrists and psychologists who travel to the ashrams of India. (At the Neuropsychiatric Institute, where I work, at least one resident psychiatrist each year takes a sabbatical to do exactly that.)

MODERN LABORATORY STUDIES OF SENSORY DEPRIVATION

The experiences which result from solitude and isolation are subjective, and were considered an unsuitable topic for objective scientific study until Admiral Byrd, in his book *Alone*, described his six months of isolation in the Antarctic snows. He had expected to taste the "goodness of peace and quiet and solitude," but the experience proved to be a lurid nightmare. He was overcome with so deep a lassitude that he lay in bed for uncounted hours, hallucinating, losing his sense of identity, floating like a "disembodied spirit in timeless space." Eskimos are aware of such dangers of solitude in the frozen north, for they do not generally venture on kayak trips unaccompanied. Sometimes those who have done so apparently developed a trance-like state in which they kept paddling far out to sea to their deaths. Admiral Byrd recommended that isolation be studied by behavioral scientists, and that task was undertaken first by Donald Hebb of Canada's McGill University. In a multitude of studies, volunteer subjects were asked to remain in sensory deprivation chambers, where they lay on comfortable beds, wearing translucent goggles, cotton gloves, and earphones emitting a constant masking noise. The volunteers were paid twenty dollars a day for as long as they would remain in the booths (generally no more than two or three days). During that time they experienced many extraordinary phenomena, including a variety of visual and sometimes auditory hallucinations. At first, they reported seeing colors and geometric forms, rather like wallpaper patterns. These changed into what were described as "dreams while wide awake," for example, "a procession of squirrels with sacks over their shoulders marching purposefully across a snowfield and out of the field of vision"; "prehistoric animals walking around in a jungle"; and "a miniature rocket ship shooting pellets at my arm." There were also reported strange body sensations, in which some subjects felt that they had two bodies, overlapped, lying side by side, or that the mind seemed "to be a ball of cotton wool floating above the body."

Do such descriptions sound familiar? For those of us who have had experience with psychedelic drugs, our reactions on reading such sensory deprivation experiences might be, "Man, he was on a real trip!"

ANCIENT INTOXICATIONS: PLANTS AND POTIONS

Another universally discovered path to other realms of the mind in both ancient and modern times, has been that of intoxication. Lost in prerecorded history are the names of the mind-altering plants brewed into potions by the oracles of Babylon, Egypt, and Greece; but under scientific investigation today are the ingredients used by the shamans of Siberia, the Bushmen of Australia, and the Indians along the Amazon. Long known for their alteration of consciousness are such plants as the cactus of the American Indian, the poppy of China, and the cannabis of India (hasheesh in the Near East, marijuana in Mexico).

Don Juan, the Mexican curandero with whom anthropologist Carlos Castaneda studied, tried through the use of his specially prepared jimson weed, psylocybe and peyote to help Castaneda "make a crack between worlds." In his attempts Castaneda did penetrate into the "Van Allen belt" of the mind, and saw there a jaguar who spoke two languages, a black dog who became transparent, so that the water he drank was seen as an irridescent fluid shooting out of each of his hairs, and a witch woman who changed into other creatures. Castaneda himself experienced growing the legs, wings, tail, and beak of a crow and then extending his wings. "Did I really fly? Did I really take off like a bird?" asked Castaneda of Dan Juan in a torment of uncertainty.

There are indications that mind-altering plants may produce another phenomenon, perhaps related to these visionary or hallucinary experiences. Sometimes, it seems, the intoxicated person receives previously unknown information which is subsequently found to be true. American investigator Dr. William McGovern, who took *caapi* (a brew made from a jungle vine) with the natives of an Amazon village, reported:

> Certain of the Indians fell into a particularly deep state of trance, in which they appeared to possess telepathic powers. . . . On this particular evening, the local medicine man told me that the chief of a certain tribe in the far-away Pira Pirana had suddenly died. I entered this statement in my diary and many weeks later, when we came to the tribe in question, I found that the witch doctor's statement had been true in every detail. Possibly these cases were mere coincidences.

Tremendous impetus to the development of mind-altering drugs came in 1954 when the Swiss chemist Albert Hoffman accidentally ingested a little-used chemical, lysergic acid, to which he had added a "tail" of a diethylamide group. Puzzled by the fantastic effects he experienced, he deliberately swallowed a tiny amount of the drug the next day. In his words:

> I lost all control of time; space and time became more and more disorganized and I was overcome with fears that I was going crazy. . . . Occasionally I felt as being outside my body. I thought I had died. My "Ego" was suspended somewhere in space and I saw my body lying dead on the sofa. I observed and registered clearly that my "alter ego" was moving around the room, moaning.

That is a description of the first LSD trip in history.

In its wake, there emerged a host of synthesized psychedelic drugs from chemists' laboratories: THC (the active ingredient of marijuana), psilocybin (the active ingredient of the Mexican mushroom), STP, DMT, and an array of other initials and nicknames for the uppers and downers of the drug culture. Used indiscriminately, these drugs have created the havoc of psychosis, brain damage, suicide, and murder. Used judiciously, they have elicited experiences of gorgeous visual imagery, creativity, and transcendental states which have been likened to genuine religious or mystical experience.

Typically the psychedelic experience begins with the appearance of beautiful colors and geometric shapes, which evolve into complex "dreams while awake" (we have already heard this kind of experience from volunteers in the sensory deprivation studies). Here is one LSD experience, as reported by film producer Ivan Tors:

> I closed my eyes and saw patterns of indescribable colors which kept flowing one into another in exquisite patterns. I felt detached from the visions. Almost as if I were not a person, but rather as if I were part of the beauty of the Universe, of Creation. I began to think of the sameness of the microcosm and macrocosm. It was as if I saw the structure of the universe, and I saw that the positive and negative charges within the atom are the only building blocks, out of which grows everything that exists. Suddenly I went through evolution, from the original explosion through primordial worlds in which I felt myself to be a reptile, a bird, a beast; on until the first independent thought was created in the mind of the beast. I walked to a mirror. I saw the face of an ape, and also the master of the world.

Perhaps this drug experience belongs more to the realm of the collective, rather than the personal, unconscious.

HYPNOSIS: ANCIENT AND MODERN

Hypnosis, by whatever name it has been called (trance, mesmerism, jar-phoonk) probably has as venerable a history as any other technique for deliberately attempting to alter consciousness.

As generally used today, hypnosis probably began with the technique devised by Dr. James Braid of Scotland, in the nineteenth century. Braid believed the state of trance he achieved, either with spoken words or by having the patient concentrate on a shiny object like a gold watch, was a form of sleep. And in fact he named the phenomenon "hypnosis," from the Greek word *hypnos*, meaning sleep. Other doctors began to practice Braid's methods, and actually used phrases like: "Your eyes are getting heavier, heavier. . . . You are falling asleep. . . . Sleep, sleep. . . ." And with a respectable percentage of patients, it was found that their eyes would close and their breathing became deep and heavy (sometimes accompanied by snoring), and during that period of trance/sleep they became amenable to suggestions that their illnesses would improve.

Today opinion among scientists is that the state achieved under hypnosis is not sleep, either physiologically or psychologically, since certain events are known to occur in association with hypnosis which do not occur in sleep; anesthesia; performance of posthypnotic suggestions on waking, although the person remembers nothing from the trance state; and the ability (with training) to produce a profound trance simply by uttering a key word, like "blue dawn," when the subject is wide awake. Apparently with deep hypnosis, the unconscious mind can remain alert and functioning (like the subconscious mind which keeps heart and stomach regulated), even though the more superficial, conscious mind is, for the duration of hypnosis, "unconscious."

Actually, it has been found that not only the hypnotized, but also the anesthetised person can retain in his unconscious everything that occurs, without knowing it consciously. Dr. David Cheek of San Francisco has reported that some patients in the operating room absorb entire conversations being held between surgeons, even though totally unconscious. Cheek told of a patient who had undergone a relatively simple operation, without complications, who inexplicably failed to recover. By putting the patient under hypnosis, Cheek obtained almost verbatim a conversation in the operating room in which the surgeon said, "Hmm . . . tumor looks malignant." And even though the tumor was found benign, the patient clung to the thought instilled in him while he was under deep anesthesia.

When particularly strong rapport has been established between hypnotist and subject, sometimes fantastic feats occur. For example, about one hundred years ago in England, the celebrated physicist Sir William Barrett, after deeply hypnotizing an almost illiterate Irish girl, absent-mindedly popped a peppermint into his mouth, whereupon the girl suddenly exclaimed, "Why for did you put a peppermint in my mouth?" Intrigued by such an unprecedented response, Barrett devised a series of "taste" experiments. He placed himself in a closet several rooms away from the hypnotized girl, who still, again and again, accurately tasted the different foods which Sir William would put in his mouth. Barrett reported his findings at the Academy of Science, but the paper was denied publication. Scientists were loath to believe such experiments then, and they are loath to believe them now.

When I visited Czechoslovakia in 1970, I was shown a film on hypnosis, made for Czech television. In the film, an army psychiatrist performs essentially the same experiment as that of Sir William Barrett, except that it is done with controls, and with the use of electrophysiological equipment to record the EEG, EKG, etc. of both hypnotist and subject. At the start, the subject is put into deep hypnosis, so deep that when he is pricked sharply with a pin, he shows no sign of feeling it. Then the hypnotist chooses, randomly, one of six envelopes, in each of which has been placed a slip of paper containing the name of a food substance (salt, sugar, pepper, honey, lemon, vinegar, all of which are present on a small table). As we watch, the hypnotist opens the envelope he has chosen, which contains the word "pepper." The hypnotist puts some pepper in his mouth. One can see the subject, sitting several feet in front of the hypnotist, making little motions with his mouth as if he were tasting something. When asked what he is tasting he replies, "Pepper." I obtained a copy of this film, and showed it at a hypnosis symposium held at UCLA in 1971. The symposium was attended by experts in hypnosis from all over the country, and most of them refused to accept the film as anything but a fraud.

Both Jack Gray (our fine hypnotist/volunteer) and I have attempted to validate the experiment by reproducing it in the lab. We have used several volunteer subjects over a period of months and have had no success at all. Whether this form of telepathy (or tasting at a distance, as some prefer to call it) is a genuine and repeatable phenomenon remains for further research to determine.

Other kinds of laboratory research with hypnosis have provided fascinating, if frustrating data. Psychologist Bernard Aaronson reports a study in which deeply hypnotized subjects were given the suggestion on one occasion that their world on waking would have *no depth* and on another occasion that the world would have *expanded depth* (as if looking through a stereoscope). Under the no-depth condition, the subjects reported feeling bored, withdrawn, and with no sensitivity to touch. Under the expanded-depth condition, one subject described a world of super-reality:

> Riding in a car was like taking a wonderfully exhilarating roller coaster ride to everywhere. The landscape was at once a gargantuan formal garden and a wilderness of irrepressible joyous space. Even now, I feel dumbstruck and preposterous in trying to describe this perceptual miracle which has somehow been given to me.

Quite often, as a subject is descending into an hypnotic state, he will report seeing brilliant colors and geometric patterns, a report we have had from sensory deprivation and psychedelic drug subjects. Hypnosis, then, appears to be another method for reaching deeper levels of the mind.

TRANCE STATES: ANCIENT

Perhaps the most commonly experienced altered state, other than dreaming, is a form of light trance. It may be that you have become so absorbed in an exquisite sunset, a piece of music, or the act of love, that for some moments you have felt transported beyond yourself into. . . . ? Usually we attribute such exalted states to the experience which evoked the feelings. On very rare occasions, experience of ecstasy occurs for seemingly no reason, and that realm of mind to which one has been mysteriously transported seems so magnificent, and *real* that one wants to spend his life in search of its meaning. That is what happened to a Canadian psychiatrist, R. M. Bucke who, at the turn of the century, reported this experience while returning home in a hansom cab after a pleasant, but unremarkable, evening:

> All at once, without warning of any kind, I found myself wrapped in a flame-colored cloud. For an instant I thought of fire, an immense conflagration somewhere close by; the next, I knew that the fire was within myself. Directly afterward there came upon me a sense of exultation, followed by an intellectual illumination

impossible to describe. Among other things, I did not merely come to believe, but I saw that the universe is not composed of dead matter, but is on the contrary, a living Presence; I became conscious in myself of eternal life. . . . The vision lasted a few seconds and was gone; but the memory of it and the sense of reality of what it taught has remained during the quarter of a century which has since elapsed.

Dr. Bucke collected as many similar experiences as he could find in world literature and from among his friends (in particular the poet Walt Whitman) and published them in an anthology, *Cosmic Consciousness*, the name to which he gave this state of being.

Throughout history there have been rare persons whose experiences of trance are a frequent phenomenon throughout life. At first they come unbidden (perhaps through illness), and then sometimes, through discipline, are brought under voluntary control. Among several primitive peoples, such persons may deliberately train themselves by solitude, fasting, or other techniques to attain trance states voluntarily. If they succeed, they are elevated to the rank of shaman, or holy man, because while entranced they are presumed to communicate with people far away, with spirits, or with the gods themselves.

However, the trance state need not be associated with mystical or religious experience. Some persons in the contemporary Western world experience trance states during which voices (seemingly not their own) speak through them. Such persons, who retain no memory of the trance, are called "trance mediums" by psychical researchers. One such trance medium, an indefatigable psychical researcher in her own right, was Mrs. Aileen Garrett. She could put herself into trance during which her "guides" spoke through her, answering questions put to her by eminent psychiatrists and psychologists. Yet Mrs. Garrett knew nothing of what occurred while she was in trance. Another famous American medium, Edgar Cayce, also learned, through a form of self-hypnosis, to put himself into trance. He was totally unaware of what transpired during trance, yet a voice spoke through him for forty years, giving diagnosis and treatment for people whose illnesses Cayce knew nothing about.

In our laboratory, a young psychic, Barry Taff, has on many

occasions put himself into trance through hyperventilation. During his trance state, our electrophysiological data have revealed that his body metabolism dramatically changes. Barry, too, remembers nothing of these trance periods, but in occasional experiments in the lab, while entranced, he will be given the name of a person unknown to him, and as he returns to consciousness, he has at times been able to describe that person with accurate detail.

Trance states, then, can be elicited in many ways, and result in a variety of experience. But they seem to share a common attribute: The entranced person seems to leave this dimension of space-time and frequently obtains information beyond his conscious knowledge.

GROUP TECHNIQUES TO INDUCE TRANCE

Primitive societies have developed sophisticated methods to evoke trance, including the use of special herbs and potions, magnetic passes, fasting, and isolation (which we have already discussed). Other techniques require the participation of the whole community, where the use of rhythmic chanting, music, and dancing are apparently vital accessories to the ecstasy. Anthropologist Shirokogoroff describes this experience with the Tungus of Siberia:

> The rhythmic music and singing, and later the dancing of the shaman, gradually involve every participant more and more in a collective action. When the audience begins to repeat the refrains together with the assistants (of the shaman), the tempo of the action increases. . . . The shaman with a spirit is no more an ordinary man or relative, but is a "placing" (i.e., incarnation) of the spirit; the spirit acts together with the audience and this is felt by everyone. After shamanizing, the audience recollects, various moments of the performance, their great psychophysiological emotions and hallucinations of sight and hearing which they have experienced. They then have a deep satisfaction—much greater than that from theatrical and musical performances of the European complex, because in shamanizing, the audience at the same time acts and participates.

Similarly in the Near East, the whirling dervishes participate in a mass dance, the tempo of which increases at an incredible rate, until one and another of the dancers drop to the floor, entranced, seeing visions of other realms (or perhaps simply hallucinating). Halfway around the world, in India and Tibet, Bon and Tantric disciples perform a stylized series of movements (called mudra), which when performed can result in prolonged trance ecstasy. In Africa and Australia, a rhythmic drum beat is still used to rouse celebrants into states of exaltation. Chanting in unison is an effective means of achieving trance, as was discovered many centuries ago by the Chinese, and by American Indians. This technique is being rediscovered today by groups like Bahia, Subud, and the Pentacostal and Fundamentalist religions. (Political leaders, notably Hitler and Mussolini, have found this to be an effective technique to arouse mass enthusiasm, or hysteria.)

The effects of thus altering one's state of consciousness can be "speaking in tongues," "possession," shaking of the entire body (like an epileptic seizure) and other paranormal or occult phenomena, which can spread like a contagion even to the skeptical spectator.

An eminent psychiatrist told me of attending a spiritualist church in Alabama. As the "spirit" (whatever it is) began to travel through the congregation, he himself felt so caught up in it that he had to hold onto the arms of his chair with all his physical strength to keep from being overcome by a force over which he felt he had no control.

And that is the danger of such techniques: once "possessed," the person loses control. Sometimes he may fall prostrate and motionless for hours, lost in visions of Heaven or Hell; but at other times he may be propelled with the group into debauchery, rioting, or, as is infamous in our history, into lynching. Certain ancient societies long ago became aware of these dangers, and carefully differentiated between true possession, or trance, and forms of mental aberration, probably hysteria and psychosis. This distinction has *not* been made in many of the more modern sects. For example, the Shakers of Pennsylvania believed that the uncontrolled shaking and trance achieved by its members through dance and rhythm were manifestations of the Holy Spirit, but the Samburu of Kenya, who also achieve shaking and trance, consider them to be sometimes merely reactions to tension or danger. Among the Arctic Tungus uncontrolled possession (speaking in tongues, emotional outbursts, etc.) is considered an illness. The Tungus permit only those persons who "possess" their spirits to become shamans; if the spirit "possesses" the person, he is considered unfit to be a religious leader. This is a crucial distinction, not yet appreciated by some of our psychiatrists, religious leaders, or parapsychologists.

TECHNIQUES TO CONTROL TRANCE STATES

Arduous disciplines have developed in various cultures to obtain control over deeper levels of the mind. In India, one such discipline is known as yoga. It is conventional in the West to think of yoga as a complex series of gymnastics, such as standing on one'e head, or sitting in the unconscionably uncomfortable "lotus" posture. But this is only one form of yoga, hatha yoga, in which one attempts to learn such mastery over· the body that one can at will stop his heart from beating, prevent blood from flowing from an open wound, or immure himself for days in a coffin with far less oxygen than is considered necessary by science for survival. For a long time such feats were dismissed by scientists as legerdemain performed by fakirs. (Didn't Harry Houdini, America's great magician, perform similar tricks which he insisted were mechanically contrived?)

Very recently experts in hatha yoga have demonstrated their capacities in our laboratories. At the Menninger Foundation, under the supervision of Dr. Elmer Green, the Swami Rama of India has undergone extensive, controlled testing in the laboratories. In his first study, Dr. Green learned that the Swami had

> exquisite differential control over arteries in his right hand. We had "wired" him for brain waves, respiration, skin potential, skin resistance, heart behavior (EKG), blood flow in his hands, and temperature. While thus encumbered he caused two areas a couple of inches apart on the palm of his right hand to gradually change temperature in opposite directions (at a maximum of about 4°F.). The left side of his palm, after this perfor-

mance (which was totally motionless) looked as if it had been slapped with a ruler a few times, it was rosy red. The right side of his hand had turned ashen grey.

In another series of experiments, the Swami, similarly wired into equipment, demonstrated control over brain wave patterns. He was able to produce 70 percent alpha rhythm (between 8 and 11 cycles per second) at will, and after several such sessions he reported that "alpha isn't anything." This is a statement with which Dr. Green and other EEG specialists strongly concur. Almost everyone, simply by closing his eyes, can produce alpha rhythm. (This information may come as a surprise to those people who have been reading the advertisements of various commercial institutes claiming that control of alpha can cure your problems and make you creative, telepathic, and a healer.) A slower brain wave is theta (between 6 and 8 cycles per second), which has rarely been brought under control in this country. Swami Rama produced theta by "stilling the conscious mind and bringing forth the unconscious" and reported that it was a noisy, unpleasant state. He then offered to produce delta waves (slower still, between 4 and 6 cycles per second), which, according to EEG experts, occur only in deep sleep. Dr. Green told this to the Swami, who replied that people would think he was asleep, but that he would be fully conscious of everything that was happening. Dr. Green described this session:

> After about five minutes of meditation, lying down with his eyes shut, the Swami began producing delta waves. . . . In addition, he snored gently. Alyce, without having told Swami that she was going to say anything (she was in the experimental room observing him during this test) then made a statement in a low voice, "Today the sun is shining, but tomorrow it may rain." Every five minutes she made another statement and after 25 minutes the Swami roused himself.

According to Dr. Green,

> He gave her statements verbatim, except for the last half of the fourth sentence, of which he had the gist correct

but not the words. I was very much impressed because in listening from the control room, I had heard her sentences, but could not remember them all, and I was supposed to have been awake.

It is possible that the new technique of biofeedback will help us to develop similar capacities. In training subjects to release muscular tensions, several investigators have reported that, unexpectedly, subjects begin describing the appearance, in their inner vision, of beautiful colors and geometric forms, followed by vivid imagery. (We have already observed these phenomena appearing in the early stages of sensory deprivation, psychedelic drug experience, and hypnosis. Perhaps this appearance of color and geometric form is a signal of the threshold to a deeper level of mind.)

With each of these techniques to achieve deeper realms of the mind, we have seen that there has been produced some kind of paranormal manifestation: a prophetic vision, knowledge of an event occurring at a far-off place, the apparent ability to know what someone else is thinking, the "possession" of someone in trance in which information is obtained about which the entranced person consciously knows nothing. Such phenomena have been called variously telepathy, clairvoyance, precognition, and trance mediumship. Recently they have been grouped under the contemporary scientific label of "biocommunication."

When Madame David-Neel returned from her many years of study in Tibet, she gave a series of lectures to the College of France, summing up her conclusions in these words:

> Everything that relates to psychic phenomena and to the action of psychic forces in general should be studied just like any other science. There is nothing miraculous or supernatural in them, nothing that should engender or keep alive superstition. Psychic training, rationally and scientifically conducted, can lead to desirable results. That is why information gained about such training constitutes useful documentary evidence worthy of our attention.

Let us take the advice of Alexandra David-Neel and learn what we can of biocommunication.

7 Telepathy and Clairvoyance

Telepathy: Communication to mind from mind.

Clairvoyance: Communication to mind from an unknown channel.

A PARADOX

In today's world we accept as commonplace that radio and television will bring us information over vast distances. But some of us find it impossible to accept that one man's mind can transmit information to another man's mind without a mechanical device. Such persons dismiss the concept of telepathy as "magical thinking."

Ironically, some primitive communities find it difficult to accept television and radio (magic!), but they accept as a matter of course that they can communicate with each other over long distances. That at least is what anthropologists have reported about certain societies in various parts of the world. For example, Rosalind Heywood, an English writer (and psychic), in her valuable book *The Sixth Sense*, tells of an incident in which an African student, studying in London, was asked to name one by one the cards a friend would be looking at in another room. The student agreed to the task and performed it with "staggering correctness." Then he asked, politely, what was of interest in so simple a task?

Anthropologist Ronald Rose spent several years studying the aborigines of Australia. He reports in his book *Living Magic* several instances of apparent telepathic communication between members of families, over long distances. They usually involved a family crisis and sometimes were received in symbolic form:

Bert Mercy and his wife Bea said they saw plovers circling over their hut one night. Bert said to his wife, "I suppose old uncle's dead." His uncle had, in fact, died in Coff's Harbor (two hundred miles distant) that night, as they later learned. Plovers were his uncle's totem, Bert explained. He knew the plovers he and Bea had seen were not real but were "mind" birds.

Another anthropologist named Pobers, while studying natives of the West Indies, became curious about a custom he frequently observed, that of persons speaking into a tree, listening and then talking back to it. One day he stopped a woman native after such a "tree talk," and asked if she would be kind enough to explain why she talked into the tree? The lady answered, rather apologetically, that she liked to gossip with a friend on another island and that she talked into the tree only because she was poor. If she were rich, she would talk to her friend over the telephone.

The aborigines believe they can do it; so do people in Africa and the West Indies. Can they? Can we? Psychical research societies have been trying for almost one hundred years to find out.

EARLY INVESTIGATIONS INTO TELEPATHIC COMMUNICATION

The first major work of the SPR and ASPR was the Census of Hallucinations in 1890 (a study which has been repeated in several countries). Its purpose was to look for evidence of telepathic communication through questionnaires sent to a representative sample of the population. Among the first investigators was the formidable scholar F. W. H. Myers, whose work *Human Personality and Its Survival of Bodily Death* remains a classic of psychical research, as well as a superb analysis of the subliminal mind (a word he coined, along with "telepathy"), which bears much resemblance to the unconscious mind described by Freud during that same period of time.

Over 20,000 replies were received from the Census questionnaires. This massive collection was studied intensively, and revealed that there were certain *classes* of phenomena, repeatedly reported by individuals in different parts of the world, uncannily similar in experiential detail. One interesting aspect of this research was that telepathy seemed to manifest more frequently in an altered state of consciousness. Culling from SPR and ASPR files, we find examples of spontaneous telepathy, received in different states of consciousness:

1. England. 1883. Dream

Received from Canon Warburton, known as a gentleman of integrity to several members of the SPR.

> I went up from Oxford to stay a day or two with my brother, a barrister. When I got to his chambers I found a note on the table apologizing for his absence, and saying that he had gone to a dance somewhere in the West End, and intended to be home soon after one o'clock. Instead of going to bed, I dozed in an armchair, but started up wide awake exactly at one, ejaculating, "By Jove! He's down!" and seeing him coming out of a drawing room into a brightly illuminated landing, catching his foot in the edge of the top stair, and falling headlong, just saving himself by his elbows and hands. (The house was one which I had never seen, nor did I know where it was.) Thinking very little of the matter, I fell a-doze again for half-an-hour, and was wakened by my brother suddenly coming in and saying, "Oh, there you are! I have just had as narrow an escape of breaking my neck as I ever had in my life. Coming out of the ballroom, I caught my foot, and tumbled full-length down the stairs."
>
> It may have been "only a dream," but I always thought it may have been something more. . . . This is my sole experience of the kind.

2. France. 1868. Trance (and Automatic Writing)

The celebrated French physician/hypnotist Dr. A. A. Liebault wrote to Myers about an experience of one of his patients, whom he described as an excellent hypnotic subject who developed automatic writing, a subject about which we will learn in a later chapter.

On February 7, 1868, Mlle. B felt an impulse—it was what she called a *trance*—and she rushed off at once to her large notebook, where she wrote in pencil, with feverish haste, the same words again and again, that a person called Marguerite was thus announcing her death. The family at once assumed that a young lady of that name, a colleague in the Coblenz High School, must have just expired. They came immediately to me, and we decided to verify the announcement that very day. Mlle. B wrote to a teacher at the school, taking care not to reveal the real motive of the letter. By return of post we received an answer, expressing surprise at Mlle. B's unexpected letter. But at the same time the correspondent made haste to announce to Mlle. B that their common friend, Marguerite, had died on February 7, at about 8 p.m.

3. United States. 1886. Via a Trance Medium

William James, the great American psychologist and parapsychologist, spent several years personally investigating a Boston housewife named Mrs. Piper, who "was subjected to every kind of test to eliminate the possibility of fraud—including having both Mr. and Mrs. Piper 'watched or shadowed' by private detectives, with the view of discovering whether Mrs. Piper received letters from friends or agents conveying information. This inquiry was pushed pretty closely, but absolutely nothing was discovered which could throw suspicion on Mrs. Piper—who is now aware of the procedure, but has the good sense to recognize the legitimacy—I might say the scientific necessity—of this kind of probation."

James recorded numerous instances of telepathic information conveyed to himself and family when Mrs. Piper was entranced. Here are two:

(1) My mother-in-law, on her return from Europe, spent a morning vainly seeking her bankbook! Mrs. Piper, on being shortly afterwards asked where this book was, described the place so exactly that it was instantly found.

(2) During a sitting at which Mrs. James and Professor James' brother were present, they were told that Professor James' "Aunt Kate," who was then living in New

York, had "passed over" that morning between two and half past, and that Professor James would be made acquainted with the fact upon his return home. Commenting on this incident, Professor James says, "On reaching home an hour later I found a telegram as follows: 'Aunt Kate passed away a few minutes after midnight.' "

4. Brazil. Date Unknown. Drug Intoxication

Colonel Morales, while deep in the Amazon, drank the Indian brew, yage, as an experiment. During the drug session he became conscious of

> the death of his sister in a house far away from where he was located. The house was in Rio de Janeiro, some 2,900 miles distant, as the crow flies, from the remote village where he then was. A month later a runner brought him a letter . . . telling him his sister had died about the same time Morales had drunk the infusion of the yage plant.

Such visions of actual events occurring at a distance, while the person having the vision is under the influence of drugs, have been reported anecdotally in several civilizations. An early laboratory investigation was undertaken at the Pasteur Institute in Paris, using mescaline (derived from peyote, the cactus used by American Indians). The staff member conducting these experiments, Dr. Bascompte Lakanal, reports the swirling colors and geometric patterns typical of the early stages of intoxication, and adds:

> The most extraordinary result was that, when telepathic experiments were carried out with the mescalinized volunteers, they could produce words, sketches, and musical notes, pronounced, sung, or drawn by other people in a distant room of the same institute.

EARLY EXPERIMENTS IN TELEPATHY

Naturally, the founders of the SPR and ASPR, being primarily scientists, were not satisfied with anecdotal material, however convincing the story or unimpeachable the source. Such happenings, barren of controlled laboratory conditions, could never be more than fascinating anecdotes. Although the evolution of good experimental methodology was slow, some of the early research gave excellent *qualitative* results. One of the most extraordinary of these semiexperimental studies was carried on over a period of fourteen years, from 1910 to 1924, by Gilbert Murray, professor of Greek at Oxford University. Murray was the most prominent classical scholar of his era and had drafted the covenant for the League of Nations. Here is an excerpt from Professor Murray's presidential address to the SPR in 1952, about those early experiments:

> Fraud, I think, is out of the question; however slippery the behavior of my subconscious, too many respectable people would have had to be its accomplices. . . . The method was always the same. I was sent out of the drawing room to the end of the hall, the doors of course being shut. The others remained in the drawing room; some one chose a subject which was hastily written down, word for word. Then I was called in and my words written down.

Using this process, Professor Murray obtained a variety of results, including remarkable hits like this:

> Mrs. Arnold Toynbee (transmitter): Savonarola having his pictures burnt in Florence and standing up and a crowd around.

> Dr. Murray: It's Italian—I think it's something in a book. Well, this is the merest guess and may have something to do with a spark that came out of the fire—I get a smell of burning, the smell of a bonfire—I get Savonarola burning the pictures in Florence.

More often he would get bits of information, but distorted and in symbolic form, as is typical of primary process thinking:

> Mrs. Davies (agent): Jane Eyre at school standing on a stool, being called a liar by Mr. Brocklehurst. The school spread out below her and the Brocklehurst family "a mass of shot purple silk pelisses and orange feathers."

Dr. Murray: My mother being at her French school being labelled "*impie.*" [Dr. M. explains his mother had once been punished at school, being made to wear a sign saying "impie"] . . . I reject that. . . . Girl standing up and a group or a family coming in and denouncing her. I think it's English.

And frequently this would happen:

Mrs. Arnold Toynbee (transmitter): Lord Jim being tried at Aden in Conrad's book. The scene in the law court.

Dr. Murray: No, not a glimmer.

Regarding the state of consciousness in which Dr. Murray performed, he said, "the only effort I make is a sort of attention of a quite general kind. The thing comes out through practically any sense channel, or is invented much as an hallucination is invented."

During the years these qualitative experiments were performed, the only available statistic was the rather naive one of percentages, which were tallied for "direct hits" (the Savonarola example), "failures" (the last example is clearly that), and "partial hits" (Jane Eyre being called a liar was transformed into Murray's mother being branded "impie," in typical primary process distortion). Using those groupings for the 800 trials, 34 percent were judged hits, 25 percent partial hits, and 41 percent failures. Like a great baseball player, Professor Murray's lifetime batting average was .340. His strikeout record was .410, and he was able to get on base with the help of an error of some kind the rest of the time. Percentages like these are interesting, but cannot tell the odds against such a performance. One might say, "Well, if he can only do it one third of the time, that's not much."

But what is it that Gilbert Murray did successfully a third of the time? He could tell what someone was thinking. How often in life can anyone do that? Probably everyone has had the experience of being about to pick up the phone when it rings, and the caller is the person he was about to call. Another common experience is that of being about to say something, when someone else says exactly what you were going to say. Generally we dismiss those experiences as coincidences.

Is it just possible that they may not all be coincidences? In Dr. Murray's experiments, it would seem that something happened beyond the reach of coincidence. But percentages are not a good statistical assessment of that possibility. More sophisticated statistics were required by psychical researchers, and as we have already learned, it was Dr. J. B. Rhine who supplied them.

THE ESP CARD STUDIES

Years before Dr. Rhine evolved his "hot dice" tests for PK, he had developed, with the help of Professor Zener, a standard deck of ESP cards (ESP is short for extrasensory perception). The deck consisted of 25 cards, each bearing one of five symbols (star, cross, circle, wave, square), five cards for each symbol. Probability theory insists that if the cards are randomly placed in five boxes, each labeled with one of the symbols, 5 hits can be expected, just by chance. A single run might produce 8 hits out of 25 cards, which is better than chance. But the next run might produce only 2 hits, and the next 6 hits, and after a great many runs the average score would be close to the expected 5 out of 25 for each run.

Now suppose someone were to achieve an average score of 7 hits out of 25 cards, over a total of 85,000 trials? The odds against such a record would require a whole paragraph of zeros. But that is exactly what Dr. Rhine discovered, when he totalled the 85,000 trials of the many subjects whom he tested in the early years. Those results were published in a modest monograph by the Boston Society for Psychical Research in 1934. Usually such monographs are virtually ignored by the scientific community, and never read at all by the general public.

The science editor of the *New York Times*, however, happened to read it, and gave it a favorable review, which set off an explosive reaction in the news media, among the general public, and most particularly among scientists. The attacks on Dr. Rhine, especially from scientists, were often vicious; he was accused of falsifying his data, of using fraudulent techniques, of cheating, of using poorly controlled experimental procedures, and of making statistical errors. With enormous patience, Dr. Rhine tried to answer each charge by tightening controls, using double blinds, performing the experiments over long distances, and hiring the best statisticians in the field. These precautions were often ignored or denied by his critics. A typical scientific attitude of the period is described by Arthur Koestler in his autobiography. Koestler, in a conversation with an outstanding mathematician, Hans Reichenbach, mentioned that he was interested in Dr. Rhine's ESP research. Reichenbach replied that it was all hokum and that the statistics were totally inadequate. Koestler denied this, and Reichenbach asked, "Who has checked the statistics?" Koestler replied, "R. A. Fisher in person." (Fisher, you may remember, was the acknowledged expert in probability statistics at that time.) Reichenbach seemed not to hear Koestler's answer, so Koestler repeated Fisher's name. When he did, Reichenbach turned pale and explained, "If that is true, it is terrible, terrible. It would mean I would have to scrap everything and start from the beginning."

ONE BATTLE AGAINST RHINE

During this controversial period, Dr. Rhine was invited to lecture at Barnard College, where psychologist Bernard Reiss questioned Rhine so sharply that Rhine said Reiss was in effect calling him a liar. Rather than defend his experiments, Rhine suggested to Reiss that he try a similar experiment, employing all the controls Reiss believed necessary. Urged on by his students, who found for him someone who claimed to be psychic, Reiss arranged a study in which the young lady agreed to guess from her home the cards Reiss would be looking at in his home, a quarter of a mile away. Over a period of several months, the subject performed 74 runs of the 25 cards (1,850 trials) and averaged *18 hits out of every 25 cards*. (This is the most spectacular series ever reported in the card-guessing studies.)

In 1938, the American Psychological Association organized a symposium on ESP. Its object, according to its chairman, Dr. J. F. Kennedy, was "driving the last nail in the coffin of ESP." When Reiss was called upon to defend his experiment, he said:

> There can be no criticism of the method used. I had the deck of cards on my desk, shuffled them, and at the stated time turned them over one by one, making a record of each card. I kept the records locked up in my

desk and sometimes it was a week before I totalled up the scores and found the number of high scores she was making. . . . The only error that may have crept in is a possibility of deception, and the only person who could have done the deceiving was myself since the subject at no time knew how well she was doing nor had any idea of cards which were being turned by myself in my room a quarter of a mile away from where she was working.

The last nail had not been driven into the ESP coffin; but scientists kept trying, and still do try. A book was recently published which demonstrated how several famous ESP studies over the past fifty years *could* have been faked. A respected British psychologist, Professor H. J. Eysenck, neatly summed up the contretemps:

Unless there is a gigantic conspiracy involving some thirty University departments all over the world, and several hundred highly respected scientists in various fields, many of them originally hostile to the claims of the psychical researchers, the only conclusion the unbiassed observer can come to must be that there does exist a small number of people who obtain knowledge existing either in other people's minds, or in the outer world, by means as yet unknown to science.

THE CAPRICIOUSNESS OF ESP

Dr. Gardner Murphy, a former president of both the American Psychological Association and the Parapsychology Association, tells of a young lady who came to his laboratory at Columbia University for ESP testing. She was left alone, and the person who would transmit was placed in a distant room. The young lady started out by scoring 15 correct out of 15 trials. (The odds against this happening by chance are about 30 billion to 1.) The experimenters rushed into the room where the young lady was working and asked if she had any idea what she was doing. She answered that she had been looking at the radiator and had seemed to see the symbols rise up in the shimmering heat waves from the radiator. This was not a helpful clue, and the interruption was as unhelpful as anything that might be imagined.

When the testing was resumed, her performance fell to chance and stayed that way. Circles and crosses and stars no longer rose up in the radiator waves.

In my own ESP card studies, similar problems have arisen. Over a period of several months two undergraduates gave superlative results, with odds again of astronomical proportions (10^{-14} to 1). Then, gradually, Harry (the receiver of information) lost his ability, and after several weeks of fruitless attempts to rekindle it (including the use of hypnosis), the work was stopped. Like so many star performers, Harry did not know whether he was performing well or badly until the results were tallied. ESP seems to be a totally unconscious process, as yet beyond voluntary control.

LABORATORY STUDIES OF "EMOTIONAL" TELEPATHY: UCLA

As the illustrations at the begining of the chapter make abundantly clear, strong emotion frequently seems to carry the message from transmitter to receiver in spontaneous telepathic experiences. Noting this fact, researchers began to talk of creating targets with strong emotional appeal, and as an experimenter who had once been an actress, I found the idea of emotional targets intriguing.

When, as a graduate student at UCLA, I discussed the idea of "emotional ESP" almost everyone with whom I talked said, "You're crazy." But no one said, "Don't do it." So I did it. With the invaluable help of Dr. J. A. Gengerelli, an experimental psychologist of impeccable reputation. Always encouraging and interested, he was nonetheless nearly insatiable in his demands for rigorous controls. When the first study, involving 96 subjects, was completed and gave promising statistical results, Dr. Gengerelli not only offered to write the difficult section on the statistical analysis, but also agreed to put his name to the article as junior author. He was at that time a full professor and I a graduate student! His name on the article, I believe, was primarily responsible for its publication in the *Journal of Abnormal Psychology*, an eminent professional journal which has published perhaps ten studies on ESP in its seventy-five-year history.

My first job for this experiment was to create "emotional episodes" for the transmitter to send. For example, I selected eight gruesome pictures of Nazi concentration camp victims, and to intensify the horror, I taped cacophonous music, an excerpt from *Iron Foundry* by Mossolov, played at too shrill a pitch. By contrast, hoping to arouse an erotic feeling, I selected slides of nude women in the *Playboy* genre, which were shown to the accompaniment of David Rose's *The Stripper*. Several such pairs of emotional episodes were contrived. Another pair consisted of an outer-space episode (scenes of astronauts and rocket ships, accompanied by an eerie section from Holst's *The Planets*) and its companion episode, called *Drunk* (slides starting with a huge drink and a little man and ending with a large drunk with a wine glass on his head). A third pair contrasted the serenity of several paintings of Madonna and Child (musical accompaniment, *Silent Night*), with the chaotic paintings of Van Gogh (accompaniment, Ravel's *La Valse,* interspersed with a man's voice saying "Van Gogh! Van Gogh!" in louder and louder tones).

Such were the emotional targets. How did we use them? Luckily, I found the Neuropsychiatric Institute laboratory with its isolation booth (still used by us for all kinds of experiments). The booth was ideal to house the transmitter, who sat alone, a captive audience. Over his ears he wore a set of earphones through which he could hear the sound accompaniment to the slides that were flashed on the screen which was facing him, inside the booth. The transmitter was told to watch the "show" as if in a theater, and at the end of each episode, he was asked to give his reactions, all of which were recorded on tape.

The receiver was taken to a dimly lit room (about seventy-five feet down the hall), where he was asked to lie down on a comfortable reclining chair. He was told that his partner, the transmitter, would be "experiencing" certain things and that his job, as receiver, was simply to relax. He was then given these instructions:

> If you have any kind of feelings, thoughts, images—any free associations—please speak them into the microphone. When you're finished, I'll show you a pair of slides, only *one* of which was actually seen by your partner. Please choose the one that best corresponds with your impressions. If you have no impressions, just guess which one you think is correct.

Typically we used four pairs of episodes in an experimental session, which generally lasted about half an hour. A complex random selection procedure was used to determine which episode from each pair was to be shown to the transmitter by one experimenter, who remained outside the booth. A second experimenter, who remained with the receiver in another room, never knew which episode was going to be shown.

Naturally, just by pure guess, the receiver had a 50 percent chance of being correct on each trial. But as we have learned from statistics, if the percentage of correct "guesses" is significantly larger than 50 percent, it is assumed something besides chance is involved. In the sixteen experiments we performed with these emotional targets, we achieved statistically significant results (often with odds better than 1,000 to 1) in ten studies. In an ambitious long-distance experiment arranged with the cooperation of parapsychologists in New York and Sussex, England, our statistics were just as impressive as when the receivers were only seventy-five feet down the hall.

More gratifying than the statistical success was the nature of the qualitative, or descriptive, data of the receiver's "free associations." On rare, exciting occasions, a receiver would give an accurate description of what the transmitter had seen. For example, when the *Drunk* episode had been shown, a receiver said, "This one has a champagne feeling. Champagne waltz. That's all." When she was shown the two slides (astronaut in space, and drunk with wine glass on his head), she laughed and said, "The man with the champagne glass on his head. Definitely. (Laughter)" On another occasion, when the *Space* episode was shown in the long-distance study, a receiver in Sussex said, "I could see the world as if I were in a space ship." Nothing could have been clearer, and of course he selected the correct slide.

Obviously if such responses had come frequently, there would have been little doubt of telepathic communication. But far more often the message from the receiver came in the typical distorted, symbolic form we have come to recognize as primary process.

PRIMARY PROCESS: SYMBOLISM AND DISTORTION

Let's briefly review primary process thinking. Everyone probably has experienced it in dreams. For instance, you might dream of a man with a moustache like your uncle's, but dressed in a Boy Scout uniform, standing in a sailboat. In the dream it somehow makes sense, but if you remember it on waking, you dismiss it as nonsense. In his study of dreams, through free association, Freud learned that a dream like that might express a wish, such as "If only uncle would take Jimmy on a boat trip next weekend." Actually primary process, by whatever name, has been used by professional dream interpreters since biblical times. We have already mentioned Joseph's interpretation of the seven fat and seven skinny cows as seven years of plenty followed by seven years of famine. Another example of primary process in a dream, interpreted by a soothsayer, is one attributed to Alexander the Great, which he dreamed during the siege of the city of Tyre (*Tyros* in Greek). Alexander dreamed of a satyr dancing on a shield. This was recognized as a pun by the interpreter (puns and word plays are frequent in dreams, as any psychoanalyst will tell you). The interpreter explained to Alexander that the Greek word for satyr (*satyros*) could also be read as Sa Tyros, meaning "Tyre is yours." Fortunately, Alexander captured Tyros; otherwise we would probably not now know the story. Another much more recent example is Professor Murray's impression of his mother being punished at school, rather than the target of Jane Eyre accused of lying by her school staff.

Our receivers frequently would give primary process distortions of what the transmitter was experiencing. For instance, when the Madonna and Child episode was shown to the transmitter, the receiver said, "A feeling of calmness . . . serenity. Very slow elegance. Sort of a *My Fair Lady* bit." When shown the Madonna and Child, and the Van Gogh slides, she laughed and said, "The Madonna. I could hear the music of *My Fair Lady*. Strange!" Another receiver, when the same pair was used, reported, "Some sort of excitement. I seem to see a sun thing. Occasionally a light disc." When she saw the Madonna and Van Gogh slides, she said, "Van Gogh. Because I saw the colors like a sunburst." One of the most delightful episodes of primary process occurred when an undergraduate psychology major reported, "All I see is an open field with a lot of bunnies running around." When he saw the two slides, Nazi concentration camp and the nude, he laughed and said, "It would have to be the girl from *Playboy* magazine. After all, I saw 'bunnies'!" (A good example of primary process punning.) Another episode that gave rise to considerable primary process was one of *Disneyland.* One receiver said, "I see balloons . . . and then I was riding around in a teacup. Honestly! It felt so strange, riding around in a teacup!" There was one slide in that series showing the Mad Tea Cup Ride, but in none of the slides were there balloons. Another receiver, for the Disneyland episode said, "So many things. The Swiss Alps, especially the Matterhorn. And those little cable cars. And ice cream cones. Little boys." Never, in any of the experiments, interestingly, was the actual word Disneyland, or nude, said by any of the receivers, although statistically these were two of the most successful episodes.

In these sixteen experiments, more than 800 persons participated, usually only for one set of four trials. One subject who participated in three of the studies proved to be a gifted psychic and one of our star subjects. He has volunteered for many experiments over the four years he has been working in the lab.

DISCOVERING A STAR SUBJECT THROUGH "PSYCHOMETRY"

Barry Taff was introduced to me when he was an undergraduate psychology major at a nearby university. Since childhood Barry had had many psychic experiences, and when I met him was proclaiming his talents as a trance medium and psychometrist, to almost anyone who would listen. Psychometry, in psychical research, means the ability to receive impressions about the life and experiences of the owner of an object simply by holding the object in one's hand. At our first meeting, Barry spoke voluminously about his exploits, until I interrupted him, handing him my key chain and asking if he could read it. Without a word, Barry took the key chain, held it for several moments, and then began to give quite specific pieces of information. He said, for example, that he "saw" two friends of mine, very similar in that both had blonde hair, were rather heavy, about the same age, extroverted, with lots of humor, and were named Shelley and Valerie. This was an uncannily accurate description of two friends of mine named Shelley and Valerie. (I have often wondered how much valuable research might have been lost if on that first occasion Barry had failed at the psychometry, as he frequently has failed in subsequent attempts.)

The psychometry test had proved useful, and I have continued using it to ferret out potential psychics. My key ring has provided a variety of information, not only about ESP, but about the psychological characteristics of the individual giving the reading. Some illustrations may help make the point clear. A psychiatrist phoned me about a patient of his whom he believed, after several startling experiences, was a gifted psychic in spite of her emotional problems. (Neurosis, and even psychosis, can accompany psychic gifts, as we shall see.) The young woman came to see me and discussed some of her experiences, which sounded genuine. Then I handed her the key chain, and asked for a reading. She had never attempted a task like that before, but she willingly followed my suggestions that she relax and make herself passive and receptive to any impressions or images that might occur in her mind's eye. After some hesitation, she began describing correctly the house in which I am living. But more particularly, she described a young girl, "about nineteen or twenty years old, with dark straight hair and brown eyes. She usually wears brown, a long brown coat, and I see her in the kitchen a lot, cooking, and sometimes she gets into loud arguments in the kitchen, but most of the time she is away at college." This was an extremely accurate picture of my daughter who is fond of cooking, is quick tempered, and is away at an Eastern college most of the year, where she dresses in a long brown coat.

Holding the same key chain on another occasion was a graduate student in psychology who agreed to try the demonstration in a seminar. He received impressions of a steel grey filing cabinet against a wall which was otherwise empty; but on top of the cabinet was, incongruously, a large leafy plant in an orange/brown container. After the seminar I took him back to the lab, where he saw for himself a steel grey filing cabinet against a blank wall, on top of which was the plant in an orange/brown container.

On another occasion, with the same key chain, a wealthy business executive described a bank vault, and a safe-deposit box, which he felt had nothing to do with me. I suggested he look inside the safe-deposit box, where he "saw" another box which contained something so unlikely that he did not want to mention it. (When a person feels some impression is incongruous or unlikely, it is not uncommon that he has latched onto a genuine piece of information, which gives more importance to a reading than the usual items like "a blue car" or "a white house with bushes out in front.") I urged him to describe what he saw. It was a long blue velvet rope of some kind, on which was encircled a pearl necklace. Then he quickly added, "But that's absurd. I know you're not the kind of person who would keep jewels in a vault!" That was true enough; I seldom wear jewelry, and habitually dress in slacks. But the fact is that I have a safe-deposit box in which are kept my mother's jewels, which she bequeathed to my daughter, and in the box is a blue velvet strand on which are placed, not pearls, but several rings which could easily give an impression of a necklace. (Here again, in this psychometry reading, we find an example of primary process distortion.)

The salient feature about these various impressions is psychological rather than parapsychological: each of the persons received information which seemed to resonate to his own personality. Barry Taff is very interested in girls, and he described two attractive blondes, correctly giving their names. The psychiatrist's patient was a college student, and her most vivid impressions were of my own college student daughter. The graduate student in psychology saw aspects of my lab, where many psychology experiments have been conducted by graduate students. And the affluent businessman saw a bank vault, and valuables. These quite different pieces of accurate information all arrived from the *same* key chain. In further discussions about psychics, we will see that their personality characteristics often determine the nature of the impressions which they receive.

EXPERIMENTS WITH BARRY TAFF

In the years that followed our first meeting, Barry completed his college work and is now obtaining a master's degree in psychology. All during that time he has volunteered for every kind of ESP study our lab has performed. One of his finest pieces of work was in a long series of emotional telepathy studies, using a wide variety of transmitters. Usually Barry was sent to my office on the ground floor of the Neuropsychiatric Institute, accompanied by an

experimenter who tape-recorded his impressions of what the transmitters were experiencing, either in the isolation booth in the lab
(five stories above my office), other places on campus, or in the
village of Westwood where UCLA is located. Barry's performance
is among the best in the lab's experience, although his success rate
of 25 percent in telepathy is *less* than Gilbert Murray's 34 percent.
Like Murray, Barry is sometimes remarkably accurate, as in this
example when the transmitter (a young girl) was asked by the
experimenter to "dress up like a hippie." The experimenter *took
out of a small suitcase* some scarves, a kaftan, and *several strands
of beads,* which she put on a table. Their impromptu conversation
was recorded on tape:

> Miss K (transmitter): I think Barry would appreciate me
> more with nothing on!
>
> Experimenter: Would you prefer to *take things off?*
>
> Miss K: (Laughing) NO!!

Barry's remarks during this episode were as follows:

> Barry: Somebody *pulling something out of a suitcase* or
> briefcase . . . *like pouring something on a table* . . . *like
> beads* or small little things. . . . They told her to *take
> something off,* and she made a joke about it, like
> clothing or something.

Much more frequently, Barry gave the primary process distortions
we have observed in other experiments, such as this example in
which the transmitter was handed a freshly plucked pansy and
asked to "send" it to Barry:

> Miss K: Pretty colors, yellow with a brown center . . .
> very soft and pretty.
>
> Experimenter: What are your associations?
>
> Miss K (Laughing): Pansy! (She makes a gesture signify-
> ing a homosexual.)
>
> Barry: Something round, a concentric thing, *gold-*
> looking. . . . A gentle mixing of *multicolored* things,

like a whirlpool of liquids . . . but it's not moving, it's stationary. . . . This also refers to *a phallic symbol*, something that wouldn't be thought of as a phallic symbol unless you're a weird person.

The colors of the pansy are described, and its phallic connotation if you're "weird," but again, the pansy is never mentioned explicitly.

TELEPATHY IN DREAMS

In several of Freud's late papers, he discusses the "telepathic dream," with the suggestion that psychoanalytic techniques of dream interpretation might be of help in deciphering the primary process and the symbolic content of the telepathic dream. Since Freud, several psychoanalysts have reported "presumptively telepathic dreams" from their patients. Sometimes they have analyzed the primary process distortion, but at other times the telepathy in the dream is transparently clear. As an example, Rosalind Heywood reports how a young psychoanalyst, with some embarrassment, told her of going to bed with his future wife for the first time, shortly before their marriage; on that special occasion, she wore an extremely unusual nightdress. A day or so later, a patient reported to the young psychoanalyst a dream in which he described exactly the unusual nightdress that had been worn by the analyst's fiancée.

Both therapists and patients have told me of telepathic dreams during therapy. Probably the most striking was the one confided in me by a UCLA professor in therapy with a psychiatrist at the Neuropsychiatric Institute. One weekend he had dreamed that his therapist had taken a boat to Catalina Island and had then returned to San Diego, where he seemed to be enjoying the spectacle of monkeys gamboling in diapers. This most peculiar imagery, monkeys in diapers, is easily susceptible of psychoanalytic interpretation involving toilet training, or id impulses, but the fact was, as the professor learned in a following session, that his therapist on that particular weekend had gone to Catalina in a sailboat with his family and had returned to San Diego, where the whole family spent a pleasant afternoon at the open zoo, watching among other things, baby monkeys cavorting in diapers.

Many such telepathic dreams have been reported as arising spontaneously in the therapeutic situation. But the dream had never been deliberately created in psychical research into telepathy, until psychiatrist Montague Ullman and psychologist Stanley Krippner at Maimonides Medical Center in Brooklyn undertook probably the most sophisticated series of contemporary studies in controlled emotional telepathy.

THE MAIMONIDES DREAM LABORATORY

At the specially created Dream Laboratory in Maimonides, a subject can sleep through the night with electrodes attached to his scalp, which will indicate on EEG equipment when he is dreaming. In all of these studies, the sleeper was the receiver. He was told that after he fell asleep, the transmitter, a person in another part of the hospital, would try to send him a message which he might be able to pick up in a dream. Each time the dreamer had a dream, he would be wakened and asked to report his dream into a microphone. Since almost all of us dream four or five and even seven or eight times each night, the Maimonides Dream Laboratory was clearly no place to get a good night's sleep! Nevertheless, the investigators were able to select carefully, from a large number of volunteers, persons who claimed to dream frequently, and to remember their dreams. In the morning, the dreamer was also required, along psychoanalytic lines, to give his free associations to each of his dreams.

The transmitter's job was to select, by a complex randomization process, one envelope from a group of one hundred envelopes, each of which contained a reproduction of a famous painting. Then the transmitter was taken to an isolated room, where he had to remain, alone, for the entire night. Once confined to the room, he could open the sealed envelope to see what picture he was to "send" to the dreamer. The transmitter was permitted to do anything he liked to help the transmission: draw, visualize, act out, meditate. He was notified by buzzer each time the experimenter (who was monitoring the EEG equipment) recognized that the receiver was entering a dream period, so that he could intensify his transmission at those times.

The results of thirteen formal studies, using this experimental model, gave a total of nine statistically successful experiments. Of more interest than the quantitative data were the qualitative data: the descriptive reports of the dreamers' dreams. There were, on rare occasions, remarkably accurate dreams of the painting being transmitted. For example, a distinguished psychologist from the University of Virginia Medical School, Dr. Robert Van de Castle, spent eight nights as a receiver in the Maimonides Dream Lab. One of those nights, the painting being transmitted was by Cezanne, *Trees and Houses*, showing a white house on a hill covered by barren trees, with no people to be seen. In one of his dreams, Dr. Van de Castle reported, "There was a house. . . . There were no people involved and nothing was going on. . . . It was just this isolated house." This, of course, was a direct hit. The Van de Castle study was one of the most successful, both qualitatively and quantitatively, of the series.

As we have come to expect, there were many more instances of primary process distortion than there were direct hits in the dreams. One such example came from a Maimonides star subject, the English psychic Malcolm Bessent, who agreed to an experimental long-distance telepathy experiment. Two thousand people (an audience at a concert given by the Grateful Dead forty-five miles away) were asked to transmit a painting (shown as a slide) of Scralian's *The Seven Spinal Chakras*, which depicts a man in the yogic lotus posture, in which seven "energy centers" are vividly colored, and a brilliant yellow circle of light radiates from the top of his head. Bessent's dreams, recorded on tape, included these statements:

> I was very interested in . . . using natural energy. . . . I was talking to this guy who said he'd invented a way of using solar energy and he showed me this box. . . . He was suspended in mid-air or something. . . . I'm remembering a dream I had . . . about an energy box and . . . a spinal column.

Numerous examples from the Maimonides studies are available in journal articles and in the recently published book *Dream Telepathy*. More recent research by Krippner, Ullman, and associates has been expanded to include telepathy in such other altered states of consciousness as hypnosis, drugs, and meditation. All of these show the same phenomena of direct hits and primary process distortion.

TELEPATHY STUDIES IN THE SOVIET UNION

In view of our own recent interest in primary process material found in telepathy, it comes as a nice surprise to learn that the Soviet Union, in more than fifty years of laboratory research with telepathy, has consistently reported "symbolic distortion" from their receivers. As long ago as 1923, Russia's pioneer parapsychologist L. L. Vasiliev described an experiment in which the transmitter was to send as his target "a strongly illuminated block of cut glass." The receiver reported: "Reflections in water . . . iceberg . . . icefloes in the north illuminated by the sun . . . rays are broken up." In his recently translated work, *Mysterious Phenomena of the Human Psyche*, Vasiliev compares telepathic reception with Freud's description of the unconscious mind and its processes. This is a remarkable statement from a Soviet scientist, since Russian research for decades has followed, not Freud, but the brilliant path blazed by Pavlov and his conditioning techniques.

CONTEMPORARY BIOCOMMUNICATION STUDIES IN RUSSIA

Telepathy, now called biocommunication, continues to be researched in the Soviet Union, with more and more complex technology. Moscow's Society of Radio, Electronics and Biocommunication has contributed remarkably interesting studies, under the supervision of physicist I. M. Kogan, whose research area is information theory. Professor Kogan has carried out long-distance studies using two of Russia's star telepaths, a biophysicist named Uri Kamensky, and an actor named Karl Nikolaev. I met these gentlemen in Moscow, and they described some of their personal experiences during those studies. On one occasion Kamensky in Moscow was asked to transmit to Nikolaev in Leningrad the image of a draftsman's compass. Nikolaev reported impressions of "metallic luster . . . thin . . . chromium-plated rod . . . rod is bifurcated . . . like a thin scissors." Again, fragments about the object were correct, but the object was compared to a scissors, rather than being named a compass. An amusing and interesting sidelight is that a third subject, unknown to either Kamensky or Nikolaev, was asked to "bug" the message. He reported that it was "something that pricks the finger ... a compass," thereby achieving a direct hit and picking up an actual behavior, since Kamensky, in order to make the object more vivid in his transmitting, had deliberately pricked his fingers with the points of the compass.

Kogan's research has become very sophisticated. In another study, both Kamensky in Leningrad and Nikolaev in Moscow were hooked into electrophysiological equipment, which monitored simultaneously the brain waves, heart beats, and other physical parameters of both men. The pair had practiced yogic breathing exercises and visualization techniques in order to "tune in" with each other. Kamensky, who always serves as transmitter, was asked to visualize having a boxing match with Nikolaev, aiming heavy blows at Nikolaev's body. There would be "long rounds" lasting forty-five seconds, and "short rounds" lasting fifteen seconds. Each long round was to be decoded as a dash, and each short round as a dot. By means of this special Morse code, a four-letter word, "Ivan" was to be transmitted from Leningrad to Moscow. Each element, that is, each dot or dash, was transmitted fifteen times, the redundancy (as information theory argues) considered vital so that a "majority vote" could be taken to determine whether a particular element was a dot or a dash. For example, if Nikolaev reported a particular symbol as a dot nine out of the fifteen times, then that symbol was voted to be a dot. The experiment worked, and the word was successfully decoded.

In discussing this study with the telepaths, they emphatically agreed that the "boxing" experiments were the least pleasant to do. Nikolaev told how, during one boxing bout, he had felt so strongly hit in the stomach that he fell off his chair, upsetting the electrodes that had been carefully placed around his body.

CLAIRVOYANCE

There is a variant of biocommunication: Instead of information traveling from mind to mind, there seem to be occasions when information arrives that apparently has not been transmitted from another mind. This phenomenon might be likened to a television camera which has been set up on the moon or Mars. Even though no one is there we can nevertheless receive information about what is happening simply by watching our TV screens. On rare occasions there seems to be the equivalent of a TV screen inside our heads, bringing information about what is happening somewhere else. There are both anecdotal and laboratory data to demonstrate this phenomenon.

THE CASE OF EMANUEL SWEDENBORG'S "VISION"

Probably the most famous and well-documented case of supposed clairvoyance is that of the eminent Swedish scientist Emanuel Swedenborg, as reported by the equally illustrious German philosopher Immanuel Kant:

> The following occurrence appears to me to have the greatest weight of proof, and to place the assertion respecting Swedenborg's extraordinary gift beyond all possibility of doubt. In the year 1759, towards the end of September, on Saturday, at four o'clock p.m., Swedenborg arrived at Gothenburg from England, when Mr. William Castel invited him to his house, together with a party of fifteen persons. About six o'clock, Swedenborg went out, and returned to the company quite pale and alarmed. He said that a dangerous fire had just broken out in Stockholm, at the Sodermalm (300 miles from Gothenburg) and that it was spreading very fast. He was restless and went out often. He said that the house of one of his friends, whom he named, was already in ashes, and that his own was in danger. At eight o'clock, after he had been out again, he joyfully exclaimed, "Thank God! The fire is extinguished, the third door from my house." . . . On Sunday morning, Swedenborg was summoned to the governor, who questioned him about the disaster. Swedenborg described the fire precisely. . . . On Monday evening a messenger arrived at Gothenburg, who was despatched by the Board of Trade during the fire. In the letters brought by him, the fire was described as precisely in the manner stated by

Swedenborg. On Tuesday morning the royal courier arrived [with news] ... not the least differing from that which Swedenborg had given at the very time when it happened; for the fire was extinguished at eight o'clock.

It might be argued that this is not a case of clairvoyance, but rather that the people in Stockholm, panicked by the havoc of the uncontrollable fire, might have (unconsciously, of course) been sending that telepathic message, which Swedenborg's mind tuned in on. Then this would be an example of telepathy, not clairvoyance. Not so simply explained is the following case.

A CASE OF CLAIRVOYANCE INVESTIGATED BY WILLIAM JAMES

In 1898, Miss Bertha Huse of Enfield, New Hampshire, suddenly disappeared without a trace. More than a hundred men searched the nearby woods and lake, fruitlessly, for two days. The next evening, a woman named Mrs. Titus, who lived in a neighboring village, alarmed her husband by making dreadful noises while she was dozing, after supper. Her husband had a hard time rousing her; and when he did, his wife was angry because, if she had been left undisturbed, she believed "she would have found the body." She asked him not to disturb her again, even though she made strange sounds while asleep. That night, according to James' report:

Mr. Titus was roused by the screams of his wife. He got up, lit the lamp, and waited, obeying his wife's instructions. She, during the following interval, *though not awake*, spoke as follows: "She followed the road down to the bridge, and on getting part way across it, stepped out onto that jutting beam which was covered with white frost. . . . She slipped on the log, fell backwards, and slid in underneath the timber work of the bridge. You will find her lying, head in, and you will only be able to see one of her rubbers projecting from the timber work."

Early the next morning, Mr. Titus gathered a group to investigate, and the body was found exactly where Mrs. Titus had described it in her trance state. What mind could have conveyed that information which apparently no one knew?

Similar cases have recently been reported by the police of Holland, based on the work of a remarkable clairvoyant, Gerard Croiset.

CROISET AND PROFESSOR WILLEM TENHAEFF

Ever since 1926, a Dutch grocer named Gerard Croiset has been intensively studied by the founder of the Parapsychology Institute of Utrecht University, Professor Tenhaeff. During those years, the police of Holland have frequently asked for Croiset's services to trace missing persons. This case, confirmed for Tenhaeff and Croiset on a tape recorder by Sergeant J. Aanstoot of the state police is typical:

> Aanstoot: We had a drowning case, and I rang you to tell you that a boy of thirteen was drowned in the river Waal and that we had not been able to find the body. You did not even ask a single question but you said that the body could be found 10 to 12 meters west of a beacon and that the beacon had a dent in it. You continued by telling me that the body lay 30 to 50 meters eastward of a jetty. And further you said there was a ship athwart the river, on the northern side.

> Croiset: Then we said to each other: That must be a ferry.

> Aanstoot: Yes, and knowing that much, I went to the ferry at Zuilichem. But when I came to the dyke, I thought to myself, this is not possible, because the accident happened downstream. A body would not drift upstream. Then I remembered Drakel, downstream, and I went there on the motor bike. I arrived at the ferry, and to my right, I saw a beacon with a dent in it. The distance was correct, for the beacon was about 50 meters out from the jetty. . . . We stood waiting for the ferry. It scarcely made any headway. And then we saw it. They had fished him out; they had found the body.

When I visited Professor Tenhaeff in 1965, he told me that Croiset was particularly gifted with finding missing children and persons who had drowned. Perhaps this is because Croiset, himself an orphan, had almost drowned as a child.

My meeting with Tenhaeff was memorable. When I arrived, unannounced, I was put off by his formal, almost stern attitude. I know how beleaguered parapsychologists are by kooks and curiosity-seekers; I suppose Tenhaeff assumed that I, being an American, must be one or the other. I explained that I had done some ESP experimentation and had found curious distortions, and plays on words, similar to Freud's primary process. All at once Tenhaeff's forbidding, bearded face suffused with pleasure. "My dear lady," he said, "you have learned a profound truth. In order to interpret the material given to me, by even the best of my psychics, I had to study intensively the works of Freud." He went on to tell me of examples from his experience, in which Freud's book, *The Psychopathology of Everyday Life,* made clear to him how puns, and plays on words come into the images of not only dreams, but the visions of psychics. As we know, such impressions often arrive as visual images, which can easily be misinterpreted.

In one of Tenhaeff's cases, a psychic working for the police said, "I see the picture of a mill. Now I see a man who is powdered with flour. Is the man's name by any chance Meel or van Meel?" (Meel is the Dutch word for flour.) It turned out that one of the persons involved in the case was named van Meel. Tenhaeff pointed out that a less experienced psychic might have said from those images that the man was a miller.

His favorite example (and mine) is of a psychic who got an impression of six glasses of beer which were magically transformed into six little rum glasses. Tenhaeff was able to interpret this correctly by consulting a map and locating the Frisian village of Sexbierum (six, beer, rum; in Dutch zes [sex], bier, rum).

In Professor Tenhaeff's forty years of research, there are several carefully documented cases of clairvoyance. Of particular, practical interest is the case of the missing pearl necklace. The necklace, insured by Mrs. S. of the Hague, had been lost, and Mrs. S. believed it could have fallen into the watercloset. Were this the case, the insurance company reasoned, the necklace could not still be in the drainpipes, and would have to be considered lost. The company called on one of Tenhaeff's psychics for help. The psychic arrived in the home, and received the impression that the necklace had slipped down the toilet. Then he walked around the house and gave an exact description of the place where the necklace was stuck in an outlet drain. In spite of the plumbers' skepticism, the drain pipe was opened. There was the pearl necklace, exactly as the psychic had seen it clairvoyantly. The insurance company wrote a letter expressing its gratitude: "We do not wish to finish this case without expressing our appreciation of Mr. G's work. . . . Supplied with the single fact that a pearl necklace was missing he was faced with an almost superhuman task. The fact that he indicated correctly where the necklace was to be found deserves special mention."

In Tenhaeff's opinion, much of the error found in psychical research could be due to an inaccurate interpretation of the visual symbols which the psychic receives. I agree, and must add that this is a problem still far from solution.

CLAIRVOYANCE IN THE LAB

Oddly, the controversial 1934 Rhine publication, *Extrasensory Perception*, contained more data on clairvoyance than telepathy. In response to criticisms charging collusion, fraud, and inadequate controls, Rhine added so many safeguards that the experiments became remarkable for their ingenuity. One standard procedure that emerged for clairvoyance testing was the Down Through test. Here the experimenter, after shuffling and cutting the ESP cards (either manually or by machine), placed the deck face down on a table. The deck remained there untouched until the subject in another room or building completed guessing the sequence of the twenty-five cards, down through the deck. In one famous study using the Down Through technique, the subject made twenty-five runs through the deck and scored an average of more than nine hits per run. The odds against this happening by pure chance are millions to one.

Actually, the clairvoyance experiments proved easier to evolve than ones for telepathy. Quoting Dr. Rhine:

> In the clairvoyance tests, telepathy had been excluded.
> It had been ruled out by the simple expedient of having
> a card which no one knew. Incredible as it now seems, it

had never been thought necessary to eliminate the possibility of clairvoyance when a telepathy test was designed. . . . It is surprising that during a half century of investigation no one challenged the adequacy of the telepathy procedure.

Dr. Rhine met this challenge by having the transmitter *think* of a card, without the card actually being there. In any event, the Rhine laboratory was able to isolate telepathy from clairvoyance, and obtained equally successful results with each method.

Basically, all the studies discussed in this chapter offer only statistical results to demonstrate the existence of ESP without offering any information about the *process* which makes this biocommunication possible. Furthermore, despite the ingenuity of the Russians in transmitting the message "Ivan" from Leningrad to Moscow, thus far we can only lament the primitiveness of this mode of communication. After all, it is far easier and expeditious to pick up a phone, dial a number, and say "Ivan." And, as the Yogis and Sufis tell us, this kind of biocommunication is a kindergarten use of the mind. But that is as far as we have gone in the Western world.

"GESP"

In his ever-evolving laboratory research, Dr. Rhine deduced that extrasensory perception fell into special categories which included not only telepathy and clairvoyance but also information arriving outside the linear time sequence we all know. He called information received from future time "precognition" and from past time, "retrocognition," linking these together under the category of general extrasensory perception, or GESP, for short.

We have looked at telepathy and clairvoyance. Let us now turn to the remaining two fields, which will require that we explore some of the mysteries of the fourth dimension, time.

8 Precognition: What Happened Tomorrow

For us believing physicists, this separation between past, present and future has the value of mere illusion, however tenacious.

—Albert Einstein

A DREAM ABOUT THE FUTURE

Recently a young man telephoned, asking to see me. He explained that as a scientist working at a local cancer research institute he was skeptical of parapsychology, but that he would like my opinion about a very disturbing event. Because such requests are rare from scientists (probably 80 percent of our calls are from crackpots or frankly psychotic people), I was happy to arrange an appointment. When the young man appeared in my office, he brought with him a large picture, which he said he preferred not to show me until after he explained the tragic circumstances surrounding it. He then proceeded to tell me that, about a month before, his sister, who was living with their parents in San Diego, had had a vivid dream that so terrified her she told the family about it in the morning. In her dream she had seen herself seated in the front seat of a car, being driven along a freeway, when suddenly a small car hurtled over the narrow freeway divider, crashing headlong into the car she was in. She saw the left front wheel of her car fly up into the air, and change into a skull's head. At this point she woke up, convinced that she would be killed in a similar accident. Her parents tried to persuade her that "it was only a dream," probably prompted by the emotional problems for which she had been seeking psychiatric help.

Here the young man paused, obviously having problems with his own emotions. Then he went on, saying his sister had been so distraught by the dream that she had made a drawing of it. He then showed me the picture he had brought with him. It was obviously a drawing by an amateur, but one could appreciate the strong emotions portrayed and observe the details of the auto accident, with the left front tire thrown into the air, the skull superimposed on it. I studied the picture, waiting for the rest of the story. With a shaking voice, the young man went on to say that two weeks after the dream—and shortly before he telephoned me—his sister had been in a car accident on the freeway, in which a Volkswagen, apparently out of control, had hurtled across the narrow freeway barrier into the opposite lane, crashing headlong into the car containing his sister and a few of her friends. His sister had been instantly killed but all the others survived. On impact with the VW the front left tire had been tossed in the air, and had been found a short distance away.

The young man very much wanted to know if this dream of his sister, portrayed in the drawing, might have been a prophetic dream, a dream about the future? I told him that I thought it was. He then wanted to know how such a thing can happen, how someone can dream about her own death two weeks before it occurs. I could only answer that although the files of the SPR and ASPR, the Rhine laboratory files, and our own files contain reports of literally thousands of such dreams, which are called precognitive dreams, we have no explanation for *how* they can happen. The only thing we know is that they *do* happen and that apparently they have always happened—on rare occasions.

VARIETIES OF PRECOGNITION IN HISTORY

Like the other paranormal phenomena we have been studying, the ability to foretell the future (whether called divination, sooth-saying, prophesying, or precognition) has been accepted as a reality in ancient civilizations, whether primitive or sophisticated. The medicine man, the shaman, the witch doctor, as well as the oracles and priestesses of ancient Egypt and Greece, were all presumed to have developed the art of prophecy to a degree that it was a factor in making political and personal decisions. We have already mentioned two historical examples of the prophetic dream and its interpretation: the Pharaoh's dream of the seven emaciated cows devouring the seven fat cows, which Joseph predicted meant seven years of plenty followed by seven years of famine; and Alexander's dream of a satyr dancing on a shield (*Sa Tyros*), interpreted as foretelling Alexander's capture of Tyros.

There are many, many such precognitive events recorded in more recent history, manifested in various states of consciousness.

Saint Joan's "Voices" and Visions

The Inquisition of Saint Joan by the Catholic Church has provided extremely detailed accounts of Joan's experiences. (In the words of F. W. Myers, "Few pieces of history so remote as this can be so accurately known.") It was recorded that Joan saw in a vision, and heard her voices tell her, that the siege of Orleans would be raised; that the Dauphin would be crowned King of France at the cathedral in Rheims; and that she would be wounded in battle. These prophecies were fulfilled. She also received the message that France would win a great victory over England within seven years. This prophecy was *not* fulfilled. This is an important item. Probably very few people in history have been as gifted, psychically, as Joan of Arc, yet she, too, was apparently sometimes wrong in her interpretations of the visions and voices.

Abraham Lincoln's Dream

Shortly before his assassination, President Lincoln dreamed of his own death. Fortunately the details of his dream were recorded by the U.S. Marshal for the District of Columbia, Ward Lamon, who was at a gathering in the White House to celebrate the news of Lee's surrender. Apparently Lincoln was unusually quiet and withdrawn. When reprimanded by his wife, he told of his dream, which was written in Lamon's diary as if in the President's own words:

> About ten days ago, I retired very late. . . . I soon began
> to dream. There seemed to be a deathlike stillness about
> me. Then I heard subdued sobs, as if a number of people

were weeping. I thought I left my bed and wandered downstairs. . . . I went from room to room. No living person was in sight, but the same mournful sounds of distress met me as I passed along. It was light in all the rooms; but where were all the people who were grieving as if their hearts would break? I was puzzled and alarmed. Determined to find the cause of a state of affairs so mysterious, and so shocking, I kept on until I arrived in the East Room, which I entered. There I met with a sickening surprise. Before me was a catafalque, on which rested a corpse in funeral vestments. Around it were stationed soldiers who were acting as guards; and there was a throng of people, some gazing mournfully upon the corpse, whose face was covered. . . .

"Who is dead in the White House?" I demanded of one of the soldiers.

"The President," was his answer. "He was killed by an assassin."

A Waking(?) Vision

From the English SPR files there is a report from Mrs. F. C. McAlpine who, in 1884, while waiting to meet her sister's train, went walking in the countryside one hot summer day:

I wandered under the shade of the trees to the side of the lake. Being tired, I sat down to rest. My attention was quite taken up with the extreme beauty of the scene before me. There was not a sound or movement, except the soft ripple of the water on the sand at my feet. Presently I felt a cold chill creep through me, and a curious stiffness of my limbs, as if I *could* not move, though wishing to do so. I felt frightened, yet chained to the spot, and as if impelled to stare at the water straight in front of me. Gradually a black cloud seemed to rise, and in the midst of it I saw a tall man, in a suit of tweed, jump into the water and sink.

In a moment, the darkness was gone, and I again became sensible of the heat and sunshine; but I was awed and felt "eerie." On my sister's arrival I told her of the occurrence; she was surprised, but inclined to laugh at it. About a week afterwards, a Mr. Espie, a bank clerk (unknown to me), committed suicide by drowning in that very spot.

This account was confirmed by the sister, and by a newspaper account of the suicide. (It is of some interest to note that Mrs. McAlpine reports an inability to move, a sudden feeling of cold, and a compulsion to stare at the water; all can be symptoms of a trance state.)

Two Dreams of Dr. Prince

One of the ASPR's most distinguished investigators was Dr. Walter F. Prince, who was deeply interested in dreams. In fact, he kept a diary of his own dreams which, on rare occasions, demonstrated that he had dreamed about an event which had not yet occurred. Here are the details of one such dream, told in Dr. Prince's words:

> Towards morning, I dreamed I was looking at a train, the rear end of which was protruding from a railway tunnel. Then suddenly, to my horror, another train dashed into it. I saw cars crumple and pile up, and out of the mass of wreckage arose the cries, sharp and agonized, of the wounded persons. And then what appeared to be clouds of steam or smoke burst forth, and still more agonizing cries followed. At this point I was awakened by my wife, since I was making noises indicative of distress. . . .

Dr. Prince told the dream to his wife before going back to sleep. To continue his story:

> At 8:18 that morning, probably no more than four hours after the dream, the Danbury express train, standing with its rear end at the entrance of the Park Avenue tunnel in New York City [the dream occurred in New Haven, about 75 miles distant] was struck by a locomotive at the head of the White Plains local train. The crash, according to the newspapers, was heard half a mile away. And then, one account states, "to add to the horror of it all, the steam hissed out from the shattered engine upon the pinned down unfortunates and rose up in clouds from the tunnel opening."

Dr. Prince reports this dream "simply and solely as a coincidental one."

As a young girl, my mother had a very vivid dream, which she remembered to the end of her life: One night, she saw in a dream a train crossing the bridge over a river, leading to the Bridgeport, Connecticut, railroad station. As she watched, she saw the bridge collapse and the train plunge headlong into the river, while the persons aboard screamed in terror. The next morning, she learned to her horror that exactly that same train accident had occurred on the bridge, one of the worst disasters in local history. (This was probably more a telepathic than precognitive dream: the actual times were never compared.)

Dr. Prince's second dream has a much more bizarre, symbolic content. On November 27, 1917, he dreamed that a woman voluntarily brought him an order for her own execution, saying she was willing to die, if he would only hold her *hand:*

> [The woman] was slender, had blonde hair, and was rather pretty. Then (in the dream) the light went out. . . . Soon I felt her hand grip mine (my *hand*) and knew that the deed was being done. Then I felt one *hand* (of mine) on the hair of her head, which was severed from her body. Then the fingers of my other *hand* were caught in her teeth, and the mouth opened and shut several times as the teeth refastened on my *hand,* and I was filled with horror of the thought of a severed but living head.

Next morning, November 28, Dr. Prince told this gruesome dream to his secretary, who corroborated the event. He also told it to his wife on the morning of November 29. In the *Evening Telegram* of the 29th, there was this news account:

Head Severed by Train As Woman Ends Her Life

> Deliberately placing her head in front of the wheels of a train that had stopped at Long Island Railroad Station at Hollis, L.I., so that the wheels would pass over her when it started, a woman identified as Mrs. Sarah A. Hand, ended her life. A letter written by her said, in part, "My body is alive without my head and my head is alive without my body."

This second dream is, of course, replete with primary process distortion: *Hands* play an important part in the dream, though the woman is not identified as Mrs. *Hand;* she talks about her "voluntary execution" (suicide), and her severed head bites Dr. Prince's hand ("my head is alive without my body"). Dr. Prince obtained an interview with Mrs. Hand's husband and mother, and confirmed that the death occurred at 11:15 P.M. on November 28, twenty-four hours *after* his dream.

Dr. Prince offers three hypotheses to account for such a dream: that the dream and the event are a combination of coincidences (this is the most frequent explanation); that there is a possible psychoanalytic interpretation; and that the dream is a precognitive experience, somehow involving travel forward in time.

RETROCOGNITION: EXPERIENCES FROM THE PAST

Another phenomenon, less well documented, is the experience of suddenly finding one's self observing an event which has taken place many years—even centuries—ago. Here are a few examples, as experienced in different states of consciousness.

A Vision While Awake

The novelist L. A. Strong reports that while standing at the back of the hall in a friend's home, he heard the front door open and saw a man enter and go into the sitting room. He followed, and was astounded to find the sitting room empty. When his friend, a schoolmaster, returned, Strong described in detail the "visitor," his clothing, brown moustache, and the music papers he carried under his arm. His friend replied that the "visitor" was the former schoolmaster, Wilfred Alington, now deceased, who had played the organ in the sitting room, when he had lived in the house. Strong, in discussing this extraordinary experience, states that he is certain of one thing: that "the spirit of the dead schoolmaster was not walking. I was, so to speak, playing a gramophone record."

(It is perhaps pertinent to mention here that recent experimentation with infrared photography has developed a process whereby it's possible to record on film what *has been* in a space several hours before: For example, an empty car park, photographed by this special process, will show on film cars that *had been* parked there several hours before. In our files, we have an infrared polaroid picture taken by a technician at the Neuropsychiatric Institute, of an empty playroom at a motel. The picture shows, albeit dimly, a man in army uniform behind a Ping Pong table. Apparently by accident, there was recorded on film the man who wasn't there, but who perhaps *had been* there, several hours before.)

PSYCHIC PHOTOGRAPHY

Psychoanalyst and parapsychologist Dr. Jule Eisenbud has devoted several bedevilled years to research with psychic Ted Serios, a man who is admittedly an alcoholic and a psychopathic personality. Yet for four years, while Serios lived as a guest in the Eisenbud home, there were conducted many strenuously controlled studies, in which a host of eminent scientists participated (as well as professional photographers and magicians, who claimed that Serios was a fraud, and that they could reproduce his pictures through trickery. In spite of Dr. Eisenbud's urgent requests that they duplicate Serios' type of picture taking, no one has as yet been able to do so.)

One of Serios' most impressive feats was that of recording on Polaroid film scenes of various places, *some of which no longer exist,* simply by looking into the lens of the camera, and signalling for someone else to snap the picture when he felt "hot," which was usually after several cans of beer, or shots of whiskey.

On one occasion, with Serios' heart "pounding away like a trip-hammer," his success became apparent, in Dr. Eisenbud's words, "the instant we stripped the developed print away from its backing. Glowing in the center of a murky but nonetheless quite distinguishable 'photograph' were the letters STEVENS on an illuminated sign over the marquee of the old, no-longer-standing Chicago Hotel (it had burned down some years before)."

Serios unconsciously made an extraordinary prediction about his work with Dr. Eisenbud. When he began this research, he confessed (as so many psychics do) that he had no idea *how* he got the pictures which appeared at times on the film. Then he added,

"You know, doc, one day I'll wake up and I won't be able to do it any more—and it'll be curtains." After years of research with Eisenbud, at the end of one strenuous session, Serios produced a vivid picture of what looks like a theater proscenium, with velvet curtains caught in the act of swirling together, closing. That picture, as Dr. Eisenbud has told many audiences, was the last picture Serios produced for him. It had, indeed, been "curtains."

WHAT ABOUT TIME?

Is it unreasonable to assume that on rare occasions a few persons obtain a glimpse, however distorted, of an event which has not yet occurred or which occurred years ago? Most people will probably say it is not merely unreasonable, it is preposterous, for one cannot travel forward or backward in time.

Interestingly, Freud stressed that *there is no time in the unconscious*. In a dream, for example, you may be with your grandmother, now dead, who is playing with your son who was not yet born when your grandmother died. Time past and time present are all mixed up. In hypnosis and under drugs time past is frequently experienced as if in present time, much as brain surgeon Dr. Penfield described the experiences of patients when he placed electrodes on the exposed cortex. For them, events were relived as if "a tape recorder were being played" (which is how the English novelist described his experience of the schoolmaster who wasn't there). Most such regressions under hypnosis or drugs are replays of the person's own life experience, although there are cases of subjects, under hypnosis, correctly giving the next day's headline, or of being regressed so far back in time that they seem to be reliving a previous life. All such experiences hint at that most popular of science fiction themes: time travel. Obviously, non-fiction scientists have not yet invented a time-traveling device. Yet, some observations about the nature of time, from eminent scientists, offer interesting speculations.

In attempting to make clear Einstein's theory of relativity, scientists have used the neat example of twin brothers, one of whom goes traveling for several years through outer space and on his return finds that he is considerably *younger* than his twin brother, who remained on earth. This oddity of time presumably has to do with the curvature of space. A more dramatic example of the time puzzle is given by the French astronomer Alexander Ananoff, who has written:

> On account of the enormous distances which separate us from the stars, and the length of time which the light of a star takes to reach us, the image of the star which we see is the image of the star which started out, several thousand years ago. Thus . . . it is possible we are looking at a star which does not exist any longer, in which case we may think that to study astronomy is to study the history of a past which has disappeared.
>
> If we found ourselves on a star, and if, from there we could see the life on our planet, we should not see modern civilization. We should for example see the events occurring in Egypt at the time of the Pharaohs.

Thus, two of our most rigorous sciences, physics and astronomy, offer examples of the evanescence and elasticity of time.

Most of us think of time as proceeding in a straight line, from past to future. And, as physicists tell us, time is the fourth dimension. Conceive then, if you will, that we are existing only in the fourth dimension, on a time line. The kind of time line that students are asked to draw to pinpoint events in history. Let us assume that this time line travels from left to right, like this:

| 1900 | 1920 | 1940 | 1960 | 1980 | 2000 | 2020 | 2040 |

Presumably you are now at the dot, which is somewhere between 1960 and 1980 (provided there has not been a time warp and it is now, as you are reading, the year 3649 o.z.). Let us further agree that at the present moment you can see exactly where you are, and you can also look back at events of the 1970s, 1960s, 1950s, etc. (Some events on the line may be obscured, but generally your vision is pretty good.) However, from that dot where you are, you cannot look *forward* to the 1980s, or 1990s (so far as you know). In other words, you know the present, you remember the past, but you can only guess about the future. At least, that's what your experience tells you clearly, day after linear day.

But, as we are aware, our raw experiences are often deceptive. In spite of what we see when we look around us, we know that earth is not flat and that is is not stationary and that the sun does not move across the sky from morning to evening. Similarly, if we touch a concrete wall, we feel with our hands how very solid it is. Yet physicists tell us that the wall is not the least bit solid; it is composed primarily of space scattered ever so thinly with atoms continually performing their cosmic dance. However, if we try to drive a car through those airy spaces that make up the concrete wall. . . . Similarly, if we look at a drop of pond water, we see a transparent liquid devoid of life. But if we place a drop of that water on a slide and look at it through a microscope, we will see that it is teeming with fantastic animal life. Putting our eye to a telescope reveals galaxies upon galaxies that, without a telescope, simply do not exist for us. Our senses, clearly, are far too crude to enable us to perceive the physical realities of the world in which we live.

For the moment, let us assume that our experience of time suffers from similar limitations. And let us return to the time line and the dot representing where you are right now.

————————————————•————————————————

Let us further suppose that a brilliant scientist has invented a time machine which can lift you above the time line like a helicopter lifting you above the earth:

Suddenly you can see not only the present and past but the future as well, and you can see them simultaneously, just as in a plane you can see not only where you are and have been, but where you are *going*.

Or consider another possibility: A scientist, equally as talented as the one who invented the infrared photographic process which reveals what *has* occupied a space, invents a photographic process that reveals what *will* occupy a space.

There has been as yet no theory devised to explain the mystery of time (just as there has yet been no theory to explain satisfactorily the mysteries of electricity or hypnosis). Nevertheless, it may be profitable to pursue the phenomenon of precognition as it has been reliably reported.

SOME CONTEMPORARY PRECOGNITIVE DREAMS

As must be obvious, the majority of precognitive dreams already reported here have dealt with harrowing, tragic experience, typically death. Such precognitive dreams seem to be most common among the persons who have visited me. Many are so disturbed by their few precognitive dreams of deaths to members of their families, that they have asked how they can stop such dreams from occurring. A few of these persons have felt that by the very process of having the dream, they may in some way have been responsible for the death. Unfortunately, we do not know how to turn off such dreams, any more than we know how to turn them on.

Occasionally, on the other hand, persons have told me of precognitive dreams that were pleasant, and even financially rewarding. The most remarkable of these is not just one isolated dream, but a *series* of dreams which continued for more than four months. About ten years ago a school psychologist and personal friend, Mrs. Sammie Hudson, began to have extremely vivid dreams, in color, which she remembered clearly for several days. This was unusual for her, since she seldom remembered her dreams after waking. Eventually she described one such dream in detail to her husband during breakfast. In the dream she had been watching a horse race, and as the winning horse crossed the finish line, she heard the track announcer give the horse's name in a clear, strong voice. The name of the horse meant nothing to her, and neither had the names of horses in previous dreams. Her husband, being an enterprising man, asked her to tell him if she had any more such dreams. That afternoon, he gathered together a list of all the races being run in the country and discovered, to his astonishment, that a horse with the same name was to run in a race on the opposite coast. The next day he looked up the results and learned that the horse had, indeed, won. For the next four months, two or three nights each week, Mrs. Hudson dreamed of horse races, in which the announcer loudly and clearly announced the name of the winner as it crossed the finish line. Her husband located the tracks at which the announced horses would be running, and bet on them. Eventually they won enough money to buy a luxury automobile. Immediately after they bought the car, her dreams of horse races stopped, and she has never dreamed of horses since. (Several years later, Mrs. Hudson told me of a persistent and vivid dream about winning jackpots at Las Vegas. She and her husband promptly went to Las Vegas, where she won seven hundred dollars on jackpots in various casinos.)

On another occasion, an insurance broker and his wife visited the lab to discuss the frequent psychic experiences the wife had had since childhood. Prominent among the psychic happenings were dreams about horse races. This was most odd for this particular woman, a devoted mother, part-time bookkeeper, and practicing Catholic, never went to the races. Nevertheless, for years she had had dreams in which she would be watching a race and see the winning horse cross the finish line. No announcer named the horse, but she could clearly see the number on the winning horse each time. She had often told her husband about the dreams, and he had been eager to test her psychic talents at the track. She had always been reluctant to go, because gambling was against her religious principles, but one morning she announced that if they went to the track that day and played the daily double, they might win a thousand dollars. She had seen two races being run in one dream, and she remembered vividly not only the horses' numbers but the odds on the daily double. They went to the track. Her description of that day at the races was wonderfully funny, because she did not remember the sequence of the two races; thus it was crucial for her to study the horses in order to place correctly the right numbers with the right horses in the first and second. Eventually the daily double bet was made, and for their two dollars, they received nearly one thousand dollars, just as she had dreamed.

After telling about these two precognitive horse-race dreams at a lecture, I was told of another by a woman in San Diego whose husband races horses. She said that one morning she woke up remembering an unusually vivid dream in which she saw the name of a winning horse posted on the tote board. The dream lingered with her, and just as her husband was leaving for the track, she told him about it. That evening at dinner, he remarked that her dream had come true, even to the detail of the odds paid, as shown on the tote board.

On still another occasion, I told these horse-race dreams to a Los Angeles television producer who was interested in doing a TV series about psychic phenomena, and the producer grinned and said, "It's a relief to know I'm not unique." And then he told me about the *only* precognitive dream in his life. It also involved a horse race, a sport which interested him not at all. In his dream, he saw the race from start to photo finish, described by a TV announcer, who grew more and more excited as the race was fought to the wire by the two horses. The name of the winner remained with him next day, because it had a familiar ring to it, which he could not place. He puzzled over the name, until he remembered a friend who had once owned a horse with a similar name. Rather sheepishly he phoned his friend to ask about the horse, only to learn that the horse had been sold and its previous owner no longer knew its whereabouts. That would have been that, except for the fact that, on a hunch, the producer searched in the evening paper for the races being run next day. He saw the horse listed as running in the fifth race. Fortunately for psychic research, the next morning he told his office staff about the dream, and they all decided to take pieces of a large bet on the horse to win. The TV producer reported that watching the race on television was one of the uncanny experiences of his life because he had already seen it in his dream. As in his dream, the announcer's voice mounted with excitement as the race drew to a photo finish, and his horse was the winner.

Why this detailed recital of horse-race dreams that have come true? Even if well documented, they are basically trivial anecdotes. The chief reason I include them is, once more, for their *psychological* value. Just as in the psychometry readings of my keychain, I believe that the contents of these four dreamers' dreams reveal how the personality influences the style of the message. One was a *bookkeeper*/housewife who in her dreams saw the winning *numbers* of the horses as they crossed the finish line. The TV producer in his dream watched the race run as a *televised* event, with the excitement of the announcer at the photo finish adding drama to the show. The wife of the race track professional saw the horse's name on the *tote board*. And the school psychologist heard the *names* of the winners, perhaps as pupils' names are called when taking the roll. (This last is the least clear.) These details lend credence to the theory that biocommunication arrives at an unconscious level, and must rise up through the personal unconscious, receiving on the way to the surface the distortions of primary process, molded by the personality of the receiver.

LABORATORY EXPERIMENTS IN PRECOGNITION

The scientifically oriented reader of these accounts may justifiably feel discontented with this recital of what may be nothing more than hearsay—anecdotes which have been verified, but have not been subjected to stringent laboratory controls. Agreed. But how can one obtain, in the laboratory, evidence to indicate that people can make accurate statements about events which have not yet occurred? On the surface, this appears to be an almost impossible job.

Actually, like so many discoveries in science, precognition in the laboratory was found quite by accident. After Dr. Rhine's 1934 publication of *Extra-Sensory Perception*, an outspoken English critic decided to see if he could substantiate Rhine's claims about ESP with card experiments. This gentleman, Dr. G. H. Soal, advertised for subjects, tested 160 people, and achieved no success at all. This long series of studies included tests with a volunteer named Basil Shackleton, who had arrived in Soal's office saying he had come to prove the existence of ESP. Despite his confidence, Shackleton's performance in 800 trials had given no better than the expected one-out-of-five hits which is chance. After compiling three years' data, which did not exceed chance expectation, Soal was prepared to refute Rhine's claims (at least with English subjects), when the English parapsychologist Whately Carington asked Soal to reexamine his data. He asked Soal to look for a consistent displacement in *time*. It was an odd request, but it was based on Carington's own research.

Carington, a Cambridge University scholar, had developed a special technique for telepathy experimentation. He had asked his receivers (who eventually totaled 250 people, living all over Great Britain), while in their homes, to draw their impressions of targets Carington placed on his desk in London. In a typical Carington study, each day for ten days, he would open a large dictionary at random and look for the first noun on the page that could be easily drawn. Carington himself then made the drawing, which no one else saw, and placed it on his desk before leaving that evening, locking the door behind him. In eleven studies, Carington collected about 20,000 such drawings which included enough good likenesses to the target pictures to exceed chance expectation. But a more interesting, totally unexpected discovery was made by Carington: He noticed that if, for instance, the target for Wednesday night had been a pyramid, several pyramid-like drawings would be sent in for that Wednesday evening and also for Tuesday and Thursday evenings. It was as if, somehow, the receivers had unconsciously anticipated the target or delayed in picking it up. Carington believed this to be a genuine effect, which he called "time displacement." He was keen to learn whether the same time displacement might have occurred in Soal's card-guessing studies, and he kept urging Soal to reexamine his data.

Naturally Soal was loath to plow through his enormous number of score sheets in search of such an unlikely finding as time displacement. But eventually he did. He found that Shackleton had scored with astonishing statistical success if each of Shackleton's calls were paired, not with the card the transmitter was actually sending, but with the card the transmitter was to send *next*, a card the transmitter had not yet seen.

For example, suppose this was an actual sequence of cards transmitted and received (instead of the traditional ESP symbols, Soal's cards contained pictures of a lion, an elephant, a zebra, a giraffe, and a pelican):

Shackleton: (zebra) lion   pelican   elephant   giraffe
Transmitter: (zebra) zebra   lion   pelican   elephant

By the usual pairing, Shackleton's score would be one correct out of the five, or no better than chance. But suppose Shackleton's calls were paired with one card *ahead* each time:

By this pairing, Shackleton would have a score of four correct out of five. And that is exactly the effect Soal found when he reexamined Shackleton's 800 trials. This "displacement effect" so intrigued Soal that he asked Shackleton to tackle another, longer series of trials. Shackleton agreed, and in 1941, a total of 3,789 trials were completed. Shackleton scored only at chance with the usual, direct pairing, but if each of Shackleton's calls was paired with the card which was to come next, his score was 1,101 hits. The odds against this happening by chance are an astronomical 10^{-35} to 1.

A fascinating phenomenon occurred when someone suggested that Shackleton's calls be speeded up (the average time for his calls was reduced from 2.8 seconds to 1.4 seconds). When these speeded-up calls were scored, it was learned that Shackleton had scored only at chance with the card immediately ahead (the "+1" card), but he had performed with brilliant success with the card two ahead (the "+2" card)!

Slowing down the calls gave no striking results. Apparently like Miniver Cheevy who was "born too late," Shackleton "called too soon."

With the publication of Soal's experiments with Shackleton (and another equally good "time displacer," Mrs. Gloria Stewart), parapsychologists began to use the card experiments to study precognition. Telepathy could be ruled out because no one knew what the next card was going to be. In fact, for the next decades, the Rhine laboratory found that the precognition method was the preferred method of ESP testing with cards.

Interestingly, the precognition method of testing has been particularly useful for demonstrations to skeptics, since the subject can fill out entire score sheets (250 trials per sheet), long before the cards are shuffled. The skeptic can then be presented with score sheets already filled out, and he himself can shuffle the cards and do the scoring. Thus charges of fraud, collusion, or improper controls can be kept at a minimum; in fact, the skeptic himself would have to be the trickster.

It was learned that a certain few subjects, like Shackleton and Stewart, can consistently predict the sequence of cards *not yet prepared.* These subjects are rare, of course, but no more rare than good telepathy subjects.

PRECOGNITION PUT TO PRACTICAL USE:
THE BRIER-TYMINSKI STUDIES

As we know, a common complaint directed against psychical research is that it has no practical application. Robert Brier, a research fellow at the Rhine laboratory, together with Walter Tyminski (whose book *Winning at Casino Gaming* contains an interesting description of the relationship between parapsychology and gaming psychology), evolved an ingenious method of putting precognition to work in gambling casinos.

First, Brier and Tyminski asked a subject, known to perform well on precognition tests, to fill out score sheets with a simple two-choice discrimination: either R for red or B for black. Then, using the majority-vote technique from information theory, which tries to clarify a weak signal by repeating it many times (the same principle used by Professor Kogan of the Soviet Union in his Morse code message of the word "Ivan"), Brier and Tyminski determined which color, red or black, got the majority of votes for their particular targets—which had already been selected. They were to be a series of roulette throws at a specified table, in a specified casino, beginning at a specified time on a future date. There were several technical problems that had to be considered, one of which is the phenomenon of "psi missing." In gambling, as everyone knows, there are people who seem cursed with psi missing; they're known as "born losers." Even the best ESP subjects have psi missing occasionally, and will score significantly below chance. As yet, there is no way of knowing *when* a subject will score high or low. It has also been clearly established that subjects rarely (if ever) score ten out of ten, or zero out of ten. An average of seven out of ten is considered hitting, and three out of ten, missing. Therefore, Brier and Tyminski chose to *watch*, without betting, the subject's first twenty-five calls, as compared with the first twenty-five spins of the roulette wheel, to determine whether the subject was hitting or missing. If he was hitting (which was considered thirteen or more correct out of twenty-five), then for the next twenty-five spins, bets were placed exactly as the subject called them. But if he was missing, the bets would be reversed; this is, if the subject had called red, the bet would be placed on black. In a series of gambling studies, which included not only roulette but craps and baccarat, Brier and Tyminski showed that their selected subjects had demonstrable, and profitable, precognition.

Warning! This is the barest description of a complex experimental procedure. The amateur at gambling and ESP testing is well advised *not* to try it.

PRECOGNITION STUDIES AT MAIMONIDES DREAM LABORATORY

The celebrated experiments in dream telepathy by Drs. Krippner and Ullman at Maimonides, described earlier, recorded on tape the dreams of a sleeper on the night that a transmitter, in another part of the hospital, was trying to convey the contents of a painting. On one occasion, a subject reported a dream in which there was this excerpt:

> There was a friend of mine, Harold, who I haven't seen for about twenty years—oh, I guess well over twenty years. . . . He was being set up for the next experiment.

This excerpt was ignored, because it had nothing to do with the painting that was being transmitted. But a week later, the staff at Maimonides received a letter from that subject:

> This is to inform you that as "predicted" in my dream of last Friday night, I met a friend of mine named Harold. . . . I was sitting with an acquaintance [in a restaurant] and had just told him of the dream and that I had not seen Harold for about twenty years. . . . We got up to leave, and there, standing in the line near the doorway, was Harold.

There were other spontaneous precognitive events recorded by the Maimonides group. Of particular interest was a letter sent from Germany by Alan Vaughan (editor of *Psychic* magazine, and a gifted psychic himself), in which Vaughan cited several dreams he had had, which he felt were premonitions of Robert Kennedy being assassinated. This letter was received by Dr. Krippner on June 4, two days before that terrible event actually occurred.

Such incidents were so striking that Drs. Ullman and Krippner decided to search for precognition in their dream studies, using a modification of their dream telepathy experiments. In their first study they used as subject the talented Malcolm Bessent, who had performed so well in the long-distance "Grateful Dead" telepathy study. Their experiments contained as many controls as the most rigorous scientists might wish, including an elaborate randomization system to select a target *word*, which was to be used to create an experience for Bessent to have the day *after* he had spent the night in the lab, where each of his dreams had already been recorded. In other words, Bessent was asked to dream about what was going to happen to him the next day. An example is perhaps the simplest way to describe this complex experiment.

Each time he was found to be dreaming, Bessent was wakened in order to record his dreams (which were not transcribed until several days later). One night he described a dream in which "there was a large concrete building ... and there was a patient from upstairs escaping. ... This patient from upstairs ... had a white coat on, like a doctor's coat." His associations to this were: "The concrete wall was sort of a sandy color, like a carved wall. ... I felt that the patient had escaped ... or just walked out and got as far as the archway." With no knowledge whatsoever of the dreams reported by Bessent, the next day the experimenter (Dr. Krippner on this occasion) went through the complex random procedure to find the word which he was to dramatize: It was the word "corridor." Dr. Krippner then went to a collection of art reproductions in the lab and chose *Hospital Corridor at St. Remy* by Van Gogh, which portrays a lone figure in the corridor of a mental institution, · which is constructed of concrete and contains archways.

On another night (during a second study), Bessent dreamed about sky, water, and birds. He reported associations that included "experiments with birds, Bob Morris doing research ... with birds. ... He's taken me out to see his sanctuary place where all the birds are kept. ... I remember seeing different kinds of doves. There were many, many different varieties. ... I just have a feeling that the target material will be about birds." The next day, Bessent was asked to experience the target, which proved to be a series of slides showing birds on water, land, and in the air, birds of many varieties, accompanied by various bird calls played on tape.

These were the two best of Bessent's efforts. But in general, he did so well dreaming about future events that in two separate studies, judges were able to match dreams and targets to a statistically significant degree. In short, the precognitive dream has been obtained in the laboratory by the Maimonides investigators under controlled conditions, with statistical significance.

PRECOGNITION AT THE UCLA LABORATORY

Our lab has made no special attempt to study precognition, but precognition has popped up spontaneously, both in lab studies and in unexpected ways.

For instance, during our "emotional episodes" telepathy experiments, with the transmitter in an isolation booth and the receiver in another room giving free associations, the following event took place. (It is important to emphasize that the experimenter, showing the episodes, never knew which episode was to be shown next; the sequence was determined, one by one, using a random selection process, the simple tossing of a coin.) The transmitter was shown three episodes, and asked to give her reactions to each.

Episode 1: "Ocean" (Slides of ocean scenes, from morning to evening.)

Transmitter: Well, the water gave me a calm, kind of restful, spacious . . . free, wide feeling. It was free and open.

Receiver: First I felt as if I had slumped over, and then I heard songs in my head—it's called the *Summer of His Years* . . . and then I was thinking about President Kennedy. And a water color painting.

Episode 2: "Kennedy Assassination" (Slides showing the events at Dallas, the President slumped over in his car, the funeral in Washington. Music: *The Summer of His Years.*)

Transmitter: Well, the song was kind of a sad ballad. And seeing what happened to him—the destruction that killed all he wanted to do. Just sadness and pain.

Receiver: All of a sudden I thought of coldness and a little girl, cold and frightened and huddling in one corner of the room.

Episode 3: "Cold" (Transmitter keeping her foot in a bucket of ice and water as long as she could bear it.)

Transmitter: Ugh ... it's terrible, so cold, co-old! It hurts all over.... I can't take it any more.

As in the Shackleton study, the receiver was consistently one target ahead. He gave accurate impressions of the Kennedy assassination (even naming the title of the song!), but he gave them one episode ahead, when the ocean scenes were being shown. Then, when the transmitter was watching the Kennedy assassination, the receiver was describing the cold that the transmitter was *going to experience* in the next episode. This receiver, like Shackleton, was receiving accurate information, but at the wrong time.

We, too, have occasionally been able to verify precognition. One of our research associates (now a clinical psychologist) was at the time in psychotherapy and was required to keep a record of her dreams as material for her therapeutic hours. At the time, she needed a paying job, and was scheduled to meet a professor about summer employment on the next Monday. The Thursday before her appointment, she dreamed she went to meet the professor in his office, but he was not there. Instead, his secretary told her she was to see Margaret. In the dream, she asked, "Where's margaret?" and was told that Margaret was "in room 806, down the hall." During her Friday therapy, she tried to associate to the dream, but could find nothing related to "Margaret" or "room 806." On Monday, she went for her appointment, only to find that the professor was not in his office; instead, his secretary told her she was to see Margaret. She asked, "Where's Margaret?" and was told, "in room 806, down the hall." Suddenly she remembered the dream, which fortunately for psychical research had been recorded in her dream book and discussed with her therapist. This precognition seems unusual because it is so trivial: no major catastrophes, just a fragment of a scene. But of psychological significance, perhaps, is the fact that she badly *needed* the job; thus her motivation may have prompted the dream. The question arises: How many of us have fragments of dreams, promptly forgotten, that might contain similar precognitive information?

Another odd precognitive event was documented when, during the course of my duties at the Neuropsychiatric Institute, I was called as a consultant on a special psychiatric problem. Sometimes I am asked to evaluate ESP in patients, who usually turn out to be more psychotic than psychic. In this particular instance, a social worker asked my advice about a thirteen-year-old girl on the adolescent ward, who was being given a thorough work-up because of her "incorrigible behavior." The girl had continued to be incorrigible on the ward, using rituals involving incantations, herbs, and "magic potions" which she claimed enhanced her ESP. As one might expect, the other adolescents on the ward had become frightened by her nightly performances, which were stopped. This had disturbed not only the patient but her mother, who insisted that her daughter's ESP was genuine and that the rituals were necessary to protect her paranormal "powers." The social worker told me that she knew nothing about ESP and would like my opinion about the girl's "powers."

In interviewing the girl, I learned that since early childhood she had had experiences typical of "born psychics": She had had dreams about things that came true; she would know, when a person came in a room, what had just happened to him; and she had been to seances, where she would "fall asleep" and talk in different voices, telling people at the seance things which she did not remember after waking up. She knew that this was a trance. With sudden emotion she told me she *hated* the trances, because while waking up, she would find herself "walking through hell, with devils all around, and it was *horrible!*" (This kind of voyage through the unconscious, as we have learned, is not unlike a bad LSD trip, or the Devil Land of the Buddhists.)

The girl also volunteered the information that she often gave readings for friends and neighbors, for money, which "paid the bills." To test her ability, I asked if she could give me a reading. She made no request for her paraphernalia (the incense, herbs, or potions), nor did she go into a trance. She simply grew quiet, looked down, and said, "Duane. That mean anything to you?" It didn't, and I asked her to spell it. "D-U-A-N-E. He works with you. Research. Like you do." I remembered that several months before, a volunteer whose first name was Dwayne had worked with us in the lab a few weeks. I gave her the benefit of the incorrect spelling, and said I might know such a person. She went on: "Duane. I can see him. He has a high hairdo, and he wears glasses, gold ones, and he's maybe five ten, and he's doing special work for you." That description did not at all fit the Dwayne who had been in the lab. The girl volunteered nothing more, and I dismissed the "reading" as a fantasy produced by the child to show off a talent, which she might have to a limited degree. That evening at home, I received a call from a doctor whom I did not know. He had been referred from the Veteran's Administration Hospital, where he worked. He said, "Since you don't know me, let me introduce myself. I'm Duane C___, and I'm calling about . . . (The rest involved an article he wished to publish about our research.) Actually, I interrupted him (rudely, I'm sure) to say, "I hope you won't think me odd, which you will. But are you about five feet ten inches tall, with gold-rimmed glasses and a high hairdo?" The doctor laughed and acknowledged that the description was accurate, particularly the "high hairdo," because in fact he wore an Afro natural.

That adolescent girl on the ward had accurately named and described someone whom I had *not yet met*, who (as she also predicted) was going to do "special work" with us.

Such instances of precognition are frequently dismissed as coincidences. But when they occur like this, in such bizarre and unexpected ways, the concept of coincidence becomes, at least to me, untenable as a total explanation.

PRECOGNITIONS THAT DON'T COME TRUE

Not for one moment should you get the impression that the precognitive dream, or vision, or hunch is usually correct. Quite the contrary. Our files containing predictions that have proved false bulge far fatter than those which have come true. To illustrate apparent precognition, we have included in this chapter accounts of dreams of terrible train and automobile accidents which subsequently did actually occur. I can give many examples of such dreams which have *not* come true.

My favorite instance is that told by a well-known movie actor who dreamed one night that he arrived at an airport to take a plane to the East, and as he entered the building he heard the announcement, "Flight 647 to New York leaving at gate 7; Flight 647 to New York leaving at Gate 7." In his dream, he boarded that plane at Gate 7, and in the air, suddenly the plane burst into flames and started plummeting to earth, at which point he woke up. A few days later, he was actually en route to the airport, to fly to New York, and as he walked into the terminal, he heard the announcement, "Flight 647 for New York leaving at Gate 7." He suddenly, in panic, remembered his dream, and promptly changed his flight for a later one. His later flight was calm and pleasant; but Flight 647, from Gate 7, also arrived in New York after an uneventful trip.

To satisfy my curiosity about the general success of popular prophets, for three years I kept a tally of their predictions, which are usually published in newspapers at the beginning of a new year.

Many of these predictions are guaranteed "safe": a flood in Asia, an earthquake in California, a volcano eruption in the Pacific, etc. It would be a rare year when such events do *not* occur! I tallied only the more specific predictions, such as: "A cure for cancer will be announced in October from Canadian scientists"; "An epidemic of smallpox will break out in Uruguay in May, and thousands will perish"; "An attempt will be made on the life of—— (name of some world celebrity)." Of such predictions, from several famous psychics, *less than 5 percent* actually occurred. A small percentage, indeed.

Yet these are predictions by persons confident enough to publish them in the press. If they are wrong so much of the time, how accurate can the corner fortune-teller be, to whom people flock in droves, money in hand, to learn about their futures?

Genuine precognition is rare, extremely rare.

CURRENT ATTEMPTS TO COLLECT AND VERIFY SPONTANEOUS PREMONITIONS

So many claims are made, *after* the fact, that people have had visions or intuitions foretelling a tragic event, like the Nicaraguan earthquake, or the assassination of Martin Luther King or President Kennedy. How often, if ever, do such premonitions actually occur? Attempts are now being made to verify prophecies which come spontaneously to people, and therefore cannot be verified in a lab. There exist premonition bureaus, like the Central Premonitions Registry, Box 482, Times Square Station, New York, 10036; people are urged to write down, in detail, any dreams, visions, or premonitions they may have, and to mail the information to the registry. The postmark on the letter will, of course, indicate whether the premonition actually occurred before the event. Thousands of letters have been received, with all kinds of predictions. Dismissing the crackpot material, which inevitably arrives with such investigations, and freely granting that a majority of the predictions do *not* come true, the registries claim a few examples of information about an event before it has actually occurred. For instance, when the English psychic Malcolm Bessent first arrived in New York, he experienced several dreams and visions which he felt might be predictions about the future. He was urged to send these to the Central Premonitions Registry, which he did. Here is one of his predictions received by Robert Nelson, the Registry's director, on December 7, 1969: "A Greek tanker, black in color, will be involved in a disaster having international significance within four to six months' time. (Onassis connected—perhaps the danger is symbolic, but I feel the ship may represent him personally.)" In February 1970, the *Arrow*, an Onassis-owned oil tanker, was wrecked off Nova Scotia, spilling its cargo of oil. This became an international incident, since the oil slick contaminated the beaches. A trivial precognition, certainly, but one that was documented by a letter postmarked before the event occurred.

OTHER KINDS OF BIOCOMMUNICATION

We have been examining GESP, or general ESP: telepathy, clairvoyance, precognition, and retrocognition. But these do not constitute by any means the whole range of information arriving spontaneously from an unknown source. There remain bewildering channels through which information arrives, providing the child prodigy, the creative artist, and many other kinds of people with answers to questions they might never have asked. These pieces of information, arriving often in sudden completeness, have been called "automatisms" by F.W.H. Myers. Let's explore those channels next.

9 Inspiration, Idiots Savants, and Information from Unknown Sources

The child prodigy; the creative artist; and information arriving through automatisms such as table tipping, ouija boards, and automatic writing.

HOW DO WE KNOW WHAT WE KNOW?

One of the most strenuously studied areas of human behavior is: How do we learn what we know? For more than a hundred years, psychology has struggled with this problem, evolving methods which include the conditioned reflex of Pavlov, the operant conditioning of Skinner, and numberless studies of rats learning their ways through mazes. Much has been gained from this research (from behavior modification therapy to brain washing), but certain phenomena continue to elude these traps of the psychologist. Long ago, for example, it was discovered that a few rats could perform a difficult task, such as finding their way through a complex maze, the very first time it was presented. The feat came to be called "one-trial learning"; and such rats became known as "maze bright" to distinguish them from their "maze dull" brothers. Then special selective breeding was inaugurated to produce maze-bright and maze-dull rats, and it was found that the bright rats so produced learned significantly more quickly than the dull ones.

But this did nothing to explain one-trial learning, a phenomenon which also occurs in people, especially children, and sometimes to an astonishing degree.

THE CHILD PRODIGY

A fascinating mystery is the child who can do incredibly diffi-cult calculations in his head, although he cannot explain *how* he arrives at his answers. In 1837, ten-year-old Mangiamele produced the answer to the cube root of 3,796,416 in 30 seconds for the examiners of the French Academy, who were angry because he did not tell them how he did it. (He didn't know.) F. W. Myers made a study of thirteen such child prodigies, which included not only Mangiamele (whose general intelligence was only average and whose mathematical gift lasted only a few years) but also geniuses like Ampere and Gauss, whose gifts remained with them through-out their lives. Another of Myers' case histories was the child Dase, who was of very low intelligence and never could grasp "the first elements of mathematics," but who was employed for his life-time—before the age of computers—by the Hamburg Academy of Science to make tables of factors and prime numbers, "a task which few men could have accomplished without mechanical aid." Today we call such people as Dase "idiot savants" (French for "wise idiots," a label which explains nothing).

A delightful incident about a child prodigy is presented by Myers, who received the information in this letter from a promi-nent Edinburgh engineer, in 1892:

> My brother very early manifested a marvelous power of mental calculation. When 6 years of age, Benjamin was walking with Father before breakfast when he said, "Papa, at what hour was I born?" He was told 4 A.M.
>
> Ben: "What o'clock is it at present?"
>
> Answer: "7:50 A.M."
>
> The child walked on a few hundred yards, then stated the number of seconds he had lived. My father noted down the figures, made the calculations when he got home, and told Ben he was 172,800 seconds wrong, to which he got the ready reply: "Oh, Papa, you have left out the two days for the leap years 1820 and 1824," which was the case.

The phenomenon of the child prodigy is still very much with us. In the 1970 Russian film *Seven Steps beyond the Horizon*, a Soviet youth is given extraordinarily complex mathematical problems to solve, which he does in seconds, the answers being confirmed, also in seconds, by a computer. Similarly, on a recent American TV program, the two children of a university professor (ages four and six) are shown, together with a class of university students, successfully working problems in advanced calculus.

From where does such knowledge derive? In his discussion, which can be found in *Human Personality*, Myers offers the views of Lamarck (acquired characteristics), Darwin (the mutant or sport, to account for the evolution of new species), and Plato (who believed that man does not learn, but "remembers" what he has learned before his present incarnation). Then Meyers offers his own hypothesis: The subliminal mind contains within it unknown, perhaps infinite capacities, which occasionally break into consciousness in a "subliminal uprush," which he also believes can account for certain artistic creations.

INSPIRATION AND THE CREATIVE ARTIST

Composers, sculptors, and writers have reported that their works, on occasion, come unbidden, and complete, and unexpectedly. John Keats said that he had "not been aware of the beauty of some thought or expression until after he had written it down." It had then struck him with astonishment and seemed rather the production of another person than his own. In discussing his poem *Milton*, William Blake wrote: "I have written this poem from immediate dictation, twelve or sometimes twenty or thirty lines at a time, without premeditation, and even against my will." Mozart (who was also a child prodigy, having composed sonatas at the age of four) described some of his works as coming into his inner hearing, sudden and complete: "Nor do I hear in my imagination the parts *successively*, but I hear them, as it were, all at once."

Often the artist will describe his inspiration as arriving in a different state of consciousness. Richard Wagner, for example, "discovered the opening of the *Rheingold* during a half-sleep on a couch in a hotel"; and in a letter to a friend he refers to the "blissful dream state" into which he falls when composing. Similarly Tchaikowski describes his experiences: "It would be vain to try to put into words that immense sense of bliss which comes over me directly a new idea awakens in me. I forget everything and behave like a madman. . . . It frequently happens that some external interruption wakes me from my somnambulistic state. . . . Sometimes they break the thread of inspiration so that I have to seek it again—often in vain."

Probably the most infamous interruption of an inspiration befell Samuel Coleridge, who while in another altered state of consciousness (under the influence of a drug—perhaps opium) had this experience, told in his own words:

> In the summer of the year 1797, the Author, then in ill health, had retired to a lonely farm-house between Porlock and Linton. . . . An anodyne had been prescribed, from the effects of which he fell asleep in his chair at the moment he was reading the following sentence:
> "Here the Khan Kubla commanded the palace to be built, and a stately garden there unto. . . ."
> The Author continued for about three hours in a profound sleep, at least of the external senses during which he has the most vivid confidence that he could have composed not less than from two to three hundred lines; if that indeed can be called composition in which all the images rose up before him as *things* . . . without any sensation or consciousness of effort. On awakening . . . taking his pen, ink, and paper, he instantly and eagerly wrote—

about seventy lines of the poem "Xanadu," when he was interrupted by a businessman from Porlock. After his visit, Coleridge could remember no more of the poem, which had disappeared "like the images on the surface of a stream into which a stone had been cast." Thus was created one of the world's great, unfinished works of art.

Another celebrated English poet, Robert Browning, said that sometimes his pen would write as if of his own volition, occasionally producing works which even he did not understand.

"When I wrote that," he is reported to have said to Elizabeth Barrett when she inquired about the meaning of a particular passage, "perhaps only God and I understood it. Now only God knows what it means."

In his book *Talks with Great Composers*, Arthur Abell writes of an evening spent with Johannes Brahms in 1896, when Brahms confided his special creative process (on the promise that Abell would not publish it until fifty years after his death, a promise Abell kept). Brahms seemed to deliberately seek a special state of consciousness:

> To realize that we are one with the Creator, as Beethoven did, is a wonderful and awe-inspiring experience. . . . I always contemplate this when I begin to compose. This is the first step. [Then] I feel vibrations that thrill my whole being. Those vibrations assume the form of distinct mental images. . . . Straightway the ideas flow in upon me. And not only do I see distinct themes in my mind's eye, but they are clothed in the right forms, harmonies, and orchestrations.

Contemporary artists still describe such experiences. Noel Coward wrote what is considered his best play, *Private Lives*, over a weekend. And Arthur Miller, after struggling for years with an idea for a play which eluded him, eventually poured forth in a week, effortlessly, the Pulitzer Prize-winning play *Death of a Salesman*. And in a newspaper interview, Richard Bach, author of the exquisite *Jonathan Livingston Seagull*, describes how this book came into being: "I saw the story happen in what appeared to be rather a vivid dream before I slept. The book was not, as some accounts have suggested, dictated to me by a vaporous talking seagull." (Another example of information arriving in an altered state of consciousness.)

NOT ALL "INSPIRATION" IS ART

Probably a very small percentage of real art is produced by such "uprushes" from the unconscious. Artists may feel "inspired" or "transported"—and produce trash. One outstanding example of this phenomenon occurred to that eminently fine writer, Voltaire, who described the experience in a letter to a friend:

> Five acts (of a play) in a week! I know this sounds ridiculous; but if men could guess what enthusiasm can do—how a poet, in spite of himself, devoured by his genius, can accomplish in a few days a task for which without that genius a year would not suffice; —in a word, if they knew the gift of God—their astonishment might be less than it must be now.

That particular work of "genius," *Catilina,* is considered by critics to be an unreadable and unactable tragedy.

Inspiration, then, can produce art or rubbish, but the fact is that an entire play, novel, or symphony may emerge, full-blown into consciousness, from an unknown source. Indeed, the artist sometimes feels that he is an imposter, as in this confession by Robert Louis Stevenson: "The whole of my published fiction should be the single-handed product of some unseen collaborator," or in the words of George Sand, "It is the *other* who sings as he likes, well or ill, and . . . I am nothing, nothing at all."

Thus, whether in the solving of mathematical problems, or in the creation of art, information may come of itself, from a deep level of the unconscious perhaps, but surely from a source unknown to the conscious mind. An analogy might be made to the phenomenon of automatic writing, which we will be examining after briefly reviewing a few "automatisms" which frequently evolve into automatic writing.

PECULIAR PRACTICES FOR BRINGING INFORMATION FROM AN UNKNOWN SOURCE

Although a much more popular pastime in the early twentieth century than today, there are still many occasions when people gather together for a table-tipping seance to obtain "messages from beyond" either for comfort or for help with personal problems. A typical procedure is for several people to assemble around a table, each sitting in his own chair. Each places his hands lightly on the table so that his own thumbs are touching and his little fingers touch the little fingers of the person next to him. Usually the lights are turned out, and the seance begins with music or singing. Perhaps after a time the table will begin to vibrate and one leg of the table will seem to rise of itself into the air and fall back to the floor. Thus, the table has tipped. Experienced sitters will then usually ask the table to tap once for yes, twice for no, and questions will be asked, the table tapping out its answers. When the table becomes lively, it is frequently asked to spell out messages, using the code of one rap for A, two for B, three for C; etc. On very, very rare occasions, meaningful messages have reportedly been produced in this fashion.

In the rich files of the SPR there is an interesting example of such table tipping from Mrs. Georgiana Kirby, in a letter to F. W. Myers, from Santa Cruz, California, received in 1886. Mrs. Kirby first learned of table tipping from "two intelligent men in town, Dr. McLean and the Reverend Dryden" who reported that in some "strange experiments, spirits tipped the table and they said sentences were spelled by the use of the alphabet." Mr. and Mrs. Kirby tried the experiment themselves, and since they "were given to understand that three or four persons would be more likely to succeed than two (since magnetism or electricity was drawn from them)" an illiterate ranch hand and former sailor from England, Thomas Travers, agreed to participate. In Mrs. Kirby's words:

> We had not held our hands one moment on the table before it tipped very decidedly, and I forthwith proceeded to repeat the alphabet. The table tipped promptly to the letters, spelling out "Mary Howells." As I knew no such person, I asked if she were a friend of Mr. Kirby's? Ans: No. Of Tom's? Ans: Sister. Are you married? Ans: No.
>
> I exclaimed, "It's all falsehood and nonsense. Here is someone professing to be Tom's sister who says her name is Howells, and that she is unmarried. Of course her name would be Travers."
>
> Tom said in a low tone, "That's her name. Mary Howells." (Tom, looking extremely confused and astonished, explained he had changed his name to Travers

after running away from a whaling ship in San Francisco.) The table then proceeded to spell the following words:
"I — have — a — child — a — girl — she — is — seven — years — old — and — now — in — a — house — of — ill — fame — in — Cat — Street — I — want — my — brother — to — bring — her — away — from — there."

This was a painful message to convey. "She says she has a little girl seven years old," I began. Here Tom removed his hands quickly from the table, and counting on his fingers, he observed, "Yes, mum, that's so. She's seven now." When I gave him the rest of the message he begged me to assure his sister that he would send 50 dollars the next month and have the child removed to a better place.

"But is it true that there is a street called Cat Street?" I asked. "Yes, mum, and it is the worst in the city."

The following day he acknowledged to me that his sister was a woman of the town.

In another letter, answering several questions put by Myers, Mrs. Kirby wrote that fraud was most unlikely on Tom's part, since she not only had repeated the letters in her *mind* while the table tapped, but also because Tom could neither read nor write. She added that after Tom returned to England, to take charge of his sister's daughter, the Kirbys were never able to produce any further table tipping; she believed it was Tom who had supplied the "electrical help." Finally, she gave the information that "Cat Street was in Plymouth, England. If it has given place to another, the fact of its former existence could be verified." In his thorough manner, Myers inquired of the Postmaster of Plymouth, and received this reply: "Sir, I beg to inform you that a few years ago there was a street named Catte Street but it is now called Stillman St."

SPIRITUALISM AND SPIRITUALISTIC SEANCES

It is not known how this peculiar practice of table tipping originated, but the impetus for the Victorian (and post-Victorian) fad of "spirit communication" via seances and mediums probably came from Hydesville, New York, where in 1847, the Fox family moved into a house with the reputation of being "uncanny." Strange rapping sounds, inexplicable footsteps and movement of furniture, doors and windows rattling on windless nights—all were supposed to occur in the house. None of these strange happenings particularly disturbed the Fox family, until one March night in 1848 when, according to a testimony given by Mrs. Fox:

> Noises were heard in all parts of the house. My husband stationed himself outside the door while I stood inside, and the knocks came on the door between us. We heard footsteps in the pantry, and walking downstairs. The children, who slept in the other bed in the room, heard the rappings and tried to make similar sounds by snapping their fingers.
>
> My youngest child, Cathie, said, "Mr. Splitfoot, do as I do." clapping her hands. The sounds instantly followed her with the same number of raps. I then thought I could put a test that no one in the place could answer. I asked the noise to rap my different children's ages, successively. Instantly each of my children's ages was given correctly, pausing between them sufficiently long to individualize them. . . . By the same simple method I ascertained that [the spirit] was a man, aged thirty-one years, that he had been murdered in this house and his remains were buried in the cellar.

These phenomena continued, and the Foxes were able to demonstrate the rappings to several neighbors. Eventually, digging in the cellar, they found human hair and bones which medical men claimed were those of a human skeleton.

Shortly afterward, events within the house took on the character of a genuine haunting: Night after night were heard "the sound of a death struggle, and the heavy dragging of a body around the room." Mrs. Fox's hair turned white as a consequence of these ghoulish occurrences, and soon after, the family left the house, with the children Kate and Margaret going to separate homes. The raps then occurred in each of the homes where Kate and Margaret had been sent. Soon curiosity seekers began to gather at these homes to listen to the raps and to watch the odd movements of the tables at which the children sat. Soon a few enterprising persons made capital of the Fox sisters by organizing "spiritualistic seances," in which raps from the table spelled out messages to those present. The Fox sisters became famous (notorious?), and for the next decades, the inevitable controversy raged: fake or real?

FAKE SEANCES AND FAKE MEDIUMS

Communications from "spirits" by means of seances held in the dark can easily be arranged, and charlatans everywhere proclaimed themselves "spirit" or "physical" or "trance" mediums and began offering a wide variety of seances for handsome fees. Seances became a worldwide fashion, more popular perhaps than the current fashion of "occult supply shops" with their Tarot cards, incense, magic potions, I Ching, and crystal balls.

A few celebrated mediums, like Eusapia Palladino, were rigorously tested time after time by psychical research investigators, who often disagreed among themselves over whether the phenomena produced were genuine. (Of all the mediums tested, only D. D. Home, whose physical mediumship and levitations we have already discussed, was never found to be involved with trickery.) So outrageous were some of the frauds perpetrated at fake seances that Harry Houdini, the famous magician, spent several years of his life exposing phony mediums and their tricks. Houdini himself would stage fascinating seances, featuring "spirit voices" coming from trumpets levitated in the air, "ectoplasmic manifestations," and other "manifestations from the beyond." At the conclusion of such seances, he would demonstrate to the impressed audience how each of those effects had been theatrically contrived.

THE GENUINE VERSUS THE FAKE MEDIUM

It is fairly easy to distinguish the genuine medium from the fraud. The genuine psychic generally uses no gimmicks, rarely asks for a fee, states that he does not know whether he will obtain any information and that the information, if obtained, may be false. The psychic who is also a medium will go into trance to obtain information—information about which no memory is retained after returning to consciousness. Noel Coward, in his witty play *Blithe Spirit,* offers the character of Madame Arcati, a medium who goes into trance, during which time all hell breaks loose (poltergeists breaking furniture, spirits appearing with devastating effects). Then, when Madame Arcati awakens from the trance, she asks with genuine interest, "Well, that's that! Did anything happen?"

The fake medium, by contrast, has all kinds of special effects, as carefully planned as a good theatrical production. At such seances, total darkness is demanded and spectators are cautioned not to move from their seats, and in particular, not to touch the medium, because to touch the medium in trance can be disastrous. (This last is, in fact, true, as we will later learn.) The charlatan medium usually has his particular specialty, one of the most popular being the "trumpet seance." A trumpet is placed on the table, and during the course of the seance it will rise into the air and seemingly float about the room; from it will emerge "spirit voices" with their messages. At one trumpet seance I attended, the medium excused himself before the session and applied a medication (perhaps belladonna) to dilate the pupils of his eyes so that he could see better in the dark. In the total darkness, with an immobilized audience, he was free to manipulate the trumpet with wires, and to use a variety of voices which, like a good ventriloquist, he could throw so that they appeared to be coming from the trumpet as it "floated" across the room.

Another seance specialty is the "materialization of ectoplasm." Ectoplasm is, presumably, a greyish substance which is sometimes emitted from the entranced medium, forming itself into a "spirit body." In the fake seance, the "ectoplasm" is in fact a large piece of cheesecloth draped over an assistant who cavorts around the room. That peripatetic parapsychologist Dr. Andrija Puharich once attended such a seance, requesting first that he be permitted to film the proceedings. Since the seance was to be held in total darkness, the medium smiled, saying that nothing would appear on the film, but that if he wished to bring his movie camera, he was at liberty to do so. Dr. Puharich did so, using infrared film, which of course can take pictures in total darkness. The resulting short film he made is a classic expose of fake seances. At a signal from the "entranced" medium, two assistants are seen to appear from behind a cabinet (a stock piece of equipment at such events), they are clad in voluminous cheesecloth, which they wave about. One of the assistants, a jovial fat man, seemed very much to enjoy tickling with his cheesecloth one or another member of the audience.

Today charlatan "psychics" are to be found everywhere, advertising in newspapers, giving lecture/demonstrations, and appearing in nightclubs and on TV. One of the surest signs of a fraud is use of this trick: The psychic asks that a dollar bill be held up from a member of the audience and he reads off, in correct sequence, the serial number of the bill. Astonishing feat—which any good magician can do, since it is merely a trick. The fake psychic will also tell you the correct color, suit, and number of a playing card from a new deck of cards, and he will invariably be correct. It is another magician's trick. One of the most spectacular demonstrations is the use of double and triple blindfolds, with coins placed over the eyes underneath the blindfolds. The "psychic" will then read out questions handed him on a slip of paper, and supply an answer. He usually holds the slip of paper at his waist, giving him a fine opportunity to look straight down, in spite of the blindfolds, and read clearly what is written. Try it. It is astonishing how clearly the eyes can see through that tiny millimeter of space.

Probably the best "seance" you can attend today is at the Magic Castle in Los Angeles, a private club for professional magicians. One special event for private parties at the Magic Castle is their "seance dinner." For a price, a group can eat dinner in a specially designed room, where rappings will be heard around the walls, trumpets will float in the air, spirit voices will be heard, and as the grand climax, the dining table will rise up in the air. Audiences are usually delighted with the evening, all the events of which have been computer-programmed and are executed with special electronic equipment. It's undoubtedly the best seance available. And of course, it's pure hokum.

THE OUIJA BOARD

Like a table tipping, the planchette and its modern derivative the ouija board have produced a wild assortment of phenomena. A ouija board can be purchased today for a nominal price in almost any toy store. Recent figures report that more than two million ouija board "games" are sold in the United States each year. (Warning! For certain persons, the ouija board is *no game* and can cause serious dissociations of personality.)

For anyone unfamiliar with the contraption, the board is the size of an ordinary game board, and has printed on it all the letters of the alphabet, all the numbers from 0 to 9, and the words *yes* and *no*. With the board comes a small object called the "pointer." To "work the board" requires from one to as many persons as can fit one finger on the pointer. When all the persons have their fingers ever so lightly placed on the pointer, they sit—silently or not, it does not seem to matter—and wait. Sometimes that's all there is to the game. Nothing happens. (The same is true for certain groups who try to tip tables.) At other times, there seems to come some kind of energy which causes the pointer to move, apparently of its own volition, from letter to letter. Frequently this movement produces nothing but gibberish: XLMVTEJKI, etc. Less frequently, the pointer spells real words and answers specific questions, which is exciting to the participants until they find out that the information thus obtained is false. Much less frequently, the pointer will deliver an accurate piece of information, for which it is difficult to produce a totally satisfactory explanation.

For example, the question might be asked: "How many coins does Betty have in her purse?" And the pointer will move swiftly to the numbers 1 and 4, indicating she has fourteen coins.

Betty opens her purse, and lo! fourteen coins are counted. Most parapsychologists dismiss this as a form of telepathy, or, perhaps more plausibly, as unconscious muscle movements. It is presumed that Betty knows, consciously or unconsciously, how many coins she has, and through unconscious (or conscious) muscle movements she has guided the pointer to provide the right answer. Obviously, if just one person working the ouija board is so motivated, fakery becomes simplicity itself.

I cannot deny, however, that I have participated in some ouija board sessions where the pointer was active and the information made sense. Sometimes the information can be uncannily, and frighteningly, accurate. For example, a personal friend, not too long ago, telephoned in a state of strong anxiety. His wife had been getting fearsome messages on the board about a relative who had dined with them on Thanksgiving Day, and shortly after dinner, had left to drive back to a San Francisco university. Later in the evening the wife brought out for the remaining guests, as a novelty, a ouija board she had purchased the previous day. Everyone sat down to try the game, and the pointer immediately became active, spelling again and again the word "Help." Eventually, more information came, to the effect that the relative had had an automobile accident on his way back to San Francisco, and was wandering in the dark, not knowing where he was. The next day there arrived the terrible news that the relative had been killed in an automobile accident.

Although frightened, the wife had continued to work the board, getting more and more peculiar "messages" from the deceased relative. Her husband became worried that this preoccupation with the ouija board might be a possible danger to his wife, and he wanted a professional opinion about the quality of the information being produced. After I had participated in a ouija board session with them, it seemed clear to me that the first night's message may have been genuine (it is hard to conceive that it was not genuine) but that the ensuing "messages," expressed chiefly in symbolic language, were psychological rather than parapsychological in their origin.

Of much more interest than either table tipping or ouija boards is the phenomenon which both activities have frequently elicited—that category of biocommunication called "automatic writing."

FROM TABLE TIPPING TO AUTOMATIC WRITING: THE CASE OF THE REVEREND WILLIAM STAINTON MOSES

An Oxford graduate, clergyman, and schoolmaster of unblemished reputation was W. Stainton Moses. He was also a personal friend of F. W. Myers, who tells us that as a schoolboy Moses occasionally walked in his sleep (this is a more common "motor automatism" than the ones we have been discussing). On one occasion, his mother saw Moses "go down into the sitting room and write an essay on a subject which had puzzled him on the previous evening, and return to bed without waking."

While a schoolmaster at University College, in the 1870s, Moses became interested in the spiritualist movement. He held regular seances with a small group of friends, during which many physical manifestations, including table tipping and levitation, presumably occurred. Finding that tapped-out messages were tedious to receive, Moses learned that he could obtain similar information simply by holding a pencil in his hand, which wrote with no effort on his part. Of the development of this automatic writing, Moses was explicit:

> At first the writing was very small and irregular, and it was necessary for me to write slowly and cautiously; otherwise the message soon became incoherent. . . . In a short time, however, I could dispense with these precautions. The writing, while becoming more and more minute, became at the same time very regular and beautifully formed. As a rule it was necessary that I should be isolated, and the more passive my mind, the more easy the communications. It is an interesting speculation whether my own thoughts entered into the subject matter of the communications. But I cultivated the power of occupying my mind with other things during the time the writing was going on, and was able to read an abstruse book, while the message was written with unbroken regularity.

This technique—keeping the mind occupied with the reading of a book while the hand writes of itself—has proved immensely useful in my own research. People will often come to the lab, claiming proficiency with automatic writing. Generally such persons are deluded into the belief that the writing is coming from some outside source, whether divine or demonic, when in all likelihood it is coming from a barely subliminal region of mind. I usually suggest that they try some automatic writing right there in the lab, and they are frequently pleased to do so until I ask that they read aloud from a book so that the automatic writing may be given free flow. As they read aloud, almost invariably the "automatic writing" automatically stops. For such persons, the practice of any automatism, whether through ouija board, pendulums, planchettes, table tipping, or automatic writing, can be dangerous because it can lead to dissociation.

A CASE OF DISSOCIATED PERSONALITY

A few years ago I received a letter from a woman who claimed to have developed automatic writing after practicing the ouija board (this is a typical progression from one automatism to another). Asking for an analysis of her writing, she enclosed several samples of her "messages." These indicated to me that she was using the "automatic writing" to dissociate herself from an emotional problem. I answered her letter, gently suggesting psychotherapy and strongly suggesting that she immediately discontinue the writing.

About a year later, this woman appeared in my office, insisting that she must speak with me alone. Her husband, who stood behind her, looked very disturbed. I suggested he wait in the reception room, while his wife talked to me, and he agreed. As soon as we were alone, the woman, with a look of triumph, told me that her "guide" had a message for me. Whereupon the woman promptly closed her eyes, reopened them, and announced that she was now the Virgin Mary and that the woman through whom she was speaking was going to follow in her footsteps. Nothing else that was said was intelligible, so I asked the "Virgin" if I might talk again with the woman. The "Virgin" graciously agreed, her eyes closed and reopened, and the woman was herself again—ecstatic at the miracle she had wrought. I excused myself and went to talk with her husband. His story was simple and sad. He had been in Viet Nam for two years, and had received frequent, happy letters from wife and children while he was away. Then, unexpectedly, he had received his discharge, and as a surprise he arrived home unannounced, soon to be greeted by the Virgin Mary. This is not a difficult case for a psychologist to interpret (it is probably equally easy for a non-psychologist). The lady obviously had certain sexual hang-ups and had found this neat dissociation of herself into the Virgin Mary in order to make sex an impossibility. Her automatic writing had helped to begin the split in her personality, which led to the schizophrenia for which she was hospitalized.

FROM THE OUIJA BOARD TO AUTOMATIC WRITING: MRS. PEARL CURRAN, AKA PATIENCE WORTH

Mrs. Pearl Curran, a St. Louis housewife with an eighth-grade education, was invited one summer day in 1912 to play the "ouija board game" with a group of friends. As soon as she joined them, the board became very active indeed. The friends continued the game for about two years, sometimes getting nonsense, but occasionally "receiving a message" that could be verified. Then suddenly, one day, came the statement: "Many moons ago I lived. Again I come. Patience Worth my name." Patience Worth stayed for five years, first with Mrs. Curran and friends at the ouija board, and then with Mrs. Curran alone, through automatic writing. Patience Worth "dictated" more than a million and a half words, in sixteenth-century English, prose and poetry, novels and stories, which critics hailed as having high literary merit. Most of these are extant and are available at libraries. One poem, "Telka," (of about 70,000 words) is written in a dialect used three centuries ago, containing a high percentage of Anglo-Saxon words. An analysis of the language made by Professor C. H. S. Schiller of London University demonstrated that the vocabulary contained no word used later than the year 1600. Schiller comments: "When we consider that the Authorized Version [of the Bible] has only 70% Anglo-Saxon, and it is necessary to go back to Layomon [1205] to equal Patience Worth's percentage, we realize we are face-to-face with a philological miracle."

Parapsychologist Dr. Walter F. Prince made a lengthy study of Mrs. Curran and published his observations as *The Case of Patience Worth*, with this conclusion: "Either our concept of what we call the subconscious mind must be radically altered so as to include potencies of which we hitherto had no knowledge, or else some cause operating through, but not originating in, the subconscious of Mrs. Curran must be acknowledged."

FROM MEDITATION TO AUTOMATIC WRITING

One very special state of consciousness is that developed through meditation. (The final chapter of this book will be devoted to an exploration of meditation in its various forms.) Some who have practiced meditation, whether as a religious exercise or for their own spiritual development, have experienced a profound alteration of personality, and sometimes an influx of knowledge so far transcending that which the person has conceived that he is filled with awe and astonishment. Occasionally this knowledge has arrived through automatic writing, as happened to St. Theresa of

Avila, who wrote volumes concerning her illuminations, often without her conscious knowledge of what had been written by her hand. An illustration is offered in the experience of the Mother Superior of the convent at Toledo, where Theresa stayed for a time. The Mother Superior entered Theresa's cell with a message for her, and "was terrified to see that the saint, after removing her spectacles to listen to the message, was then siezed in a trance lasting several hours. The nun dared not move or go away, but remained staring at Theresa until she finally came to her senses. The blank sheet of paper was by this time covered with her writing."

A much more recent, and more lengthy, communication was received by an American, Mrs. Alice A. Bailey, from "the Tibetan." Their collaboration began in 1919 and continued for more than twenty years. In her *Unfinished Autobiography*, Mrs. Bailey thus describes her initial encounter with the "Tibetan":

> I had sent the children off to school and went out on the hill close to the house. I sat down and began thinking ... and heard a voice which said "There are some books which it is desired should be written for the public. You can write them. Will you do so?" Without a moment's notice I said, "Certainly not. I'm not a darned psychic and I don't want to be drawn into anything like that."

A period of three weeks elapsed before another encounter took place, at which time Mrs. Bailey reluctantly agreed to give it a try. In her words:

> I would like to make it clear that the work I do is in no way related to automatic writing. Automatic writing, except in the rarest of cases (and, unfortunately, most people think their case is the rare exception) is very dangerous. ... We have had to handle many cases of obsession as the result of automatic writing.
> In the work I do, I assume an attitude of intense, positive attention. I simply listen and take down the words that I hear and register the thoughts which are dropped one by one into my brain. ... I have never changed anything that the Tibetan has ever given me.

The work of the Tibetan has greatly intrigued people and psychologists everywhere. They dispute as to what is the cause of the phenomenon, and argue that what I write probably comes from my subconscious. I have been told that Jung takes the position that the Tibetan is my personified higher self and Alice A. Bailey is the lower self. Some of these days (if I ever have the pleasure of meeting him) I will ask him how my personified higher self can send me packages all the way from India, for that is what He has done.

By 1949, at the time of Mrs. Bailey's death, this collaboration had produced more than twenty volumes on esoteric subjects, from healing and telepathy to the astral and etheric bodies. All these volumes are extant today and are widely read by persons interested in occult philosophy.

What can we make of this strange terrain we have been exploring, in which information arrives spontaneously and unexpectedly to a bewildering assortment of people: children, artists, housewives, schizophrenics, clergymen, and mystics? Such persons have not yet been subjected to laboratory investigation; there seem to be no tools or methods with which to measure or comprehend these extraordinary events.

In many instances it would seem as if the information comes from a very deep level of consciousness, so deep that the author of the event has no knowledge of how the information has arrived, and often feels no relationship to that which has been produced. And in some instances, the information seems to have arrived from a totally different person than the one delivering the message. How can we examine this division of mind and/or personality? It might be wise to start with what we know about mind and personality, from the researches of our psychiatrists and psychologists.

10 From Multiple Personality to "Possession"

Amnesia, fugues, dissociation, "possession," trance states, and the phenomena each produce.

LITTLE FUGUES

"I think, therefore I am," declared Descartes, and the Age of Reason began. But this dictum overlooks a host of events in which I apparently *am*, but I do not think at all. A commonplace example of this phenomenon is the inveterate smoker—Dwight Eisenhower was one—who finds he is smoking two or three cigarettes at the same time, without having been aware that he had lit any one of them. Another example is the driver of an automobile who suddenly becomes aware that he has driven ten or twenty miles with no remembrance of the journey. A less common, but still familiar example is that of a person who "blacks out" at a party after drinking too much liquor yet may continue to talk, take leave of his host, drive safely home, and find himself in his own bed the next morning—perhaps with a woman whom he has never seen before. Something within him has performed all those functions without his conscious knowledge. Psychiatry calls such a temporary loss of consciousness a "fugue state"; when the loss of consciousness continues for weeks, months, or even years, it is labeled "amnesia." Victims of amnesia are a favorite subject in fiction, but genuine cases of amnesia are sometimes much stranger stories.

THE CASE OF ANSEL BOURNE

Ansel Bourne was born in New York in 1826. At the age of seven, his father and mother separated, and the boy's life became one of poverty and hard work. Eventually he became a carpenter, married, had children, and to all appearances led an unremarkable life except, perhaps, for the fact that he was a convinced atheist. One day, when thirty-one years of age, Bourne suddenly became very ill, and was unconscious for two days. His doctor claimed he had suffered a severe sunstroke. Three weeks later, seemingly recovered and while taking a walk, Bourne, for no apparent reason, felt a strong urge to go to church. Immediately he felt such revulsion at the idea that he thought to himself he would rather be "struck deaf and dumb forever" than go inside a church. A few minutes later, Bourne felt dizzy, sat down and was instantly deprived of sight, hearing, and speech. He had to be led home. Over the next several days he recovered his sight, but could neither hear nor speak. Remembering vividly how he had thought he would rather be "deaf and dumb forever" than go to church, he repented and wrote a message that he wanted to be taken to the Christian Chapel and be converted. This was done, but he remained deaf and dumb. He asked to be taken a second time to the church, and on that occasion he stood up while his conversion statement was read aloud. While he was standing, his hearing and speech were restored to him.

Thus far, the case might be considered one of hysterical deafness and muteness brought about by a religious conflict. And, in fact, the next thirty years passed uneventfully. Then, in January, 1887, Bourne left his home for a routine business trip to Providence, Rhode Island, and did not come back. His family and the police searched for him, but he could not be found. Eight weeks later, as Bourne remembered it, he heard a "loud shot," and woke up early one morning, to find himself in a strange room, in a strange bed. He did not know where he was, or what had happened to him. He walked out of the room and met a strange man (Mr. Earl), who said, "Good morning, Mr. Brown." The following conversation then took place:

Bourne: "Where am I?"

Earl: "You're all right."

Bourne: "I'm all wrong. My name is not Brown. Where am I?"

Earl: "Norristown."

Bourne: "Where is that?"

Earl: "In Pennsylvania."

Bourne: "What time in the month is it?"

Earl: "The fourteenth."

Bourne: "Does time run backward here? When I left home it was the seventeenth."

Earl: "The seventeenth of what?"

Bourne: "The seventeenth of January."

Earl: "It's the fourteenth of March."

Earl thought that Brown had gone out of his mind, and sent for a Doctor Read, who listened to Bourne's story, and wired his family, asking if they knew an Ansel Bourne. The family hastily wired back that Ansel Bourne was very real, and had been missing. Bourne returned home; he remembered nothing at all of the eight weeks he had been "A. J. Brown," who had opened a small business in Norristown, where he had become known as a respectable and honest merchant.

At Harvard, Professor William James heard of this strange case and wondered if, by means of hypnosis, Bourne might learn what had happened to him during those blank eight weeks. Bourne agreed to the investigation, and traveled to Boston, where James proceeded to hypnotize him, using magnetic passes. Bourne proved a good subject and easily fell into trance, during which time he gave a complete account of his life as A. J. Brown. However, under hypnosis, Brown knew nothing of Bourne, and Bourne knew nothing of Brown. According to James, attempts were made "to produce a deeper trance in which the 'Brown' and 'Bourne' personalities might be unified. We could get no manifestation of either personality while the other was to the front, and at the end of our experiments, Bourne and Brown seemed as far as ever from realizing that each belonged to the other."

MULTIPLE CASES OF MULTIPLE PERSONALITY

The Bourne/Brown case is an interesting one of amnesia and double personality. There are other cases on record, not of just two personalities, but three, four, five, and even sixteen personalities occupying the same body. These, naturally, present more puzzling problems.

It has been estimated that in the past seventy years there have been about 150 cases of multiple personality reported in medical literature, including the famous "Miss Beauchamp" of Dr. Morton Prince, and Professor Janet's "Leonie." Until recently the most famous multiple personality case on record was the one described by psychiatrists Thigpen and Cleckley in their book *The Three Faces of Eve,* which was later made into an absorbing movie. Their patient, Eve White, was originally seen for psychiatric treatment because of severe headaches and occasional black-outs which had not responded to medical treatment. The authors describe Eve White at the first meeting as "a neat, colorless young woman," married and with one child. Gradually, over the course of an uneventful treatment, Eve's headaches lessened and she reported feeling much better, and after a year treatment was discontinued. A few months later an outraged husband, and a bewildered Eve, asked urgently to see the psychiatrists. Eve, it seemed, had gone on an unprecedented shopping spree during which she had bought expensive, seductive evening clothes which she would never have occasion to wear. Eve herself was aghast, saying she had no idea where the clothes had come from or how they had gotten into her closet. During a private interview, Eve grew troubled, confessed that she was "hearing voices," and said she was deeply afraid of going crazy. Even as the doctor was trying to reassure her, suddenly (in the authors' words) "Eve seemed momentarily dazed. Her body slowly stiffened. Closing her eyes, she winced as she put her hands to her temples. A slight shudder passed over her entire body." Then, with "a bright, unfamiliar voice that sparkled," the woman said, "Hi, there, doc!" This was the dramatic entrance of Eve Black, who knew all about Eve White and had nothing but contempt for her. When she was conscious, Eve White knew nothing of Eve Black. Eve Black had used the headaches as a way to "get out," which included having a good time buying expensive clothes, going to bars, and flirting with men—all without Eve White's knowledge.

During the following phase of the therapy, the two personalities would alternate, obligingly, for the doctors, until—just as suddenly—a third personality, who called herself Jane, emerged. Jane denied having even the slightest knowledge of either Eve White or Eve Black, commenting frequently that she had just been "born." Yet Jane seemed more intelligent, more aware, and more integrated than either of the Eves, who never knew that a third personality had arrived. Jane, however, quickly became familiar with the actions of both Eves, going with Black to dance halls, and with White to work, acting always as an observer without participating in their actions, having empathy for the problems of both. For almost a year the three personalities continued to exist in the one body, independently of each other. Eventually, the three seemed to coalesce, with Jane the surviving entity. Thigpen and Cleckley made an extensive survey of the literature on multiple personalities, made films demonstrating the two dramatically different Eves, offered various ideas about what may have happened, but confessed that they could not explain the phenomenon.

Very recently, at the UCLA Neuropsychiatric Institute, a young married woman named Ellen was admitted as an in-patient, with a history of black-outs and headaches, as well as suicide attempts. Like Eve, Ellen was a pretty, but colorless girl. But one day the resident psychiatrist, who was treating her, entered his office for a therapy session and was confronted by a mischievous, witty young woman who knew all about Ellen and detested her. It was this second personality, Letty, who had tried to kill Ellen during one of Ellen's black-outs, by rushing out into the middle of a freeway where cars were speeding by in both directions, and then "leaving" Ellen to fight her way to safety. Like Eve Black, Letty enjoyed "getting out," buying pretty clothes which Ellen would not buy, and having "fun." Shortly after Letty's appearance, another per-

sonality "got out." This third personality was very mu
Eve's Jane, in that "Number 3" was vicious and fierce
threatening to kill her therapist. It is considered that she n
made one attempt on his life. Number 3 was totally insens
pain: In a video tape which shows the three different personalities,
the psychiatrist sticks a pin deeply into Number 3's arm (as in a
test for deep hypnosis), with no reaction at all from the lady. The
goal of this resident psychiatrist was, like Professor James', to
integrate these personalities. And at this writing, he seems to have
had success.

· Oddly, over the next twelve months, three more cases of
multiple personality appeared on the wards of the Neuropsychiatric Institute.

Thus far, there is no satisfactory explanation for the multiple
personality, although several hypotheses have been offered. One is
that the patient is merely "role playing"; cleverly *acting* the
various personalities in order to attract special interest and attention from doctors and staff. Another idea, derived from psychoanalytic theory, suggests that the personality has "split" into the
trilogy of ego, id, and superego. For example, with both Eve and
Ellen, the first personality was a weak ego, and this made possible
the eruption of the id. The id is primarily interested in gratifying
its sexual drives in "having fun" or simply expressing anger, after
which the superego makes its appearance. The superego can act as
a form of conscience which may eventually dominate and direct
the other two aspects of the personality. A third hypothesis
maintains that these are "dissociative states," which can occur in
fugue, amnesia, under hypnosis, and in altered states of consciousness. The rationale here is that we all are different personalities:
We can be father, husband, employee, athlete, politician, chef,
etc., and any one of these parts of the personality can become cut
off from the others, causing a dissociation which might become
permanent. All of these explanations fit the forms of classical
psychology. There is another hypothesis, however: that a multiple
personality may be a form of "possession," the one body being
occupied by "spirits" of one kind or another.

The concept of "possession," while probably not at all satisfactory to explain the multiple personalities here described (or the

most recent case of Sybil, who in a lengthy psychoanalysis managed to fuse sixteen different personalities), is nevertheless one which may be worth examining.

CASES OF "POSSESSION"

The idea of being "possessed by spirits" is an ancient one. And as we have learned, in certain communities in Siberia and among certain Indians of South America and Eskimos, when an individual "possesses" his spirits, he is elevated to the rank of shaman or holy man, but when his spirits "possess" him, he is considered a sick person, unworthy of becoming a shaman.

We do not have this tradition in our Western culture. Those unfortunates who have been considered "possessed" have at certain periods of our history been burned at the stake as witches, and at other periods been confined to mental institutions. On rare occasions, medical men treating such persons have written in detail the case histories. One such history, again from the files of the ASPR and investigated by William James, is that of an eighteen-year-old girl treated by Dr. Ira Barrows, toward the end of the nineteenth century.

The Case of Miss Anna Winsor

Dr. Barrows was called in to treat Anna Winsor in 1890, after she became ill with typhoid fever. Her condition worsened, until Dr. Barrows described her as suffering from "hysteroepilepsy," with protracted, violent convulsions and intervals of "insane delusions." Here are excerpts from Dr. Barrows' extensive case history:

> June 16. Apparently unconscious of everything around her. She began, with her forefinger, to form letters on the sheet as if trying to spell some word. It was suggested that paper and pencil be given her. She began to write names of persons long since dead. Then about her own sickness, "It (always using the third person singular) will be a long time sick; lose her sense of smell, be blind for many months, doubtful if she ever walks again. Her sickness will develop many phases and strange phenomena."

Sept. 24. Complains of great pain in right arm, when suddenly it falls down by her side. She looks at it in amazement. Thinks it belongs to someone else. Cut it, prick it, she takes no notice of it. (For nearly 5 years, the hallucination remains firm. She believes that her arm is a foreign object, and a nuisance. She bites it, pounds it, calls it "Stump," saying, "Stump" has got this or that or the other that belongs to her.)

November 13. While sleeping, personates "Aunt Chloe," writes for flour, mixes and makes some biscuits, *uses both hands when asleep, when awake has no power to move the right.*

January 1. Raving delirium: pulls her hair nearly out of her head. *The right hand protects her against the left as much as possible.*

February 11. Commences a series of drawings with her right (paralyzed) hand, "Old Stump." Also writes poetry with it. I have sat by her bed and engaged her in conversation, and drawn her attention in various ways while the writing and drawing have been uninterrupted. She has never exhibited any taste for, or taken any lessons in drawing.

March. (She became blind, 4th January; is still blind) Sees as well with her eyes closed as open; keeps them closed most of the time. Reads and draws with them closed.

May 31. Imagines herself a dog; barks, growls, howls; sets dogs in the street to barking; laps water.

January, 1893. At night and during sleep, Stump writes letters, poetry, both asleep and awake. *This arm appears to have a separate intelligence. When she sleeps it writes or converses by signs. It never sleeps;* endeavors to prevent her from injuring herself or her clothing when she is raving."

This very sad case has an odd parallel in the fictional character of Dr. Strangelove, whose right hand constantly attempts to strangle his own throat and is prevented by his left hand, producing a struggle very similar to that described in Anna Winsor by Dr. Barrows.

According to shamanistic tradition, this would be a case of the spirit possessing the person. And so would the next case:

"The Watseka Wonder"

Lurancy Vennum, a fourteen-year-old girl in Watseka, Illinois, became ill with "fits" (possibly epilepsy), in which she would remain unconscious for hours; on regaining consciousness, she would speak of dead persons she had been visiting. Friends believed the girl had gone insane and should be committed, and Dr. E. W. Stevens was called in to examine her. When he first saw Lurancy, she told him she was an old woman named Katrina Hogan; later she said that she was a young man named Willie Canning. Eventually, Dr. Stevens hypnotized her, and she became calm, saying she had been controlled by evil spirits. Dr. Stevens suggested she had better control, and Lurancy obliged by "becoming" Mary Roff.

Indeed there had been a Mary Roff in Watseka, but she had died in 1865 when Lurancy had been one year old. This delusion that Lurancy had "become" Mary Roff persevered and intensified. Mary Roff's bereaved parents still lived in Watseka, and soon learned about Lurancy's delusion. Mrs. Roff, together with her daughter, Mrs. Minerva Alter, decided to visit the Vennums. As they came in sight, walking down the street, Lurancy/Mary saw them and exclaimed, "There comes ma and sister Nervie!" which is what Mary had called her sister Minerva as a child. Mary/Lurancy became so "homesick" for her "family" that the Roffs agreed to accept her into their home as their own daughter Mary. At the Roff's home, Mary/Lurancy seemed to know "every person and everything that Mary knew 12 to 15 years ago, calling by name friends and neighbors of the family." What is more, during the next four months, she did not recognize her own parents, the Vennums, nor their neighbors. Then, one day, "Mary called Mrs. Roff to a private room, and there in tears told her that Lurancy Vennum was coming back. . . . She sat down, closed her eyes, and in a few moments the change took place, and Lurancy had control of her own body. Looking wildly around the room, she anxiously asked, 'Where am I? I was never here before.' " Shortly afterward,

Lurancy returned to her own parents' home, apparently recovered. She continued to live with them until her marriage, and was never troubled by a recurrence of her illness. Lurancy's mother, Mrs. Vennum, wrote the following testimony:

> We give credit of her complete cure and restoration to her family to Dr. E. W. Stevens, and Mr. and Mrs. Roff, by their obtaining her removal to Mr. Roff's where her cure was perfected. We firmly believe had she remained at home, she would have died, or we would have been obliged to send her to the insane asylum; and if so, she would have died there. . . . Several of the relatives of Lurancy, including ourselves, now believe she was cured by spirit power, and that Mary Roff controlled the girl.

What can we make of this extraordinary case? We find the use of hypnosis to alleviate "fits and hallucinations"; during the hypnotic trance, a phenomenon remarkably like that called "possession" occurred. Instead of trying to repress that phase of the psychosis (if that's what it was), the doctor chose to accept it, and use it to eventuate a cure.

A much more recent, and possibly more complex case was reported by psychiatrist James McHarg at the Edinburg Parapsychology Conference in 1972. McHarg had been treating a fifty-eight-year-old woman for paranoid schizophrenia, which had begun in 1958, when her general depression suddenly erupted into hallucinations which she described as "malevolent agents bent on invading, down through the chimney and through the roof, her flat and her very person." (McHarg labelled this "Delusion 1.") These hallucinations continued so vividly that eventually she was admitted to the hospital, where five months later she began to feel that there was a "beast" inside her she had to "hawk up. She had gone around hawking and spitting into ash trays and plant pots over a period of fourteen months. Thereafter this delusion (Delusion 2) faded away." Next, in September 1963, the patient began to experience hallucinatory noises in her left ear, which she attributed to a "beast, eating its way into her brain" (Delusion 3).

After several years of unsuccessful treatment, McHarg discovered that a male patient, recently transferred to his care, had been complaining of persistent, peculiar noises in his left ear and that this patient was a long-estranged, younger brother of the woman patient. Neither brother or sister knew of the whereabouts of the other. This remarkable synchronicity (Jung's term for apparently unrelated, acausal events which occur together) led McHarg to study the progress notes of both patients, who had been treated for several years, by different doctors.

Quoting from McHarg's paper:

> The case records indicated, indeed, that the hallucinatory noises in the woman patient's left ear and the symptomatic noises in her brother's left ear had both come on in September 1963. It seemed also that the patient's increased apprehension about the supposed beast had developed concurrently with the increased apprehension of her brother about his own left-sided ear symptoms (until he became totally deaf in the left ear) and that the eventual subsidence of the patient's apprehension had taken place concurrently with the brother's apprehension as he became reconciled to his deafness.

This denouement concerning Delusion 3 inevitably drew McHarg's attention to Delusion 2: that of "hawking up beasts" by spitting into ash trays, etc. Again, in McHarg's words:

> Enquiry into this brought out that it had developed with the development in the brother of a productive cough which had eventually been found to be due to a bronchial carcinoma. It seemed, furthermore, that the maximum agitation of the patient about the beasts she believed she was expectorating had been reached in February, 1961, just prior to the operative removal of the brother's carcinoma. The complete resolution of this delusion, which followed, seemed to have coincided with the brother's complete recovery following the operation.

This left Delusion 1 to be explained, the threatened invasion by the "beasts" into her flat through the roof and chimney. McHarg points out that this threat of invasion could be interpreted to show a symbolic correspondence to the actual beginning of the malignancy, which the surgeon had established as having occurred sometime between 1957 and 1959 (the woman patient's first hallucinations having occurred at the midway point, in 1958). McHarg acknowledges that these correspondences, "each and all" may have been simply fortuitous; and he recommends that other psychopathological syndromes be investigated for similar findings. (Indeed, his case in some respects might be likened to the "possession" of Lurancy Vennum, or to Miss Anna Winsor's "Stump.")

ANOTHER TYPE OF "POSSESSION"

Thus far we have been examining very sick persons who seem to have been possessed in one way or another. In the shamanistic view, this is characteristic of sickness, when the "spirit" possesses the person. But, according to this same view, when the shaman "possesses" the spirit, he can obtain useful, otherwise unobtainable information. Obviously we lack this tradition in our culture; but we have had, and continue to have, trance mediums through whom "spirits" are presumed to speak. We have already emphasized the charlatanism of most "spirit communications" from trance mediums at fake seances.

But we have not discussed the fact that there are today, and there have been in the past, genuine trance mediums who seem to have the ability to go into an altered state of consciousness (trance), and in that state make statements, which have been verified, about events totally unknown to the medium. Furthermore, on returning to consciousness, the medium usually has no knowledge of the statements that have been made while entranced. This split in consciousness may be similar to the split that occurs in amnesia, multiple personality, and hypnosis, but in at least one respect, there is a difference. The trance medium generally has control over one factor: He decides when, and where, he will go into trance.

TRANCE MEDIUM: MRS. AILEEN GARRETT

Aileen Garrett developed the ability to go into trance, at will, early in her life, and kept the ability until her death in 1971. She confesses in her autobiography, *Many Voices,* that the phenomenon never ceased to bewilder her. In her efforts to under-

nd the nature of the two "guides" who spoke through her
uring trance (one named Abdul Latif, the other Uvani), Mrs.
Garrett undertook a thorough psychoanalysis with the distinguished psychiatrist Dr. Adolph Meyer. She also permitted researcher Hereward Carrington to monitor her with physiological
equipment during her trances. It was learned that Mrs. Garrett's
metabolism in her normal state was distinctly different from the
metabolism of Uvani, in trance, and both Mrs. Garrett and Uvani
gave a different metabolism than Abdul Latif, the other guide
during trance. There was never any explanation found for the
phenomenon, although Mrs. Garrett was untiring in her cooperation with laboratory investigations.

In 1930, in an English laboratory, she went into trance and
Uvani promptly appeared. But suddenly the voice changed and
announced itself as Flight-Lieutenant H. Carmichael Irwin, captain
of a dirigible which had crashed in France two days before. A
transcript of the Irwin voice was made, in which minute details of
the accident were reported. This transcript was later sent to British
Air Minister Sir John Simon, who verified the communication,
which included details unknown to anyone, to be correct in a
line-by-line analysis.

Mrs. Garrett gave many such seances, frequently producing
nothing verifiable, but occasionally producing material like that in
the Irwin case. About these "guides" or "spirit controls," Mrs.
Garrett had a definite opinion:

> I prefer to think of the controls as principals of the
> subconscious. . . . I long ago accepted them as working
> symbols of the subconscious. I definitely believe the
> entities are formed from the spiritual and emotional
> needs of the person involved. They are able to watch
> over, and in a sense, guard against the outside or inside
> menacing influences. Without these aspects of person-
> ality, I might not have made such extensive effort to-
> ward understanding the nature of mind. For myself, I
> have never been able wholly to accept them as spirit
> dwellers on the threshold, which they seem to believe
> they are.

Mrs. Garrett was never aware of anything these guides said when
they "spoke through her"; but it seems she made efforts to keep

them in perspective, and under control, rather than have them dominate her life. According to the shamanistic view, she may not have possessed her spirits, but neither did she permit them to possess her. And for the whole of her long life, she contributed of herself, and of her finances, to further the progress of psychical research.

TRANCE MEDIUM: ARTHUR FORD

Very much like Aileen Garrett, Arthur Ford for over forty years cooperated with scientists who studied him in both normal and trance states. Experiments ranged from work with Sir Oliver Lodge in the 1920s, to work with scientists in 1968, who used the same telemetry equipment on Ford that is used to monitor the physiology of astronauts in space. Unlike Mrs. Garrett, Ford believed that the guide who spoke through him during trance was a true spirit being.

Like many psychics, Ford learned as a child that he often knew what other people were thinking, but believed that everyone had a similar faculty. It was not until his participation in World War I that he appreciated how unusual his talent was, for he found that he would frequently dream he was reading casualty lists, noticing the names of fellow-soldiers, and the next day would find his dream to have been altogether too accurate. (Again, we find biocommunication coming precognitively, in the dream.) After his discharge from the service, Ford began to study for the ministry, and was fortunate in finding that rara avis, a professor of psychology who was not only interested in his psychic experiences but also conversant with research in parapsychology. This research encouraged Ford to further his own experimentations, and he soon discovered that he could go into trance, during which reliable information would be produced. Like most true trance mediums, Ford was totally unconscious during the trance periods and never knew what was spoken through him until notes taken during the trance were read to him. Quite suddenly, in 1924, a "guide" broke into a trance, saying: "When Ford wakes up, tell him from now on I will be his control, and that I go by the name of Fletcher." Fletcher remained with Ford until his death, providing astonishingly accurate information at times, but totally failing at other times. Ford, being scientifically oriented, wanted as much verification of Fletcher's identity as possible and asked sitters at seances to inquire about Fletcher in detail. Fletcher willingly supplied information, which included his last name, the military unit in which he served during World War I, and the manner in which he had been killed in action. All these details were verified.

Far more impressive than this demonstration (which could easily have been faked) was Fletcher's contribution to the Houdini challenge. Harry Houdini, the reader may remember, had spent years of his life exposing false mediums. He had done more than that: He had made a pact with his wife, Beatrice, that the one to die first would attempt to communicate to the other a message (via a medium), using the complex code they had employed in their magic act, a code which no one in the world but the Houdinis knew. Houdini died in 1926, and Beatrice Houdini was flooded with alleged messages from her decreased husband, none of which were in the least accurate. In 1928, during Ford's seances, Fletcher began to speak extensively about Houdini, and the message for his wife. Eventually Beatrice Houdini agreed to participate in a series of seances, which were attended by reputable people, including an editor of *Scientific American*. Everything said during the seances was transcribed by an expert in shorthand. At the conclusion of the seances, Mrs. Houdini made a public statement verifying that "the long, precisely worded communication" had been delivered in the complex code which had been used in the Houdini's vaudeville act.

Mrs. Houdini's statement made headlines in the news for weeks. Arthur Ford was suddenly world-famous, and he was promptly denounced by skeptics everywhere as a fraud. Ford constantly offered to demonstrate his talents for scientists and for universities, and sometimes the results were like those in the incident described below, which took place at a midwest college noted for the quality of its scholarship and the integrity of its faculty. Records were kept which included this report:

> At one point, Ford said, "I get a name something like Brazil. Brazila. It is a person's name...." He said this has to do with a scholarship and with the name Brazila. No one spoke up and after a few more attempts, Fletcher dropped the subject with obvious frustration.

After the sitting one of the professors present said to another who had been present, "You know, when Arthur Ford was talking about Brazila? Well, I don't believe in any of this stuff so of course I refused to speak up. But I knew exactly what he was talking about. The college used to have an award that was called the Brazila scholarship."

This kind of audience behavior still bedevils psychical research. Occasionally the reverse behavior occurs. Instead of denying the known, some persons pursue the unknown, as in this instance given by Dr. M. Edmund Speare, former professor at Harvard and an editor of the Oxford University Press. Speare kept detailed records of his six sittings with Ford in 1966 (a year after the death of the professor's wife, Florence). Here is an excerpt from Dr. Speare's report:

Every word at these sittings was tape recorded; for some messages it has taken me months to verify, [and] the great majority of them proved correct. Statements are always Fletcher's. Comments of mine are in parentheses.

1. Florence says, "There is a person here who knows about you. His name is David Little; he was Curator of the Harvard Theatre collection; he was Master of Adams House at Harvard. Did you know him?" (Speare: No, I never heard of him. There was no Adams House in my Harvard days.)

(Comment. I phoned the Curator and asked, "Who was David Little? Was he ever a Curator of the Harvard Drama collection?" Her answer: "No, he was never Curator, but he did much curatorial work during his life at Harvard. He died before I came here; he was Master of Adams House here—a House built long after you taught at Harvard.")

Like most genuine mediums, Ford never promised that he could obtain the requested information, but he was always ready to accept a challenge. Probably the greatest of his challenges was his appearance on a Canadian TV program in 1967 with Bishop Pike. Pike's interest in psychic phenomena had strongly increased after the death of his son, Jim, and the strange events which followed, documented in Pike's book *The Other Side.* In Pike's words, "The plan of the program was that Ford would attempt to go into trance and we would see what—if anything—happened." Ford did go into trance, for two hours on TV, during which time Fletcher gave several details, not only about Pike's son, but other persons known to Pike, some of whom he barely remembered. Headlines in the world's newspapers made a travesty of the television program, claiming it had been a melodramatic stunt in which Bishop Pike had been duped by a clever charlatan, who played shamelessly on Pike's emotional travail over his son's death. The Bishop was very much aware of the possibility of fraud, and several months later arranged for another private session with Ford. Again there was a flow of information from Fletcher, sometimes vague, sometimes specific, as in this tape-recorded statement: "Tell George Livermore—you'll be seeing him soon—that Caroline will be coming over soon." So much other material was presented in the seance that the Bishop ignored this datum, not really knowing who "Caroline" was. Shortly afterward, at a Christmas service, Pike saw George Livermore and spoke with him briefly. Six weeks later, he learned from his secretary that Mrs. Livermore had died. Suddenly, the Bishop remembered the words of Fletcher, and asked if his secretary remembered Mrs. Livermore's first name. She did, and it was Caroline.

For Bishop Pike, Fletcher's performance was convincing; it was quite the contrary for skeptics who saw or read about the television program. Arthur Ford, who died in 1971, was very much aware that he had never found a way to convince the nonbeliever. No one ever has.

TRANCE MEDIUM: EDGAR CAYCE

One January day in 1912, a Harvard professor named Dr. Hugo Munsterberg traveled by train to Hopkinsville, Kentucky, drove to Edgar Cayce's home, introduced himself to the thirty-four-year-old man, saying, "I have come here to expose you." Munsterberg had in his possession several news clippings about Cayce, including one from the *New York Times,* which Cayce had not seen. Its heading read: "Illiterate Man Becomes Doctor When Hypnotized—

Strange Power Shown by Edgar Cayce Puzzles Physicians." The article contained a paper presented to the American Society of Clinical Research in Boston, by Dr. Wesley Ketchum, "a reputable physician of high standing and successful practice." Here are excerpts from the *Times'* article:

> Dr. Ketchum is not the only physician who has had the opportunity to observe the workings of Mr. Cayce's subconscious mind. For nearly ten years his strange power has been known to local physicians of all recognized schools. Dr. Ketchum's paper starts: "About four years ago I made the acquaintance of a young man 28 years old, who had the reputation of being "a freak." They said he told wonderful truths while he was asleep. As I was "from Missouri," I had to be shown.
>
> "And truly, when it comes to anything psychical, every layman is a disbeliever from the start, and most of our chosen profession will not accept anything of a psychical nature, hypnosis, mesmerism, or what not, unless vouched for by some M.D. away up in the profession. . . .
>
> "My subject simply lies down and by auto-suggestion goes to sleep. While in this sleep, he becomes unconscious to pain of any sort, and strange to say, his best work is done when seemingly he is 'dead to the world.'
>
> "I give him the name of my patient and the exact location of same, and in a few minutes, he begins to talk as clearly and distinctly as anyone. His language is usually of the best, and his psychological terms and descriptions of the nervous anatomy would do credit to any professor of nervous anatomy; which is to me quite wonderful, in view of the fact that while in his normal state he is an illiterate man, especially along the lines of medicine, surgery, or pharmaceutics.
>
> "The cases I have used him in have, in the main, been the rounds before coming to my attention, and in six important cases which had been diagnosed as strictly surgical he stated that no such condition existed, and outlined treatment which was followed with gratifying results. One case, a little girl, daughter of a gentleman prominent in the American Book Company of Cincinnati, had been diagnosed by the best men in the Central

States as incurable. One diagnosis from my man completely changed the situation, and within three months, she was restored to perfect health, and is so to this day."

The article goes on to tell how Ketchum had once asked Cayce, in trance, to give the source of his knowledge. The reply came:

Edgar Cayce's mind is amenable to suggestion, the same as all other subconscious minds. Further, the subconscious mind is in direct communication with all other subconscious minds. In addition, Cayce's mind has the power to interpret to the objective mind of others what it acquires from the subconscious mind of others.

Ketchum concluded his paper by saying that Cayce had given "more than 1,000 readings, but had never turned his wonderful powers to pecuniary advantage."

Munsterberg waited for Cayce to finish reading the article and then asked Cayce how he did his "tricks." Cayce referred him to the subconscious mind being in direct communication with all other subconscious minds. (Here we might interject that this concept bears a striking resemblance to Carl Jung's concept of a "collective unconscious," an idea which Jung had not yet formalized on paper.) Munsterberg's answer to Cayce was simple: "The story of the subconscious mind," he said, "can be told in three words: there is none."

Munsterberg remained in Hopkinsville to talk to the local townspeople about Cayce and to witness a reading by Cayce, given in the standard way. Dr. Ketchum brought his patient to Cayce's home, where he was taken to a small room. Munsterberg was permitted to observe the proceedings, and a stenographer recorded everything which transpired, for Cayce, like so many mediums, knew nothing of what happened when he was in trance. Cayce's father, Leslie, was also present, standing at the head of the couch. Cayce proceeded to sit on the edge of the couch, loosen his shoelaces, undo his tie, and unfasten his cuff links. Then he lay down on the couch, flat on his back, closed his eyes, and folded his hands over his abdomen. Gradually his breathing deepened until he seemed to be asleep. Then Leslie Cayce read aloud from a notebook: "You will have before you the body of (the patient's name), who is present in this room. You will go over the body carefully, telling us the conditions you find there, and what may be done to correct anything that is wrong." For several minutes there was silence. Then a mumbling, which was incoherent, followed by Cayce's suddenly clearing his throat and speaking in a strong voice: "Yes, we have the body here." There followed a long description of the patient's condition and what should be done to remedy it, everything being transcribed in shorthand. Finally Cayce's voice said, "We are through for the present." Leslie Cayce gave the suggestion he return to normal consciousness, and after a few minutes Cayce yawned, opened his eyes, and sat up. Dr. Munsterberg suddenly turned to the patient and asked, "What do you think of this man?" The patient replied that Cayce had described his condition better than he could have himself. Then Munsterberg said slowly: "If I were you . . . I would do exactly as he says. From what I have heard from the people I have talked to . . . some extraordinary benefits have come."

Munsterberg had spent his time in Hopkinsville interviewing several of the persons Cayce had helped. One of the most impressive cases he heard about came from the mother of a fifteen-year-old girl named Aime Dietrich. According to Aime's mother, when her daughter was two years old, she had caught the grippe, after which she had developed severe convulsions, which continued and resulted in brain damage. The damage worsened over the next two years in spite of treatment by medical experts in several cities, one of whom had told Mrs. Dietrich that Aime was suffering from a rare brain affliction which was invariably fatal. Aime was brought home to die; and only then did Mrs. Dietrich go to Edgar Cayce, about whom she had been skeptical, since she had known him as a local youth of very little schooling. Cayce, in trance, had said that before Aime had caught the grippe, she had suffered a spinal injury in a fall (which fall was corroborated by Mrs. Dietrich, although she had considered it a minor incident). He then gave specific information about where the lesion in the spine was and what should be done to correct it. According to Aime's mother, at the end of the first week of treatment, the child, who had lost the power of speech, suddenly called out the name of a doll she had loved. This was the beginning of a cure that brought her swiftly back to the mental level of a normal five-year-old. At the age of fifteen, Aime was a normal, healthy girl.

Dr. Ketchum also discussed Cayce's work with Munsterberg, giving remarkable details about an early case, in which Cayce had suggested a medication called "Oil of Smoke." Ketchum had never heard of the preparation, nor was it listed in the pharmaceutical catalogs, and so another reading was held in which he asked Cayce where the medication could be found. The name of a drugstore in Louisville, Kentucky, was given, and Ketchum wired for the preparation. The manager wired back saying he had never heard of it. So a third reading was held, and it was learned that on a shelf in the back of the drugstore, behind another preparation (which was named) would be found a bottle of "Oil of Smoke." Ketchum wired this to the manager of the Louisville store, who wired back, "Found it." And the medication was sent.

Stories like these left Munsterberg bewildered and bemused. He told Cayce he would like to know more about these phenomena, because he would hesitate to pass judgment without a long and thorough investigation. But Munsterberg left Hopkinsville, and never returned.

Others had come to investigate Cayce before and after Munsterberg, some of them not so gentle in their methods. Several years before, for example, a group of local doctors had invited Cayce to give a demonstration at a monthly meeting of their club. At the meeting, as usual, Cayce put himself to sleep on a couch, and was then given the name and address of a patient of one of the doctors present. (This was all the information that was ever required.) After some minutes came the words, "Yes, we have the body." This was followed by the statements, "He is recovering from an attack of typhoid fever. The pulse is 96; the temperature 101.4°." The doctor of the patient then said the diagnosis was correct, and a committee of three went to check on the patient's temperature and pulse. While the committee was gone, an argument developed as to the state of consciousness Cayce was in; to find out, in spite of protests from Cayce's associates, one of the doctors stuck a needle in Cayce's arms, hands, and feet. Since there was no response, another doctor took a hatpin, which he thrust entirely through Cayce's cheeks. Still no response. Another doctor said something to the effect that Cayce was probably "hardened to all that" (?!), then took out his penknife, with which he lifted Cayce's nail from his left forefinger. Again, no response.

However, shortly afterward Cayce woke up and immediately felt sharp pain, and became angry. The doctors explained that they were merely performing "a few scientific tests." His temper getting the better of him, Cayce denounced the scientists, saying he had permitted various doctors to make various kinds of "tests," but that the tests were performed simply to prove that he was a fake. He vowed then that he would never again submit to such tests or try to prove anything to the medical profession. (Incidentally, his nail never again grew normally.)

In spite of that uncharacteristic outburst, Cayce did submit time and time again to many investigations during his forty years of mediumship.

How did Edgar Cayce develop his extraordinary ability? As has often been the case, by chance, through hypnosis. As a young man, he had suffered from a chronic throat ailment which forced him to speak in little more than a hoarse whisper. He had gone to many doctors but had obtained no relief. During this period, a stage hypnotist named Hart arrived in Hopkinsville, met Cayce, and offered him a proposition: He would use hypnosis to cure Cayce's ailment; if he succeeded, he was to be paid two hundred dollars; if not, there would be no fee. Cayce agreed, and with friends observing the procedure, Cayce was quickly hypnotized. Under hypnosis, he was able to speak in a healthy, clear voice. But when he returned to consciousness, his hoarseness immediately returned. (This is not an uncommon occurrence in hypnotherapy today; but at that time the phenomenon was not well known.) Eventually, a report of Cayce's case was sent to an expert hypnotist, a medical doctor in New York with the delightful name of Quackenboss. Remarkably, Dr. Quackenboss became sufficiently interested in Cayce's case to travel to Hopkinsville, where he succeeded in inducing a "very very deep sleep" in Cayce, so deep that no one, including Quackenboss, was able to waken him for twenty-four hours. When Cayce eventually did wake up, spontaneously, his voice was no better. Quackenboss returned to New York, but continued to mull over the case. Fortunately, Quackenboss was a scholar, and remembered early experiments conducted in France by the Marquis de Puysegur. The Marquis had been able to deeply hypnotize a peasant boy named Victor, and under hypnosis Victor had been able to diagnose and treat the sick. (We have already discussed a similar situation, in Phineas Quimby's early work with mesmerism: He had been able to hypnotize Lucius deeply, and under hypnosis Lucius—never Quimby—had been able to diagnose and treat the sick, including Quimby himself.)

Quackenboss wrote to Cayce, suggesting that a hypnotist try to get Cayce to do what Victor and Lucius had done: diagnose and treat himself. Obviously, this was a long shot. And in Hopkinsville there were no hypnotists, except for an amateur named Al Layne. Despite family objections, Cayce and Layne agreed to try just one experiment. Cayce would put himself to sleep (he had learned to do this when others had tried to hypnotize him). Then, when Layne saw that Cayce was well into his "auto-suggestion," Layne would ask Cayce to describe the condition of his own throat. This procedure was followed one afternoon in 1901. After Layne's suggestion was repeated many times, Cayce began to mumble incoherently; then suddenly in a clear voice, for the first time, came those strange introductory words: "Yes, we have the body." The voice went on to describe the throat condition, and to prescribe the remedy, which was for the circulation to increase in the afflicted parts. While Cayce continued to sleep, and onlookers watched, Cayce's throat, neck, and chest turned first pink, then red. Twenty minutes passed, and then Cayce, still in trance, spoke again: "It's all right now." When Layne brought him back to normal consciousness, Cayce's voice was clear and strong. And it remained that way.

(Here we might remember that, seventy years later, the Swami Rama, at the Menninger Laboratory, demonstrated that he could so manipulate the circulation of the blood in his palm that, in Dr. Green's words, "the left side of his palm had turned rosy red, and the right side of the palm ashen gray." Too, the reader may remember that after biofeedback training, laboratory mice could control differential blood flow to each ear. It would seem that under hypnosis, Cayce was similarly able to control the circulation of blood to his neck and throat.)

Gradually, as news of Cayce's cure spread, others began to ask for his trance "readings," and despite his reluctance (he never knew what happened to him in trance and was afraid he might do harm), his help was sought by ever-increasing numbers of sick people. Right up to his death, in 1945, Cayce continued to give readings, records of which were meticulously kept. Today, more than 30,000 such reports are available for research purposes at the Association for Research and Enlightenment at Virginia Beach.

Cayce was always puzzled (and sometimes alarmed) by his mysterious gift. Every reading began with, "Yes, we have the body." But Cayce never learned who the "we" were who had the body, or where they had it. Only gradually did he learn to trust the readings which, when he first read them in his conscious state, he could not understand, having had only a seventh-grade education. Attempts were always made to follow up on the cases he treated, but as medical science knows too well, follow-ups are difficult to obtain. The problems here were even more difficult, since the majority of readings were done at a distance, in reply to letters received by Cayce from all over the world.

It is probably true that Cayce helped many people, but in all likelihood he failed as often as he succeeded. I met one former Cayce patient, now a psychologist, who as a child accidentally cut his eye with scissors. The doctors insisted his eye had to be removed, but a Cayce reading recommended application of special poultices, and the eye was saved. When I met him, he was middle-aged and did not wear eyeglasses. I also met another man who had gone to Cayce for a reading, followed his suggested treatment, and almost lost his life as a result, or so he believes.

Although Cayce never charged a fee, and was always poor, he was constantly under suspicion and occasionally in trouble with the law for practicing medicine without a license. Several licensed doctors, like Ketchum, came to Cayce for help with difficult cases, but Cayce and his family longed for genuine scientific validation. During one reading, they asked what the best method for scientific investigation would be. The information obtained said that should a student stay, day after day, watching the readings and examining the constant stream of mail, checking with the patients and physicians, the work could be proved, but only to that one student. He would not be able to convince others. Apparently it has ever been thus, in psychical research. I have often found myself in the same position with colleagues, whether the research be in skin vision, ESP, or Kirlian photography.

After Cayce's death, some scientists did become interested in the work he had done. Dr. William McGarey, of Phoenix, Arizona, studied the Cayce readings relating to specific cures for specific illnesses, and he discovered that a rare skin disease, sclera derma, considered incurable by modern medicine, had been diagnosed and successfully treated by Cayce. McGarey tried the treatment suggested in the Cayce readings, and in 1969, reported that he had obtained remission of sclera derma in eight cases which had been diagnosed as incurable.

Cayce's scholarly son, Hugh Lynn, was particularly anxious to validate his father's work. One day a book he had sought (long out of print) was finally located. When it arrived, Hugh Lynn read *Principles of Nature, Her Divine Revelations* with mounting excitement for it contained biographical details of a man who, although he had lived more than seventy-five years before his father, had done almost exactly the same kind of work!

TRANCE MEDIUM: ANDREW JACKSON DAVIS

By this time, surely, the reader will be able to describe how as a boy, A. J. Davis developed his psychic ability. Should there be anyone in doubt, the story is as follows: A mesmerist came to Poughkeepsie, New York, in the 1830s, and demonstrated the phenomenon of mesmerism to volunteers from his audience. Andrew was a volunteer who was *not* successfully mesmerized. After the stage performer had gone on to other lectures, a local tailor experimented with Andrew. And, like Lucius for Quimby, and like Victor for de Puysegur, Andrew fell into a deep trance, during which he developed remarkable clairvoyant powers. After several months of demonstrations, the boy said in trance that his powers were to be used to help the sick. This injunction was obeyed, and eventually a skeptic and medical doctor, S. S. Lyon, became convinced of Davis' gift, and was for many years his devoted associate. Like Cayce, Davis could use his healing skills only in mesmeric trance (induced by passes). His work continued for thirty-five years, at which time Davis decided to study medicine. When sixty years of age, he received his M.D. degree and began legitimate medical practice. But he continued to obtain his best results psychically, by placing his fingertips against the palm of his patient's hand. (Like Quimby, but unlike Cayce, he no longer needed the trance.) Andrew Jackson Davis died at the age of eighty-four, after writing several books based on his readings. Most had little to do with medicine, but much to do with metaphysics.

Hugh Lynn Cayce pored over Davis' book with his father. Both men were struck by the startling similarity between Davis' life and Edgar Cayce's. Hugh Lynn suggested that with such corroborative evidence, science would have to pay attention to the phenomenon. Edgar Cayce shook his head in disagreement, saying that if Andrew Jackson Davis, and Victor, and Cayce were all to give readings on the same case, and were they all to agree, and if a medical doctor called in by scientists, were to state that the diagnosis was correct—the scientists would probably hang the doctor as a fraud, and run the others out of town.

Perhaps Cayce's diagnosis in this instance was as correct as others he had made.

FROM FUGUE TO ?

We have looked at a range of behaviors, from brief lapses of consciousness to long trance-like states, sometimes voluntarily induced. We have seen evidence that during trance accurate and sometimes remarkably helpful information may be channeled through the entranced person, who, on his return to a normal waking state, remains unconscious of what has been said through him.

We have learned that in primitive communities, communications which arrive in trance are accepted as precious messages when given by the shaman who "possesses" his spirits; but other utterances in trance, when given by someone whom the spirit "possesses," are considered the ravings of a sick person. Contemporary medical science holds for the most part to this latter view, that "voices" heard or unheard are either auditory hallucinations or the ravings of a schizophrenic.

It is suggested that in the next section we entertain the earlier hypothesis: that messages received in trance states, or from other levels of consciousness, may on occasion contain information of value, information which arrives from as yet uncharted realms of the mind.

Part III: Other Realms

11 On the Limitations of Science

A thought that sometimes makes me hazy:
Am I—or are the others crazy?

—Albert Einstein

TWO TYPES OF SCIENTIFIC INQUIRY

Thus far in our explorations of ineluctable phenomena we have generally been able to offer either controlled experiments or well-supported anecdotal evidence. And we have seen that parapsychologists, whenever possible, have employed rigorous scientific methodology to validate in the laboratory the observations that have been made in natural surroundings. Not that science is always able to follow that course. Phenomena like earthquakes and exploding stars, for example, have not yet been created under laboratory conditions. But, when an accident occurs, such as a meteorite falling from the sky, the phenomenon is intensively studied for all the information it offers. Thus, what the meteorite reveals about its journey can help us better understand the nature of that space through which man now travels.

Interestingly, during the eighteenth century, meteorites were the subject of considerable controversy, for most physicists of that era believed it impossible that stones should fall from the sky. The great French scientist Anton Lavoisier, who almost single-handedly created the science of chemistry from the mystique of alchemy, was asked by the French Academy of Science to investigate an alleged fall of a meteorite. Here is an excerpt from his report on that event:

True physicists have always been doubtful of the existence of these stones. However, we shall faithfully report the fact communicated to us, and we shall then see what conclusions we can draw.

On September 13, 1768, at half-past four in the afternoon, a sharp thunderclap was heard which resembled the report of a gun. Then, a considerable whistling sound was heard in the air, without any appearance of fire. Several crofters looked up and saw an opaque body describing a curve, and falling on a meadow. They all ran up to the spot and found a sort of stone about half buried in the earth, but it was so hot and burning that it was impossible to touch it. [Eventually] M. l'Abbe Bachelay, having procured a piece of this stone, expressed a wish that its nature might be determined.

We shall give an account of the experiments we have made with the object. . . . Having reduced the stone to powder we combined it directly with black flux and obtained a black glass. After calcination, we proceeded to reduction. We only obtained a black alkaline mass, and hence concluded that the metal contained in the stone is iron, combined with alkali.

[More analyses were made, on the basis of which we] must conclude therefore that the stone *did not fall from the sky*. The opinion which seems to us the most probable and agrees best with the principles accepted in physics is that this stone was struck by lightning. We can only conclude that lightning falls by preference on metallic substances.

On the basis of Lavoisier's laboratory analysis, despite witnesses who saw the stone *fall*, it was decided by scientists that there was no such thing as a meteorite; and museums around the world threw away their "stones struck by lightning." It was thirty-five years before Lavoisier's opinion was reversed.

SCIENCE OUTSIDE THE LABORATORY

Obviously, not all discovery has been the result of controlled laboratory experiment. Who can say by what methods man first evolved the wheel, the use of fire, and the extraordinary wisdom of placing seeds in the ground and then waiting six or eight months for the emergence of food?

In this next section we will be examining some presumed phenomena for which there is little or no laboratory experimentation, much less corroboration. Those few scientists who are interested have not yet found adequate methods to investigate such oddities as poltergeists, ghosts, ectoplasm, journeys out of the body, or life after death. To most rational men, these belong to primitive "magical thinking," to the hallucinations of a disturbed mind, to conscious or unconscious deception, or to the overwhelming desire in most of mankind to believe in its immortality.

This is a rational point of view. But is it correct? Remember Lavoisier's analysis, and his conclusions based on "principles accepted by physics."

THE POSSIBILITY OF OTHER REALITIES

Might there be realms of existence about which we know almost nothing? Today we are much concerned with space travel and the possibility of life in other solar systems (and elsewhere in our own), life which may exist in forms very different from life as we know it. We hear, year after year, of UFOs, which are generally dismissed as meteorites or mirages, helicopters or hallucinations, swamp gas, comets, or exploratory models of new flying machines. That intrepid explorer of the psyche, Carl Jung, once published a paper on UFOs, explaining them as projections we make of our unconscious fears or desires. In 1958, after the paper was published, Jung tells us in *Memories, Dreams and Reflections* of a dream he had:

> I caught sight from my house of two lens-shaped metallically gleaming discs which hurtled down to the lake. They were UFOs. Immediately after, another came speeding through the air: a lens with a metallic extension which led to a box—a magic lantern. It stood still in the air, pointing straight at me. I awoke with a feeling of astonishment. Still half in the dream, the thought passed through my head: "We always think that UFOs are

> projections of ours. Now it turns out that we are their
> projections. I am projected by the magic lantern as
> Carl G. Jung. But who manipulates the apparatus?"

Jung's dream is reminiscent of the remark made by a Chinese sage who, on waking from sleep, said: "I have been dreaming I was a butterfly—or is it that I am a butterfly now dreaming I am a man?"

The question concerns reality. What is reality? Is this world, and its inhabitants, the only reality? Or might there be other realms, with their own kinds of reality, very different from our own? Since science concerns itself primarily with the dimensions of the physical world, it has developed no method to examine other possible, nonphysical realms. Therefore we must rely chiefly on anecdotal data and the myths in our world cultures. These myths, we will come to learn, often give remarkably similar descriptions of other realms.

The reason for such similarity might be, perhaps, a psychological or even physiological one. For instance, scientists have long known that there are dramatic individual differences between people and that such differences can create a drastically different reality. On a simple level, the reality of an eight-foot-tall basketball player must be extremely different from that of a pygmy. The world of the deaf must be different from the world of the hearing, and the world of those with no taste buds different from that of a gourmet. Scientists have recently learned that a few members of the youngest generation can see into the ultraviolet region, a region which for most of us is invisible. Certain American Indians can see different colors of black, and have given those colors (which look the same to us) different names. It may be that the shaman or psychic lives in a different reality than most of us know; he may experience phenomena too subtle for our more gross senses.

But of course, we can only rely on their subjective reports, which are soft data. And since many readers may have little patience with soft data, dismissing it to the realm of fiction, let me borrow from that genre and give a synopsis of the science fiction story *Preposterous* by Frederic Brown. In the story an irate Mr. Weatherwax castigates his wife, at breakfast, for permitting their son to read trash like "Astounding Stories" with such "impossibly wild" ideas as telekinesis and travel in other galaxies via space warps. Then he leaves the apartment, steps into an "antigravity" shaft, floats gently down two hundred stories to the street, where he luckily finds a free atomcab, whose robot driver heads directly for Moonport. This permits Mr. Weatherwax to settle back and tune in on the "telepathecast." Unfortunately, no information is available about the Fourth Martian War, just a routine bulletin from Immortality Center. Rather than tune in on that, our hero "quirtles."

Rather than read the next chapters, there may be readers who, like Mr. Weatherwax, will prefer to quirtle.

12 Can We Get Out Of Our Bodies?

> The notion that the physical body of man is as it were the exteriorization of an invisible subtle embodiment of the life of the mind is a very ancient belief. Conjectures concerning it vary with every stage of culture and differ within every stage. But the underlying conception invariably holds its ground. . . .
>
> I am persuaded that, the more deeply modern research penetrates into biology, psychophysiology and psychology, the more readily will [it] coordinate the mental, vital and physical phenomena of human personality which otherwise remain on our hands as a confused and inexplicable conglomerate.
> —G. R. A. Mead

DISTORTIONS OF BODY IMAGE

Behavioral scientists have long been familiar with the schizophrenic who describes weird changes taking place in his body: He may feel as if his body has become very, very small or enormously tall; his head may feel detached from his body; or, as in the case of Anna Winsor and her "Stump," he may be convinced that an arm or leg does not belong to him. People who are not mentally ill, but under temporary stress (psychological or physical), sometimes report feeling similar distortions in their bodies or feeling no consciousness of body at all.

As we have already mentioned, someone blacked out from too much alcohol may carry on all kinds of activities, but be absolutely unconscious of having done so. The reverse is also possible: One's body may lie totally inert, as in profound sleep, coma, or hypnosis, but one's consciousness may travel. We find vivid descriptions of this phenomenon in certain altered states of consciousness, reported both as anecdotes and as experiments under laboratory conditions.

For example, as the reader may remember, during his six months of total isolation at the South Pole Admiral Byrd described how, while lying inert on his bed, he sometimes felt as if he were "floating like a bird in disembodied space." In subsequent laboratory studies of sensory deprivation, subjects reported drastic changes in body sensations. One man reported that he felt as if he had "two overlapping bodies, side by side," and another man experienced his mind as "a ball of cotton wool floating above the body."

Under hypnosis, too, strong distortions of body image can be elicited. The subject can be told that his arm or leg has disappeared or that his hand is made of iron, and he will feel and behave exactly as if these suggestions were the reality. On some occasions, after a hypnotic session, a subject may describe feeling as if he had been "floating above his body," observing what was happening even though his eyes were closed. Similarly, under self-hypnosis, auto-suggestion, or in the early stages of meditation, it is not uncommon for the person to feel strange sensations of bodily distortion, as if his head were endlessly expanding or as if his body had become weightless and he was floating in space.

In her autobiography Saint Theresa described how during spiritual exercises, "one feels one has been wholly transported into another and different region. The soul is suspended in such a way that it seems to be completely outside itself."

Drug experiences may at times elicit the same kind of experience. Chemist Albert Hoffman reported on that first famous LSD trip: "My ego was suspended somewhere in space and I saw my body lying down on the sofa." When Carlos Castaneda smoked Don Juan's psychedelic mixture, he describes how, when his nose was running, he tried to wipe it with the back of his hand, and his upper lip was rubbed off; then, in wiping his face, his flesh was wiped away, or melted; terrified, he tried to grab onto a pole with both hands, but his hands went right through the pole. He staggered back against the wall, and his whole body melted into it. Eventually, under Don Juan's guidance, Castaneda began to feel as if he were moving with "tremendous lightness and speed in water or air. . . . I contorted and twisted and soared up and down at will . . . and I began to float like a feather back and forth, down, and down, and down." After the experience, Castaneda told Don Juan he felt as if he had lost his body. Don Juan said of course he had. Such flights (trips) are not uncommon in psychedelic sessions, and according to Masters and Houston (who have conducted numerous LSD sessions), when a subject experiences this sensation, he "seems to project his consciousness away from his body and then is able to see his body as if he were standing off to one side of it or were looking down on it from above." Before this occurs, some subjects describe seeing an aura or "energy force field" surrounding their bodies.

This last description may remind the reader of the explorations being made with Kirlian photography, which show emanations or "energy fields" surrounding leaves, animals, and people; Soviet biologist Inyushin suggests that this may be the "bioplasma body" contained in and surrounding the physical body. Currently there is a resurgence of interest in what has been described for thousands of years as the "energy" or "astral" body, and the experiences obtained while in this second body.

WHAT ABOUT THE ENERGY BODY?

All around the world's cultures, the concept of such a body can be found. In ancient Egypt, frescoes depicted sculptures of the "ka," which was presumed to be a birdlike double of the person that leaves the physical body at death. In the sacred Tibetan book *Bardo Thodol* (the Tibetan "Book of the Dead"), there are given specific instructions to the dying person on how to release the "energy" body as death comes: "When thou art recovered from the swoon [of death] . . . a radiant body resembling the former body, must have sprung forth. This Bardo-body . . . is endowed with the power of miraculous motion." Today, in British Guiana, the Akawaio Caribs believe that their shaman's spirit, in trance, detaches itself from his body and flies up into the skies. And in Venezuela, the Yaruro Indians believe that when their shamans journey to spirit lands, their spirits leave behind just the "husk" of their physical bodies. Among the Arctic Tungus, there is a belief that the soul can leave the body, causing unconsciousness, and that after death, this soul goes to the world of the dead. In ancient Greece a similar belief existed that the psyche, or soul, is transformed at death into the *eidolon*, a tenuous, insubstantial image of the once-living person. In the *Odyssey*, the hero meets his dead mother and tries to embrace her, but, like Castaneda's hands grabbing at the pole, his arms go right through her, and he cries, "Is this but a phantom (*eidolon*) that Queen Persephone has sent me, that I must lament and groan the more?" His mother replies that it is not a deception, but that "this is the way with mortals when they die."

Among the Buddhists it is firmly believed that a holy man may develop powers (*siddhi*) which permit his "radiant body" to pass "without feeling any resistance, through a wall, a rampart, or a hill as if it were air; to walk upon the water without sinking in it." Saint Paul, in the New Testament, writes: "There is a natural [physical] body and there is a spiritual body."

The Greeks called it the eidolon, the Tibetans the radiant body, the Egyptians the ka, the Germans the dopfelganger, the Norwegians the verdoger, the occultists the astral or etheric body, Inyushin the energy body. Descriptions of this subtle body, whatever it is called, are remarkably similar. Specifically, quoting from Yogi Ramacharaka:

The Astral Body, belonging to every person, is an exact counterpart of the perfect physical body of the person. It is composed of fine ethereal matter, and is usually encased in the physical body. In ordinary cases, the detachment of the astral body from its physical counterpart is accomplished only with great difficulty, but in the case of dreams, great mental stress, and under certain conditions of occult development, the astral body

> may become detached. . . . It also leaves the body under
> the influence of anesthesia, or in some deeper phases of
> hypnosis.

Many readers will almost certainly be tempted to say: "Absurd, impossible." I remember having exactly that reaction in my early forays into parapsychology.

Let me suggest that we be reasonable (not rational), and instead of instant denial, let us look for evidence that such bodies exist. Let us examine subjective reports of both spontaneous and directed out-of-the-body experiences as described by persons in the states outlined by Ramacharaka: hypnosis, anesthesia, dreams, severe stress, and occult or spiritual development.

HYPNOSIS

Once more, hypnosis furnishes curious clues about paranormal events, this time in relation to the "energy body." During the nineteenth century, the French investigators Albert de Rochas, Henri Baraduc and other colleagues made many experiments using mesmerism to achieve what was called the "exteriorization of sensibility." This group of researchers believed that under mesmerism both sensory and motor "currents" could be projected beyond the body. (Their research is reminiscent of the recent work by Harold Burr, Leonard Ravitz, and the scientists at the Prague convention who reported detecting energy fields around the body with the use of sensitive instruments.) After mesmerizing a subject, de Rochas would suggest that the subject would feel sensations at a distance from his body. Then he would prick the air with a pin, and the subject would frequently describe a sensation of pain at a point on the body roughly corresponding to the pinprick. These early studies were not well controlled, nor could they be duplicated by other research workers, and were soon discarded.

More than fifty years later, the experiment was revived by Dr. Jarl Fahler, president of the Finnish SPR, first at Helsingfors and later at the parapsychology laboratory at Duke University. Dr. Fahler used hypnosis rather than mesmerism, and in all his experiments, which ranged over a ten-year period with literally hundreds of subjects, he achieved success with only one person, a "Mrs. S."

With this special subject, Fahler carried out a series of rather dramatic experiments called "water glass" tests. The tests were done in the presence of six to eight witnesses and were recorded by a secretary. Here is a verbatim report of one conducted in 1953:

> The subject was brought into deep hypnosis. Two similar glasses, both filled with the same amount of water, were placed on the table in front of her. The experimenter [Dr. Fahler] took one glass and put it between the subject's hands. He then gave verbal suggestions that "all sense of feeling and pain were being drained" from her arms and hands, into the water glass, and that the arms and hands, at the same time, were becoming insensitive to feeling.
>
> After repeating these suggestions a few times, the results were tested by sticking a needle into the water in the glass. The subject reacted with a jerk of the arms and hands. The needle was then stuck into her arms and hands, but there was no reaction whatever. [Author's note: The standard test for depth of hypnosis is sticking the subject with a pin or needle; if genuinely, deeply hypnotized, the subject will feel nothing; hence the usefulness of hypnosis in surgery.]
>
> The experimenter then took the glass from the table and went into an adjoining room, from which he could not be seen by any of the persons in the experimental room. There he pushed the needle into the water glass ten times. The subject reacted with pain ten times. Another person, Dr. M., took the glass from the experimenter, went out into the entrance hall. The persons present in the room noticed that the subject reacted with a jerk four times consecutively. When Dr. M. returned, he stated that he had pushed the needle into the water glass four times.
>
> During the experiment, it was noticed that the reactions of the subject became stronger if a spoon was substituted for the needle.

Fahler goes on to report that the "water glass" tests were successful on many other occasions, even when the glass was taken three rooms away, or outside the apartment. However, he stresses that he has not been able to find any other subject to duplicate these effects. Once more we find it is only the exceptionally gifted person who achieves paranormal phenomena. In my own experience, teaching hypnosis, I have worked with hundreds of subjects, but could achieve deep trance with a very few, and of those few, only one seemed to experience a paranormal event (not exteriorization), which will be discussed in a later chapter.

If we accept these Fahler results as genuine, they would indicate at the least that one's senses can be stimulated at a distance away from the physical body. Interestingly, Aristotle supported this view, writing that "the spirit body (or energy body) contains in it all of the senses: it is, for instance, not the ear, nor even the membrane or drum of the ear, that is the hearing sensory. Eyes, ears, and nostrils are sense organs only. They are the means whereby sensible experience is referred to the spirit." Similar descriptions are found in Buddhist and yogic texts about the astral body.

ANESTHESIA

As we have read, Ramacharaka suggests that the detachment of the astral body may occur spontaneously under special conditions, such as anesthesia. Infrequently, during surgery, there have come reports from patients of extraordinary sensations of being suspended in space—usually hovering under the ceiling—looking down at the operation being performed on their bodies. Hereward Carrington offers, in *The Phenomena of Astral Projection*, the case of Mrs. H. Schmidt of Daytona Beach, Florida, who was operated on under ether:

> After the operation I was placed in a private room and my husband and a special nurse were sitting beside me, one on each side of the bed. . . . I was still unconscious from the ether and my body seemed lifeless. Suddenly I saw the family physician step to the open doorway of my room. . . . Afterwards, when I became my normal self, my husband, the nurse and the doctor could not understand how I had known that anyone had stood in the doorway, since I was physically unconscious and my

eyes were closed and focused the other way. But this is what I really experienced: when the doctor came up to the door, I saw myself sit erect in the bed. I mean that it was the real 'seeing' myself which had raised itself up; I did not see this from my physical body.... I still remember this as if it had happened yesterday. My physical body was flat in bed when I sat up in my other body. In fact, I was unable to raise myself up physically for two weeks, and then had to be assisted.

Very recently, the sister of one of my students was admitted to the UCLA Hospital for a routine appendectomy. She told her brother, who hurried to tell me, that under the anesthetic she saw, from above, the operation being performed, and after the operation, the doctor swabbing her wound with some red medicine before putting on the bandages. When the bandages were removed, the red marks were found, as she had previously described them.

DREAMS

Borrowing once more from the remarkable collection of the SPR, we find this case reported in 1863 by Mr. and Mrs. Wilmot of Bridgeport, Connecticut. The case is extraordinary in that a third person verified the phenomenon, having observed it himself. In Mr. Wilmot's words:

I sailed from Liverpool for New York, on the steamer *City of Limerick.* On the evening of the second day out, a severe storm began which lasted for nine days. Upon the night of the eighth day, for the first time I enjoyed refreshing sleep. Toward morning I dreamed that I saw my wife, whom I had left in the U.S., come to the door of the stateroom, clad in her night dress. At the door she seemed to discover that I was not the only occupant in the room, hesitated a little, then advanced to my side, stooped down and kissed me, and quietly withdrew.

Upon waking I was surprised to see my fellow-passenger leaning upon his elbow and looking fixedly at me. "You're a pretty fellow," he said at length, "to have a lady come and visit you this way." I pressed him for an explanation, and he related what he had seen while wide awake, lying on his berth. It exactly corresponded with my dream.

The day after landing I went to Watertown, Conn., where my children and my wife were visiting her parents. Almost her first question when we were alone together was, "Did you receive a visit from me a week ago Tuesday?" "It would be impossible," I said. "Tell me what makes you think so." My wife then told me that on account of the severity of the weather, she had been extremely anxious about me. On the night mentioned above she had lain awake a long time thinking about me, and about four o'clock in the morning it seemed to her that she went out to seek me. She came at length . . . to my stateroom. "Tell me," she said, "do they ever have staterooms like the one I saw, where the upper berth extends further back than the under one? A man was in the upper berth looking right at me, and for a moment I was afraid to go in, but soon I went up to the side of your berth, bent down and kissed you, and embraced you, and then went away." The description given by my wife of the steamship was correct in all particulars, though she had never seen it.

STRESS

Sometimes, with severe illness, a person may experience this strange detachment, or dissociation, from the physical body. Here is a case reported by a soldier during World War I:

I was stationed in Aden in 1913 and was seriously ill with dysentery. I got to the stage of having to be lifted from side to side, as I was too weak to move myself in bed. From the instructions I heard the M.O. give the orderlies (we had no nurses in Aden then) I gathered that a collapse was expected and that in the event of the occurrence I was to be given a saline injection via the rectum.

Shortly afterwards, I found myself lying parallel to the bed, about three or four feet above it and face downwards. Below me I saw my body and witnessed the giving of the rectal injection. I listened to all the con-

versation of the two orderlies and of a strange M.O. who
was directing affairs. . . . I well remember that the saline
came from an enamel kind of vessel which was connected to a rubber tube—the vessel being held up at
arm's length by an orderly.

I found myself next back in bed, feeling much better.
I told my story to the orderlies, who were quite skeptical. I particularly inquired about the strange M.O. I
found there had been one; he was en route to Bombay, I
think, and had called at the hospital in time to help. . . .

On reading the above, I find I have omitted to mention that the orderlies said I couldn't possibly have any
knowledge of the matter, as I was quite unconscious
before and after the operation.

Another case report from a soldier, this time from World War II,
seems to have occurred as the result of a violent shock:

I was an armoured-car officer engaged in medium and
long-range reconnaissance work with the 21st Army
Group. At about 2:30 p.m. on August 3, 1944, I was in
a small armoured scout car which received a direct hit
from a German anti-tank gun. Our car, which was full of
various explosives, grenades, phosphorus bombs, etc.,
blew up. . . . The force of the explosion threw me about
twenty feet away from the car and over a five foot
hedge. My clothes, etc., were on fire, and there were
various pieces of phosphorus sticking to me which were
also burning. . . . I imagined for a split second that I had
gone to hell, and I quickly tried to recollect some
particular vice which might have been my qualification.
It is interesting to notice that I did not see any rapid
"trailer" of my past life as, I believe, drowning persons
report. All this took a fraction of a second, and the next
experience was definitely unusual. I was conscious of
being two persons—one, lying on the ground in a field
where I had fallen from the blast, my clothes, etc., on
fire, and waving my limbs wildly, at the same time
uttering moans and gibbering with fear—I was quite
conscious of both making these sounds, and at the same
time hearing them as though coming from another person. The other "me" was floating up in the air, about

twenty feet from the ground, from which position I could see not only my other self on the ground, but also the hedge, the road, and the car, which was surrounded by smoke and burning fiercely. I remember telling myself "It's no use gibbering like that—roll over and over to put the flames out." This my ground body eventually did, rolling over into a ditch under the hedge where there was a slight amount of water. The flames went out, and at this stage I suddenly became one person again.

Another, seemingly much rarer experience is the one reported by an aviator, also in World War II, when "someone out-of-the-body" saved his life in a miraculous fashion. This incident is reported in a biography of the famous Capucin monk Padre Pio:

> During World War II, a young Italian air force officer started off on a squadron mission, but was forced to bail out when his aircraft caught fire. The parachute failed to open, and the young man would have been killed instantly had not a friar caught him in his arms and carried him the rest of the way down to earth. That same evening the young officer told the story to the C.O. who needless to say did not believe a word of it. Instead the C.O. thought it wise to give the young flier a short leave to recover from the shock of the experience.
>
> When he reached home, he told his mother about the experience. "Why," exclaimed the mother, "that was Padre Pio. I prayed to him so hard for you!" Then she showed him a picture of the Padre. "Mother," he said incredulously, "that is the same man!"
>
> The young flier was so impressed with what had happened that he decided to go to Padre Pio's church, San Giovanni Rotondo in the town of Foggia, to thank the monk. He was further astounded when the Padre said to him, "That is not the only time I have saved you. At Monastir, when your plane was hit, I made it glide safely to earth." It was a fact that the young man's plane *had* been hit at Monastir, and that he had also managed to glide safely for a landing. But there seemed no way for Padre Pio to have known about this at the time.

Possibly the greatest stress any of us can experience is that of an illness which has been judged by the attending doctors as in its terminal stages. This report of an out-of-the-body experience (referred to as OBE, for short) can be found, of all unlikely places, in a medical journal, the *St. Louis Medical and Surgical Journal*, published in 1889 and written by, of all unlikely people, a medical doctor, A. S. Wiltse. This doctor obtained sworn depositions from the witnesses who were part of the experience. Dr. Wiltse had been ill with typhoid fever, and was believed to be in the last stages of life:

> Feeling a sense of drowsiness come over me, I straightened my stiffened legs, got my arms over my breast, and soon sank into utter unconsciousness.
>
> I passed about four hours in all without pulse or perceptible heart beat, as I am informed by Dr. S. H. Raynes, who was the only physician present. [During that time] I came again into a state of conscious existence and discovered that I was still in the body, but the body and I had no longer any interests in common.
>
> With all the interest of a physician, I beheld the wonders of my bodily anatomy, intimately interwoven with which, even tissue for tissue, was I, the living soul of that dead body. I watched the interesting process of the separation of soul and body. By some power, apparently not my own, the Ego was rocked to and fro, laterally, as a cradle is rocked, by which process its connection with the tissues of the body was broken up. . . . I felt and heard, it seemed, the snapping of innumerable small cords. When this was accomplished, I began slowly to retreat from the feet, toward the head. . . . As I emerged from the head, I floated up and down and laterally like a soap bubble attached to the bowl of a pipe until at last I broke loose from the body and fell lightly to the floor, where I slowly rose and expanded into the full stature of a man. I seemed to be translucent, of a bluish cast and perfectly naked. . . . As I turned, my left elbow came in contact with the arm of one of two gentlemen, who were standing at the door. To my surprise, his arm passed through mine without apparent resistance, the severed parts closing again with-

out pain, as air reunites. I looked quickly up at his face to see if he had noticed the contact, but he gave no sign—only stood and gazed toward the couch I had just left. I directed my gaze in the direction of his, and saw my own dead body. It was lying just as I had taken so much pains to place it. . . .

Without previous thought and without apparent effort on my part, my eyes opened. Realizing that I was in the body, in astonishment and disappointment, I exclaimed: "What in the world has happened to me? Must I die again?"

I was extremely weak, but strong enough to relate the above experience. . . . I made a rapid and good recovery, for having travelled some hundreds of miles during the interval, as I close this paper my pulse stands at eighty-four and strong, just eight weeks from "the day I died," as some of my neighbors speak of it.

There are plenty of witnesses to the truth of the above statements, in so far as my physical condition was concerned. Also to the fact that just as I described the conditions about my body and in the room, so they actually were. I must, therefore, have seen these things by some means.

ON THE PATH OF SPIRITUAL DEVELOPMENT

Throughout Oriental religions and philosophies, both ancient and modern, there are accounts of holy men who "travel" to help the sick and those in need. A recent report of one such OBE is described by Arthur Osborne in his biography of the twentieth-century spiritual leader Ramana Maharshi. This incident was related by a disciple of the Maharshi, who while

sitting in meditation, felt distracted and longed intensely for the presence and guidance of the Maharshi. At that moment the Maharshi entered the temple. Ganapati prostrated himself before him and, as he was about to rise, he felt the Maharshi's hand upon his head and a terrifically vital force coursing through his body from the touch.

Speaking about this incident in later years, the Maharshi said: "One day, some years ago, I was lying down and awake when I distinctly felt my body rise higher and higher. I could see the physical objects below growing smaller and smaller until they disappeared and all around me was a limitless expanse of dazzling light. After some time I felt the body slowly descend and the physical objects below began to appear. I was so fully aware of this incident that I finally concluded that it must be by such means that Siddhas [sages with powers] travel over vast distances in a short time and appear and disappear in such a mysterious manner. I found myself on a high road and at some distance was Ganapati temple and I entered it."

OBE AND LSD

One last anecdote: A psychiatrist friend of mine recently told me of an LSD session during which he suddenly felt keen longing to visit his parents, who lived in Europe. He described how, suddenly, he heard "a roaring sound, like wind" and felt as if he were traveling with the speed of light. When this sensation ended, he found himself in his old room. He could see through the wall which separated that room from his parents' room, and as he looked, he saw that his parents were sleeping quietly. He looked around his own old room, and picked up a once-favorite book. As he held it in his hand, feeling its weight and texture, he was overcome with the thought that he might be able to return to his body, in the lab, carrying the book with him. This was such a terrifying idea that he put the book down abruptly; within moments he found himself back in the lab in which he was having the LSD "trip." Shocked at this denouement, I asked him *why* he had not made the experiment of holding onto the book for his return trip. He answered, solemnly, that had he done so, and had the book been in his hand when he "came to" back in the lab, that one fact would have destroyed his entire concept of how the world is structured, and that prospect had been too fearsome.

OBE AS A LEARNED, VOLUNTARY PROCEDURE

We have been discussing involuntary, spontaneous OBE. But prolonged practice, in a variety of disciplines, has presumably bled certain men to learn how to leave their bodies at will. ⁄sons in the Western world who have acquired this ability seem to be very few. We have already discussed the work of Phineas Quimby, who learned how to achieve, in himself, the deep trance state that he was able to impose on the young Lucius. As he grew more expert, Quimby experienced the sensation of visiting patients in their homes, and several of his patients reported actually seeing him and feeling his touch during these "absent treatments," as they were called. As we know, Edgar Cayce also taught himself to go voluntarily into deep trance, a phenomenon which constantly puzzled him and about which he sought to learn more. In one trance the question was asked: "What is meant by personality?" And the answer given was: "The personality is that which is known on this physical plane as the consciousness. When the subconscious controls (as in hypnosis), the personality is removed from the individual and lies above his physical body. This may be seen here in my own case." But to those present on that occasion, there was nothing to be "seen." However, on a later occasion, both dramatic and alarming, there was a vivid demonstration of that other consciousness or "astral body."

Cayce's son, Hugh Lynn, told me of the incident, which he himself observed while conducting a public session with his father in trance. During that session, a man in the audience scribbled a note and handed it to Hugh Lynn, reaching across the body of the entranced Cayce. Cayce instantly stopped talking and fell into a deep catalepsy. This had never happened before; Hugh Lynn did not know what to do; so, sensibly, he did nothing. After several hours of total immobility, which caused great consternation to those present, Cayce's body suddenly did an incredibly swift "jackknife," and Cayce catapulted to his feet. At a subsequent reading, an explanation was requested about the incident, and the answer was given that during trance the "personality," or astral body, is lifted above the physical body, and on that particular occasion, the man leaning across Cayce's body to hand Hugh Lynn the note had thrust his arm through Cayce's astral body with an impact equivalent to a "kick from a horse." (This is probably the reason it is universally advised never to touch a medium in trance.)

None of the healers we have discussed—Quimby, Andrew Jackson Davis, Edgar Cayce, or Harry Edwards of England—gave much attention to the capacities of the astral body, being primarily interested in the healing of patients. However, there are at least three Americans who devoted a great part of their lives exploring the nature of the astral body, and obtaining a measure of control in their OBE. One of these Americans was, oddly, a state prisoner in an Arizona jail.

ED MORRELL, THE "STAR ROVER"

Ed Morrell's story is one of the most remarkable on record, in that his OBEs all occurred while he was in a double straitjacket, which would seem to eliminate the possibility of fraud. In the Arizona prison to which he was confined for four years during the early twentieth century, a standard punishment for the intractible prisoner was being trussed into not one, but two straitjackets, one tightly laced outside the other. When the prisoner was thus encased, water was poured over the jackets, which then proceeded to shrink, causing the prisoner to feel as if he were being "slowly squeezed to death by a boa constrictor." Before his first jacket punishment, Morrell had been advised by a veteran of the experience to "give up and die." Indeed, Morrell found the pain so excruciating that he tried to do exactly that. He had the sensation that he was slowly smothering, when suddenly he found he had somehow detached from his physical body, and his consciousness was roaming free, beyond the walls of the prison. When his jailers came to release him from the ordeal, Morrell did not show any of the customary anguish. In an effort to break his spirit, his jailers put him back in the jackets time and time again, on one occasion for 126 consecutive hours. For Morrell, these experiences were an exquisite release, in which he could travel wherever he wished, observing events as they were actually transpiring, events which he told fellow prisoners, wardens, and eventually even the governor of Arizona, W. P. Hunt. Morrell's psychic travels were substantiated time and again; and at least one of his precognitive experiences proved to be correct, for Morrell predicted the exact day and hour of his release.

Morrell wrote about his experiences in a book, *The Twenty Fifth Man;* and Jack London, who became an intimate friend of Morrell, wrote a fictionalized account of Morrell's experiences in his fine novel *The Star Rover* (also titled *The Jacket*), which unfortunately is out of print and almost unobtainable today. While serving the last part of his sentence, Morrell was not subjected to the jacket punishment, and though he tried repeatedly to project his consciousness as he had done when confined, he was never successful. Apparently for Morrell, one of the necessary conditions for the release of the energy body was the terrible stress of being encased in the jackets.

SYLVAN MULDOON:
THE PROJECTION OF THE ASTRAL BODY

The Projection of the Astral Body (first published in 1929 and reprinted steadily since then) is a collaboration of Sylvan Muldoon and psychical researcher Hereward Carrington. The book evolved as a result of a previous work by Carrington in which he had discussed astral projection (or OBE), quoting almost exclusively from the writings of a Frenchman, M. Lancelin. Carrington considered the material inadequate, but it had been all that he "had been able to unearth." After reading Carrington's work, Muldoon promptly wrote a letter to Carrington which is quoted in the introduction to their book: "I have been a 'projector' for twelve years, long before I knew that anyone else in the world did such things. . . . What puzzles me most is that you make the remark that M. Lancelin has told practically all that is known on the subject. Why, Mr. Carrington, I have never read Lancelin's work, but if you have given the gist of it in your book, then I can write a book on the things Lancelin does not know!" And that's exactly what he did, after Carrington satisfied himself that Muldoon's claims were genuine. In his introduction, Carrington writes:

> No wild or preposterous claims are anywhere made in this book as to what has been accomplished during these "astral trips." Mr. Muldoon does not make claim to have visited any distant planets—and return to tell us in detail their modes of life; he does not claim to have explored any vast and beautiful "spirit worlds"; he does not pretend to have penetrated the past or the future; to have relived any of his past "incarnations. . . ." He asserts, merely, that he has been enabled to leave his

physical body at will, and travel about in the present, in
his immediate vicinity, in some vehicle or other, while
fully conscious.

Muldoon wrote the major portion of the book, which includes
descriptions of his various trips and the many techniques he
developed to release the astral body. His first, totally unexpected
and terrifying OBE occurred to him when, as a boy of twelve, he
was taken by his mother to a Spiritualist camp in Iowa. At that
time, Spiritualism was still a strong movement in America, and
Muldoon's mother had decided to see for herself whether what
was claimed by the Spiritualists was "fact or fiction." The family,
on this particular night, retired at an early hour in a rooming house
where there were lodged half a dozen widely known mediums.
Muldoon wrote:

> I dozed off to sleep, and slept for several hours. At
> length I realized that I was slowly awakening. . . . I
> knew I existed somewhere . . . but *where* I could not
> understand. . . . I tried to move, only to find that I was
> powerless, as if I *adhered* to that on which I rested. . . .
> Eventually the feeling of adhesion relaxed, but was
> replaced by another sensation equally unpleasant—that
> of floating. Occurring at the same time, my entire rigid
> body commenced vibrating at a great rate of speed, in
> an up-and-down direction. All this to me was like some
> queer nightmare. Amid this pandemonium of bizarre
> sensations—floating, vibratory, zigzagging—I began to
> hear, and then to see. When able to see, I was more than
> astonished! I was floating in the very air, rigidly hori-
> zontal, a few feet above the bed. . . .

Muldoon then found himself standing upright in the room, but six
feet above the bed. He was able to get to a standing position on
the floor, however. Then he turned toward the bed he had been
in:

> There were two of me! I was beginning to feel myself
> insane. There was another "me" lying quietly on the
> bed! My two identical bodies were joined by means of

an elastic-like cable, one end of which was fastened to the medulla oblongata. . . . I attempted to open the door, but found myself passing through it. Going from one room to another I tried fervently to arouse the sleeping occupants of the house. I clutched at them, called to them, tried to shake them, but my hands passed through them as though they were but vapors. I started to cry. . . . As I recall it, I prowled about for perhaps fifteen minutes when (the cable) pulled. I began to zigzag again under this force. . . . It was the reverse procedure of that which I experienced rising from the bed. Slowly the phantom lowered, vibrating, then it dropped suddenly, coinciding with the physical body.

After this initiation, Muldoon had literally hundreds of astral projections, during which he learned how to maneuver the cable and the astral body. He also learned how to induce such trips through special techniques, which he offers the reader who might like to try them out. One such technique he has called "dreaming true":

It is very important to observe yourself in the process of falling asleep. If you conduct experiments of this character on yourself, you will be enabled gradually to keep conscious control; and this self-observation—the con- sciousness of going to sleep—is extremely interesting. When you have learned to do that, then construct mentally a definite scene, which you must hold firmly in mind; and at the very last moment—before you fall asleep—consciously transfer yourself into the scene. One must have movement of self outstanding in the dream— not merely standing back and looking on.

A word of warning! If you are neurotic, easily influ- enced, lack "will" and are fearful—do not try astral projection. Turn toward physical culture rather than psychical culture.

In another passage Muldoon corroborates what we have learned about the nature of the astral body: that it houses all the senses. He reports that at times he seemed to "see" out of different parts of the energy body. For example, he might be lying upon his back in the air and see what was taking place below him, even though looking in the opposite direction with his eyes.

As almost inevitably happens, Muldoon found out that the great majority of people simply did not believe his experiences. In his words:

> My associates—yes, even members of my own family— ridiculed the very suggestion of such an "impossibility" as they called it. . . . So within me arose a determination to learn what brought about the projections. One night in bed I had been concentrating upon different parts of the body, and came to rest upon my heart. I noticed that it did not seem to be beating at the speed it should.

Muldoon, therefore, went to a doctor, who examined him and found that his heart was beating steadily, but very slowly: only 42 beats per minute. (Some athletes have this slow heart beat.) The doctor prescribed a cardiac stimulant, which Muldoon took for the next two months. During those two months, he could not induce a projection, although during the previous year he had managed at least one OBE each week. He then stopped taking the medication, and within a short time was able to induce the experience. In this interval, Muldoon made an interesting discovery: "I could control my pulse rate by means of my mind! After retiring and relaxing, I would concentrate upon my heart, and in less than two weeks I could speed up the heart beat or slow it down at will." It seems that Muldoon had learned a technique of biofeedback (or Hatha Yoga) without formal instruction. Indeed, the concept of biofeedback had not been developed at that time.

ROBERT MONROE: JOURNEYS OUT OF THE BODY

In 1971, a respected business executive of radio and television, Robert Monroe, published an account of his OBEs in the book *Journeys out of the Body*. Unlike Muldoon, Monroe did not begin having OBEs as a boy, or even as a young man. In fact, he had been living "a reasonably normal life with a reasonably normal family" until 1958. Shortly after the family brunch one Sunday afternoon "a severe, iron-hard cramp" seized him across the diaphragm, a solid band of unyielding pain. The next morning nothing remained of the cramp except a muscle soreness. On a Sunday three weeks later, while he was lying on a couch, he saw "a ray seem to come out of the sky." In his words, "It was like being struck by a warm light. . . . The effect when the beam struck my entire body was to cause it to shake violently or 'vibrate.' I was utterly powerless to move." (This inability to move and the strong vibrations sound like Muldoon's experiences.) Similar episodes recurred several times over the next weeks, and Monroe began to think he might have some illness: heart, epilepsy, or even insanity. He went to his family doctor, who could find nothing at all wrong with him. Months passed, with the same kinds of phenomena occurring spasmodically until "they almost became boring." One night in bed when the "vibrations" came on, Monroe, whose hobby was gliding, happened to think how nice it would be to take a glider up the next day:

> After a moment, I became aware of something pressing my shoulder. . . . My hand encountered a smooth wall. . . . I immediately reasoned that I had gone to sleep and fallen out of bed. . . . Then I looked again. Something was wrong. This wall had no windows, no furniture against it, no doors. . . . Identification came instantly. It was not a wall, it was the ceiling. I was floating against the ceiling, bouncing gently. I rolled in the air, startled, and looked down. There, in the dim light below me, was the bed. There were two figures lying in the bed. To the right was my wife. Beside her was someone else. . . . I looked more closely, and the shock was intense. *I* was the someone on the bed!

Like Muldoon, Monroe had never heard of travels outside of the body, and he went through years of doubt about his own sanity. He had many interviews with psychiatrists and psychologists; he became familiar with what he terms the "underground" of psychical research groups all over the United States; he also met with professional parapsychologists. But from these sources he found little guidance. Gradually, through trial and error, he learned to induce the "vibrations" at will and to direct his travels. With practice, he was able to do so successfully about 50 percent of the time.

In 1964, the noted psychic and author Harold Sherman, who was then visiting Los Angeles, telephoned me to ask if I would like to meet, and perhaps invite some professional colleagues to meet, Robert Monroe. At that time I had very little belief in the reality of the astral body, but I was delighted at the opportunity of listening to Monroe's experiences. About twenty people met at my home that evening. Sherman introduced Monroe, who spoke for about two hours about his "travels," answering all questions that arose as he spoke. One of the experiences he related that night is told in his book:

> I floated upward, with the intention of visiting Dr. Bradshaw, who was ill in bed with a cold. I thought I would visit him in his bedroom, which was a room in his house I had not seen and if I could describe it later, could thus document my visit. . . . After a while the uphill travel became difficult, and I felt I wouldn't make it. With this thought, an amazing thing happened. It felt precisely as if someone had put a hand under each arm and lifted me. I rushed quickly up the hill. Then I came upon Dr. and Mrs. Bradshaw. They were outside the house. I didn't understand this, because Dr. Bradshaw was supposed to be in bed. He was dressed in light overcoat and hat. They seemed in good spirits, and walked past me unseeing. I floated around in front of them, waving, trying to get their attention, without result. . . .
>
> We phoned Dr. and Mrs. Bradshaw that evening. I made no statement other than to ask where they were between four and five that afternoon. Mrs. Bradshaw stated that roughly at four twenty-five they were walking out of the house toward the garage. Dr. Bradshaw was wearing a light hat and a light-colored topcoat. However, neither "saw" me in any way. The coincidences involved were too much. It proved to me—truly for the first time—that there might be more to this than normal science and psychology and psychiatry allow—more than

an aberration or hallucination—and I needed some form of proof. It is a simple incident, but unforgettable.

When, at length, Monroe had finished reporting his experiences to our group, and no one had any further questions to ask of him, he turned to us and said quietly: "Now I'd like to ask all of *you* a question. What do you think has been happening to me?" There ensued a very, very long pause. Across from him, sitting on a large sofa, were five psychologists. They looked at each other rather uncomfortably, and then one of them, as if acting as spokesman for the group, said, in as kind a way as possible, "Frankly, if I were you, I'd see a psychiatrist. I think you're psychotic." In his book, Monroe discusses that evening and comments wryly: "Several half-seriously stated that I should run, not walk, to the nearest psychiatrist. (None present offered his services.)" He then put to us a second question: "Would you, personally, take part in experiments that would lead to the creation of such unusual activity in yourself?" Remarkably, about half the people there (all of them scientists) said they would. Including me.

SCIENTIFIC STUDIES OF OBE

For the most part scientists have avoided giving any considera-tion to the phenomenon of OBE. Those few who take the concept seriously have until very recently relied on the methodology of the SPRs: to collect and analyze anecdotal data. One study of this kind, undertaken by Celia Green, director of the Institute of Psychophysical Research at Oxford University, was published in 1968. The data were obtained by means of an appeal via the press and the British Broadcasting Company for "first-hand accounts of experiences in which the subject had appeared to himself to be observing things from a point located outside his physical body." Questionnaires were sent to the 400 persons in England who replied, and more than half that number returned the question-naires. This was not a sufficiently large population for the desired statistical analysis, but the author believes the anecdotes provide a characteristic model for the experience. Many subjects, inde-pendently of each other, reported that they generally were lying down when the event occurred; they frequently experienced some sort of paralysis at some time during the experience; they quite often described the sensation of occupying an "exact duplicate" of the physical body; and they usually experienced a "floating" sensation, hovering above the scene. Frequently they expressed surprise at the sensation of looking down and seeing one's own inert body, or of trying to touch objects like lamp switches or door knobs, and feeling one's hand go right through the object. Feelings of lightness, freedom, vitality, and health were characteristically reported.

The most prolific collector of OBE is Robert Crookall, by profession a geologist. Crookall has already published six volumes of anecdotal material (including *The Techniques of Astral Projection, The Study and Practice of Astral Projection,* and *Case Book of Astral Projection*) and does not seem about to stop.

Interesting as these case histories are, they do not contribute to our scientific knowledge. For that, it is necessary to perform controlled experiments in the laboratory with subjects who can at will leave their bodies and later return to them. Obviously, to perform such experiments the first requisite is analagous to that which is asked for in the famous recipe for turtle soup: First catch the turtle.

LABORATORY INVESTIGATIONS OF OBE

Dr. Charles Tart at the University of California at Davis was the first professional to catch not one, but two "turtles." One who was willing and eager to be caught was Robert Monroe. The Monroe experiments have been interesting but far from conclusive, for like most psychics, Monroe feels deeply the constraints of the laboratory with its cumbersome apparatus. This is the way he describes one of his nights in Dr. Tart's lab:

> By nine-thirty in the evening, all electrodes had been attached by the technician, who was the only person present when I arrived. Experienced usual difficulty in getting head comfortable. As a "side sleeper" each side was equally uncomfortable due to the electrodes attached to the ears. I attempted to relax naturally, but was unsuccessful.

Various techniques developed by Monroe were tried without success. Finally, to continue in Monroe's words,

> I fell slowly, and could feel myself passing through the various EEG wires. I could "see" the light coming through the open doorway to the outer EEG rooms. I went slowly through the doorway. I was looking for the technician, but could not find her. She was not in the control console room, and I went into the brightly lit outer room. And suddenly, there she was. However, she was not alone. A man was with her, who was about her height, with curly hair. Feeling something calling for a return to the physical, I slipped back. Reason for discomfort: dry throat and throbbing ear.
>
> I opened my eyes, and sat up, and called to the technician. She came in, and I told her that I had seen her, however, with a man. She replied that it was her husband. That he came to stay with her during these late hours. I expressed the desire to meet him. The technician removed the electrodes, and I went outside with her and met her husband. He was about her height, curly haired.

Monroe added that the experience was verified by the technician:

> In a report to Dr. Tart, the technician confirmed that she was in the outer hall with her husband at the time. She also confirmed that I did not know he was present, and that I had not met him previously. Dr. Tart states that the EEG shows definite unusual and unique tracings during time of activity.

In lab lingo, this is "soft data." Anecdotal. What proof is there that there was no collusion between the technician, her husband, and Monroe? Thus far, there has been no "hard data" from the Monroe studies.

But Dr. Tart's other subject, a professional nurse, provided hard data. She had confided to Dr. Tart that she had an OBE almost every night when she was falling asleep and that she had done so ever since she could remember. However, as a child she had once confided to a chum about one of her "trips" during sleep, and the little girl had called her a liar, among other things. This had confused her very much because she had thought everybody did it. When she learned that just about nobody did it, she stopped talking about it. When Dr. Tart asked if she would be willing to come to his lab, sleep, and try some experiments during an OBE, she said she would. Tart's experimental design was straightforward. The young woman was to be hooked into the EEG equipment and then go to sleep for the night. Since electrodes were pasted to her scalp, she could not move more than six or seven inches (otherwise the machine would have a kind of epileptic seizure and invalidate the entire experiment—as well as wreck Dr. Tart's lab). While asleep, her job was, should she get out of her body, to rise to the ceiling, and look down at a very high shelf, where Dr. Tart had previously placed a placard on which he had written a five-digit number, obtained from a random number table. She was to report to Dr. Tart what the five numbers were.

For several nights she had no success. The strange environment, the uncomfortable electrodes, all the things that had disturbed Monroe also disturbed her. Each night, after she had been put to bed, Dr. Tart placed a different placard of five digits on the shelf. Toward six o'clock in the morning on the fourth night, Dr. Tart was at the EEG machine (having spent the night monitoring the equipment), when he was snapped out of a light doze by the young woman, who was still attached to the machine, but awake and exclaiming excitedly, "Charley, I've got it!" And she rattled off five numbers. Dr. Tart was so sleepy that all he did was murmur, "Fine, go back to sleep," before he suddenly realized that the numbers were correct, and in the correct sequence! The statistical probability of getting five numbers right, just by chance, is one in a hundred thousand.

This study was published in the *ASPR Journal*, in 1968 and aroused a storm of criticism not only from the skeptics, of course, but also from parapsychologists. Skeptics visited Dr. Tart's lab and pointed out that with certain angles of refraction, under certain lighting conditions, etc., the numbers on the placard could have been reflected off the glass face of the clock in the sleeping room, and thus the young woman could have seen them from her prone position. Parapsychologists were highly critical because Dr. Tart himself had obtained the five-digit number from the random number table. Since *he* knew the number, it was more reasonable to assume that the subject had obtained the number telepathically than as the result of an OBE. In any event, clairvoyance could not be excluded.

Such are the thorns of the researcher. Apparently there is no foolproof procedure for any experiment ever devised in the behavioral sciences. Criticisms from opposite camps are often one as valid as the other. And when other labs try the seemingly identical procedure, they sometimes obtain diametrically opposite results.

But Dr. Tart's pioneer work succeeded in interesting other parapsychologists in the possibility of laboratory studies involving OBE. Recently, Dr. Karlis Osis, director of research for the ASPR, has found some gifted subjects who have been able to report accurately targets he has placed in his lab, which the subject "visits" from home, sometimes hundreds of miles away. In these studies, as in all OBE studies thus far, the objection can be raised that it is not OBE, but telepathy or clairvoyance that is being investigated. Nevertheless, the hunt is on for those rare individuals who claim to have the OBE technique under voluntary control.

And there the phenomenon of OBE rests, today, from the scientific point of view. The implications inherent in the phenomenon, should it prove to exist, are vast.

Does a mind or spirit inhabit the body, which can leave the body during sleep, voluntarily, and perhaps at death?

Is this the energy body, astral body, etheric body of ancient, occult, and primitive beliefs?

If the mind/spirit or second body can vacate the body, does the body remain available for other kinds of experience—such as possession by spirits, or aspects of the collective unconscious emerging in personalized form? Would this account for the "guides" of the trance mediums? And if the mind/spirit leaves the body, can it make itself known, in the manner of apparitions, or ghosts?

13 Hallucinations? Or Apparitions and Ghosts?

Glendower: I can call spirits from the vasty deep.

Hotspur: Why, so can I, or so can any man;
But will they come when you do call for them?

—Shakespeare, *Henry IV*

THE ENERGY BODY

We have been considering a preposterous notion: that a second body, made of a fine energetic stuff, inhabits the physical body but can leave it occasionally to travel great distances, perhaps even traversing through time, and into other dimensions. In support of this notion we have brought into our discussion the experiences of persons who, under great stress or as the result of a shock, have found themselves apparently looking down at their inert physical bodies from a second body which felt to them more real than the physical bodies they usually occupy.

Let us briefly recapitulate the characteristics of this etheric, or energy, body. Generally it is invisible to others. But to the person (or consciousness) that occupies that second body, it seems to be an identical and visible counterpart of his physical body. Apparently it is weightless, or very light in weight, so that characteristically it floats to the ceiling of the room, or up into the sky. Occasionally this sensation of "flying" occurs as a vivid dream, such as those described by the Senoi Indians, or for that matter, in the flying dreams of all of us. Moreover, it is composed of such stuff that it can apparently pass effortlessly through walls, encountering no obstacle in its passage. These are interesting characteristics, for not only does this energy body seem to be the "stuff that dreams are made on," but it seems also to correlate with another preposterous field of inquiry among parapsychologists: that of phantoms, apparitions, ghosts, or as some prefer to label them, hallucinations.

HALLUCINATIONS

There seems to be no generally accepted definition of an hallucination. Let us use, then, the one given by the *Encyclopaedia Britannica:* "It is generally and rightly assumed that the hallucinatory perception of any object has for its immediate correlate a state of excitement which, as regards its characteristics and its distribution in the elements of the brain, is entirely similar to the neural correlate of the normal perception of the same object. The hallucination is a perception, but a false perception." This is a rather complex way of saying that the hallucination is like all mental phenomena (ideas, thoughts, cerebrations, etc.): an excretum of the neurons in the brain. The cerebral cortex fires, and creates our imagery whether from the external world or from our internal electrical/chemical actions.

But this definition runs afoul of actual experience. An alcoholic in the throes of delirium tremens sees pink elephants and other fantasia which he has never seen before, and for which there have been no "neural correlates of normal perception." The same can be said for the hallucinations of the psychedelic experiences of Castaneda, Huxley, and countless others who report seeing colors never seen, sights never experienced, sounds never heard. From where and from what "neural correlates" do these experiences arise?

Gestalt psychology has tried to answer that question by suggesting that the "new" image is merely an amalgam of parts of objects we have experienced. As in the dream, you might find yourself talking to a composite woman who has the eyes of your mother, the hair of your secretary, and the body of Marilyn Monroe. Somehow, in the dream, you have put together these discrete pieces of people into a Gestalt which you have never actually seen; but all the separate *parts* have been experienced. Surrealist painters seem to create works of art on a level something like this: a melted clock in a desert, with a purple apple at one side, containing one enormous, unblinking eye. The Gestalt explanation may be satisfactory for dream hallucinations. But other phenomena seem more difficult to explain.

For example, it is not uncommon for schizophrenics to describe in detail creatures that occupy what to the observer is empty air. And psychics occasionally will do the same thing. The question is: How much of what is seen is an hallucination? As illustration, the English psychic Douglas Johnson once told me about one of his most extraordinary experiences, which occurred in a commonplace situation, when he was sitting with an acquaintance in a London cafe. He happened to look up at the bar and saw sitting there an elderly dark woman, who seemed to be very much out of place, for she was dressed in the peasant clothes typical of the tropics. The woman beckoned to Johnson, insistently, and he excused himself to join her. She informed him in poor but understandable English that she was the mother of the young man sitting with him, and that she was very worried because her son was planning an illegal and dangerous mission for that evening. She implored Johnson to dissuade her son from the undertaking. Very much against his common sense, he said he would try to help. After returning to his table, he looked back at the bar, but the dark woman was no longer there. Eventually, feeling foolish, he brought into the conversation a casual, but detailed description of the woman who had been at the bar. To his astonishment, he learned that his description exactly tallied with the young man's mother, who had been dead for some time. (The young man was so distressed by the incident that he confessed to his plan of robbery, and vowed that he would abandon the scheme.)

Hoax? Hallucination? Or something else?

THE CENSUS OF HALLUCINATIONS

As we have learned, the first major study undertaken by the SPR was the Census of Hallucinations. There was only one question asked, requiring a simple Yes or No answer: "Have you ever, when believing yourself to be completely awake, had a vivid impression of seeing or being touched by a living being or inanimate object, or of hearing a voice; which impression, so far as you could discover, was not due to any external physical cause?" To those answering "Yes," another questionnaire was given, asking for a detailed description of the event(s). Similar censuses were later conducted in the United States, Germany, and France. In all, more than 27,000 persons replied; and of that number, over 10 percent answered in the affirmative and gave accounts of their "hallucinations."

Then came the enormous job of analyzing and corroborating the data.

Gradually there emerged a totally unexpected lode of rich material, soon christened "crisis cases." These were characterized by the apparitions of specific persons, who were "seen" at the time of death, even though the death might have occurred without previous warning and at a distance sometimes thousands of miles from the person seeing the apparition.

Could such hallucinations, appearing at such a specific time, be coincidences? Inevitably this is the first question to arise in ESP research. In order to answer it, the researchers devised an ingenious statistical approach, based on the probability of a particular death occurring together with such an hallucination. As the basis for calculating this probability, the average annual death rate for England was ascertained for the decade 1881-1890, which proved to be 19.5 deaths per 1,000 persons. The probability that any *specific* person would die on a specific day of the year was 19.5 in 365,000, or 1 in 19,000. Therefore, if these apparitions were coincidences, they should be occurring at the rate of once in every 19,000 cases of apparitions reported. Instead, it was found to happen once in every 43 cases. This ratio of 1:43, instead of 1:19,000 is "statistically significant," essentially ruling out (as statistics always try to do), the probability of chance, or coincidence.

But far more convincing than these statistics, which can be argued (as can most statistics), were the striking similarities appearing in the anecdotes which were reported, independently, by persons who did not know each other and who often lived in different countries. Since those first censuses, there has been a steady stream of spontaneous cases received by the SPRs and parapsychology centers, and these similarities have continued to appear for more than a century.

Naturally these data are suspect. Psychologists have found that unusual anecdotes typically became exaggerated in the telling and retelling. All the same, it might be useful to offer here a few documented crisis cases from several countries around the world.

Case 1. 1869. Italy

The British SPR verified the date of his death from official records and received corroboration of the reported vision from the lady's husband, who was with her and comforted her at the time of this experience:

> At Fiesole, on March 11, I was giving my little children their dinner. On raising my head (as much from fatigue as for any purpose), the wall opposite me seemed to open, and I saw my mother lying dead on her bed. Some flowers were at her side and on her breast; she looked calm, but unmistakably dead, and the coffin was there. It was so real that I could scarcely believe that the wall was really brick and mortar, and not a transparent window.... I was so distressed by the vision that I wrote to my mother, entreating her to let me know how she was. By return of post came the statement that she had died on March 5, and was buried on the 11th.

Case 2. 1890. United States

One morning in Chicago, Mrs. Paquet woke up feeling gloomy, and could not shake the feeling. Her brother was a stoker plying a tug in the Chicago harbor, but she had no reason to feel alarm for him. In an effort to dispel her unusual depression, she went into the pantry to make tea. Here, in her words, is what she saw there:

> My brother Edmund—or his exact image—stood before me and only a few feet away. The apparition stood with back toward me, or, rather, partially so, and was in the act of falling forward—away from me—seemingly im-

pelled by a loop of rope drawing against his legs. The vision lasted but a moment, but was very distinct. I dropped the tea, clasped my hands to my face, and exclaimed, "My God! Ed is drowned!"

She also noted that the legs of his pants were rolled up, showing their white lining. The tragedy happened as she saw it, about six hours earlier.

Case 3. 1917. India

In its investigation, the SPR learned that the aviator, seen in the following vision by his sister, had been shot down and killed on March 19, very early in the morning.

At the time [March 19th], the baby was on the bed. I had a very strong feeling that I must turn around; on so doing I saw my brother, Eldred Bowyer-Bower. Thinking he was alive and had been sent to India, I was simply delighted to see him, and turned around quickly to put my baby in a safe place on the bed, so that I could go on talking to my brother; then turned again and found he was not there. I thought he was only joking so I called him and looked everywhere I could think of looking. It was only when I could not find him I became very frightened and the awful fear that he might be dead. . . . Two weeks later I saw in the paper he was missing. Yet I could not bring myself to believe he had passed away.

Case 4. 1967. United States

The only documentation for this instance is the word of my aunt, who had the vision. She was visiting relatives in Los Angeles on vacation from Connecticut, and was startled awake one morning about 4 A.M. At the foot of her bed she saw her nephew, my brother. Astonished, she exclaimed, "Charles! What are you doing here?!" He did not answer, and seemed to disappear. The next morning, at the breakfast table, my aunt told her sister and brother-in-law about the experience. Later in the day, our family had the difficult task of calling this home to tell of the totally unexpected death of my brother during the night.

CHARACTERISTICS OF THE HALLUCINATIONS

In these anecdotes from four countries, ranging over almost a century, we see obvious similarities. The hallucinations are so much like human beings that they are frequently mistaken for the actual person. The apparitions do not appear because the percipient is consciously anxious or worried about them. In our sample cases, the apparition usually arrives suddenly, while the person is engaged in simple household tasks. Although vividly seen, with details of clothing and facial expressions, these crisis apparitions are soundless, and disappear as suddenly as they appear.

CARL JUNG'S "HALLUCINATIONS": TWO MORE CASES

As we know, Jung was deeply convinced of a collective unconscious, in which we are all of us interconnected. His interest in psychical research was active for many years, perhaps because of his own experiences. In his autobiography, *Memories, Dreams, and Reflections,* he describes two incidents which are similar in some respects to the cases already presented.

On one occasion, as he lay awake one night thinking of the unexpected death of a friend whose funeral had been the day before,

> I felt that he was in the room, that he stood at the foot of the bed and was asking me to go with him. In all honesty I had to ask myself, "Suppose it is not a fantasy, suppose my friend is really here and I decided he was only a fantasy—would that not be abominable of me?" Yet I had equally little proof that he stood before me as an apparition. . . . [Eventually Jung decided to "play along" and followed his friend in imagination.] He led me to his house, and conducted me into his study. He showed me the second of five books with red bindings which stood on the second shelf from the top. Then the vision broke off.

Jung was so intrigued by the vision that the next morning he went to his friend's widow and asked to look for something in the library, where he had never been. He found the five books with red bindings, the second volume of which was *The Legacy of the Dead,* by Zola. Jung draws no conclusion, but considers the event provocative.

Similarly provocative was another occasion when, at two in the morning, he awoke with a start and "had the feeling that someone had come into the room." At that time he was concerned about a former patient whom he had relieved of a deep depression. The patient had subsequently married and as a result of which, or so Jung believed, had relapsed into a new depression. Jung immediately turned on the light, but no one was in the room. As he lay awake, he remembered feeling a dull pain.

> [It was] as though something had struck my forehead and then the back of my skull. The following day I received a telegram that my patient had shot himself. Later I learned that the bullet had come to rest in the back wall of the skull. . . . In this case the unconscious had knowledge of my patient's condition. All that evening, in fact, I had felt curiously restive and nervous, very much in contrast to my usual mood.

POSTMORTEM CASES

Jung conveys the impression that both his former patient and his friend may have been trying to convey information to him. In similar types of anecdotes in their collections (which comprise a smaller percentage than crisis cases), the SPRs have observed that the phantom or apparition was seemingly trying to convey specific information, unknown to the percipient. These hallucinations, more often than not, occurred weeks, months, or even years after the death of the person, and thus were classified by Tyrrell as postmortem cases. The postmortem case, then, is sometimes characterized by auditory hallucinations, or even sensations of touch or texture. Not infrequently, the presence is heralded by an intense feeling of *cold.* Here are a few examples:

Case 1. 1838. Scotland
One day a Presbyterian Scotswoman, Anne Simpson, called upon Father McKay, in a state of "utmost anxiety," for as she

explained, a woman named Maloy, recently deceased, had "appeared to her for several nights," urging her to go to a priest, who would pay a debt of "three and tenpence" owed to an unspecified person. McKay wrote, in a letter to the Countess of Shrewsbury:

> I made inquiry and found that a woman of that name had died, who acted as washerwoman and followed a regiment. . . . I found a grocer with whom she had dealt, and on asking him if a female named Maloy owed him anything, he turned up his books, and told me she did owe him three and tenpence. I paid the sum. Subsequently the Presbyterian woman came to me, saying that she was no more troubled.

(Not all exorcisms have proved to be so simple.)

Case 2. 1890. Russia

This correspondent, Baron von Driesen, begins his report by stating that he has never believed, and does not believe, in the supernatural and that he is inclined to attribute the episode to his "excited fancy."

> My father-in-law died after a long and painful illness. I had not been on good terms with him. Different circumstances had estranged us, and these relations did not change until his death. He died very quietly, after having given his blessings to all his family, including myself. A liturgy for the rest of his soul was to be celebrated on the ninth day. On the eve of that day, I read the Gospel before falling asleep. I had just put out the candle when footsteps were heard in the adjacent room—which ceased before the door of our bedroom. I called out, "Who's there?" No answer. I struck a match . . . and saw my father-in-law standing before the closed door. Yes, it was he, in his blue dressing gown, lined with squirrel furs. I was not frightened. "What do you want?" I asked. M. Ponomareff stopped before my bed and said, "I have acted wrongly toward you. Forgive me! Without this I do not feel at rest there." I seized his hand, which was long and cold, and answered, "God is my witness, I have never had anything against you." [The ghost of] my father-in-law *went through the opposite door* and disappeared. . . . The

liturgy was celebrated by the Rev. Father Basil. When it was over, Father Basil led me aside and said to me in a rather solemn voice, "This night at three o'clock, M. Ponomareff appeared to me and begged of me to reconcile him with you."

This account was substantiated by the Reverend Father Basil.

Case 3. 1928. England

On rare occasions the message comes from an apparition of someone totally unknown to the percipient, months or years after his death. One such case is reported by Aileen Garrett who, in spite of a lifetime of personal psychic experience, and strenuous research, admits to her bewilderment about the phenomenon. In a characteristic passage she writes: "Although I can attest to the actuality of my experiences, I am unable to explain or interpret them. So long as [science] does not extend itself to cover this field of the mind, I must always retain a slight distrust of these mental phenomena, and therefore of myself." She then describes this event (here abbreviated):

On release from the hospital, I was taken back to my apartment, in order to recuperate. . . . I cannot tell you what woke me. I know only that I awoke, and I looked across the room. I saw hands extending towards the gas fire. I could see the blood circulating through them, and on the little finger of the right hand there was a ring, and on it the initials E.H.D. I then removed my gaze from the initials and looked at the feet extending beyond the chair to the floor. They were a man's feet, in evening slippers. He wore two pairs of socks, black over red, as though to keep his feet warm. He looked pale and worn, about fifty; he was good-looking with a thin moustache and very blue eyes in a gaunt face. As I looked I heard him cough, and he hit his chest and said to me: "You see what it has done to me. It will also kill you if you remain here. This damp place is over an arm of the canal, and it throws off 'telluric rays' which will undoubtedly make you ill." Then with deliberation he walked out of the open doorway. [I told] Dr. Young when he called later that morning. He exclaimed, "By God! That is my old patient who died three months ago. If I may have your permission, I would like to tell his widow." This lady came to see me, and told me that her husband did die, having had bronchial asthma for a long time; that the ring on his finger had been removed before he died and was now in her possession. I inquired if the house was built on swampy soil, and found that there was indeed a delta under the house.

Mrs. Garrett asks, "How can this be explained, and what was it I saw, if it was not a ghost?" Her question remains unanswered.

GHOSTS AND HAUNTINGS

This last case brings us to the third category of apparitions, as classified by Tyrrell: cases in which the ghost seems to occupy a particular locale. Indeed, the haunted house, graveyard, or burial ground seems to be universally recognized by cultures of all eras; and just about every country today has its favorite haunting grounds, whether among the stately homes of England, in the jungles of South America, or the forests and deserts of the Orient.

As anthropologists have repeatedly demonstrated, certain cultures have evolved special techniques for mollifying malignant or recalcitrant ghosts. The noted Tibetan scholar W. Y. Evans-Wentz writes of a European planter who died in the Malabar jungle of southwest India and was buried there. Years later a friend of the planter visited his grave and found that it was fenced in, and littered with empty whiskey and beer bottles. Knowing that the natives were religious and therefore never drank liquor, he asked for an explanation of the condition of the grave. He was told that the "dead sahib's ghost had caused much trouble and no way had been discovered to lay the ghost until an old witch doctor declared that the ghost craved whiskey and beer, to which it had been long habituated when in the flesh." The people then had purchased the dead man's favorite brands of drink and to the accompaniment of their ritual for the dead, they had poured the alcohol on the grave, leaving the bottles there. It had been an expensive but effective remedy.

A STATELY GHOST OF ENGLAND

Lest the reader dismiss hauntings as mythology from ancient cultures or primitive peoples, it may be worth describing in some detail a ghost who is apparently still very much in residence in England. According to the history of Longleat Manor, as related by the Marquess of Bath, in the middle of the eighteenth century Lady Louisa Carteret fell in love with a man other than her husband, and as was the custom in that romantic era, one night her husband fought a duel with her lover. The duel took place on the third floor of the manor, and the lover was slain. Lady Louisa, known as the Green Lady Ghost, has presumably been wafting through the manor house for more than two centuries.

Generally such legends are listened to, chuckled at, and dismissed. But in 1964, NBC Television decided it might be an interesting entertainment for the American public to be introduced to some famous haunted houses of England. An experienced film director, Philip de Felitta, was sent to England to research and film the documentary. De Felitta's daughter, Aileen, and my son, Leland, were high school chums at the time, and Leland told me of De Fellita's extraordinary adventures while making the film. In those years I was much more skeptical of astral bodies and ghosts, and did not inquire further. Nor did I see the television show, "The Stately Ghosts of England," when it appeared in 1965.

As my interest grew, however, I visited De Felitta with two psychical research workers, one a physicist, the other a psychiatrist, and we obtained a first-person report of the happenings of Longleat Manor. We sat in his lovely home on top of the Hollywood Hills, drinking wine, listening to stereo music in the background, and looking down at the panorama of the city below. But as our host warmed to his subject (he was grateful for sympathetic ears, for no one had ever really believed his story), this sophisticated background gradually transformed into the eerie atmosphere of Longleat Manor. Apparently De Felitta had, with thoroughgoing skepticism, gone to England expecting to provide the American public with an interesting view of England's exquisite old homes, and aristocracy, and nothing more. Indeed, nothing in the least ghoulish did occur as his expert English camerman and crew traveled the countryside, capturing on film several splendid old mansions. They were accompanied by a psychic who, because of his expertise and knowledge of England's famous haunts, had been hired as a consultant. This gentleman, let's call him James, was considered generally as something of an eccentric, and definitely excess baggage.

Until they arrived at Longleat Manor. Almost immediately that the crew had set up their equipment, bizarre things began to happen. Lights blew up, and the telephone went dead. A heavy piece of equipment anchored on the third floor, where the duel had been fought, somehow broke loose, rolled down the hall, and crashed over the spiral staircase to the floor below, almost killing someone standing in the stairwell.

"But that was just the overture," said De Felitta, pausing to sip his wine. "Fortunately we had a crackerjack crew, who reassembled the equipment quickly. And on the first day's shooting we got what we believed was an excellent day's rushes. We sent the film down to London that night, to be developed. We always did that, to make sure our footage was usable before we left the location."

Another pause. "When the rushes came back, we were all shocked. Nothing like that film had ever been seen by any of us, and we were all veterans in the business. From start to finish, all that we saw was a sickly greenish-yellow haze. Not black film, or spotty film, or any of the defects that can occur in developing. Just a yellowish-green nothing. The cameraman checked his camera and could find nothing wrong with it, but we sent for another camera anyhow. And I called Kodak personally, to ask that they bring down fresh film, which they would guarantee to be in mint condition. They agreed, and the film was brought down. But I was beginning to get worried. You see, we had set up a camera on the third floor landing, with infrared film, to do time-lapse photography all through the night, one frame every fifteen seconds. And when we had gone to get the film, we found that the camera had been turned off. No film had run. It was easy to say that someone had been playing a practical joke, but the crew swore up and down they had left the camera functioning perfectly. And the night watchman on duty had had orders to let no one in or out while the shooting was going on. And he kept assuring us that no one had been there.

"Anyhow, we shot everything again the next day with a new

camera and fresh film, which I personally took with me to London, with a friend who agreed to develop the film with me right there."

Another pause, while his listeners waited eagerly for the development.

"The second batch of film turned out exactly like the first batch. Greenish-yellow haze from start to finish." (As we will see shortly, it is almost classic that certain haunts, and/or poltergeists, can affect electricity, telephones, light bulbs, and film.)

"What did you do?" asked the physicist.

"You won't believe it. I can hardly believe it myself. But driving back from London for the third day's shooting, I was thinking hard. These delays were costing NBC a lot of money, we were way over schedule, and I didn't feel like calling New York to say we were having trouble because of some ghosts. Anyhow, there was James, our psychic consultant, sitting in the car, not saying much. But I had a hunch that he could tell me how to handle it. So, as we're driving, I said to him, 'James, we won't get it today either, will we?' And he said, 'No.' And then I took the plunge. 'OK,' I said, 'What do I do now?' "

Another pause. We all drank some more wine.

"This guy James," De Felitta continued, "was a wise fellow. He wasn't pushing for power; he wasn't smirking with an 'I-told-you-so.' He just said, seriously, 'You really should ask them for permission.' That was a jolt. I didn't see how I could ask a ghost I can't see for a favor, but I was in so deep, I just nodded and said, 'OK, how do I do that?' "

We laughed. Rather nervously.

"James said it would be best for *me* to do it, alone. And he recommended the third-floor library, because it seemed to him to be a 'focal area of activity.' I said, 'Third-floor library it is. When?' And he answered, quietly, 'Well, it's generally best done in total darkness. I personally find midnight a good time. And whatever you do, I recommend that you speak respectfully.'

"I kept thinking about his idea all day while we were shooting. Because I knew that day's shooting wouldn't be any better."

"Was it?" I asked.

De Felitta shook his head. "Same green haze. Anyhow, that night I explained to the watchman that I wanted to be in the Manor, alone, on the third floor. He arranged it, and then he left me." De Fallita shook his head and smiled. "You know, I was scared. But more than scared, I felt so damn *foolish!* All this was happening, and I couldn't deny it was happening, but still, some part of me couldn't accept it. You get brainwashed into believing there's no such animal as a ghost. Ghosts are for Hallowe'en, for horror movies. But for Christ's sake, they can't screw up a TV show! But there I was, walking into an empty library at midnight to have a talk with some ghosts. And believe me, I talked seriously and respectfully."

"Can you remember specifically anything you said?" I asked.

He laughed. "I can quote it almost word for word. Because I was telling it like it was. I said, 'Whoever you are, I think you should know we don't want to do you any harm. We just want to show Longleat Manor to the world, because it's a beautiful home. And I'm only trying to do my job. If you keep me from doing it, I'll lose my job, and so will the other good people who are working with me. We are simply working men trying to earn our livings. And we ask, with all respect, that you permit us to get on with our work.' And that was that."

"Did you get any kind of an answer?" I asked.

"Absolutely nothing. I said my piece, and it was quiet. No raps, no lights, just empty silence. I didn't know if I had accomplished anything or not. But I felt better. Because I had done what I thought was right."

Pause. I think we were each wondering what we would have done in a similar situation.

"The next day I just had the feeling everything was going to be ok. And it was. The film came out beautifully—with a special bonus! That time-lapse camera on the third floor had worked all night long. And when we developed it, we saw the ghost! Or a manifestation of *something*. Here it is." De Felitta showed us stills, taken from the infrared film of the third-floor camera. They revealed what looked like a blob of light emerging from a door at the far end of the hall, gradually floating down the hall, then disappearing through a door near the camera.

De Felitta added, as we studied the photographs, "I don't know if this is significant or not. I like to think it is. But those lights came on the film around 1 A.M., shortly after I spoke my piece in the library. . . . Maybe they were cooperating. . . . Anyhow, we ran this piece of film when the show aired, in 1965."

Thus, for all the world to see, NBC showed a manifestation of the stately ghost from Longleat Manor.

MACKENZIE'S CASES

In 1968 the English parapsychologist Andrew MacKenzie appeared on BBC-TV and discussed his research into apparitions. He was rewarded with a rash of responses from viewers who claimed experiences with ghosts and apparitions in their homes. Of the letters he received, MacKenzie found forty-nine promising cases, all of which he personally investigated, publishing the results in his book *Apparitions and Ghosts.* Of particular interest are those cases he reports of ghosts which are seen by more than one person at the same, or different, times. Such "collective" cases are not so rare as one might suppose and offer a new set of problems, well presented by Professor H. H. Price in his introduction to Tyrrell's excellent book *Apparitions:* "Surely a telepathic hallucination ought to be a purely private phenomenon, experienced only by the person for whom the telephatic communication was intended. But in fact it is sometimes experienced by indifferent bystanders as well. The notion of a *public* hallucination is a very strange one, almost as strange as the notion of a public dream." Sometimes mass hypnosis is hypothesized to explain the collective case. However, in this next case, taken from MacKenzie's collection, it is difficult to discover who is doing the hypnotizing, since there is no one in the vicinity but husband, wife, dog—and the phantom.

In his letter to MacKenzie, the husband reports noticing "the figure of a man walking frequently past the kitchen windows towards the coach house, invariably at dusk. Mary [his wife] once walked accidentally into 'him' and has not forgotten the experience of intense cold. She noticed he wore glasses and walked unsteadily. He never walked further than the entrance to the coach house. Our dog used to bark and follow him, then would suddenly stop, always at the entrance to the coach house, looking around very surprised at having lost the visitor." This apparition was first seen two days after the couple had moved into their new home, and was seen at odd intervals up to the time of book publication (1971). On a few occasions the figure was seen inside the house, twice downstairs, once on the upstairs landing, and once coming out of the bathroom, "stripped to the waist, with a towel over his 'arm.' "

The husband's opinion was that the "repetitive pattern [of the walk to the coach house] suggests to me a single event being repeated again and again." MacKenzie's investigation revealed that the son of the previous owner fitted the description of the ghost. According to the villagers, this young man had often come home drunk, and then would sleep in the coach house. However, to complicate matters, the son had left home some years before, and had been reported dead in another part of the country. MacKenzie learned that the coroner's verdict, at the time of the inquest, was suicide. For several years, then, this young man had not been in the vicinity, and the new owners of the home had not known of his existence, nor his eccentric behavior, nor, indeed, what he looked like.

"HAUNTED HOUSES" AND OUR LAB

Over the years our lab has discovered that the type of haunting just described, witnessed by two or more persons in a particular locale, is not unusual. At least, not in Los Angeles. We receive on the average of two calls a month from persons who believe their houses are haunted. As a result (and in self-defense), we have become rather skilled at taking a detailed case history before proceeding with a formal investigation. For, in the bulk of these cases, as we learned in early field trips, it is not the house, but the persons living in the house who are "haunted"—haunted by their own neuroses or psychoses, which they project into the surroundings in which they live. Yet, on a few occasions, we have been subjectively convinced that something very much like a collective haunting is being experienced. Interestingly, and in contrast to popular superstition, Los Angeles "haunted houses" are not old, abandoned mansions. They are typically middle-class, recently built, comfortable homes which are lived in by several members of a family, most of whom have had some experience with the apparitions.

As an example, here are excerpts from a long typewritten letter which we received in May of 1972:

In September 1971, my husband and I purchased the house we are presently living in. The house is six years old, a trilevel, with the master bedroom located up a short flight of stairs (5) and three bedrooms and bath up a flight of 10 stairs.

My husband and I sleep with the bedroom door open so we can listen for our little boy, C——(3½). One night something woke me (I don't know what; as far as I can remember I hadn't been dreaming). I saw a red light, which seemed to be about 5 or more feet in height and 3 or more feet in width, moving slowly up the stairs. I became frightened and woke my husband. But when he woke, the light was gone.

The next few weeks went by normally, except for some incidents involving C——. Several times he would look up from what he was doing and say, "What, daddy? What, daddy?" as if his father was calling him, when in actuality his father was not home. I mentioned these incidents to my husband but we attached little importance to them.

It was toward the end of November when I noticed a drastic change in my feelings about the house. Before I had found it a lovely house, but my feelings went from liking to hatred. I became depressed and unhappy, which is not like me at all. Trying to trace the source brought me back to our house. Although my rational instincts told me that was ridiculous, my survival instincts told me it was true. January 4 we put our house up for sale.

During this time we would occasionally hear strange noises, nothing frightening, but when C—— would hear them, he would say, "What's that?" And we would tell him, "That's just the furnace." So after that whenever he heard any strange noise he would say, "That's the furnace."

The disturbing thing happened one Saturday, while we were watching a TV show called the Sixth Sense. It was an episode of a man who was drowned coming back to haunt his wife. He is dripping wet, but there is an unearthly quality about him. When C—— saw this apparition he exclaimed, "There's Furnace." Just after he says this, the wife on TV sees her husband and screams.

C—— says, "Furnace make lady scream." He was not in the least upset by seeing the apparition.

But perhaps the strangest thing of all is that my feelings about the house changed abruptly in mid-February. One morning I woke and felt my normal self, eager to start a new day. And I have felt that way ever since. This change of feeling occurred approximately at the time C—— said, "Furnace went out the door."

The reason for this letter to you is to find out if anyone else has reported this type of manifestation, and if your researchers have been able to come up with a common denominator for the occasions. We would appreciate any assistance or advice you can provide.

Naturally we sent investigators to interview the family, who were charming and intelligent people. But the strange activities of the house had quieted down, and there was little more to be learned, and little advice to be given. Most "haunts" we have investigated have provided little information of interest, but there have been exceptions.

A FORMAL INVESTIGATION OF A "HAUNTED HOUSE"

Our first controlled study of a haunted house began in 1965 when a rather embarrassed psychiatrist at the Neuropsychiatric Institue came to us with the news that good friends of his believed their house was contaminated by "spooks." On four different occasions, persons unknown to each other had told the owners that they had seen a strange figure around the house. The psychiatrist was not interested in this area of research, and asked if I would be willing to make an investigation. I had just returned from a parapsychology convention in New York, where I had heard a fascinating paper presented by Dr. Gertrude Schmeidler, who described an investigation of a haunted house. She told how a group of psychics had been taken through the home and then asked to show on a map where they felt a "ghost" might be lurking, and to describe the kind of ghost they felt it might be. In her paper, Dr. Schmeidler regretted she had not used a control group of nonpsychics to perform the same tasks.

This mode of investigation seemed appropriate for the haunted house on the West Coast. In order to avoid any introduction of my own knowledge, which might influence the results, I asked the psychiatrist not to tell me the location of the house, nor the names of the owners. The only information I wanted was a floor plan of the house and the names of the four persons who had seen the apparition. These were supplied, and with the cooperation of the local branch of the ASPR, a group of psychics (as well as a group of nonpsychics) were enlisted to participate. Members of the ASPR in Los Angeles interviewed each of the witnesses who had seen the apparition, and supplied me with their tape-recorded remarks.

The first witness, a journalist, was having tea at the pool with her hostess when she saw a man walk swiftly around the pool. He was middle-aged, dressed formally in a black suit, white shirt, and tie. She wondered why he was not introduced, and asked her hostess, who looked puzzled and said there was no gentleman present.

The second witness was the pool maintenance man, who one day when he had been told the owners were away, was surprised to see a man inside the house walking swiftly to the dining room.

The third witness, a screenwriter, was staying in the house while the owners were on holiday. As he was about to retire for the night, he saw at the bedroom door a man of about fifty, tall, rather heavyset, dressed in dark pants and a white shirt. The figure had a menacing demeanor, so much so that the screenwriter left abruptly, and spent the night in a motel. He added that, being Scotch, he would not have spent the money for the motel room unless he had been genuinely frightened.

The last witness was the real-estate agent who had sold the owners the house. One night, alone in the house, he saw a tall, middle-aged man, wearing dark slacks and a T-shirt, walking toward the dining room.

None of these four people knew each other then, nor to my knowledge have they met subsequently. The owners of the house had never seen the ghost, but they had been repeatedly disturbed in the middle of the night by sounds of a "dinner party" in progress in the dining room, sounds which they had recorded on tape.

Following Dr. Schmeidler's paradigm, six psychics, each individually conducted by a different investigator, were given maps and taken through the house. They were asked to locate on the floor plans where they felt a ghost might be lurking. In addition, they were asked to fill out multiple-choice questionnaires regarding the ghost (e.g., Age: teens; twenty to thirty-five; thirty-five to fifty; fifty or over) which also included physical characteristics, and clothing. To a high level of statistical significance, the psychics agreed on certain features of the ghost: that he was over thirty-five, of average to heavy build, tall, with average to heavy musculature. This description, if one is going to invent a ghost, hardly fits the conventional idea. By contrast, the control group of non-psychics showed no agreement of any kind.

One very interesting precognitive impression was given spontaneously by one of the psychics, who kept returning to the dining room because of the "strong vibrations" she felt there. She announced that a fire would break out in the dining room, forcing the owners to evacuate. Several months later, that is exactly what happened; and the firemen who extinguished the fire could not find the cause of the outbreak. This study was published in collaboration with Dr. Schmeidler, to whom we are indebted not only for her original experimental design, but for the sophisticated statistical analysis she made of the data.

THOSE WHO SEE GHOSTS AND THOSE WHO DON'T

As a footnote, let me confess that in none of the haunts on which I have made house calls and in none of the seances in which I have participated have I, personally, ever observed anything remotely resembling an apparition. Other members of the lab, on occasion, have claimed to experience phenomena such as cold spots, vaporous substances, even faces and forms. I do not discredit their claims, for it is a commonplace that at the same seance, or in the same haunted room, two or three people in a group will see and describe phenomena (on which they agree) which are invisible to the others in the party. This need not be considered a folly invented by psychical research; for very hard-headed physiologists and psychologists have carefully studied thresholds of perception and agree that what is visible or audible to one person may be invisible or inaudible to another. Differences become more pronounced between species. Dogs, for example, can hear far beyond the range of the human ear. In fact, one can purchase special dog whistles which people cannot hear.

Apparently these differences in auditory or visual perception are a question of frequency of vibration. It would seem that I, personally, am not tuned into that range of frequencies. Fortunately other parapsychologists seem to be tuned in, and they have obtained records, both on camera and on tape recorders, as mysterious as the stately ghost of Longleat Manor. Before discussing the research of William Roll, at Durham's Psychical Research Foundation, and Professor Hans Bender, head of the University of Freiburg's Department of Parapsychology, let me digress into another haunted-house investigation—with bewildering results.

THE HALF-WAY HOUSE

A few years ago I received a phone call from a social worker and friend, Bart Ellis, who at the time was conducting a half-way house for disturbed adolescents. He believed the house was manifesting disturbances typical of a haunting, including strange sounds emanating from one room, which he had recorded on tape. By then, the lab had evolved a standard procedure for such house calls, which involved the services of the lab psychic, Barry Taff. Giving him no previous information about the house at all, we would conduct Barry through each room of the house, and he would report his impressions into a tape recorder. If his impressions seemed accurate in any way, we would occasionally hold a seance to obtain further information.

As we were making plans for that evening, a staff psychiatrist from the NPI happened into my office, listening skeptically to our project, and then asked suddenly if he could join us. We were delighted. It's a rare opportunity when a professional, and skeptic—even as a lark—offers to cooperate in an investigation. That night Barry, Dr. H., and I went through the house, Barry going from room to room recording his impressions. When Barry had finished, the psychiatrist claimed that he, too, had a good imagination, and, as a control, he would like to do what Barry had done—go from room to room, giving his impressions. We agreed, and he began, with a strong dramatic flair. He described, as the hero of the house, a seventeen-year-old adolescent boy, a loner, a drug abuser, who had left home, and after wandering on beaches, getting involved in hippie groups, etc., had found his way to this house. Dr. H. walked into one bedroom, stopped suddenly at the bed, saying, "And here—on this bed—the boy committed a sexual assault on a thirteen-year-old. Homosexual assault." He went into other rooms, with no special impressions, and stopped in the largest bedroom at a particular spot in the middle of the room. He lifted his arms, then pointed down, saying, "And right here, the boy collapsed from an overdose of a drug and fell to the floor. But he was discovered in time, and survived."

Out of patience with Dr. H., who seemed to be making a travesty of the investigation, I suggested we go downstairs to compare Barry's impressions with what had been observed in the house. On the way, Bart Ellis took me aside and asked, "Who is that guy?!" He didn't point to Barry, but to Dr. H. Ready. To apologize, I answered that he was a psychiatrist. Bart interrupted excitedly, saying that while Dr. H.'s impressions had nothing to do with the haunting, they were absolutely accurate. There had been a seventeen-year-old loner in the house, a drug abuser, who had assaulted a thirteen-year-old boy in the small bedroom, and had been discovered after taking an overdose, exactly at the spot where Dr. H had stopped and raised his hands. In my opinion, this was a remarkable psychic impression received by Dr. H. But Dr. H. dismissed that idea, preferring to call it a coincidence, based on the probability of an adolescent drug abuser and sexual pervert living in a half-way house such as this one. Granting that probability, Dr. H. had nevertheless scored a high number of hits, including specific locations where specific acts had been carried out. (Although Dr. H. did not admit to his success with this psychic reading, he later served as co-investigator in an extensive laboratory study of Barry's telepathic ability.) In this particular case, we never learned anything about the "ghost," and in time the disturbances faded away.

POLTERGEISTS: THINGS THAT GO BUMP IN THE NIGHT (OR DAYLIGHT)

Generally included in the category of apparitions and/or ghosts is the phenomenon of the "poltergeist," a German word meaning a noisy or boisterous spirit. Poltergeists quite literally make things go bump and crash in the night, or in broad daylight, for that matter. From various countries, over the centuries, have come remarkably similar accounts of places in which mysterious outbreaks have occurred: stones hurtling inside houses, crockery and lamps suddenly shattering for no apparent reason, furniture collapsing or moving without apparent physical cause. Again using the SPR reports for early source material, let us look at a few cases.

Case 1. 1906. Austria

An Austrian member of the SPR, "Mr. Weinstadt" (a pseudonym) learned through newspaper reports of a blacksmith's shop in which "acts of vandalism" were being committed: Tools, pieces of iron, etc., were being flung about the shop, injuring the blacksmith and his two apprentices, none of whom could find the culprit. When Weinstadt arrived, he found the blacksmith wearing a stiff hat for protection. The blacksmith showed him a lump on the back of his head where he had been struck by a piece of iron. His two apprentices, aged sixteen and eighteen, had had similar "accidents." After several weeks of observation in the shop, Weinstadt submitted a report of his own experiences:

> The first phenomenon was a piece of iron about the size of a walnut touching me quite *lightly* on the top of my felt hat, and from there dropping to the floor. Later on I was struck by a small blade of steel on the back of the neck. . . . [On another day] I watched the boys drilling a hole in a piece of iron. Suddenly the younger of the two screamed out and was nearly bent double with pain and fright; an iron instrument had struck him pretty sharply on the left temple. I had noticed the instrument before, lying on the work bench about a yard behind the boy. . . . [On a third occasion I saw a small picture on one of the walls] *fluttering* to the middle of the shop in an almost parabolic direction. It did not *fall*, but behaved rather like a sheet of paper; it did not break on the floor.

These and other phenomena continued for about two months and then stopped, after the apprentices had been dismissed.

Case 2. 1911. Ireland

This poltergeist incident is of exceptional interest in that it was investigated by a Nobel-Prize-winner, Sir William Barrett, professor of physics at Dublin University (whom the reader may remember for his "tasting at a distance" hypnosis experiments). The poltergeist had been violently throwing objects, including the family Bible, around a Derrygonnelly cottage occupied by a farmer, his wife, and five children from the ages of ten to twenty. Here is Sir William's account of his experiences in the cottage the first night:

> I closely observed each of the occupants lying on the bed. The younger children were asleep, and Maggie [the twenty-year-old daughter] was motionless; nevertheless, knocks were going on everywhere around; on the chairs, the bedstead, the walls, and ceiling. The closest scrutiny failed to detect any movement on the part of those present that could account for the noises, which were accompanied by a scratching or tearing sound. Suddenly a large pebble fell in my presence on the bed; no one had moved to dislodge it even if it had been placed for the purpose. When I replaced the candle on the window sill in the kitchen, the knocks became even louder, like those made by a heavy carpenter's hammer driving nails in the flooring.

Similar phenomena were observed on the following two nights, with unabated intensity. At the farmer's urging, a member of Sir William's party agreed to conduct a service, in an attempt to rid the family of the "spirit." Again quoting from Sir William's report:

> The noises were at first so great we could hardly hear what was read, then as the solemn words of the prayer were uttered they subsided, and when the Lord's Prayer was joined in by us all, a profound stillness fell on the whole cottage. The farmer rose from his knees with tears streaming down his face, gratefully clasped our hands, and we left for our long midnight drive back to Enniskillen. I am afraid this does not sound like a scientific account, but it is a veracious one.

After that, there were no further disturbances in the cottage.

Case 3. 1917. England

During World War I, an Englishman had a dugout built into a small hill in his garden, for use as an air raid shelter. The builder and his assistant, a sixteen-year-old boy, complained almost daily that stones and sand kept hitting them as they worked. These complaints were ignored until one day, when the owner, alone, went to inspect the dugout. He reported:

> I closed the door at the bottom of the steps and . . . a stone came violently in contact with the inside of the door. I then cautiously proceeded to push the door open. Immediately another stone struck the door violently. In quick succession from 7 to 8 stones struck the wall. I satisfied myself that no person was near.

The builder, in a sworn statement, wrote that he

> felt something like some dirt come on my head. The boy roared with laughter as he said a brick was hovering there. As my hand got near it, it dropped on the ground near my feet. The brick weighed about ten pounds.

This episode sounds very much like that in the blacksmith's shop, where an iron as large as a walnut hovered near Weinstadt's hat. A Canadian soldier, in another sworn statement, said he had witnessed many of these phenomena, including spurts of sand emerging from near the ceiling "as if shot from a peashooter."

The news media publicized these happenings, with opinions ranging from "pure bunkum" to the suggestion that German spies were tunneling under England. Eventually a petroleum expert declared that these untoward events were the result of "natural gas," an opinion that was the one generally accepted as being scientifically sound. This opinion, incidentally, has a familiar contemporary ring: Some experts today explain UFOs as an illusion created by swamp gas.

PRESENT-DAY POLTERGEISTS

Poltergeists are still with us. Two recent outbursts have been intensively studied by parapsychologists, in collaboration with physicists using sophisticated electronic instrumentation. Their findings have only served to deepen the mystery.

Case 1. 1967. United States

When Susy Smith, a popular writer on psychical research, was being interviewed on radio in Miami, Florida, she received a phone call asking how to stop a "spook" which was creating havoc in a local warehouse, breaking numerous beer mugs, ash trays, vases, and other crockery. In her words, "It sounded as if a poltergeist had gone berserk, and there was nothing I wanted to see more than a genuine poltergeist in action." She offered to go to the warehouse to investigate—and for the next twenty-four days, together with the police, reporters, and TV and radio men, she witnessed numerous activities which no one could explain. Miss Smith then had the acumen to ask two leading parapsychologists for help. Dr. J. G. Pratt, of the University of Virginia, and William Roll, head of the Psychical Research Foundation, arrived in Miami in time to conduct a serious and strenuous investigation.

Naturally, these scientists were very much on the lookout for a trickster, someone playing a pretty hoax, perhaps a magician looking for publicity. These are the first possibilities to be ruled out. In fact, parapsychologists often employ the talents of a professional magician to duplicate observed "paranormal" activity. A magician in Miami was called on to duplicate the crashing and fallings of objects, but he could not. According to Susy Smith, "We were all finally converted into genuine unadulterated 'believers' on Monday and Tuesday, when the activity got so fast and furious that no human, unless he had been on roller skates, could have rigged up enough devices to trigger things so fast."

Both Roll and Pratt centered their interest on a nineteen-year-old shipping clerk, Julio, as a possible source of the trouble. But in his report of the case, Pratt exonerates Julio, describing how on one occasion he was alone in the warehouse with Julio when a two-quart pickle jar crashed to the floor, yet Julio had been under his constant surveillance. Pratt concluded: "The circumstances before the event and our close inspection of the situation immediately after did not reveal any normal explanation of how the jar came to break as it did." Roll brought in physicists to analyze the movements of the objects as they cavorted through the air, performing torques and twists which are not explainable according to the laws of physical motion, as understood today. Remember the brick hovering near the builder, the picture fluttering to the floor, the iron grazing Wienstadt's felt hat?

Case 2. 1968. Germany

The Rosenheim poltergeist is far and away the most famous poltergeist in history. Its activities, including frequent calls to ask for the time (four calls per minute were recorded to the local time number), so disturbed the German Post Office and Telephone Company that the telephone system was completely overhauled, and then sealed off. In fact, the postal authorities tore up the offices, and the road outside, trying unsuccessfully to find out how the telephones could ring when no one was dialing a number. The poltergeist also, obligingly, made its activities visible on film for Professor Hans Bender of the University of Freiburg. Eventually, these phenomena, which continued for several months, were given an intensive investigation by two physicists, Karger and Zicha, from the eminent Max Planck Institute of Physics. Karger and Zicha employed elaborate equipment for their research, and submitted a written report of their studies, excerpts from which are presented here:

> Examples of inexplicable phenomena given to us by the officials of the electrical works were: interference with the telephone, unaccountable turning off of safety devices, bursting of bulbs, and oscillations of lamps in the ceiling. The electrical works had tried to elucidate the disturbances in the supply circuit, finally installing their own lamps and supplies and an emergency assembly. The phenomena did not cease. The Siemens linear graph Unireg I of the electrical works was provided with a voltage-amplification additional unit. Between 16:30 and 17:48 about fifteen strong oscillations were registered. Approximately simultaneously we heard a report resembling an electrical discharge which seemed to hail from different positions. The sounds were taped.
>
> With a view to a thorough investigation the voltage was inserted parallel to the graph on a channel of a Tektronix (Type 1A4) connected to a storage oscilloscope (Type 549). On the 3 remaining channels, we

registered via corresponding probes the electrical potential and the magnetic field in the proximity of the
graph. As a result of our findings, we were forced to
dismiss the following possible explanations of the deflections in the graph:

Alterations in voltage
Electrostatic charge
External magnetic field (static)
Ultra- or infra-sound (subsequent investigation)
Manual action
Fraud and trick manipulation impossible.

We must thus conclude that the deflections occurred
in the graph in spite of the fact that we had carefully
eliminated or controlled all conceivable physical causes.
[This] agrees with the conception of a "mechanical"
influence without ascertainable cause. Thus bulbs had
burst although the filaments were intact and had not
been burnt. The civic works and CID agree in their
descriptions of plates jumping off the walls, of pictures
and calendars turning around on the walls, and the
turning of a picture by more than 90 degrees was
recorded by an Ampex videorecorder.

We are reduced to the following summing up.

The phenomena are not explicable by the available
means of theoretical physics.

The phenomena (including interference with the telephone) did not seem to be produced with the help of
electro-dynamic effects.

Not only simple events of an explosive nature take
place, but also complicated movements, e.g. curves in
the graph.

A surprisingly exact correlation unknown to physics
was found: the anomalous deflections only occur when
a certain employee, Miss Schneider, is in the immediate
vicinity. Since the events only occur in the presence of a
certain human being, a case unforeseen in physics arises
in which the investigation of the human being can
initiate new fundamental physical discoveries.

CLUES TO THE POLTERGEIST

The reader may have observed that, in addition to Miss
Schneider of Rosenheim, in every poltergeist case here described

there has been a young person on the scene between the ages of ten and twenty (Miss Schneider was eighteen years old at the time). One hypothesis is that the adolescent who is in strong emotional turmoil (neurotic, psychotic—or just in love?) can trigger some kind of energy which moves objects in their vicinity. We have already seen that certain gifted, adult psychics like Kulagina and Geller have been able at times to channel and direct this energy. The last statement by Karger and Zicha certainly parallels the objectives of the Prague conference, which were to examine the interaction of the human being with his environment.

When Julio, the blacksmith's apprentices, and Miss Schneider left their jobs, the phenomena ceased. But the question remains: What aspect of their persons or personalities might have been responsible for the bewildering movements of objects in their vicinity? Perhaps the infant science of bioenergetics may one day find a valid interpretation for "poltergeist" activity.

BUT WHAT ABOUT APPARITIONS?

Leaving aside the activities of the poltergeist, there remain without explanation that assortment of hallucinations, apparitions, phantoms, and/or ghosts. We have seen that descriptions of these whatever-they-are remain remarkably similar across centuries. What sort of explanation can be offered for these phenomena? This is not an easy question, and there is no ready answer.

Let me offer a tentative hypothesis, based on the assumption that there does in fact exist an energy body, or etheric body, and that this second body can at times disengage itself from the physical body. Let us also entertain the idea, offered by many esoteric philosophies, that this energy body—*of all of us*—leaves the physical body at death. What, then, would become of that energy body? What would its function be?

Answers to those questions have been offered by just about every culture of the world—very similar answers. I am of course referring to those fascinating concepts of survival after death, and reincarnation.

14 Survival after Death? Reincarnation?

> I laugh at what you call dissolution,
> And I know the amplitude of time . . .
> And as to you Life I reckon you are the leavings of
>   many deaths
> (No doubt I have died myself ten thousand times
>   before.)
>
> —Walt Whitman

WHAT HAPPENS WHEN WE DIE?

In a recent psychology class I asked the question: Suppose you were to die and discovered that you continued to exist; what would your reaction be? There was no response from the hundred-odd students, so I addressed the question to a girl sitting in a front row, who simply shrugged and replied, "Oh, I don't believe in that sort of thing."

"I don't doubt that," I answered, "but the question is: Suppose you were to die, and in spite of your belief, you discovered that you still existed. How would you feel?"

There was a startled moment in the room, and then an uncomfortable laugh. It was a disturbing thought to these students, most of whom had been reared in the materialistic philosophy that the end of the body is the end of everything. That day's lecture was devoted to the problem of death, and the hypotheses of what may lie beyond it. Professors of psychology who study the subject of death, (called thanatology in academic circles) generally confine their inquiries to reactions at the prospect of death. A few clinical psychologists are beginning to try to "prepare" terminal patients for the advent of death. But what is it that the dying person is being prepared to face?

SOME SURVEYS OF DEATH AND THE DYING

In 1960, the American Institute of Public Opinion conducted a poll, asking this question of a representative sample of people: "Do you believe there is, or is not, a life after death?" The results were surprising: 74 percent of the United States population answered, "There is"; 14 percent, "There is not"; and 12 percent "Can't say." With such a large majority of the population believing in something beyond death, it is surprising that so few serious attempts have been made to explore the possibilities that may exist beyond the dissolution of the physical body.

One such attempt, *Deathbed Observations by Physicians and Nurses*, was undertaken recently by Dr. Karlis Osis, research director of the ASPR. Osis sent questionnaires to 10,000 nurses and doctors, asking specific questions about the behavior of dying patients. The replies received contained information about approximately 35,000 patients observed at the time of death. Only 10 percent of those persons were conscious. (One respondent wrote dourly, "Nowadays man dies doped.") Of the 3,500 persons who were conscious and rational in their dying moments, more than 700 were described as being—far from fearful or sad—in an "extremely elevated" mood. It was further learned that the most common deathbed experience of these patients was the appearance of hallucinations: hallucinations involving persons already dead who, according to the dying patient, had come to help them make the transition into the next phase of existence. This last finding corroborates an earlier study by Sir William Barrett, *Deathbed Visions*, in which can be found the particularly interesting case of a "Mrs. B.," who in 1924 lay dying in an English hospital. Because she had been so gravely ill, she had been carefully prevented from learning about the death of her sister, Vida, just a few weeks before. As Mrs. B. was sinking, she said, "It is all so dark, I cannot see." A moment later she exclaimed, "Oh . . . it's lovely and bright. . . . I can see father; he wants me." After another moment, with a puzzled expression, she said, "He has Vida with him. . . . Vida is with him!" And within a few minutes, she died. Hallucination? Fantasy? Perception of another dimension of reality, just prior to joining it? Who can say?

THOSE WHO HAVE "DIED" AND RETURNED

Thanatologists generally discourage discussions of life after death, considering that at best they can be only theoretical or futile, since no one has ever died and returned to report his experiences. This may not be quite true, if descriptions of the afterlife such as the following are to be credited as something other than delusions.

1. Arthur Ford
Arthur Ford, in his book *Unknown But Known,* writes that he had been critically ill in a hospital at Coral Gables, and his doctors had said he could not last the night. Ford heard his doctor say, "He may as well be comfortable. Give him the needle." Then, in Ford's words:

> I was floating in the air over my bed. I saw my body but took no more interest in it than in a cast-off coat. Then total, timeless unconsciousness. . . . I awoke, with no sense of having a body. Yet it was I, *myself.* Coming toward me from all sides were people I had known and thought of as dead. . . .
>
> At one point, a court of higher beings considered my condition. They were seriously concerned about the dissipation of opportunities to accomplish what I knew I was meant to fulfill. It was made clear I would have to go back. I balked like a spoiled child and braced my feet and fought against going. . . . There was a sudden sense of hurtling through space, and I found myself—in Coral Gables. I had been in a coma for two weeks.

2. Private Ritchie
The most recent case of this kind to be published, to my knowledge, is *The Pseudo-Death of Private Ritchie,* 1963, which contains affidavits from the U.S. Army doctor and attending

nurse, attesting to the fact that Ritchie had been pronounced dead. In Ritchie's words:

> When I opened my eyes, I was lying in a little room I had never seen before. I sprang out of bed ... and I stopped, staring. Someone was lying in the bed I had just left. He was dead. The slack jaw, the grey skin was awful. Then I saw the Phi Gamma Delta fraternity ring that I had worn for two years. ... I was beginning to know that the body on the bed was mine, unaccountably separated from me, and that my job was to rejoin it as fast as I could. I tried to draw back the sheet, but I could not seize it. I thought suddenly, "This is death, this splitting of one's self."

Thus far, Ritchie's description is very similar to the one recorded by Dr. Wiltse, when he found that his energy body had separated from the physical one and that his energy body could not make contact with anything in the room. But then, Ritchie's experience took a different turn:

> The little room began to fill with light. I say "light," but there is no word in our language to describe brilliance that intense. The light which entered that room was Christ. ... But something else was present in that room, ... every single episode of my entire life, ... every event and thought and conversation, as palpable as a series of pictures. There was no first or last, each one was contemporary, each one asked a single question, "What have you done with your time on earth?" ...
>
> A new wave of light spread through the room, and all around was a very different world occupying the same space. It was thronged with people, with the unhappiest faces I had ever seen. ... Had their hearts and minds been all concerned with earthly things, and now, having lost earth, were they still fixed hopelessly here?
>
> I was permitted to look at two more worlds. The second occupied this very surface of the earth, but it was a vastly different realm. There were universities and great libraries and scientific laboratories that surpassed the wildest inventions of science fiction. Of the final

world I had only a glimpse. At a great distance I saw a city—but a city, if such a thing is conceivable, constructed out of light. The next instant the dazzling light faded, and a strange sleep stole over me. . . .

Weeks later Ritchie was able to look at his medical records:

There it was: Pvt. George Ritchie, died Dec. 20, 1943, double lobar pneumonia. Later . . . the doctor told me there was no doubt in his mind that I had been dead when he examined me, but that nine minutes later the soldier who had been assigned to prepare me for the morgue had come running to him to ask him to give me a shot of adrenalin. The doctor gave me a hypo of adrenalin directly into the heart muscle. . . . My return to life, he told me, without brain damage or other lasting effect, was the most baffling circumstance of his career.

Private Ritchie became a medical doctor himself, in practice now, believing firmly that he was returned to life so that he could "learn about man and serve God."

These two contemporary cases contain certain Christian concepts. But stripped of those specific religious references, the experiences themselves might be compared to this one, told by Plato two thousand years ago in his *Republic*. There, the warrior Er was killed in battle. On the twelfth day after his death, his body (which had not disintegrated) was placed on the funeral pyre, at which point Er returned to life and described his adventures in the afterworld:

Each soul, as it arrived, wore a travel-stained appearance . . . and those who had descended from heaven were questioned by those who had risen out of the earth; while the latter were questioned by the former about earth. The souls about to enter earth life were thus addressed:
"A new generation of men shall here begin the cycle of its mortal existence. Your destiny shall not be

allotted to you, but you shall choose it for your-selves. . . ."

It was truly a wonderful sight, Er said, to watch how each soul selected its life. The experience of their former life guided their choice. . . . It so happened that the soul of Odysseus had drawn the last lot of all. The memory of his former sufferings had so abated his ambition that he went about a long time looking for a quiet, retired life, which [had been] thrown contemptu-ously aside by the others. He chose it gladly. . . .

Now, when all the souls had chosen their lives . . . they took up their quarters by the bank of the river of Indifference; . . . each, as he drinks, forgets every-thing. . . . In a moment, the souls were carried up to their birth, this way and that, like shooting stars. Er himself was prevented from drinking the water; but how, and by what road, he reached his body, he knew not: only he knew that he suddenly opened his eyes, and found himself laid out upon the funeral pyre.

In world literature literally thousands of similar stories can be found, in which the dying or deceased finds himself in another dimension, peopled by those who have already died. Different cultures have different names and descriptions of these afterlife planes: the Happy Hunting Ground, Limbo, Hades, Heaven, Gusho, Amenti, the Sidpa Bardo, etc. These regions are each described according to the customs of a particular society, and the thinking patterns of the individual. But the *essence* of this afterlife plane seems always to be the same: It is a nonmaterial plane occupied by the "spirits" of the deceased, who stay there temporarily before going on to another phase of development.

A CONTEMPORARY DESCRIPTION OF THE AFTERLIFE PLANE

Another source of information about the afterlife plane is some of the phenomena we have studied, such as automatic writing, and the utterances of sensitives in trance. Generally the "messages" delivered through these media are a jumble of cant and nonsense, reminding one of a badly tuned radio that is receiving two or three stations at the same time, through a welter of static. On rare occasions, however, the radio seems to have been tuned in with a minimum of distortion, and some interesting material has emerged similar to that which has already been described.

To the scientifically oriented Westerner, probably the most acceptable description of the afterlife plane is the message received by Stuart Edward White, a well-known American novelist of the early twentieth century, who was married to a lively woman named Betty. Before 1919, White wrote, "I had paid occult matters little attention. I knew that spiritualism had been 'exposed.'" In that year, the Whites were invited to play the fashionable ouija board "game." They declined, but others of the party at the board reported that it kept repeating insistently the one word, "Betty." Betty was asked to join them, which she did reluctantly, and the board immediately spelled out, over and over again, "Get a pencil, get a pencil." Some days later, Betty was intrigued enough to "get a pencil" and discovered automatic writing. This was soon superseded by trance, in which Betty experienced a kind of double consciousness in which one part of her was aware of messages being relayed to another part of her from the "Invisibles." Betty spent one hour a day for many years, relaying these messages to her husband, who wrote them down verbatim. These messages, purporting to be a description of the afterworld, were published in 1937 as *The Betty Book*, which has continued to find a wide audience. White quotes one occasion in which the Invisibles said through Betty: "You have enfeebled the word 'God.' The world has grown ashamed of the spirit. It mortifies it, just as the old ascetics used to mortify the body. . . ."

Two years after the publication of the book, Betty died. Her husband fully believed that Betty continued to exist in the afterworld plane she had visited in trance. Eventually, with a group of friends, her husband arranged a series of seances to reach Betty, and they believe they did.

"There is only one universe." Betty kept insisting, maintaining that she had not *gone* anywhere. When asked to clarify, she explained that the dimensions of this world and her present world were actually interpenetrating each other but that they seemed like separate planes because of the difference in *frequency*. She used the analogy of an electric fan: When a fan is going at high

can look right through the blades as if they are not
/ are rotating so fast, they have become invisible. Simi-
/dimension which Betty now occupied was vibrating at a
,her frequency, and therefore she was invisible to people
world. "If the frequency were different for your human
focus, she is reported to have said, "you could see me. As it is,
you look through me." Betty's purpose was "to chart some kind
of course to be followed scientifically . . . to get over in terms of
mechanics the possibility of the two worlds being the same but of
a different frequency. . . . If you could discover the frequency,
you can reveal my universe."

On rare occasions, a few people believe they stumble on this
particular frequency. A Smith College professor, Dr. Ralph Har-
low, describes a time in 1960 when he and his wife were strolling
in the woods on a spring morning:

> From behind us we heard the murmur of muted voices.
> We saw nothing, but the voices were coming nearer. We
> then perceived that the sounds were not only behind us
> but above us, and we looked up. About ten feet above
> us was a floating group of glorious creatures glowing
> with spiritual beauty. As they passed, their conversation
> grew fainter until it faded out entirely, and we stood
> transfixed. We sat and I said, "Now, Marion, what did
> you see? Tell me exactly in precise detail." She knew
> my intent—to test my own eyes and ears; to see whether
> I had been the victim of hallucinations. Her reply was
> identical to what my own senses had reported. "For
> those split seconds," she said calmly, "the veil between
> our world and the spirit world was lifted."

DELIBERATE DEATH AND REBIRTH?

In the Orient, death is viewed differently than in the West,
particularly by teachers of the spiritual path. It is sometimes
reported that a highly evolved master will receive knowledge that
his death is imminent, and then the sage prepares himself and his
followers for the event. The German philosopher and mystic Lama
Anagarika Govinda, in his *Way of the White Clouds*, thus reports
the death of his teacher:

The guru had made it known that he would soon leave his body which had become a burden to him. "But," he said, "I do not forsake you. Instead of dragging on in an old body, I shall come back in a new one. You may look for me in three or four years." After this, he retired for meditation, giving instructions not to be disturbed. He maintained a state of deep absorption for ten days and then an attendant held a mirror to his face, a mirror which remained unclouded. The guru had left his body— which had remained unchanged and erect—and was kept in that position for several weeks, during which his body showed no signs of decay.

Which, as we have learned, was what Plato wrote of Er's body, after twelve days. This kind of tale goes against the experience of the Westerner, who has no evidence of bodies that do not disintegrate at death. Interestingly, a case of exactly that phenomenon occurred in Los Angeles when Yogi Paramahansa Yogananda died in 1944 and was removed for burial to Forest Lawn cemetery. Harry T. Rowe, the mortician in charge, wrote:

The absence of any visual signs of decay in the dead body of Paramahansa Yogananda offers the most extraordinary case in our experience. No physical disintegration was visible in his body even twenty days after death. No indication of mold was visible on his skin, and no visible desiccation took place in the bodily tissues. This state of preservation of a body is, so far as we know from mortuary annals, an unparalleled one. The physical appearance of Yogananda on May 27, just before the bronze cover of the casket was put in position, was the same as it had been on May 7.

A TIBETAN TRADITION: THE "TULKU"

For many centuries in Tibet it was seriously believed, and the custom actively practiced, that when a high lama, most particularly the Dalai Lama, dies, his soul passes into a newborn child, the "tulku," who must be found wherever he may be, to become the new Dalai Lama. Tibetan procedures to locate the tulku, at least as described by Govinda, would, perhaps, be approved by Western scientists as good single-blind and double-blind studies. In the case of Govinda's deceased guru, it was reported to the monastery that a baby had been born in Gangtok who insisted (as soon as he could talk) that he was not a Sikkimese but a Tibetan and that his name was "Jigme." (This was the name an oracle had said would be the name of the reincarnated guru.) A delegation of monks was sent to Gangtok when the child was four years old. In Govinda's words, the monks spread out before the boy "various monastic articles, like rosaries, vajras, bells, teacups, wooden bowls, damarus, and other things which are in daily use in religious rituals. . . . The boy immediately picked up those objects which had belonged to him in his previous life, rejecting all those which had been deliberately mixed up with them—though some of them looked far more attractive than the genuine articles."

Much more rigorous and lengthy tests are executed to locate the tulkus of the Dalai Lamas; procedures for the location of the present Dalai Lama are described in detail in Heinrich Harrer's *Seven Years in Tibet*.

REINCARNATION

The contemporary Western world has no such belief in reincarnation. But this situation did not always obtain. Both early Judaism and Christianity accepted the doctrine of reincarnation (and, since 1913, the Catholic Church has reaccepted it). The fact is that reincarnation has been a worldwide belief for millennia and is still accepted by the vast majority of mankind today.

Let us take a whirlwind, worldwide tour to explore beliefs in reincarnation, and let us begin in India, the country which anthropologists tell us has been the source from which have spread many of the world's languages, cultures, and religious beliefs. Lost in India's prerecorded history is the origin of the "ever-returning Wheel of Life." But Hindus, Buddhists, Jainists, Vedantists, and myriad sects in India describe the "endless round of lives" to be lived here on earth until the individual soul breaks through this world illusion (Maya) into reality (Nirvana). Followers of Buddha, and disciples of Zen and Tao spread this belief throughout China and Japan.

Traveling further east, across the Pacific, we find that several island cultures incorporate reincarnation into their belief systems. According to the chief librarian of the Okinawan Prefecture, Shimabuku Zenpatsu, the majority of Okinawans believe that each person has a spirit which leaves his body after death, travels to an afterworld called Gusho, and eventually returns to earth in the body of a newborn baby, generally within seven generations. Zenpatsu stresses that Gusho is a "spiritual state, where only the spirit of man exists. . . . Not mind, but spirit reincarnates, . . . mind being received by the individual through ancestral descent."

Among the Balinese, according to Margaret Mead, the belief is strong that "the individual is reincarnated over and over . . . so that the life cycle . . . merely completes one of an endless set of circles between this world and the other."

In Australia, write anthropologists Spencer and Gillen, "In every tribe without exception, there exists a firm belief in the reincarnation of ancestors. The assumption has been made that reincarnation is universal among the Australian aborigine—who is presumed to go far, far back into man's antiquity."

Concerning reincarnation beliefs on the North American continent, archaeologist Daniel Brinton writes, "This seemingly extraordinary doctrine which some have asserted was entirely unknown and impossible to the American Indian, was in fact one of their most deeply-rooted and widespread convictions."

Rasmussen and other anthropologists have pointed out that the Eskimos, Aleuts, and Tlingit Indians of the far north base their religions on reincarnation. In the far south, and throughout Africa, belief in reincarnation is also deeply rooted. According to E. G. Parrinder, author of *African Traditional Religions*, "The studies made by anthropologists . . . have revealed deep-seated beliefs in reincarnation held by many different African peoples. Death is not looked upon as an enemy: if one dies, he is believed to have been reborn on the 'other side of the veil,' and vice versa in case of birth in this world."

Perhaps this general African belief in reincarnation has its origin in Egyptian antiquity, which has bequeathed to the world, among its many treasures, the remarkable religious work titled *The Egyptian Book of the Dead*, a guidebook for the dying, to lead them into the afterlife plane of existence.

NOT ONE, BUT TWO GUIDEBOOKS FOR THE DEAD

Another equally ancient guidebook for the dead originated somewhere in Tibet, halfway around the world from Egypt, yet, to all appearances, these two extraordinarily similar books were produced independently of each other. *The Bardo Thodol,* or *The Tibetan Book of the Dead*, was translated by W. Y. Evans-Wentz, who began his task fresh from three years research in Egypt. He swiftly realized the uncanny similarity between the Tibetan and Egyptian works. In his introduction, he describes how both books give similar methods to raise the energy body (called "Ka" in Egypt, "desire body" in Tibet) from the deceased physical body. The judgment scenes in both books depict a symbolic weighing of the soul (in Tibet, black versus white pebbles; in Egypt, the "Heart" versus the "Truth"). The judge in the Egyptian book is the ape-headed god Thoth; in the Tibetan book, the monkey-headed god Sinje. Evans-Wentz further notes that the great lamas of Tibet are embalmed and mummified in a fashion very similar to ancient Egyptian royalty. He concludes that the books are "so much alike in essentials as to suggest a common origin, at present unknown."

ANOTHER REMARKABLE PARALLEL

Exploring the three concepts of reincarnation, evolution, and the collective unconscious, we find these amazingly similar writings, apparently produced independently of each other from three ancient civilizations:

1. A great Sufi poet wrote:
    I died as a mineral and became a plant.
    I died as a plant and rose to animal.
    I died as animal and I was man.
    Why should I fear? When was I less by dying?
    Yet once more shall I die as man, to soar
    With angels blest; but even from angelhood
    I must pass on.
2. A terse Herbrew aphorism in the Cabala says: "A stone became a plant, a plant an animal, an animal a man, and man a God."

3. From the poetic legends of ancient Greece there is the tale of Proteus, a god who could change his shape at will. When a man tried to grab hold of Proteus, to find out what he really was, Proteus was sleeping "like a stone." When touched, he became a plant. On being approached again, he turned into a serpent, then a man. And then, transforming into spirit, he ascended into the sky.

THE BARDOS ARE IN THE MIND

In the *Tibetan Book of the Dead* are found lengthy instructions on how the dying person should confront the formidable events which he will meet in the afterworld planes, or Bardos. These events, it is repeatedly stressed, are not realities, but events emerging from the person's *own mind*, no matter how magnificent, or horrifying, or void.

> Demons bearing various weapons will utter, "Strike! Slay!" and make a frightful tumult.... Apparitional illusions, too, of being pursued by various terrible beasts of prey will dawn.... Being terrified by them, [you] will flee, not caring whither. But the way will be obstructed by three awful precipices. They will be terror-inspiring, and one will feel as if one is about to fall down them. O nobly-born, they are not really precipices: they are Anger, Lust, and Stupidity.
>
> Others ... will experience various delightful pleasures and happiness.... [And] that class of neutral beings will experience neither pleasure nor pain, but a sort of colorless indifference.

(In a few examples from the LSD trips, and from those "returned from death," we have already found the horrors, and the delights, and the "neutral" experiences. And, as psychiatrists will tell us, such experiences of the unconscious seem to correlate very well with one's own concepts of "reality.")

A PSYCHOLOGICAL EVALUATION OF THE TIBETAN BOOK OF THE DEAD

In his foreword to the Evans-Wentz translation, Carl Jung makes the suggestion that men of the Western world might do well to read the *Tibetan Book of the Dead*—backward. For, he explains, it is characteristic of Oriental religious literature to start at the pinnacle, proceeding with diminishing climaxes. And the *Tibetan Book of the Dead* is no exception. It begins with initiation into the brilliant light of the highest Bardo and ends with entrance into the womb, for rebirth, from the lowest Bardo. Quoting Jung, in this lowest Bardo, the Sidpa Bardo,

> The dead man . . . begins to fall a prey to sexual fantasies, and is attracted by the vision of mating couples. Eventually he is caught by a womb and born again. Meanwhile, as one might expect, the Oedipus complex starts functioning. . . . The European passes through this specific Freudian domain where his unconscious contents are brought to light under analysis, but he goes in the reverse direction. He journeys back through the world of infantile-sexual fantasies to the womb. . . .
>
> Freudian psychoanalysis never went beyond the experiences of the Sidpa Bardo; that is, it was unable to extricate itself from sexual fantasies, and similar "incompatible" tendencies which cause anxiety and other affective states. Nevertheless, Freud's theory is the first attempt made by the West to investigate . . . from the animal sphere of instinct, the psychological territory corresponding to the Sidpa Bardo.

Jung adds that, in view of our existing biological ideas, efforts to travel further into the unconscious, although they "would not have been crowned with success," might have led to an exploration of the "psychological residua of previous existences. . . . But neither science nor our reason can keep step with this idea. We know so desperately little about the possibilities of continued existence of the individual soul after death, so little that we cannot even conceive how anyone could prove anything at all in this respect."

Can anyone offer even a scrap, a shred of evidence regarding previous lives?

A FEW SCRAPS OF EVIDENCE

Not infrequently people in the Western world will report sudden brief and inexplicable "knowings" of having been somewhere before, being able to describe in detail cities or towns in countries they are visiting for the first time. Several such incidents have been reported to me by students over the years. One businessman and his wife, for example, told in detail how, on their first visit to Cairo, in a rented limousine, the wife suddenly "knew" the city and directed the astonished chauffeur to obscure landmarks not generally shown to tourists. Neither man nor wife had any explanation for the event. Similarly, a clinical psychologist and colleague spoke to me, in confidence, of his experience in Firenze when, to his amazement, in that city which he had never visited before, he found himself walking purposefully in the night through familiar streets to find a particular bridge he could see in his mind. When he arrived at exactly that bridge, he looked down and saw reflected in the water the face of a Renaissance figure whom he recognized to be himself. In my own family, an aunt told me that on her first trip to Mexico, she amazed and delighted her companions on the bus going through Taxco by telling them what building, plaza, or shop they would find around each corner. She just felt that she had "seen it all before."

Generally, psychologists label this phenomenon "déja vu" (French for "seen before"), and offer assorted explanations from "physiological tricks of the retina" to hallucinations, or illusions.

Sometimes, people suddenly acquire access to a different realm of mind, as in a psychedelic drug experience, when they seem to experience in detail events of other persons in other eras, as if happening to themselves. The same effect is observed under hypnosis. But reality and fantasy seem so intricately interwoven in the drug or hypnotic experience that such data are considered too unreliable for serious study.

Of more interest, perhaps, is this experience as recorded by a twenty-six-year old German woman under the pseudonym of Inge Ammann, in 1967. While driving through Franken Province with her husband (where neither had ever been), she suddenly "recognized" the area and spontaneously exclaimed that she had lived there before, and knew exactly where everything was. Her husband became impatient when she told him her name had been Maria D. and pointed out the house she had lived in with her parents and two brothers. Stopping for refreshment in the village tavern, she was shocked to recognize the tavern keeper as the same man, much older, who had served her family. She and her husband inquired of the innkeeper about the "D. family" and learned that both parents, and the older son were dead. The innkeeper volunteered that "poor little Maria" had died the most tragic death; and as he described how Maria had been kicked savagely by a horse in a stable, Inge cried out and lost control, reliving the experience of her "previous death." She concludes, "It took me several weeks to regain my composure. Since then, my husband and I have avoided the whole subject. That's probably the best thing, all around."

Brief, inexplicable event. An anecdote, perhaps not at all reliable. But other persons have reported more prolonged adventures with "previous lives."

THE FAR MEMORIES OF JOAN GRANT KELSEY

Born into the Edwardian England of 1906, Joan Grant as a child was apparently not only psychic, but remembered "previous lives" she had lived. However, her conservative, upper-class parents discouraged her actively from anything so un-British as reincarnation. But Joan retained her psychic gifts into adulthood, and on her first visit to Egypt, she felt that shock of "knowing" the country and its characteristics. This feeling was vastly intensified when she was given an Egyptian scarab. As she held it in her hand, sudden, intense memories of ancient Egypt flooded into her awareness, memories which she recorded as they came to her, all part of a whole but disconnected, like the pieces of a jigsaw puzzle. When the writing ended, as suddenly as it had begun, she and her husband pieced it together into sequence, and the book *Winged Pharaoh* emerged in 1937. It was ostensibly a novel about Sekeeta, the daughter of an Egyptian pharaoh who lived three thousand years ago. Interestingly, scholars and critics had only praise for the accuracy of the historical detail of the book (in much the same way that the writings of Patience Worth were evaluated). But Joan Grant was not an Egyptian scholar, nor had she done any research. In fact, she believes that she *was* Sekeeta in a "previous life" and that the book was simply a record of "far memories."

Over a period of time, she learned how to voluntarily "shift levels" (again, her phrase), in order to receive impressions of other lives she believes she has lived, most of which, she reports, were quite ordinary lives, much too ordinary to make into novels. All the same, she has published a few books based on these far memories. Her most recent work, *Many Lifetimes* (1967), was written in collaboration with her psychiatrist husband, Dr. Denys Kelsey, who had believed in reincarnation long before meeting Joan. The authors gave a dramatic account of how Joan's ability to shift levels clarified a difficult situation, when a mosquito bite on her eyelid became painful and refused to heal. This was an odd occurence, for Joan had worked with her father for years at the Mosquito Control Institute, and she was quite used to being bitten by the insects. With her husband present, Joan shifted levels and reported she had once died of a fly bite on the eyelid, and from that deeper level of consciousness she gave precise directions to her husband for the treatment of the wound. (This technique of treatment may remind the reader of Edgar Cayce's trance readings.) Her husband followed the strange directions he was given, and the sore soon disappeared.

As a result of this and similar incidents, Dr. Kelsey began to use Joan's gift of far memory to help in the treatment of a few of his recalcitrant patients. In his practice, he was frequently successful in using hypnosis and age regression to recover forgotten traumae. But in some instances, when regression in the patient's present life seemed of no avail, he would ask Joan to shift levels in search of possible explanations in a "previous life." This psychiatric technique seems too bizarre to be believed; at least, that was my reaction when I first learned about it from a psychiatrist colleague, long before I knew anything about Joan Grant and her novels.

THE FEATHER PHOBIA

At an International Congress of Psychotherapy in Germany one year, I had the pleasure of meeting again a respected Dutch psychiatrist, let's call him Dr. M., whom I had come to know because of his innovative use of LSD in psychotherapy. One night, as we were dining together, Dr. M. told me of a recent remarkable, if inexplicable, case he had treated. The patient had been suffering for years with a rare phobia: He would be overcome with panic whenever he found himself near *feathers!* Most phobias (of elevators, airplanes, snakes, spiders, etc.) can be seen to have some basis in reality: Actual disasters have been known to occur in their vicinity. But feathers? My Dutch friend had worked on the case diligently, but without success. Finally, he decided to take his patient for consultation to a sanatorium in the south of France run by Dr. Kelsey and his wife. At this point, Dr. M. broke off his narrative to ask if I knew of the Kelseys and the work they did. I confessed that their names were unknown to me. Dr. M. hesitated, then looked at me a long moment, and apparently decided he could give me his confidence. It was then that I first learned about Joan Grant's ability to shift levels and obtain far memories. I remember I listened carefully, and nodded, but I was inwardly, immediately skeptical, exactly as my more conservative colleagues typically respond to me.

Dr. M. told me that when he presented his patient to Joan Grant, she was able to shift levels, and began to describe a medieval battle on a field in Italy, where she saw one particular soldier fall, badly wounded, and left for dead by his companions when the battle ended. Joan Grant kept watching the soldier as he lay mortally wounded and unable to move; he looked up and saw a vulture, whose black *feathers* grew more and more menacing as it circled closer and closer. . . .

This episode apparently struck a responsive chord in Dr. M.'s patient, who from that time on was relieved of his feather phobia. My Dutch friend smiled as he finished his story. And then he said, "It was a cure. But was the cure due to a previous life trauma? Or to a fantasy? Or suggestion, or spontaneous remission?" He did not answer his question, and neither did I.

A "PREVIOUS LIFE" UNDER HYPNOSIS

Not too long ago, at a symposium near Sacramento, California, I learned of a similar cure effected by a hypnotherapist. A woman had come to him for relief from persistent, painful migraine headaches which no conventional medical treatment had been able to control. The patient proved to be an excellent hypnotic subject, and when deep trance was achieved, the hypnotist requested her to go to the *source* of her headaches. Almost immediately the patient, a small, slender woman, felt herself to be a giant of a man, a Roman gladiator, in fact, who was being savagely beaten about the shoulders and head by his master. To the astonishment of the hypnotist the patient "relived" this experience with intense emotion. When the catharsis was ended, the hypnotist returned her to normal consciousness, with the suggestion that she need never suffer from her migraine headaches again. And she never did.

But the patient, Ann Armstrong, continued to work with that hypnotherapist, doing research in altered states of consciousness, and developed into a gifted psychic. I have talked with Miss Armstrong, and I have heard her lecture. On both occasions I was impressed that when she was asked the inevitable question of whether the Roman gladiator was an incarnation or a fantasy, she replied quietly that she did not know.

THE BRIDEY MURPHY AFFAIR

The beginnings of this notorious episode involving hypnosis and reincarnation go back, oddly, to Edgar Cayce. Although Cayce was a devout Protestant, admitting of Heaven and Hell but denying reincarnation, at the age of forty-six he was forced to reexamine his beliefs. During a reading, the entranced Cayce was asked by a gentleman named Arthur Lammers several metaphysical questions, questions that had never been put to him before. Later, when the contents of the session were read back to Cayce, he was shocked to learn that in trance he had stated categorically that reincarnation, far from being the "half-baked myth" he believed it to be, was a "fundamental fact of the Universe." Later readings gave more and more information about other planes of existence, and reincarnation.

Years later, a young lawyer visited Virginia Beach, expressly to expose Cayce as a fraud. (What a familiar story, the converted skeptic!) After studying the readings, particularly those dealing with reincarnation, the lawyer, whose name was Morey Bernstein, returned to Colorado with the idea of using hypnosis in order to look for evidence of "previous lives." Bernstein eventually found, in Mrs. Virginia Tighe, an excellent subject who swiftly regressed to infancy, prebirth, and a "previous life," when she suddenly began speaking in an unfamiliar Irish brogue of nineteenth-century Belfast. Bernstein tape-recorded all six sessions, in which Mrs.

Tighe claimed to be Bridget Kathleen Murphy, born in 1798 to Duncan and Kathleen Murphy. She reported that she married a "barrister," said that she shopped for foodstuffs at "Farr's" and "John Carrigan's," and gave other specific details of her home and surroundings. Eventually, she said she was "ditched" (buried) in 1864.

Bernstein published this material, with verbatim tape transcripts, as *The Search for Bridey Murphy*, in 1956. The book unexpectedly became a runaway best seller and caused an angry furore among scientists, religionists, and the news media. Investigators were sent to Ireland, and found no records of Bridget Kathleen Murphy's birth, marriage, or death. But they did find (after diligent research by a Belfast librarian) that there had been both a "Farr's" and "John Carrigan's" food stores at that time, and that the Irish used the word "ditched" colloquially during that period, as a synonym for "buried." However, so many sensational exposes appeared in the press and scientific journals that gradually the Bridey Murphy affair came to be regarded as nothing but an elaborate hoax. This is the general opinion today despite the scholarly detective work of Professor C. J. Ducasse of Brown University, who published his findings in 1962. Ducasse concluded that none of the articles, scientific or journalistic, about Bridey Murphy "had succeeded in disproving, or even in establishing a strong case against, the possibility that many of the statements of the Bridey personality are genuinely memories of an earlier life of Virginia Tighe over a century ago in Ireland. . . . On the other hand, the verifications . . . of obscure points in Ireland, mentioned in Bridey's six recorded conversations with Bernstein, do not prove that Virginia is a reincarnation of Bridey, nor do they establish a particularly strong case for it."

Which leaves Bridey Murphy in the same limbo as the other cases we have discussed.

Actually, hypnotists both before and after Bernstein have successfully regressed subjects into "previous lives" and obtained interesting data, data which are just about impossible to verify. For, contrary to the schizophrenic who will claim to be Napoleon, Jesus, or Cleopatra, persons regressed under hypnosis usually give themselves such commonplace names and places of birth that they are all but impossible to trace. Like Bridey Murphy.

Another difficulty is that the subject under hypnosis is still bound by his individual fears and problems, which sometimes will stop the research almost before it has begun, as in the next example.

AN AGE REGRESSION EXPERIMENT AT UCLA

One day a young man telephoned our lab, offering to volunteer for ESP experiments. We receive a great many such calls, very few of which we accept. But in this instance, in our initial interview, we were favorably impressed. The young man told us he had been totally blinded in a high school chemistry class, when a vial he was holding in his hand exploded, burning his face and destroying his eyes. Despite that handicap, he had become a successful musician. He was also well-read, knowledgeable in parapsychology, and had had what seemed to us a few genuine psychic experiences. He expressed particular interest in hypnosis, which he had studied superficially, and was eager to try age regression, and possible "previous lives."

Since I had never attempted hypnosis with a blind person, asked Jack Gray (our volunteer hypnotist) to perform the induction, and of course he agreed. On the day of our experiment, the three of us went into the isolation booth, where Jack skilfully and swiftly took the subject into a deep level of hypnosis. Jack then transferred the subject to me and left the booth. I suggested to the subject that he travel to whatever time or place he wished. There was silence for a short time. Then a strange, moaning sound began to come from him, starting softly but changing quickly into a shriek of terror. I had no idea what had happened, and asked him to describe where he was. He answered, in a terrified tone, that he didn't know, that it was very, very dark. Suddenly he shrieked again, "Help! Help me! I can't find my way!" I started to assure him I would bring him back, but suddenly a total change came over him, and he began to curse the enemies who had murdered him and left him to wander in the blackness. I wondered if this could be a symbolic reference to his blindness and started to speak, but he again interrupted me to describe the "south pyramid" and the rampart where he now found himself to be standing, seeing his enemies creeping up behind him to hurl him from the rampart to his death below. He screamed, beads of sweat poured down his face, and he flung himself prone from the sitting position he had taken. Then as if cleansed of an emotional storm, he fell into a calm sleep. Jack had returned during this dramatic episode; and after a few moments we decided that Jack should bring the subject to his normal state. As he worked, Jack stressed that the subject, on waking, could remember everything that had happened, or nothing that had happened, or only as much as he wished to remember; the choice of remembering was completely the subject's. Jack also suggested that on waking, the subject would feel relaxed and refreshed.

When the young man sat up, he did look refreshed for a moment, but then the memory of his experience flooded into his consciousness. Eventually he said that the experience had "scared the hell out of him" and that he did not wish to continue with the experiments. This was not surprising to us. We have frequently had to stop ESP experiments, for such reasons. Typically a psychic will give a reading and make a few correct (occasionally indiscreet) hits, and the subject will stop the session abruptly. At other times we ourselves stop the experiment if the subject grows afraid. Fear must be respected, for it is often an unconscious defense against untoward, violent eruptions from the unconscious, which is apparently what was occuring in the case of this blind man.

Once again we are left with a question: What was the meaning of the strange drama of "a murder on the south pyramid"? Fantasy? A previous life? Primary process distortion of the "darkness" (blindness) caused by the chemical explosion?

IAN STEVENSON'S RESEARCH INTO REINCARNATION

The best contemporary research into reincarnation is undoubtedly that of Dr. Ian Stevenson, professor of psychiatry at the University of Virginia. Dr. Stevenson has traveled around the world, gathering data with meticulous diligence from persons (usually children) who claim to remember a previous life. Dr. Stevenson's files contain more than 1,200 cases which he has personally investigated in places as remote from each other as India, Alaska, and Lebanon. In 1966 he published *Twenty Cases*

Suggestive of Reincarnation, and is now preparing a second book, with more extensive findings. Dr. Stevenson is too conservative a scientist to claim that he has "proved" reincarnation, but his evidence is striking, as these cases (selected from many) will illustrate.

Case 1. 1964. Lebanon. Imad Elawar

When Imad was two years old (in 1960), he began to speak of his previous life, with special reference to his lovely mistress, who still lived in a village only twenty-five miles away from where Imad was born (or "reborn"). The child kept referring to the time "when he was grown up" and had been a man named Ibrahim, who had died of tuberculosis in 1949. Dr. Stevenson traveled with Imad and his family to Ibrahim's village, and tabulated fifty-seven items the child told him about his life as Ibrahim before he died. The boy was proved correct on fifty-one of the fifty-seven, ten of which had been told Dr. Stevenson on the drive to the village.

Dr. Stevenson does not discount the possibility of collusion between the two families (the distance between villages was, after all, only twenty-five miles), but he does question what purpose or benefit such collusion would have provided, since no publicity or reward came of the investigation.

Case 2. 1954. India. Jasbir/Sobha

This case, in some respects, is similar to that of the Watseka Wonder, Lurancy Vennum/Mary Roff. If the reader will remember, Lurancy became ill with "fits," began to impersonate people she saw around her (whom no one else saw), and finally "became" for a period of four months Mary Roff, the deceased daughter of the Roffs, who permitted Lurancy/Mary to live with them as her daughter for that interval.

Here, in India, Dr. Stevenson found Jasbir, an Indian boy of the Jat caste, who at the age of three and a half years had contracted a severe case of smallpox and was declared dead. The boy revived, however, and after his recovery he insisted he was a twenty-two-year-old Hindu, Sobha Ram. This was painful to Jasbir's family, not because of the idea of reincarnation, which is accepted among Indians of every sect, but because the child refused to eat anything but Brahmin food, which is repulsive to Jats. Jasbir's family grew resentful, to the point where they refused to permit Jasbir to meet his "widow."

Dr. Stevenson tried to learn from Jasbir/Sobha how the transition from one personality to the other was made. He was told by the boy that Sobha had met a holy man, after death, who had advised him to "take cover" in Jasbir's body. According to Stevenson, "Although the apparent 'death' of Jasbir occurred in the period April/May, 1954, we do not know that the change in personality of Jasbir took place immediately on the night when his body seemed to die and then revived. In the following weeks, Jasbir was still perilously ill with smallpox and not able to express much of any personality."

Case 3. 1946. Alaska. Victor Kahkody

The Eskimos, the Aleuts, and the Tlingit Indians all believe in reincarnation. In particular, the Tlingit Indians believe the dead return to their immediate families and can be identified by particular "sympathy scars" which the deceased brings back into the baby's body. Of the thirty-six cases studied by Stevenson among the Tlingits, probably the most striking is that of Victor, of the Kahkody tribe, who a year before he died, told his favorite niece that he would return as her child. He promised she would recognize him by the scar on one side of his nose, and another on his back, from an operation. Eighteen months later the niece, Mrs. Chotkin, had a baby boy with exactly those birthmarks. When the boy was thirteen months old, being taught by his mother to say his name, he exclaimed, "Don't you know me? I'm Kahkody!" When he was two years old he identified his own "widow" and his son. Victor could remember his previous life vividly until the age of nine, but then these memories gradually faded.

In a recent paper (1973), Dr. Stevenson reports that among his present, now much larger collection of "previous life" personalities suggestive of reincarnation, he has repeatedly found similar characteristics in cases occurring in remote communities, far distant from each other. In today's world, with communication between nations so swift, similar events occurring in places far distant from each other do not seem as remarkable as in antiquity. Nevertheless, Dr. Stevenson's research is provocative.

LIFE AFTER DEATH AND/OR REINCARNATION: WHAT DOES IT MATTER?

We can be very sure that almost no one in this world has any remembrance of a previous life, or any experience of an existence after death. Even assuming that the Buddhist view of the interim afterlife, with subsequent innumerable incarnations, is more accurate than the Christian view of an eternal life spent in either Heaven or Hell, and that the Christian view is more accurate than the view of nothing at all beyond death—so what?

For that vast number of people who accept the reality of reincarnation there has evolved one of two approaches in dealing with the present life on earth. One point of view maintains that whatever happens in this life is because of one's "karma," evolved from previous existences, against which one is helpless. This attitude frequently leads to a life of apathy and indolence, for how can one challenge the gods? The other approach is based on the idea that one can improve his chances in the afterlife, and the next life on earth, by behaving with morality and honor, and by observing fastidiously the rituals of one's particular religious belief. Both points of view have many adherents.

But according to the sages of every age, both views are false, and have arisen from ignorance of the supreme Reality, knowledge of which can be achieved in this life, perhaps, through one or another discipline of meditation.

Suppose, now, we examine the teachings of the masters of meditation, past and present, to learn what they tell us about all that we have been discussing: bioenergy, biocommunication, and, in fact, every kind of paranormal power, as well as possible other realms of existence.

15 Toward a Different Dimension of Being

> The mind is restless, turbulent, strong and stubborn
> . . . and as difficult to restrain as the wind.
>
> —Bhagavad Gita

A WAY TO SELF

In the early decades of this century, a man lived in a cave, in India, near a hill called Arunachala. He taught no classes; he gave no lectures; there was no publicity about him. Yet visitors came from all around the world to learn from him a path toward peace and spiritual understanding. What can account for this phenomenon?

According to the little that is known of his early years (he seldom spoke about his personal life), he was the son of well-to-do parents, and a normal schoolboy like others in India, until the age of seventeen. Then one afternoon while studying, as he described the experience,

> I was sitting alone in my uncle's house. I seldom had any sickness, and on that day there was nothing wrong with my health, but a sudden violent fear of death overtook me. . . . I just felt, "I am going to die" and began thinking what to do about it. . . .
>
> The shock of the fear of death drove my mind inwards and I said to myself mentally, without actually framing the words: "Now that death has come, what does it mean? What is it that is dying? This body dies."

And I at once dramatized the occurrence of death. I lay with my limbs stretched out stiff as though rigor mortis had set in. . . . I held my breath and kept my lips tightly closed so that no sound could escape, so that neither the word "I" nor any other word could be uttered. "Well, then," I said to myself, "this body is dead. It will be carried stiff to the burning ground and there reduced to ashes. But with the death of this body am I dead? Is the body I? It is silent and inert but I feel the full force of my personality and even the voice of the 'I' within me, apart from it. So I am Spirit transcending the body. The body dies but the Spirit that transcends it cannot be touched by death. That means I am the deathless Spirit." All this was not dull thought; it flashed through me vividly as living truth which I perceived directly, almost without thought process. . . . From that moment onwards the "I" or Self focussed attention on itself by a powerful fascination. Fear of death had vanished once and for all.

Shortly after this death and rebirth experience, the boy left his home and family to follow the solitary path toward self-realization.

Many months later, it was rumored that in an underground vault of a thousand-pillared temple there was a holy man, so deep in meditation that he had not moved for weeks. In India, such holy men and hermits are revered and looked after by the "ordinary people." One of these descended into the vault and was aghast at what he saw: a youth, naked, motionless, so absorbed in his meditation that he was oblivious of the vermin and rats that were gnawing at his legs and genitals. (To the end of his life the marks of those bloody and pus-filled sores remained.) The youth was lifted up and carried outside, still oblivious of his surroundings.

Gradually the Ramana Maharshi, as he came to be known, returned to the world around him. And eventually he was persuaded to settle at Arunachala, where an ashram evolved for those who wanted to be near him. The Maharshi lived for many years in the caves on the hill. He spoke seldom; when he did, his advice was simple, yet so difficult. It was to meditate on the question: "Who am I?"

An English scholar, Paul Brunton, tried to get further elucidation, on an intellectual level, and this exchange ensued:

Brunton: What exactly is this Self of which you speak?

Sri Ramana: I tell you to pursue this enquiry, "Who am I?" You ask me to describe this true Self to you. What can be said? It is That out of which the sense of the personal "I" arises and into which it will have to disappear.

Brunton: Disappear? How can one lose the feelings of one's personality?

Sri Ramana: The first and foremost of all thoughts, the primeval thought in the mind of every man, is the thought, "I." . . . If you could mentally follow the "I" thread until it led you back to its source you would discover that, just as it is the first thought to appear, so it is the last to disappear. This is a matter that can be experienced.

Brunton: What is left then? Will a man become quite unconscious or will he become an idiot?

Sri Ramana: No; on the contrary . . . he will become truly wise when he has awakened to his true Self, which is the real nature of man.

Brunton: But surely the sense of "I" must also pertain to that?

Sri Ramana: The sense of "I" pertains to the person, the body and brain. When a man knows his true Self for the first time something else arises from the depths of his being and takes possession of him. That something is behind the mind; it is infinite, divine, eternal. Some people call it the Kingdom of Heaven, others call it the soul and others again Nirvana, and Hindus call it liberation; you may give it whatever name you wish. When this happens a man has not really lost himself; rather he has found himself.

Who am I? One form of meditation, from one spiritual master.

The Ramana Maharshi died in 1950. But other spiritual leaders continue to appear, just as they have appeared for thousands of years. The message they give, in different languages and countries, has always been the same. The Greeks advised: "Know thyself." Jesus said, "The kingdom of God is within you." The yogis had maintained, long before the writing of the Bhagavad Gita: "atma-nam viddhi," which means "know the universal Self."

AN AMERICAN'S EXPERIENCE OF DEATH AND REBIRTH

Mystical literature, whether of the East or West, consistently demonstrates that a man must die to be born again. The experience may be dreadful, like the "death" of St. Theresa, who came back to life dressed in her burial shroud, or exquisite, like St. Paul's revelation on the road to Damascus; it may be swift and terrifying, like the Ramana Maharshi's sudden "death" one afternoon, or in gradual, almost imperceptible changes. However it happens, the death of the personality apparently must be experienced before the "I," the Self, can be born into consciousness, even though the Self is always there, within.

Joel Goldsmith's death and rebirth was a gradual process. A successful Jewish businessman of the early twentieth century, Goldsmith became critically ill with tuberculosis and was given three months to live. Since there was no hope from medicine, he decided to seek the help of a Christian Science practitioner, and in three months made a full recovery. (Many years later, when he was telling of this experience, a skeptic insisted he had had a wrong diagnosis, since tuberculosis can not be so dramatically "cured." Goldsmith then submitted to an x-ray examination, which showed he had only one lung; where the other should have been, there was, as he described it, "a wall of muscle.")

Remarkably, this healing seemed to have made no inner changes in Goldsmith; he had not yet died to be reborn. And for several more years he continued in the business world until, in 1928, while on a trip to Detroit:

> I was taken sick, found the name of a Christian Science practitioner, and asked him to help me. He told me it was Saturday; that day he always spent in meditation. To this I said, "Of course you wouldn't turn me out looking the way I do?"
> "No, come on in."
> He permitted me to stay two hours with him. Long before the two hours were up, I was healed of that cold, and when I went out on the street I found I

couldn't smoke anymore. When eating dinner I found I couldn't drink anymore. The following week I found I couldn't play cards anymore and I also found I couldn't go to the horse races anymore. And the businessman had died.

Within thirty-six hours after my first spiritual experience, a woman buyer said that if I would pray for her she would be healed. The only prayer I knew was "Now I lay me down to sleep," and I didn't see that that was going to do much healing.

But she insisted. So I closed my eyes and said, "Father, you know that I don't know how to pray, and I certainly know nothing about healing. So if there is anything I should do, tell me."

And very very clearly, as much so as if I were hearing a voice, I realized that man is not a healer. That satisfied me. That was the extent of my praying, but the woman had her healing, a healing of alcoholism.

Over a period of many years, Goldsmith developed from businessman to healer to spiritual teacher. His teaching followed the Christian tradition, but essentially his message was like that of the Ramana Maharshi, or any of the masters:

In reality there is only one power. It is true that as long as we are dealing with the human world in a human way there will be two powers: the power of good and the power of evil. As human beings we shall always have laws of sin, laws of sickness, laws of lack and limitation. A state of existence which transcends this is brought about as an activity of consciousness. No one can do this for us but ourselves. . . .

Prayer is then no longer words or thoughts; prayer is no longer asking God to do something. It is a state of silence in which you can be receptive to the word of God. The mind is still.

THE MODERN SEARCH FOR THE SELF

There is a strong revival of interest today in this search for knowledge of the Self, whether through psychoanalysis, biofeedback, growth centers, altered states of consciousness, drugs, religions, or courses in meditation as offered by Tibetan rimpoches, Zen masters, or yogis. Probably the most enthusiastic interest comes from the youth of the world, who have become dissatisfied with the material life: its marvelous machines with their concomitant pollutions; its abundance of foods with their preservatives and artificial tastes; its wealth of manufactured enjoyments accompanied by commercials and ready-made laugh tracks.

A strong impetus toward this search for Self can probably be attributed to the explosion of the drug culture among the youth in the 1960s. Although many of the "flower people" went on to more potent, often lethal main-line drugs, others deserted drugs in favor of the transcendental experience which can be achieved through one meditative discipline or another. The flight of these young people into communes, study groups, or even to the Orient, in search of the Self is well known. Where I work, at the Neuropsychiatric Institute, each year for the past six years at least one resident psychiatrist or psychology intern has taken a year's leave to explore the dimensions of mind which can be achieved through study with a spiritual teacher, or guru. Each has chosen according to his leaning: a Zen monastery, an Indian ashram, a Vedanta, or Sufi, or Arica center. They have all returned to their professional work, believing they can give a deeper and more constructive dimension to the treatment of their patients. One such young psychiatrist, recently returned from India, presented a talk at a UCLA symposium in 1973 titled Deeper Levels of the Mind: An Exploration of Meditation. A few years ago, one would have expected such a symposium to have gone practically unattended. Instead more than five hundred people, ranging from housewives to physicists, listened raptly and asked where and how they could learn to explore the Self through meditation. A difficult question. . . .

THE PROBLEMS OF MEDITATION

As one begins on the path toward Self-knowledge, the instructions are so simple as to seem absurd (Who am I?). Generally the novice is asked merely to sit quietly, in a comfortable position, and "still the mind." Of what use such a banal task, when one is searching for the transcendental experience? Naturally the best way to learn the answer to that question is to try the experiment.

Suppose you decide to sit in silence, without thoughts, for ten minutes each day. And you begin one morning, in the solitude of your room. That's when the fun, or torment, starts. You will probably find it just about impossible to do. You will suddenly remember all the things you *should* be doing and have left undone: phone calls, correspondence, marketing. And the more you try to banish those intrusions, the more insistent they will become. Or, you may begin to experience unexpected, unpleasant body sensations: an itch, an urge to urinate, a dull pain in the back that grows more and more disturbing. Suppose you decide to ignore, or simply observe these distractions each day, every day. It may take months or years before you can sit quietly, without distractions of body or mind, for just ten minutes. Indeed, it may never happen. This seemingly simple task is so very difficult to do that different techniques have been devised to make it easier. The neophyte may be told to repeat aloud, or silently, a specific phrase (mantram); or to focus his attention on a particular movement, such as his own breathing; or to concentrate on an object, any object: a pencil, a candle flame, a flower. In a few recent laboratory studies, such variations of meditative techniques have produced interesting results.

THREE STUDIES ON THE BEGINNINGS OF MEDITATION

Although William James wrote his provocative *Varieties of Religious Experience* more than half a century ago, scientists generally ignored his pioneering work on altered states of consciousness, perhaps because they were leery of the word "religious" in the title. Only very recently have behavioral scientists taken James' ideas into the laboratory. Probably the first study on meditation in America was that of psychiatrist Arthur Deikman in 1963.

Deikman asked volunteers, individually, to undergo twelve sessions over a period of three weeks, the first lasting five minutes, the second ten minutes, and the rest fifteen minutes (or longer, if the subject wished); all sessions were to be spent contemplating a small blue vase. Deikman did not mention meditation in his instructions, which were:

> The purpose of these sessions is to learn about concentration. By concentration I do not mean analyzing the different parts of the vase, or thinking a series of thoughts about the vase, but rather, trying to see the vase as it exists in itself, without any connection to other things. Exclude all other thoughts or feelings or sounds or bodily sensations. Do not let them distract you but keep them out so that you can concentrate all your attention, all your awareness on the vase itself. Let the perception of the vase fill your entire mind.

The results of this brief meditation were rich and varied. All subjects at one session or another saw the vase becoming a more intense, deep blue. Sometimes the vase became brighter while everything else became dark or indistinct; the word "luminous" was often used, as if the vase had become a source of light. The vase also seemed to change shape. In one subject's words, "It was always a vase, pot shaped, but there was a change symmetrically and undulating up and down"; another subject said, "The outlines of the vase shift. At that point they seem almost to dissolve entirely . . . and for it to be a kind of fluid blue . . . a very fluid kind of thing."

One subject reported, "When I really began to feel, you know, almost as though the blue and I were perhaps merging . . . I almost got scared. . . . I was losing my sense of consciousness almost." This "merging" sensation continued to occur until "at one point it felt . . . as though the vase were in my head rather than out there. . . . I almost felt at that moment as though, you know, the image is really in me, it's not out there." Another subject had this experience: "It started radiating. I was aware of what seemed like particles . . . coming from the highlights there and right to me. . . . It was radiating heat. I felt warm from it. . . . Everything was dark all around, a kind of brown, lavender, eerie color, and it was during this incandescent kind of radiating inner glow thing . . . I could feel my pulse beating in my penis and in my temples. . . . I felt there was a light coming down from above, too."

All these reactions from only twelve sessions, none of which lasted longer than thirty-three minutes. Perhaps the reader will recognize, in these descriptions of experience, a similarity to the undulating, vivid and luminous colors, and the pulsing radiations, which are found so frequently in reports of a psychedelic drug experience.

Another study in meditation was done originally for a Ph.D. dissertation by psychologist Edward Maupin and published in 1965. Maupin chose as the object of contemplation the subject's own breathing, while he sat on a chair, back straight, both feet resting on the floor. Instructions were deceptively simple:

> Let your breathing become relaxed and natural. Let it set its own pace and depth if you can. Then focus your attention on your breathing movements of your belly, not your nose or throat. Do not allow extraneous thoughts or stimuli to pull your attention away from the breathing.

In all, twenty-eight men experienced nine such meditative sessions of forty-five minutes each. Their experiences ranged from unpleasant sensations like "going under an anesthetic," "dizziness," and a "befogging" of consciousness to pleasant body sensations, sometimes erotic; sometimes "vibrations" or "waves" or sensations of bodily "suspension" were reported. And occasionally subjects felt extensive loss of body feelings and a very lucid state of consciousness, which was deeply satisfying. Again one may note a similarity to early stages of psychedelic or sensory deprivation experiences.

Several laboratory studies have been made of the technique known as transcendental meditation, taught by the Students International Meditation Society (SIMS), a vigorous offshoot of the visits made to the West by the Maharishi Mahesh. This Maharishi is not to be confused with the Ramana Maharshi, who never offered to teach the spiritual path for a price.

In a special ceremony, the initiate is given his own mantra: an *inner* sound, to be repeated over and over, silently, for twenty minutes, twice each day. That, apparently, is the essence of the technique.

Interestingly, men and women all over the United States (and other countries) have found this a beneficial, sometimes even transcendental experience. In fact, scores of people of all ages have become meditators, and the society has testimonials concerning a range of topics, from the acquired ability to lose weight just by "thinking about it" to a reported cure of multiple sclerosis (that particular gentleman has been in our lab, for photographic studies of meditation), to a developed clairvoyant or telepathic ability. These claims can no more be derided or ignored than the century-old claims of the Christian Science church or the many other Mind Cure or Mind Control movements, still popular today.

In fact, some very intelligent and curious students, who joined SIMS, have performed laboratory studies on the various effects of transcendental meditation, both psychological and physiological. One study, which served as a doctoral dissertation in physiology at UCLA for Robert Keith Wallace, was published in dignified scientific journals and pioneered the way for many further studies. Using highly sophisticated apparatus, Wallace monitored several physiological parameters on SIMS members who had been meditating for not less than four months. He reported:

> During meditation O_2 consumption, CO_2 elimination, cardiac output, heart rate, and respiration rate significantly decreased, skin resistance significantly increased and the electroencephalogram showed specific changes in certain frequencies. . . . Arterial lactate decreased markedly during meditation and remained low after meditation. These results distinguish the state produced by transcendental meditation from commonly encountered states of consciousness such as waking, dreaming and sleeping and altered states such as hypnosis and conditioning.

Simply, Wallace found that during meditation many of the body's physiological processes *slowed down* considerably, which might elicit a feeling of deep rest and relaxation. Wallace also speculates that the decrease in blood lactate may reduce anxiety.

If twenty minutes of "soundless sound" can relieve physical and mental tensions, it would certainly seem time well spent. Attempting to assess transcendental meditation's effects on physical and mental health, Wallace evaluated questionnaires given to 394 members of SIMS and found that "67% reported significant improvements in physical health, and 84% reported significant improvements in mental health."

Clearly, those 394 subjects were not a random sample of SIMS members; presumably many experiencing less satisfactory results dropped away and/or did not fill out the questionnaires. Typically only enthusiasts (for or against) will bother to report on their experiences.

Wallace has inspired other researchers to investigate the effects of meditation, and their results continue to command respect. In fact, at the 1974 American Psychiatric Association convention, research psychiatrist Dr. Bernard Glueck of Hartford's Institute for Living reported on a controlled study of transcendental meditation, compared with two other therapeutic modalities. Glueck found that with seriously disturbed patients (several of whom were schizophrenic) transcendental meditation provided a significantly greater measure of improvement than the other treatments. In particular, oddly, those patients who had chronically suffered severe insomnia—receiving little more than an hour's sleep at night, in spite of strong medication—were enjoying, after a few weeks of meditative practice, seven and eight hours of deep sleep each night with no medication at all.

It should be noted that these studies have explored the effects of meditation with beginners in the discipline. What are the experiences of persons who have devoted their lives to its practice?

THE OBJECTIVE OF DEEP MEDITATION

There have been numberless men and women—Christian, Sufi, Buddhist, Zen, whatever culture—who have made meditation their way of life. To what goal? To whatever name one chooses: enlightenment, liberation, God, transcendence, truth. The truth will set you free, in the words of Jesus. But that truth is hidden deep within one's self. Take no one's word, accept no creed, follow no prescribed rituals. In the words of Gautama:

> Do not believe on the strength of the sages of old times; do not believe that which you yourself imagined, thinking a god has inspired you. Believe nothing which depends only on the authority of your priests. After

investigation, believe that which you have yourselves
tested and found reasonable.

This advice seems comparable to that given by contemporary
science: Doubt everything, and search for objective truth. But how
can one find *objective* truth in one's own being? By stripping away
all subjective experience, which includes all fears, desires, am-
bitions, hates, loves, and habits of thought, both conscious and
unconscious. Obviously this requires ceaseless, relentless pursuit of
all one's conditioned reactions of mind and body, in order to
confront and demolish them. Liberation, or enlightenment, means
the achievement of what Buddha called "the Unconditioned
State."

The first and most arduous task of the disciple, then, is to
decondition himself. This task may strike a chord in those behavior therapists who, following the researches of Pavlov, Skinner,
Wolpe, and others, are using desensitization or deconditioning in
their practice.

DECONDITIONING AND BEHAVIOR MODIFICATION

Let us digress briefly into behavior therapy. Hypnosis and deep
relaxation (both altered states of consciousness) are often used
with patients crippled by fears or desires. For example, if a patient
feels such panic at the thought of flying that he cannot take a
plane trip, a therapist might ask him to relax in a reclining chair
and *fantasy* the various stages of driving to the airport, checking
his luggage, presenting his ticket, boarding the plane, fastening his
seat belt, and so on. If, at any of these steps the patient expresses
a feeling of anxiety, he is stopped and told to relax and begin the
fantasy again. Sooner or later he learns to remain pleasantly
relaxed while in fantasy he takes a complete trip from airport to
airport. Then the therapist may accompany him on his first actual
drive to the airport, and even onto the plane, again using relaxation if the patient begins to feel anxious. A frequent outcome of
this technique is a fairly swift deconditioning of the flying phobia.

A variation on this technique asks that the patient confront the
fear. A patient who is terrified of snakes is asked to fantasy that
she is surrounded by snakes. At first she may scream and scream

and scream her terror, but gradually, as she realizes that no harm has come to her except from the fear *in her own mind*, she may become quite tranquil as she fantasies snakes climbing all over her. At this point a real snake may be brought into the room and then eventually placed on her lap. Finally the patient can calmly hold and caress the snake without fear. She has been deconditioned by facing the fear directly.

Another variant of this therapy asks that the patient learn to harness his destructive desires. As an example, a talented musician is desperate because of an incessant, intolerable urge to exhibit himself to attractive girls in public places. He has already been arrested several times for indecent exposure, and on the last occasion was warned that his next offense would mean imprisonment. He has just been offered a good job in a different locale, but is afraid to accept it for fear his compulsion will be his undoing. Under hypnosis the patient is asked to *surrender* to his desire; it is suggested that he exhibit himself, in fantasy, again and again and again and again to every beautiful girl he can imagine. Eventually he grows bored with the fantasy and resists the request to repeat it. Thus, by yielding until satiation to the intolerable desire, he is deconditioned. Similar techniques have been used, with varying degrees of success, on other unwanted desires: to smoke, to overeat, to drink, to shoplift, and the like.

MEDITATION AND DECONDITIONING

Suppose one were to examine *every* fear and desire, both conscious and unconscious, lurking within him? It is instructive to read in both ancient and modern texts the various deconditioning techniques in meditation which have been developed to overcome such emotional problems.

In his recent book, *The Message of the Tibetans*, Arnaud Desjardins reports one type of yogic practice which strives for liberation not only from special fears, but from fear itself. As in the treatment for the snake phobia, these practices

> consist in undergoing voluntarily such and such a form of fear and are accompanied by cries, choking, shuddering and convulsions. The disciple fights with the

> monsters and terrors which he hides within himself and
> which at last are brought up to the conscious level. He
> sees them, defies them, tears off their masks and dis-
> covers that they can do no more against him. And this
> leads to freedom from all repulsion and horror, starting
> with the horror inspired by the so-called perverted or
> criminal thoughts. Since these "monsters" are part of
> us, let us face the fact.

Apparently behavior therapists of the West are beginning to appreciate the "Devil Land" of the unconscious mind, a realm which
has been known for at least two thousand years in the East.

MEDITATION AND PSYCHOANALYSIS

Desjardins, in the same book, also offers this warning and
advice:

> I can think of no word which has produced more
> confusion in people's minds than "meditation." All the
> various attempts, exercises, and efforts which can be
> classed under this heading require . . . personal guidance
> suited to the disciple. Meditation exercises found in
> books, however faithfully translated, are no more use to
> the reader than electric appliances without current and
> knowledge of the method of use. . . .
> Somebody asked [a lama]: "When one is meditating
> how can one fight against associations of ideas, thoughts
> that continually enter the mind?"
> "The purpose is to convince the disciple that it is
> impossible. If the source is there, the thoughts will
> come. Deal with the source, not with the thoughts."

Deal with the *source*. Here one is reminded of psychoanalytic
technique which, through free associations of ideas and thoughts,
attempts to get at the *source* of the conflict, often buried deep in
the unconscious.

Carl Jung makes a striking point in his introduction to the
Tibetan Book of the Dead. When the deceased traveler reaches the
last and lowest (Sidpa) Bardo, just before he is returned to a new

life, he finds himself in a terrifying realm, confronted by three precipices. But he is told that they are not really three precipices; that is an illusion. Rather they represent the person's own traits of anger, lust, and stupidity. Jung writes that those versed in Freudian theory can easily translate thus:

Anger   =   Aggression
Lust   =   Sexuality
Stupidity =   Unconscious contents of the psyche

Again it would seem that the sages of old, in the stillness of their meditations, found those same powerful instinctual drives. And apparently they learned that such fears and desires *lie within one's mind*. And when the mind is brought under control, unwanted and destructive emotions are eliminated. Psychotherapy today seems to be following this same path toward a healthy mind, freed from unwanted fears and yearnings.

MEDITATION AND SENSORY DEPRIVATION

In order to achieve liberation, the disciple can choose one of many roads. A well-trod path in the East is that of the hermit who isolates himself in a forest or cave, perhaps following a tradition set down by Milarepa, who was walled into a cave for years by his teacher. This practice may well remind us of recent sensory deprivation experiments, except that the isolation lasts for a far greater time than the three or four days spent in an isolation booth in a modern laboratory. Perhaps the reader remembers the dissociations, hallucinations, weightlessness, etc., described by subjects in those studies.

For comparison, Alexandra David-Neel gives this account of the disciple in the isolation of his cave.

In some of these abodes it is impossible to distinguish any object. According to what I have heard from men who have spent long periods of seclusion in darkness, these hermits enjoy, at times, wonderful illuminations. Their cells become bright with light, or in the darkness every object is drawn with luminous outlines, or again, a phantasmagoria of shining flowers, landscapes, and personages arise before them. . . . The kaleidoscopic mirage is considered by them entirely subjective. It is, they think, caused by the uncontrolled agitation of the mind. When the latter is brought near stillness, the phantasmagoria vanishes. There remains only a spot, which moves, but when the spot is seen as motionless and unchanging, the disciple then has achieved "one-pointedness of concentration." . . . With such concentration, mystics can achieve total anesthesia, so that the body feels nothing at all.

Our contemporary studies in sensory deprivation (as well as biofeedback and psychedelic drugs) would seem to be just a beginning.

MEDITATION AND BIOFEEDBACK

Recent studies by Budzinski and Stoyva report that learning to relax the frontalis muscle in the forehead, through conditioning techniques, brings unexpected visual imagery and a slowing of alpha rhythm, accompanied by *slow* rolling eye movements rather than the rapid eye movements typical of dreams. Eventually, control over the tension of the frontalis muscle is achieved, and tension headaches can be eliminated.

Hatha Yoga requires assuming postures of extreme tension (the lotus, the cobra); but the disciple learns to remain in those positions completely relaxed. Thus the disciple learns to relax not just one muscle in the forehead, but just about all the muscles of his body. In so doing, as we have seen, a yogi like Swami Rama can voluntarily control blood flow and brain waves and create a sharp difference of temperature on two places in the palm of his hand. On a recent TV program, a yogi in India permitted himself to be incarcerated in a vault with a minimum of oxygen. He was able to maintain a condition of deep trance, with such shallow breathing that he stayed inside the vault for hours after an ordinary person would have suffocated.

At Menninger Foundation, Dr. Elmer Green has proceeded further with relaxation and biofeedback, trying to induce a "relaxed, quiet, inward-turned" state similar to meditation. His subjects experienced visual imagery, sometimes of forgotten childhood memories, sometimes archetypal images, such as the "Wise Old

Man" or teacher who comes and offers advice. Green reports that these images can be either enjoyable or distressing. Perhaps these types of biofeedback training bring the student to the stage of meditation in which illusions or visions of one's inner being, both enjoyable and distressing, are manifested.

The ultimate purpose (by whatever path) is to absorb, or demolish, the visions so that they lose their power to either distress or delight. Zen master Huang Po summed up the "fundamental principle" thus:

> If (the disciple) should behold the glorious sight of all the Buddhas coming to welcome him, surrounded by every kind of gorgeous manifestation, he would feel no desire to approach them. If he should behold all sorts of horrific forms surrounding him, he would experience no terror. He would just be himself, oblivious of conceptual thought and one with the Absolute. He would have attained the state of unconditioned being.

Therefore, when one has achieved mastery over the mind, conscious and unconscious, so that neither the most glorious or hideous of visions can affect one's equanimity, he has achieved mind control. And what then?

MEDITATION AND PARAPSYCHOLOGY

Along this path, as one begins to acquire mastery of mind, "siddhi," or "miraculous powers" may manifest themselves. These siddhi have been enumerated by several authors, one of whom religious philosopher Mircea Eliade quotes:

> [After the student attains mastery,] firm and imperturbable, he applies his mind to the modes of the Wondrous Gift (siddhi). . . . He becomes visible or invisible; he goes, feeling no obstruction, to the further side of a wall or hill, as if through air; he walks on water without breaking through; he travels in the sky like the birds on the wing. With that clear Heavenly Ear he hears sounds both human and celestial, whether far or near.

Penetrating with his own heart the hearts of other men, he knows them. With his heart thus serene, he directs his mind to the knowledge of the memories of his previous existences.

In this one paragraph, which according to Mircea Eliade occurs "almost as a stereotype in the mystical literature of India," we find psychokinesis, out-of-the-body experiences, levitation, clairaudience, telepathy, and the ability to regress to previous incarnations. Other miraculous powers enumerated include the ability to control heat and fire, to materialize and dematerialize objects, and to master every bodily process, including that of death.

Naturally we are today inclined to dismiss such siddhi as legends, superstitions, or belief in primitive magic. But there can be found contemporary reports that such faculties do indeed exist, not only among the holy men of India and Tibet, but with some masters who have made themselves available for laboratory study.

Telepathy

In his book *Be Here Now*, former Harvard professor Richard Alpert describes his first meeting in India with the man who was to become his guru. Immediately, the guru demanded that Alpert give him his Land Rover. This confused Alpert: a holy man asking for material gifts? This confusion was further confounded when the guru said that Alpert had spent the previous night thinking about his mother, who had died the year before from a disease of the spleen. This was true, but it was something Alpert had told no one in India. Telepathy. . . ? Alpert wasn't sure, but he received further indication that it might be telepathy when the following day, the guru asked, "Where is the medicine?" The night before, Alpert had been thinking about LSD, which he had with him, and had decided to ask the guru what LSD actually was. But he did not connect medicine with LSD until someone in the group gave him the suggestion. Then he took out a bottle which contained several psychedelic drugs. The guru smiled and asked, "Gives you siddhis?" Alpert had never heard the word "siddhis," which was translated for him as "powers," and since the guru was an old man, Alpert conjectured that he might be losing his vitality and was asking for something like vitamin B12. Alpert said apologetically that he did not have any such medicine with him, but the guru simply held out his hand for an LSD pill.

Body Control

Each of the LSD pills was a very large dose. The guru took one, then a second, then a third. This was about 1,000 micrograms, an enormous dose. (Not too long ago a psychiatrist killed an elephant with an overdose of LSD.) Immediately the scientist in Alpert looked forward to a vastly interesting experience, but throughout the day nothing at all out of the ordinary occurred. The guru would simply turn to Alpert from time to time and smile, as he continued to work with his other students.

Healing

When a former colleague of Alpert's (and still a professor at Harvard) was en route to India, Alpert suggested he visit the guru. Oddly, for the professor was not interested in esoterica, he and his wife did visit the temple of the guru, which was apparently deserted. As they were leaving, though, the guru suddenly appeared on the steps, and invited them in. Several hours were spent in conversation, during which time the guru told the professor many things about the professor's childhood. But this did not convince the professor that the guru had unusual powers; after all, Alpert could have done research and forwarded the information to his master.

The next morning, however, the professor's wife woke up with a very high fever, more than 105 degrees, and no medical doctor could be found. The professor appealed to the guru, who came immediately to the hotel room, and sat down, next to the sick woman. He simply sat there quietly; but within ten minutes her temperature dropped to normal, and she soon felt quite well again.

(This professor has since announced to his graduate students that he intends to do extensive research in parapsychology.)

Precognition

Huston Smith, professor of philosophy at Massachusetts Institute of Technology, has written of an experience of his own, in which his teacher, a roshi, demonstrated precognition by accurately predicting, five years in advance, the year of his death.

Control of Heat and Fire

The ability to generate heat is called, in Tibet, "tumo," and is described by Alexandra David-Neel thus, in her *Magic and Mystery in Tibet:*

> To spend the winter in a cave amidst the snows, naked, and escape freezing is a somewhat difficult achievement. Yet numbers of Tibetan hermits go safely each year through this ordeal . . . by generating tumo, a subtle fire which . . . drives the energy, till it runs all over the body along the tiny channels of *tsas.*

(*Tsas* are defined as veins, arteries, and nerves. This energy may be similar to the ch'i of acupuncture, which is said to run along invisible meridians, then connecting to the blood and circulatory systems.)

Mme. David-Neel gives a detailed account of the discipline to acquire control of tumo, and then describes the examination which concludes the training, conducted on the bank of an icy river or lake:

> The neophytes sit on the ground, cross-legged and naked. Sheets are dipped in the icy water; each man wraps himself in one of them and must dry it on his body. As soon as the sheet has become dry, it is again dipped in the water and placed on the novice's body to be dried as before. The operation goes on until daybreak. Then he who has dried the largest number of sheets is acknowledged the winner.

A different meditative technique, used in yoga, requires that the disciple contemplate fire until he has mastered its essence. Once he has done so, the disciple can then walk on red-hot coals without harm. An acquaintance of mine (a clinical psychologist) recently told of watching such a ritual of walking on burning coals. As he watched, he became aware that he had entered a different consciousness in which he felt as if he, too, were capable of the feat. And, in fact, he became a participant in the ceremony, feeling ecstasy as he walked slowly back and forth over the coals without suffering any kind of burn.

Out-of-the-Body Experience?

A variation of tumo may be the yogic discipline of rousing the kundalini. When performed without guidance by a skilled teacher, the results can be disastrous to the student, as has recently been vividly reported by a Kashmir post office worker, Gopi Krishna. Krishna outwardly had lived the life of an ordinary, middle-class married man with a family. But, ever since failing in his university career, Krishna had resolved to acquire control over his "wandering mind." To this end, every day he would rise very early and sit in the lotus position, meditating, for several hours before beginning his day's work. After many uneventful years of this practice, the following experience was reported by Krishna:

> One morning . . . I sat cross-legged in a small room. Long practice had accustomed me to sit in the same posture for hours, contemplating an imaginary lotus. I sat, intent on keeping my attention from wandering and bringing it back again and again whenever it moved in any direction. My whole being was so engrossed that for several minutes I lost touch with my body and surroundings. This experience has happened to many people who practice meditation regularly, but what followed has happened to few.
>
> I suddenly felt a strange sensation below the base of my spine. [As soon as he paid attention to the sensation, it disappeared. But he learned to keep his concentration on the lotus when the sensation recurred.] The sensation again extended upwards, growing in intensity. Suddenly, with a roar like that of a waterfall, I felt a stream of liquid light entering my brain and spinal cord. . . . The illumination grew brighter and brighter, the roaring louder, I experienced a rocking sensation and then felt myself slipping out of my body. I felt the point of consciousness that was myself growing wider and wider. I was now all consciousness immersed in a sea of light, simultaneously conscious and aware in all directions

without any barrier or material obstacles, and in a state of exaltation and happiness impossible to describe.

Automatic Writing

That happiness did not last long. Krishna was left in a state of exhaustion. Over the next days he lost his powers of concentration and experienced an "unbearable, dry, burning fire" in his body day and night. He could neither eat nor sleep. He lost all feeling for his wife and children. It took more than twelve years of desperate suffering, which included futile visits to doctors of Western medicine as well as yogis, before Krishna learned how to harness the enormous kundalini power he had unwittingly unleashed. Once it was controlled, even more astounding events occurred. Krishna, who had never written poetry, began to "receive" poems, not only in his own language, but in German, French, and Italian—languages of which he knew nothing.

Krishna's second book, *The Biological Basis of Religion and Genius,* contains an introduction by Carl Von Weizsacker, director of the Max Planck Institute for the Life Sciences, who comments on these poems:

> I can feel the inevitably growing annoyance of my scientifically trained readers, for I felt the same way. . . . Why does the story have to end in miracles? Would anything be lacking if he were to write poems in just those languages he had learned? But I must honor the facts. Since then I have seen the [German] poem. [It] is reminiscent of a folk song, a naive communication of an unquestionable experience. A few lines out of context will serve as an example:
>
> ### German
> Ein schoner Vogel immer singt
> In meinem Herz mit leisem Ton
> Und wenn vergeist der Nachtwind auf
> Die grunen Graser seine Tranen . . .
> Dannder Vogel wacht.
>
> ### English Translation
> A beautiful bird always sings
> In my heart with a soft voice . . .
> And when the night wind sheds

> Its tears on the green grass . . .
> Then the bird is watching.

Just as the German poem is German in the way of a German folksong, so the Italian poem is written like an Italian folksong: it rhymes *cuore* with *amore*. . . .

What makes this poetic phenomenon possible and what purpose does it serve? I do not know. Honor the incomprehensible!

Creativity

At the turn of the twentieth century, an Indian reared and educated in England returned to his native country and became a political revolutionary. After thirteen years of this work, for the first time since his return to India, he met a yogi. This meeting led to the death/rebirth of Sri Aurobindo. During this transition, Aurobindo continued his political career, attending secret meetings, and giving public speeches, which last task he found increasingly difficult to do. Before addressing an audience in Bombay, he mentioned this problem to his guru. In the words of Aurobindo:

> He asked me to pray, but I could not pray. He replied that it did not matter; he and some others would pray and I had simply to go to the meeting . . . and wait and speech would come to me from some other source than the mind. [I did as I was told.] "The speech came as though it was dictated. And ever since all speech, writing, thought and outward activity has so come to me from the same source."

At length, Aurobindo was imprisoned for a year, during which period he died completely to the political life. He settled at an ashram in Pondicherry, and for six years without interruption, he effortlessly wrote a stream of literature which has been published around the world. Aurobindo insisted:

> I have made no endeavor in writing. I have simply left the higher Power to do the work and when it did not work, I made no effort at all. It was in the old intellectual days that I had sometimes tried to force things. I never think . . . it is out of a silent mind that I write

whatever comes ready-shaped from above. As soon as that happened there was an immense relief; I have felt body-strain since then but never any kind of brain fatigue.

This creative activity of Aurobindo, which evolved through the intense discipline of yoga, may perhaps remind us of those creative artists (Brahms, Mozart, Stevenson) who spoke of "merely listening," or "holding a pen" while whole compositions were received as if dictated by another. It may be that the creative process, whether occurring spontaneously or by cultivation, is the same: The intellectual mind is stilled, and a deeper consciousness makes itself known.

Levitation

There is an old Sufi story of a dervish walking along a lake front, hearing from an island a disciple mispronouncing a prayer. Feeling it his duty, the dervish took a boat to the island, where he gave the correct pronunciation to the disciple, who was grateful for the instruction. Headed back in the boat to shore, the dervish (who was feeling satisfied with his good deed) was thunderstruck to see the disciple running toward him, on top of the water, calling out humbly his excuses for having forgotten the correct pronunciation: would the dervish be kind and teach him again?

There is also an old Russian story about three old men living on an isolated island in the Arctic. A bishop decided to visit them and learn how they prayed, and he was aghast when they told him their prayer: "You are three; we are three; have mercy on us." The bishop immediately taught them the Lord's Prayer, for which they fervently thanked him. The bishop then set sail for home, soon to be startled by the appearance of strange clouds in the distance, which as they neared the boat, turned into the three old men skimming along the surface of the water. They apologized to the bishop for having forgotten the prayer, and asked to be taught again. The bishop crossed himself and told the old men to go back and "pray for us sinners."

Two different cultures, thousands of miles apart, with the same legend—not only about levitation, but about the fallacy that the *correctness* of ritual can bring spiritual grace. Is this another example of the collective unconscious?

A much more recent description of levitation is given by the well-known British author and musician Cyril Scott, who wrote three books about the teachings of his guru, who, interestingly, was an Englishman. In the second of these books, *The Initiate in the New World*, Scott describes a New Year's Eve celebration in Boston, at which the master is persuaded by his students to demonstrate phenomena. Before doing so, he said: "If I show you a few things tonight, it's to amuse you, I grant, but it's also to give you more faith. You may ask why, for the same reason, I don't take a big hall and give an exhibition? The answer is . . . the general public would merely explain everything away as conjuring tricks." (We have heard this argument over and over, and we will continue to hear it.)

When someone asked for a demonstration of levitation, the master requested a student, Arkwright, to lie down full length on his back.

> The master stood over him, placed his hand about two feet above his recumbent body, then slowly raised it and Arkwright rose in the air, as if he were being pulled up by an invisible cord. He remained for about one minute suspended a yard above the top of the platform, then slowly sank down again.

Scott's books were published in the 1930s and were as widely read (and as controversially discussed) as Castaneda's present trio of books about his guru, Don Juan. Castaneda, too, in *A Separate Reality*, describes a form of levitation in which he watched the curandero, Don Genaro, "climb" a waterfall; then, as he perched on a ledge, he seemed to slip, his whole body appearing to hang in mid-air. Later, Castaneda was told by Don Juan that Genaro had been supported by "invisible tentacles," "fibers of light" which are part of every man's body and by means of which "every man is in touch with everything else." Perhaps it was with these invisible "fibers of light" (the energy body?) that Arkwright was levitated.

Materialization

A contemporary holy man in India, Sai Baba, is famous (or notorious) for his miraculous power of materializing objects such as jewels, medallions, and a healing ash (vibuthi). In a recent documentary film, *Man and Miracles,* Sai Baba—who looks to be a young man with an Afro hair style—is shown at his ashram among his disciples, some of whom are Americans. A few of his students report, in the film, some of their extraordinary experiences with the guru. Easily the most remarkable story is that told by a Californian, Mr. Cowan, who says that he "died" in June of 1973. He describes his death, from pneumonia, in his hotel room, attended by medical doctors who told his wife that he had passed away. Cowan said he was aware that he had "died" and that his consciousness had separated from his physical body, but remained near his corpse as it was taken by ambulance to a mortuary to be prepared for burial. Suddenly, he says, his consciousness was shifted to a meeting between Sai Baba and a "judge" who decided that Cowan should return to life because he had not yet finished the work he was intended to do. (The reader may be reminded of Arthur Ford's "death," reported in the previous chapter, when after being separated from his physical body, Ford's consciousness found itself before a group of judges who sent him back, to complete his work on earth.) Cowan goes on to describe how he then found himself standing next to his lifeless body, thoroughly disliking the idea of returning into the "cesspool" of his diseased carcass. But return he did, and experienced much more intense discomfort before regaining his health. This was but one of many healings attributed to Sai Baba, not only by laymen but by scientists who admit being baffled by the experience.

Prominent in the film are occasions in which Sai Baba seems to materialize into his hands rings, necklaces, objets d'art, and healing ashes. But watching the film, a skeptic (or even someone willing to believe) can easily dismiss these "materializations" as simple sleight-of-hand tricks which any competent magician could easily duplicate. Once more we are in a quandary: Are we witnessing genuine siddhi or conjuring tricks?

GUATAMA BUDDHA ON THE SIDDHI

It is delightful to learn that the same quandary existed millennia ago, at the time the Buddha lived. He was explicit about the siddhi, explaining that miraculous powers may appear to you as you strive to obtain mastery of the mind. But, as he is quoted in the Vinaya text:

Suppose that a brother enjoys the possession of siddhi. . . . And if he were to manifest the yogic power of
divining the thoughts of others, the unbeliever could
say, "Sir! There is a charm called the Jewel charm. It is
by the efficacy of that he performs all this."

This is, of course, what we hear today when psychics or holy
men such as Geller, Kulagina, or Sai Baba demonstrate a "miraculous power." They are usually dismissed as charlatans employing a
conjuring trick, a "Jewel charm."

Instead of displaying siddhi, Gautama urged that the disciple
avoid them as a destructive (if glamorous) distraction leading away
from the main task: mastery of the mind and liberation.

MEDITATION AND SCIENCE

The aim of classical science, as was discussed at the Prague
conference, had been to study the universe *objectively*, in order to
know of what it "really" consists, and how it "really" functions.
But contemporary science has learned that such an objective view
of the universe is constantly being distorted by the unconscious,
subjective views of the observer.

The aim of classical meditation, as we have learned, is to acquire
such control of the mind that one can demolish all subjective fear,
desire, and preconceptions derived from experience and teachings.
When mastery of the mind has been achieved, one can then
transcend the illusions which go to make the world as one has
been conditioned to see it. Don Juan tried in vain to get his pupil
to "really see." Milarepa spent years alone in a dark cave in order
to rid himself of all hallucinations, whether of gods or devils, so
that he could transcend the human condition. Saint Anthony
fought the same fight with his temptations in the desert. William
Blake wrote about the glory, the transfiguration, that exists for us
when "the doors of perception are cleansed."

In her book *The Secret Oral Teachings*, Alexandra David-Neel
reports what her Tibetan teacher said about seeing truly:

All our perceptions are nothing but interpretations of a
fugitive contact by one of our senses with a stimulus.
Thus we are led to contemplate the existence of two
worlds: that of pure contact not colored by the screen

of "memories"; and that created by the interpretation. The first of these worlds represents Reality and is indescribable. [The second] consists purely of movement. There are no objects "in movement"; the objects consist of movement.

As we know, our physicists discovered this fact not too long ago: a table, they tell us, is not a solid object but consists of billions of constantly moving atomic and subatomic particles. Returning to the Tibetan teaching,

This movement is a continued and infinitely rapid succession of flashes of energy. These rapid flashes of energy are sufficiently like one another to remain imperceptible to us. Then suddenly occurs, in this series of moments, a different moment which catches our attention and makes us think a new object has appeared. This process is often explained by comparing it with a grain which remains apparently inert, then one day shows a germ, that is different from the grain. However, the inertness of the grain was only in appearance.

Today we might use the analogy of time-lapse photography, in which each static, inert frame can, as it moves through the projector, reveal the growth of a flower from a seedling, the emergence of an object which is different from the seedling.

Again, according to the teachings,

There are two theories and both consider the world as movement. One states that the course of this movement (which creates phenomena) is continuous. The other declares that the movement advances by separate flashes of energy which follow each other at such small intervals that these intervals are almost nonexistent.

And here we are, face to face with the present position of physics: Is all energy a wave (continuous movement) or is it quanta (separate packets of energy)? It is fascinating to realize that thousands of years ago, through meditation and in the stillness of mind, sages reached fundamentally the same conclusions as our contemporary physicists.

TOWARD A DIFFERENT DIMENSION

It seems not improbable that soon the two disciplines of science and meditation may join together. The process, in fact, seems already to have begun. Scientists like Jeans have already likened the universe more to a great thought than to a great machine. And with psychoanalysis, depth psychology, and the exploration of altered states of consciousness, behavioral scientists have begun to uncover the wisdom that is hidden in the depths of the psyche. In fact, they are now talking of the need to study peak experiences, transcendental states of being, and the supremely healthy individual instead of devoting themselves exclusively to the pathological states of mental illness.

Perhaps by bringing meditation into the laboratory for serious, prolonged examination and/or by persuading scientists to try for themselves the process of meditation in order to obtain a truly objective view of the world around them, we may be able to strip ourselves of our preconceived ideas of how the world is, or should be, organized. By doing so, we may find ourselves exploring strange, at first incomprehensible dimensions of experience—incomprehensible because our man-made "laws of nature" (which have needed constant revision) do not admit that such dimensions can exist.

We may find ourselves, through these explorations, approaching the next evolutionary rung of the ladder, a different dimension of being, transforming from material man into man of the spirit.

REFERENCES

Some quotations from these sources have been abridged for the sake of clarity and brevity.

Introduction
p. 1 Lindbergh, Charles, "Man's Potential," an essay contained in Charles Muses and Arthur Young (eds.), *Consciousness and Reality: The Human Pivot Point,* Outerbridge & Lazard, New York, 1972, p. 312.
p. 6 Szent-Gyorgy, Albert, *The Crazy Ape,* Grosset and Dunlap, New York, 1971, p. 15.

Part I: Bioenergy

Chapter 1. Realms of Energy
p. 11 *Proceedings of the International Conference of Psychotronics,* 2 vols., Zdenek Rejdak, Prague, 1973. Each paper is printed in the language in which it was presented (Czechoslovakian, Russian, English). All quotations from the Prague Conference may be found in these proceedings.
p. 13 Russell, Bertrand, *An Outline of Philosophy,* London, 1927.
p. 15 Shchurin, S., et al., "Communication between Cells," *Journal of Paraphysics,* 1:67-70, 1973 (in English).
pp. 16-17 Walter, E. Gray, *The Evoked Potentials,* edited by W. Cobb and C. Morocutt, Elsevier, London, 1969.
pp. 11ff. Much of this material on electricity and magnetism has been gratefully derived from Arthur Koestler's discussions in *The Act of Creation,* Dell, New York, 1967, and *The Roots of Coincidence,* Random House, New York, 1972.

Chapter 2. Bioenergy: Can It Be Seen through Kirlian Photography?
pp. 23-24 Ostrander, Sheila, and Lynn Schroeder, *Psychic Discoveries behind the Iron Curtain,* Prentice-Hall, New York, 1970, p. 199.
p. 24 V. M. Inyushin has contributed many articles to the study of bioluminescence and Kirlian photography. The 1968 paper "On the Biological Essence of the Kirlian Effect," and the proceedings of the 1969 sympo-

sium, *Problems in Bioenergetics,* were published in Russian by Kazakh State University, Alma-Ata, Kazakhstan, U.S.S.R.

p. 25 Semyon and Valentina Kirlian have also published extensively. Articles translated into English include "Photography and Visual Observation by Means of High-Frequency Currents," *Journal of Scientific and Applied Photography,* 6:397-403, 1961; and "In the World of Wonderful Discharges," published by Kazakh State University, Alma-Ata, Kazakhstan, U.S.S.R., 1958.

p. 25 Powell, A. E., *The Etheric Double,* Quest Book, Theosophical Publishing House, London, 1969.

p. 27 Several of the Soviet research articles have been translated into English, and are available from various sources. Probably the best source over several years is the *Journal of Paraphysics,* published by Benson Herbert in Downton, Wiltshire, England, from 1965 to the present.

p. 28 Szent-Gyorgy, Albert, *Bioelectronics,* Academic Press, New York, 1968.

p. 29 Prat, S., and J. Schlemmer, "Electrophotography," *Journal of the Biological Photography Association,* 7:145-148, 1939.

p. 29 Drbal, Karel, "From Professor Navratil to the Kirlians," *Proceedings of the International Conference of Psychotronics,* Prague, 1973.

pp. 32ff. Articles by our laboratory are numerous. A publications list which includes places and dates of publication may be obtained by writing directly to the publishers of this book.

p. 35 Inyushin, "On the Biological Essence of the Kirlian Effect."

p. 61 Pratt and Schlemmer, op. cit.

Chapter 3. Bioenergy and Healing

p. 62 Worrall, Ambrose, and Olga Worrall, *The Gift of Healing,* Harper & Row, New York, 1958. The quotations in this chapter from the Worralls are from this source as well as an interview given by them to *Psychic* magazine, April 1972, and Harold Sherman's *Your Power to Heal,* Harper & Row, New York, 1972.

p. 63 Olga Worrall's paper has been published in the *Proceedings of the Dimensions of Healing Symposium,* Academy of Parapsychology and Medicine, Los Altos, Calif., 1972. These proceedings also contain papers by other investigators included in this chapter: Carl Simonton, M.D.; William McGarey, M.D.; Bernard Grad, Ph.D.; Sister Justa Smith, Ph.D.; Douglas Dean; and the author.

p. 65 Sherman, Harold, *Your Power to Heal,* Harper & Row, New York, 1972, pp. 12ff.

p. 66 Spraggett, Allan, *Kathryn Kuhlman, The Woman Who Believes in Miracles,* Signet, New York, 1971.

pp. 68ff. The history of healing has been surveyed by several authors, perhaps the best and most conservative account being psychiatrist Louis Rose's *Faith Healing,* Penguin, Baltimore, 1971. An earlier survey, also recommended, is Yogi Ramacharaka's *The Science of Psychic Healing,* Yogi Publishing Society, Chicago, 1935.

p. 69 Esdaile, James, *The Introduction of Mesmerism into India,* London, 1856.

pp. 70ff. Dresser, Horatio (ed.), *The Quimby Manuscripts,* University Books, New Hyde Park, N.Y., 1969. The quotations may be found on pp. 33ff. and p. 61.

pp. 71-72 Peel, Robert, *Mary Baker Eddy: Years of Discovery (1821-1875),* Holt, Rinehart & Winston, New York, 1972. The quotations are from p. 157, and pp. 198ff.

p. 73 James, William, *The Varieties of Religious Experience,* Collier-Macmillan, New York, 1969. Quotations are from pp. 90ff. and p. 110.

p. 75 Rose, Louis, *Faith Healing,* Penguin, Baltimore, 1971.

pp. 76-77 Jung, Carl, *Memories, Dreams, Reflections,* edited by Aniela Jaffe, Pantheon, New York, 1968, p. 110.

p. 78 An excellent account of primitive remedies later given scientific validation is to be found in Robert de Ropp's *Drugs and the Mind,* St. Martin's Press, New York, 1957.

p. 79 Adamenko, V., "Electrodynamics of Living Systems," *Journal of Paraphysics,* 4:113-120, 1970.

p. 80 Yogi Ramacharaka, *The Science of Psychic Healing,* Yogi Publication Society, Chicago, 1935, pp. 36ff.

p. 82 Worrall and Worrall, op. cit.

p. 85 Dr. Grad's research has been published in various scientific journals. One such article (with bibliography) may be found in the *Journal of the American Society for Psychical Research,* 61:286-305, 1967. The incidents described in this chapter are published in the *Proceedings of the Dimensions of Healing Symposium.*

p. 88 Sister Justa Smith's work is reported in the *Proceedings of the Dimensions of Healing Symposium* and in *Human Dimensions,* 1:15-19, 1972, Rosary Hill College, Buffalo, N.Y.

pp. 89ff. Miller, Robert N., The first experiment in long-distance healing is described in detail in Sally Hammond's *We Are All Healers,* Harper & Row, New York, 1974, pp. 54ff.; the second is in *Science of Mind,* 47:12-16, 1974.

Chapter 4. Receiving Bioenergy: Dowsing, Skin Vision, Acupuncture

p. 93 Quoted in Leonid L. Vasiliev, *Mysterious Phenomena of the Human Psyche,* University Books, New Hyde Park, N.Y., 1965, pp. 151ff.

p. 94 Chadwick, D. G., and L. Jensen, "The Detection of Magnetic Fields Caused by Groundwater and the Correlation of Such Fields with Water Dowsing," Utah State University, 1971. (This article was reported in proceedings of the Prague International Conference, 1973, by Carl Schleicher.)

pp. 95-96 Vasiliev, op. cit., pp. 155-156.

p. 97 Platonov, K. *Psychology: As You May Like It*, Moscow Publishing Company, Moscow, 1968 (in English).

pp. 98ff. Mary Wimberley's experiments were reported at the 1972 Parapsychology Conference in Edinburgh, and published in the proceedings as "Skin Vision and Telepathy in a Blind Subject," *Research in Parapsychology: 1972*, Scarecrow Press, N.J., 1973, pp. 82-84. A more discursive report on Mary's work may be found in the *Osteopathic Physician*, October, 1972.

p. 108 A full report of this experimental therapy can be found in Dr. McGarey's "Acupuncture and Body Energies—A Bridge in Understanding the Healing Process," *Proceedings of the Dimensions of Healing Symposium*, pp. 93-102.

pp. 109-110 Ledergerber, Charles, "Electroacupuncture in Obstetrics," paper presented at Acupuncture Symposium, UCLA, 1973.

p. 111 Kim Bong Han's research on the "Kyungrak System" was published, presumably, in the *Journal of the Democratic People's Republic of Korea*, vol. 2, 1965. (Copies are perhaps nonexistent.)

p. 112 Burr, Harold S., *Blueprint for Immortality*, Neville-Spearman, London, 1972, p. 33.

Chapter 5. Transmitting Bioenergy: Psychokinesis

p. 118 This passage is quoted in Arthur Koestler, *The Roots of Coincidence*, Random House, New York, 1972, p. 27.

p. 120 Rhine, Louisa, *ESP in Life and Lab*, Collier-Macmillan, New York, 1967, p. 20.

p. 121 Ibid., p. 171.

p. 124 Fechner, Gustav, quoted in Charles Von Reichenbach, *The Vital Force*, Mokelumne Hill, Calif., 1965, p. 241.

p. 124 Kulagin, V. V., "Nina S. Kulagina," report delivered at the Prague Symposium of Psychotronics, 1970. Published in condensed form, in English, by Benson Herbert in *Journal of Paraphysics*, 1970, pp. 54-62.

p. 126 Schmeidler, Gertrude, "PK Effects upon a Continuously Recorded Temperature," *Journal of the American Society for Psychical Research*, 67:325-340, 1973.

p. 131 Batcheldor, K. J., "Report on a Case of Table Levitation and Associated Phenomena," *Journal of the Society for Psychical Research*, 43:339-356, 1966.

p. 137 Anisimov, V., "Autogravity," *Socialist Industries*, Moscow, 1973 (in Russian).

Part II: Biocommunication

Chapter 6. Realms of the Mind

p. 142 Miller, Neil, "Learning of Visceral and Glandular Responses," *Science*, 163:434-445, 1969. Also Leo DiCara, "Learning in the Autonomic Nervous System," *Scientific American*, 1970, pp. 30-39.

p. 145 Penfield, Wilder, *Speech and Brain Mechanisms*, Princeton University Press, Princeton, N.J., 1959.

pp. 145-146 Freud, Sigmund, *An Autobiographical Study*, Norton, New York, 1952, pp. 62ff.

pp. 147-148 Jung, Carl, et al., *Man and His Symbols*, Dell, New York, 1972, pp. 56ff.

p. 148 Eliade, Mircea, *Patterns in Comparative Religion*, World Publishing, New York, 1971.

p. 149 Masters, R. E. L., and Jean Houston, *The Varieties of Psychedelic Experience*, Delta, New York, 1966, p. 227.

p. 150 Custance, John, *Wisdom, Madness and Folly*, Pellegrini & Cudahy, New York, 1952, pp. 18ff.

p. 150 Huxley, Aldous, *Heaven and Hell*, Harper, New York, 1956, p. 14.

p. 151 Chao Pi Ch'en, quoted by Gopi Krishna in *Psychic*, February 1973, p. 18.

p. 152 Jung, Carl, *Memories, Dreams, Reflections*, edited by Aniela Jaffe, Pantheon, New York, 1968.

pp. 152-153 Findlay, A. *A Hundred Years of Chemistry*, 2d ed., Duckworth, London, 1948, p. 42.

p. 154 Rassmussen, K., *The Intellectual Culture of the Iglulik Eskimos*, Copenhagen, 1929, p. 119.

p. 154 Al-Ghazzali, quoted in William James, *The Varieties of Religious Experience*, Crowell-Collier, New York, 1969, pp. 316ff.

p. 155 David-Neel, Alexandra, *Magic and Mystery in Tibet*, Penguin, Baltimore, 1971, pp. 74ff.

p. 156 Byrd, Richard E., *Alone*, Putnam & Sons, New York, 1938.

p. 156 Bexton, W. H., W. Heron, and T. H. Scott, "Effects of Decreased Variation in the Sensory Environment," *Canadian Journal of Psychology*, 8:70-76, 1954.

p. 157 Castaneda, Carlos, *The Teachings of Don Juan: A Yaqui Way of Knowledge*, Ballantine, New York, 1968.

p. 158 Masters, R. E. L., and Jean Houston, *The Varieties of Psychedelic Experience*, Delta, New York, 1966, p. 115.

p. 158 Reported in Charles Savage and Louis Cholden, "Schizophrenia and the Model Psychosis," *Journal of Clinical and Experimental Psychopathology*, 17:405.

p. 159 Tors, Ivan, quoted in Constance Newland, *My Self and I*, Coward-McCann, New York, 1962, pp. 247ff.

p. 160 Cheek, David, "Hypnosis and Anesthesia," paper presented at Hypnosis Symposium, UCLA, February 1971.

pp. 160-161 Barrett, Sir William, quoted in Simeon Edmunds, *Hypnosis and ESP*, Wilshire Books, Los Angeles, 1968, pp. 97ff.

p. 162 Aaronson, Bernard, "Hypnosis, Time Rate Perception, and Personality," paper presented at Eastern Psychological Association, 1965.

pp. 162-163 Bucke, R. M., *Cosmic Consciousness*, University Books, New York, 1961, pp. 73ff.

p. 164 Shirokogoroff, S., "Psychomental Complex of the Tungus," quoted in J. M. Lewis, *Ecstatic Religions*, Penguin, Baltimore, 1971, p. 53.

pp. 166-168 Green, Elmer, "How to Make Use of the Field of Mind Theory," *Proceedings of the Dimensions of Healing Symposium*, UCLA, October 1972.

p. 168 David-Neel, op. cit., p. xii

Chapter 7. Telepathy and Clairvoyance

p. 169 Heywood, Rosalind, *The Sixth Sense*, Dutton, New York, 1961, p. 151.

p. 169 Rose, Ronald, *Living Magic*, condensed account in Martin Ebon, *True Experiences in Telepathy*, Signet, New York, 1967, p. 90.

p. 170 Pobers' work is reported in Louis Pauwels and Jacques Bergier, *The Morning of the Magicians*, Avon, New York, 1973, p. 167.

p. 170 Myers, F. W. H., *Human Personality and Its Survival of Bodily Death*, Longmans, Green, New York, 1954, vol. I, p. 138.

p. 172 James, William, "Notes on Mrs. Piper," quoted in David C. Knight, *The ESP Reader*, Grosset & Dunlap, New York, 1969, pp. 81ff.

p. 173 Masters, R. E. L. and Jean Houston, *The Varieties of Psychedelic Experience*, New York, Delta, 1966, p. 115ff.

p. 173 Reported by Dr. Felix Martin-Ibanez, in "Editor's Essay," *MD*, June 1965, p. 11.

pp. 174-175 Koestler, Arthur, *The Roots of Coincidence*, Random House, New York, 1972, p. 35.

p. 176 Rhine, J. B., *Extra-Sensory Perception*, Boston Society for Psychical Research, Boston, 1934.

p. 177 Koestler, Arthur, *The Invisible Writing*, Collins, London, 1954, p. 294.

pp. 177-178 The Reiss study is described fully in J. Gaither Pratt, *Parapsychology: An Insider's View of ESP*, Doubleday, New York, 1964, pp. 64ff.

p. 178 Eysenck's statement is quoted in Arthur Koestler, *The Roots of Coincidence*, p. 14.

pp. 178-179 This research was reported in "Star Subjects in an ESP Card-Guessing Experiment," an unpublished paper presented at the Foundation on the Research on the Nature of Man, Durham, N.C., 1970.

pp. 179ff. The UCLA studies in emotional telepathy have been published in various journals, including *Journal of Abnormal Psychology*, 72:341-348, 1967, and *American Journal of Clinical Hypnosis*, 13:46-56, 1970, and in J. B. Rhine (ed.), *Progress in Parapsychology*, Seeman, Durham, N.C., 1971, pp. 152-160.

p. 183 Taff's experiments have been described in detail in "Laboratory Investigation of a Psychic," to be published in *Behavioral Neuropsychiatry*.

pp. 188ff. Ullman, Montague, Stanley Krippner, and Allan Vaughan, *Dream Telepathy*, Macmillan, New York 1973.

p. 190 Vasiliev, L. L., *Experiments in Mental Suggestion*, Institute for the Study of Mental Images, Hampshire, England, 1963, p. 62.

p. 190 Vasiliev, L. L., *Mysterious Phenomena of the Human Psyche*, University Books, New York, 1965, p. 31.

pp. 190-191 Kogan, I.M., "The Informational Aspect of Telepathy," paper presented *in absentia*, at UCLA symposium, A New Look at ESP, 1969.

pp. 192-193 Kant, Immanuel, *Dreams of a Spirit Seer*, quoted in David C. Knight, *The ESP Reader*, Grosset & Dunlap, 1969, pp. 114-115.

pp. 193-194, Murphy, Gardner, and Robert Ballou, *William James on Psychical Research*, Viking, New York, 1969, p. 73.

p. 194 Tenhaeff, Willem, *Proceedings of the Parapsychological Institute*, State University of Utrecht, December, 1960, pp. 49ff.

pp. 195-196 Ibid., pp. 16ff.

pp. 196-197 Rhine, J. B., *The Reach of the Mind*, Sloane, New York, 1971, p. 44

Chapter 8. Precognition: What Happened Tomorrow?

pp. 200-201 Lincoln's dream is reported in Pratt, J. Gaither, *Parapsychology: An Insider's View of ESP*, Doubleday, New York, 1964. pp. 148-149.

p. 202 Murphy, Gardner, *The Challenge of Psychical Research*, Harper & Row, New York, 1961, pp. 28ff.

p. 204 Reported in Rosalind Heywood, *ESP: A Personal Memoir*, Dutton, New York, 1964, p. 195.

p. 205 Eisenbud, Jule, *The World of Ted Serios*, Morrow, New York, 1967, p. 33.

p. 207 Astronomer Ananoff is quoted in Alexandra David-Neel and Lama Yongden, *The Secret Oral Teachings in Tibetan Buddhist Sects*, City Lights, San Francisco, 1968, pp. 35-36.

p. 212-214 The Soal experiments are described in detail in Murphy, op. cit., pp. 125ff.

pp. 215-216 Brier, Robert, and Walter Tyminski, "Psi Application: Parts I and II," *Journal of Parapsychology*, 34:1-36, 1970.

pp. 216-218 This Maimonides material on precognitive dreams is taken principally from Montague Ullman, Stanley Krippner, and Allan Vaughan, *Dream Telepathy*, Macmillan, New York, 1973, pp. 178ff., but includes personal communications from Krippner.

Chapter 9. Inspiration, Idiots Savants, and Information from Unknown Sources

p. 227 Myers, F. W. H., *Human Personality and Its Survival of Bodily Death*, Longmans, Green, New York, 1954, vol. I, pp. 80ff.

pp. 227-119 Interesting material on the creative artist can be found in G. N. M. Tyrell, *The Personality of Man*, Penguin, Baltimore, 1960, pp. 30ff.

p. 228 Koestler, Arthur, *The Act of Creation*, Dell, New York, 1964, pp. 166ff.

p. 229 Abell, Arthur, *Talks with Great Composers*, quoted in Thomas Jay Hudson, *The Law of Psychic Phenomena*, Weiser, New York, 1968. (Introduction by Seale.)

p. 229 Bach, Richard, quoted in a newspaper interview, 1974.

p. 230 Tyrrell, op. cit., pp. 34ff.

pp. 233ff. Myers, op. cit., vol. II, pp. 149ff.

pp. 233-234 Fodor, Nandor, "The Fox Sisters and the 'Hydesville Rappings,'" in *Encyclopedia of Psychic Sciences*, reprinted in David C. Knight, *The ESP Reader*, Grosset & Dunlap, New York, 1969, pp. 22ff.

pp. 238-239 Myers, op. cit., vol. II, p. 589.

p. 241 Professor Schiller is quoted in Raynor C. Johnson, *Psychical Research*, Funk & Wagnalls, New York, 1968, p. 142.

p. 242 Tyrrell, op. cit., p. 42.

pp. 242-243 Bailey, Alice A., *The Unfinished Autobiography*, Lucis, New York, 1973, pp. 162ff.

Chapter 10. From Multiple Personality to "Possession"

pp. 244-247 Myers, F. W. H., *Human Personality and Its Survival of Bodily Death*, Longmans, Green, New York, 1954, vol. I, pp. 315ff.

p. 247 Thigpen, Corbett, and Hervey Cleckley, *The Three Faces of Eve*, McGraw-Hill, New York, 1957, p. 20

p. 250 Schreiber, Flora, *Sybil: The True Story of a Woman Possessed of 16 Separate Personalities*, Regnery, Chicago, 1973.

pp. 250-251 Myers, op. cit., p. 360.

pp. 252-253 Murphy, Gardner, and Robert Ballou (eds.), *William James on Psychical Research*, Viking, New York, 1969, pp. 52ff.

p. 253 Myers, op. cit., p. 360.

pp. 253-255 MacHarg, James, *An Enquiry into the Ostensibly Synchronistic Basis of a Paranoid Psychosis*, paper presented at Parapsychology Association Convention, Edinburgh, 1972.

p. 256 Carrington, Hereward, *The Case for Psychic Survival*, Citadel, New York, 1957.

p. 256 Garrett, Aileen, *Many Voices*, Allen & Unwin, London, 1969, p. 92ff.

p. 258 A detailed description of the Houdini seances can be found in Ford, Arthur, *Unknown but Known*, Signet, New York, 1969, p. 13.

p. 258 Ford, Arthur, *Nothing So Strange*, as reprinted in David C. Knight, *The ESP Reader*, Grosset & Dunlap, New York, pp. 211ff.

p. 259 Ibid, pp. 85ff.

p. 260 Pike, James, *The Other Side*, Doubleday, New York, 1968, p. 334.

pp. 260-262 *New York Times* article, quoted in Hugh Lynn Cayce, *Venture Inward*, Paperback, New York, 1969, pp. 36ff.

pp. 260ff. This material on Edgar Cayce has been culled from several books written about Cayce, probably the most complete biography being Sugrue's *There Is a River*. The Association of Research and Enlightenment, Virginia Beach, Va., has a complete bibliography of these works.

pp. 261-262 Sugrue, Thomas, *There Is a River*, Dell, New York, 1970, pp. 16ff.

Part III: Other Realms

Chapter 11. On the Limitations of Science

p. 273 Einstein's jingle is quoted by A. Koestler, *The Act of Creation*, Dell, New York, 1964, p. 134.

p. 274 Flammarion, Camille, *Haunted Houses*, Appleton, New York, 1924, pp. 380ff.

p. 275 Jung, Carl, *Memories, Dreams, Reflections*, edited by Aniela Jaffe, Pantheon, New York, 1963, p. 323.

p. 276 Brown, Fredric, "Preposterous," in Idella Stone (ed.), *14 Great Tales of ESP*, Fawcett, Greenwich, Conn. 1969, pp. 137ff.

Chapter 12. Can We Get Out Of Our Bodies?

p. 278 Mead, G. R. S., *The Doctrine of the Subtle Body*, Quest, Wheaton, Ill., 1967, p. 1.

p. 279 These, and many other sensory deprivation experiences, can be found in Charles Brownfield, *Isolation, Clinical and Experimental Approaches*, Random House, New York, 1965.

p. 279 E. Allison Peers (ed.), *The Autobiography of St. Theresa*, Doubleday, New York, 1960, p. 119.

p. 279 Hoffman is quoted in Charles Savage and Louis Cholden, "Schizophrenia and the Model Psychosis," *Journal of Clinical and Experimental Psychopathology*, 17:405ff.

pp. 279-280 Castaneda, Carlos, *The Teachings of Don Juan*, Ballantine, New York, 1969, p. 144.

p. 280 Masters, R. E. L., and Jean Houston, *The Varieties of Psychedelic Experience*, Delta, New York, 1966, p. 86.

p. 280 Evans-Wentz, W. Y., *The Tibetan Book of the Dead*, Oxford University Press, New York, 1969, p. 104.

pp. 281-282 Yogi Ramacharaka, quoted in Sylvan Muldoon and Hereward Carrington, *The Projection of the Astral Body*, Weiser, New York, 1969, p. 47.

p. 282 This research of Albert de Rochas, *The Exteriorization of Sensibility*, is quoted in Simeon Edmunds, *Hypnosis and ESP*, Wilshire, Los Angeles, 1968, p. 110.

p. 283 Fahler, Jarl, "Does Hypnosis Increase Psychic Powers?" *Tomorrow* 6:96ff., Autumn 1958.

p. 284 Aristotle, quoted in Mead, op. cit., p. 52.

pp. 284-285 Muldoon, Sylvan, and Hereward Carrington, *The Phenomena of Astral Projection*, Weiser, New York, 1969, p. 58.

pp. 285-286 Myers, F. W. H., *Human Personality and Its Survival of Bodily Death*, Longmans Green, New York, 1954, vol. I, pp. 682ff.

pp. 286-288 Johnson, R. C., *Psychical Research*, Funk & Wagnalls, New York, 1968, pp. 119, 121ff.

p. 288 This Padre Pio incident is reported in David C. Knight (ed.), *The ESP Reader*, Grosset & Dunlap, New York, 1969, pp. 127ff.

pp. 289-290 Myers, op. cit., vol. II, pp. 315ff.

pp. 290-291 Osborne, Arthur, *Ramana Maharshi and the Path of Self-Knowledge*, Rider, London, 1963, pp. 96ff.

p. 292 Langley, Noel, *Edgar Cayce on Reincarnation*, Paperback, New York, 1969, p. 126.

p. 293 Morrell, Ed, *The Twenty Fifth Man* (out of print), 1924, and quoted in Muldoon and Carrington, op. cit., pp. 99-102.

p. 294 London, Jack, *The Jacket*, also known as *The Star Rover* (out of print), 1914.

pp. 294ff. Muldoon, Sylvan, and Hereward Carrington, *The Projection of the Astral Body*, Weiser, New York, 1969, pp. 19, 50ff., 126, 195ff.

pp. 297ff. Monroe, Robert, *Journeys out of the Body*, Doubleday, New York, 1971. The two quotations can be found on pp. 27 and 48ff.

p. 300 Green, Celia, *Out-of-the-Body Experiences*, Ballantine, New York, 1973.

p. 301 Among Robert Crookall's works on out-of-the-body experiences are *The Study and Practice of Astral Projection*, University Press, New York, 1966, and *Out-of-the-Body Experiences: A Fourth Analysis*, University Books, New York, 1970.

pp. 301-302 Monroe, op. cit., pp. 72ff.

p. 303 Tart, Charles, "A Psychophysiological Study of OOBEs in a Selected Subject," *Journal of the American Society for Psychical Research*, 62:3-27, 1968.

p. 304 Research on Ecsomatic Experiences of Living Persons. Project described in *ASPR Newsletter*, American Society for Psychical Research, Spring 1973.

Chapter 13. Hallucinations? Or Apparitions and Ghosts?

p. 306 *Encyclopaedia Britannica.*

p. 307 A complete discussion of the Census of Hallucinations may be found in G. N. M. Tyrrell, "Apparitions," *Science and Psychical Phenomena and Apparitions* (in one volume), University Books, New York, 1961, pp. 18ff.

p. 309 Myers, F. W. H., *Human Personality and Its Survival of Bodily Death*, Longmans, Green, New York, 1954, vol. II,   p. 355.

pp. 309-310 Tyrrell, op. cit., pp. 51ff.

p. 310 *Proceedings of the Society for Psychical Research*, London, 33:168ff.

pp. 311-312 Jung, Carl, *Memories, Dreams, Reflections*, edited by Aniela Jaffe, Pantheon, New York, 1963, p. 312. The next quotation can be found on pp. 137ff.

pp. 312-314 Myers, op. cit., p. 348. The next case is also from Myers, op. cit., pp. 40ff.

pp. 314-315 Garrett, Aileen (ed.), *Does Man Survive Death?*, Helix, New York, 1957, pp. 9ff.

p. 315 Evans-Wentz, W. Y., *The Tibetan Book of the Dead*, Oxford, New York, 1969, intro., p. 1xxv.

p. 320 MacKenzie, Andrew, *Apparitions and Ghosts*, Popular Library, New York, 1971, pp. 66ff.

p. 320 Tyrrell, op. cit., p. 13.

p. 323 Schmeidler, Gertrude, "Quantitative Investigation of a Haunted House," *Journal of the American Society for Psychical Research*, 61:137-149, 1966.

p. 325 Moss, Thelma, and Gertrude Schmeidler, "Quantitative Investigation of a 'Haunted House' with Sensitives and a Control Group," *Journal of the American Society for Psychical Research*, 62:399-409, 1968.

p. 328 From the *Proceedings of the Society for Psychical Research*, quoted in G. N. M. Tyrrell, *The Personality of Man*, Penguin, Baltimore, 1960, pp. 209ff.

p. 329 *Proceedings of the Society for Psychical Research*, 25:390ff., 1911.

p. 330 Tyrrell, *The Personality of Man*, pp. 211ff.

p. 331 Smith, Susy, *Prominent American Ghosts*, Dell, New York, 1969, pp. 196ff.

p. 331 Roll, W. G. and J. G. Pratt, "The Miami Disturbances," *Journal of the American Society for Psychical Research*, 65:409-454, 1971.

pp. 332-333 Karger and Zicha's work is reported by Andreas Resch, "The Rosenheim Case," *Journal of Paraphysics*, 3:69-76, 1969.

Chapter 14. Survival after Death? Reincarnation?

p. 336 Osis, Karlis, *Deathbed Observations by Physicians and Nurses*, Parapsychology Foundation, New York, 1961, p. 16.

p. 337 Ford, Arthur, *Unknown but Known*, Signet, New York, 1969, pp. 54ff.

pp. 337-339 Ritchie, George C., M.D., "The Pseudo-Death of Private Ritchie," in David C. Knight (ed.), *The ESP Reader*, Grosset & Dunlap, New York, 1968, pp. 510ff.

p. 339 Plato, *The Republic*, Book X, quoted in Joseph Head and S. L. Cranston (eds.), *Reincarnation in World Thought*, Julian Press, New York, 1969, p. 199ff.

p. 341 White, Stewart Edward, *The Betty Book*, Dutton, New York, 1937.

p. 342 White, Stewart Edward, *The Unobstructed Universe*, Dutton, New York, 1940. pp. 59ff.

p. 342 Quoted in Arthur Ford (as told to Jerome Ellison), *The Life beyond Death*, Putnam, New York, 1971, pp. 137ff.

pp. 342-343 Govinda, Lama Anagarika, *The Way of the White Clouds*, Shambala, Berkeley, Calif., 1970, p. 113.

p. 343 Paramahansa Yogananda, *The Autobiography of a Yogi*, Self-Realization Fellowship, Los Angeles, 1968. This affadavit is published *in toto* in this book; here it is abridged.

p. 344 Govinda, op. cit. p. 164.

p. 344 Harrer, Heinrich, *Seven Years in Tibet*, Dutton, New York, 1954, pp. 291ff.

pp. 344-345 This "worldwide tour" of beliefs in reincarnation is primarily derived from Head and Cranston, op. cit.

p. 345 Budge, E. Wallis, *The Egyptian Book of the Dead*, Dover, New York, 1967.

p. 346 Evans-Wentz, W. Y., *The Tibetan Book of the Dead*, Oxford University Press, London, 1969, p. 22.

p. 347 Ibid., p. 162.

pp. 347-348 This material is presented in Carl Jung's Psychological Commentary to *The Tibetan Book of the Dead*, 1969 edition, pp. xli ff.

p. 349 Inge Ammann (pseudonym), "Now I Am Convinced," reprinted in Martin Ebon, *Reincarnation in the Twentieth Century*, Signet, New York, 1970, pp. 108ff.

pp. 350-351 Kelsey, Denys, and Joan Grant, *Many Lifetimes*, Pocket Books, New York, 1969.

p. 353 Langley, Noel, *Edgar Cayce on Reincarnation*, Paperback, New York, 1967, pp. 11ff.

pp. 353-354 Bernstein, Morey, *The Search for Bridey Murphy*, Lancer, New York, 1965.

p. 354 Ducasse, C. J., "How the Case of 'The Search for Bridey Murphy' Stands Today," *Journal of the American Society for Psychical Research*, January 1962. Reprinted in Martin Ebon, *Reincarnation in the Twentieth Century*, Paperback, New York, 1967, pp. 70ff.

pp. 356ff. Stevenson, Ian, "Twenty Cases Suggestive of Reincarnation," *Proceedings of the American Society for Psychical Research*, vol. 26, September 1966.

Chapter 15. Toward a Different Dimension of Being

pp. 360-361 Osborne, Arthur, *The Teachings of the Ramana Maharshi*, Rider & Co., London, 1962, p. 10.

p. 362 Osborne, Arthur, *The Ramana Maharshi and the Path of Self-Knowledge*, Rider & Co., London, 1963, p. 20.

pp. 363-364 Sinkler, Lorraine, *The Spiritual Journey of Joel S. Goldsmith*, Harper & Row, New York, 1973, p. 16.

p. 364 Goldsmith, Joel S., *Beyond Words and Thought*, Julian Press, New York, 1968, p. 15; and his *Practicing the Presence*, Fowler & Co., London, 1971, p. 69ff.

p. 367 Deikman, Arthur, "Experimental Meditation," in Charles Tart (ed.), *Altered States of Consciousness*, John Wiley & Sons, Inc., New York, 1969, p. 201.

p. 368 Maupin, Edward, "Individual Differences in Response to a Zen Meditation Exercise," in ibid., p. 190.

p. 369 Wallace, Robert Keith, *The Effects of Transcendental Meditation,* Students International Meditation Society, Los Angeles, 1970. p. xiii.

p. 370 Glueck, Bernard, paper presented at "Metapsychiatry" Panel, American Psychiatric Association Convention, Detroit, May 1974.

pp. 370-371 From the Kalama Sutta, quoted in Alexandra David-Neel, *The Secret Oral Teachings in Tibetan Buddhist Sects,* City Light Books, San Francisco, 1967, p. 8.

pp. 372-373 Desjardins, Arnaud, *The Message of the Tibetans,* Stuart & Watkins, London, 1969, pp. 120ff.

p. 374 David-Neel, Alexandra, *Magic and Mystery in Tibet,* Penguin, Baltimore, 1971, p. 251.

p. 375 Budzynski, Thomas, "Twilight-State Learning: A Biofeedback Approach to Creativity and Attitude Change," paper presented at the Transformations of Consciousness Conference, McGill University, 1973.

p. 376 Blofeld, John (ed. and trans.), *Huang Po, The Zen Teaching of,* Buddhist Society, London, 1968, p. 46.

pp. 376-377 Eliade, Mircea, *Yoga, Immortality, and Freedom,* Bollingen, Princeton, N.J., 1971, p. 178.

pp. 377-378 Ram Das, *Be Here Now,* Lama Foundation, New Mexico, 1971.

pp. 378-379 Smith, Huston, "Parapsychology in the Indian Tradition," *International Journal of Parapsychology,* 8:259, Spring 1966.

p. 379 David-Neel, *Magic and Mystery in Tibet,* pp. 220ff.

pp. 380-381 Gopi Krishna, *The Biological Basis of Religion and Genius,* Harper & Row, New York, 1972, pp. 10ff.

pp. 382-383 Satprem, *Sri Aurobindo: An Adventure in Consciousness,* India Library Society, New York, 1964, pp. 145, 259.

p. 384 Scott, Cyril, *The Initiate in the New World,* Routledge and Kegan Paul, London, 1971, p. 286.

p. 384 Castaneda, Carlos, *A Separate Reality,* Simon & Shuster, New York, 1971, pp. 125ff.

p. 386 As quoted in Mircea Eliade, op. cit. p. 180.

pp. 386-387 David-Neel, *The Secret Oral Teachings in Tibetan Buddhist Sects,* p. 180.

RECOMMENDED READING
Realms of Mind and Energy

Books:

Burr, Harold Saxton, *Blueprint for Immortality*, Neville-Spearman, London, 1972.

Castaneda, Carlos, *The Teachings of Don Juan: A Yaqui Way of Knowledge*, Ballantine, New York, 1973.

Castaneda, Carlos, *A Separate Reality*, Simon & Schuster, New York, 1971.

Castaneda, Carlos, *Journey to Ixtlan*, Simon & Schuster, New York, 1973.

Delgado, Jose, *Physical Control of the Mind*, Harper-Colophon, New York, 1969.

Dingwall, Eric, *Abnormal Hypnotic Phenomena*, Barnes and Noble, New York, 1968. (4 vols.)

Dresser, Horation (ed.), *The Quimby Manuscripts*, University Books, New York, 1961.

Eisenbud, Jule, *The World of Ted Serios*, Morrow, New York, 1967.

Eliade, Mircea, *Myths, Dreams, and Mysteries*, Harper, New York, 1960.

Heywood, Rosalind, *ESP: A Personal Memoir*, Dutton, New York, 1964.

Huxley, Aldous, *Heaven and Hell*, Harper, New York, 1956.

James, Williams, *The Varieties of Religious Experience*, Collier-MacMillan, New York, 1969.

Johnson, Raynor, *The Imprisoned Splendour*, Hodder, London, 1953.

Jung, Carl, *Memories, Dreams, Reflections*, Pantheon, New York, 1963.

Knight, David C., *The ESP Reader*, Grosset & Dunlap, New York, 1968.

Koestler, Arthur, *The Roots of Coincidence*, Random House, New York, 1972.

Lewis, J. M., *Ecstatic Religions*, Penguin, Baltimore, 1971.

Monroe, Robert, *Journeys Out-of-the-Body*, Doubleday, New York, 1972.

Muldoon, Sylvan, and Hereward Carrington, *The Projection of the Astral Body*, Weiser, New York, 1969.

Murphy, Gardner, and Robert Ballou, *William James on Psychical Research*, Viking, New York, 1969.

Myers, F. W. H., *Human Personality and Its Survival of Bodily Death*, Longmans, Green, New York, 1954. (2 vols.)

Ostrander, Sheila, and Lynn Schroeder, *Psychical Discoveries behind the Iron Curtain*, Prentice-Hall, New York, 1970.
Rhine, J. B., *The Reach of the Mind*, Sloane, New York, 1971.
Rhine, Louisa, *ESP in Life and Lab*, Collier-Macmillan, New York, 1968.
Rose, Louis, *Faith Healing*, Penguin, Baltimore, 1971.
Sugrue, Thomas, *There Is a River*, Dell, New York, 1970.
Tart, Charles (ed.), *Altered States of Consciousness*, Wiley & Sons, New York, 1969.
Tyrrell, G. N. M., *The Personality of Man*, Penguin, Baltimore, 1960.
Ullman, Montague, Stanley Krippner, and Alan Vaughan, *Dream Telepathy*, Macmillan, New York, 1973.
Vasiliev, L. L., *Mysterious Phenomena of the Human Psyche*, University Books, New York, 1965.
Worrall, Olga, and Ambrose Worrall, *The Gift of Healing*, Harper & Row, New York, 1965.

Journals:
Journal of the American Society for Psychical Research, 5 W. 73 St., New York, N.Y.
Journal of the Society for Psychical Research, 1 Adams Mews, London, England.
Journal of Parapsychology, Parapsychology Press, Durham, N.C.
Journal of Paraphysics (Benson Herbert, ed.), Downton, Wiltshire, England.

Recommended for Further Study
Bhagavad Gita, translated by Yogi Ramacharaka, Yogi Publishing Company, Chicago, 1935.
David-Neel, Alexandra, *Magic and Mystery in Tibet*, Penguin, Baltimore, 1971.
David-Neel, Alexandra, *The Secret Oral Teachings of Tibetan Buddhist Masters*, City Lights, San Francisco, 1967.
Desjardins, Arnaud, *The Message of the Tibetans*, Stuart and Watkins, London, 1969.
Goldsmith, Joel S., *Beyond Words and Thought*, Julian Press, New York, 1968.
Govinda, Lama Anagarika, *The Way of the White Clouds*, Shambala, Berkeley, Calif., 1970.
Herrigel, Eugen, *Zen in the Art of Archery*, McGraw-Hill, New York, 1964.
Huang Po, *The Zen Teaching of*, translated by John Blofeld, Buddhist Society, London, 1968.
Osborne, Arthur, *The Teachings of the Ramana Maharshi*, Rider, London, 1962.
Satprem, *Sri Aurobindo: An Adventure in Consciousness*, India Library Society, New York, 1964.

Sinkler, Lorraine, *The Spiritual Journey of Joel S. Goldsmith,* Harper & Row, New York, 1973.

The Sutra of Hui Neng, translated by Wong Mou-Lam, Buddhist Society, London, 1966.

Yogi Ramacharaka, *Advanced Course in Yoga,* Yogi Publication Society, Chicago, 1955.

INDEX